# Voiceless, Invisible, and Countless in Ancient Greece

# Voiceless, Invisible, and Countless in Ancient Greece

*The Experience of Subordinates, 700–300 BCE*

*Edited by*
SAMUEL D. GARTLAND AND
DAVID W. TANDY

# OXFORD
UNIVERSITY PRESS

Great Clarendon Street, Oxford, OX2 6DP,
United Kingdom

Oxford University Press is a department of the University of Oxford.
It furthers the University's objective of excellence in research, scholarship,
and education by publishing worldwide. Oxford is a registered trade mark of
Oxford University Press in the UK and in certain other countries

© the several contributors 2024

The moral rights of the authors have been asserted

All rights reserved. No part of this publication may be reproduced, stored in
a retrieval system, or transmitted, in any form or by any means, without the
prior permission in writing of Oxford University Press, or as expressly permitted
by law, by licence or under terms agreed with the appropriate reprographics
rights organization. Enquiries concerning reproduction outside the scope of the
above should be sent to the Rights Department, Oxford University Press, at the
address above

You must not circulate this work in any other form
and you must impose this same condition on any acquirer

Published in the United States of America by Oxford University Press
198 Madison Avenue, New York, NY 10016, United States of America

British Library Cataloguing in Publication Data
Data available

Library of Congress Control Number: 2023942287

ISBN 9780198889601

DOI: 10.1093/9780191995514.001.0001

Printed and bound in the UK by
Clays Ltd, Elcograf S.p.A.

Links to third party websites are provided by Oxford in good faith and
for information only. Oxford disclaims any responsibility for the materials
contained in any third party website referenced in this work.

# Acknowledgements

This work is the product of a decade of conversation and collaboration. We need first to thank Department of Classics at the University of Leeds for their support of a series of seminars under the rubric "Subordinates and Subordination in Ancient Greece," begun in the 2012–13 year. Also the Faculty of Classics Craven Fund and the Corpus Christi College Charles Oldham Fund for generous support for a conference in May 2017 "Subaltern Voices in Archaic and Classical Greece" at Corpus Christi College, Oxford. We were pleased that the group took an interest in thinking about their work in conjunction with other papers; we were grateful that Paul Cartledge urged us to consider how to expand and supplement the existing group with others who had not been able to join us at Corpus.

There are many participants and respondents whose efforts over the years have significantly impacted the nature of this collection, with especial thanks to the insights and responses from Kostas Vlassopoulos, Naoise Mac Sweeney, Josephine Quinn, Will Mack, and Lynette Mitchell. Our thanks to the press, to Charlotte Loveridge who helped us shape the volume, Karen Raith and Nadine Kolz who steered it into the production process, and to Saraswathi Ethiraju at Straive for overseeing the final stages. We are equally thankful to the reviewers for OUP, who were at once robust in their criticisms and unfailingly generous and supportive. We are very grateful to Hilary Walford's eagle-eyed copy editing of a challenging MS.

Last point: deep gratitude to our contributors from whom we continue to learn so much and to our families for cutting us some slack to get this project to the finish line. But it is appropriate to dedicate the publication of this project to the memory of the subordinates of the past, including the ones in this collection, and to the dignity of the subordinates of the present and future in a world that is not providing much in the way of protections for them.

# Contents

*List of Figures*     ix
*List of Contributors*     xi

    Introduction: Subordination in Boiotia     1
    Samuel D. Gartland and David W. Tandy

1. A Moral Economy of the *Demos* in Early Archaic Greece     17
   Julien Zurbach

2. Solon and the *Demos* in his Poetry     37
   Anthony T. Edwards

3. Reconstructing the Lives of Urban Craftspeople in Archaic and Classical Greece     67
   Sarah C. Murray

4. 'Don't tell anybody you are a thete!': Athenian Thetes: Identity and Visibility     99
   Lucia Cecchet

5. The Athenian Working Class: Scale, Nature, and Development     127
   Hans van Wees

6. The Local Slave Systems of Ancient Greece     155
   David M. Lewis

7. How to Find a New Master: The Agency of Enslaved Persons in Ancient Greece     184
   Sara Forsdyke

8. Spoken from the Grave: The Construction of Social Identities on the Funerary Monuments of Metics in Classical Athens     207
   Sara Wijma

9. Varying Statuses, Varying Rights: A Case Study of the *graphē hubreōs*     243
   Deborah Kamen

10. Strategies of Disenfranchisement: 'Citizen' Women, Minor Heirs, and the Precarity of Status in Attic Oratory     265
    Rebecca Futo Kennedy

*Index*     291

# List of Figures

| | |
|---|---|
| 3.1. Mikion's stylus | 76 |
| 3.2. Possible depiction of a goblin on a sherd from Phidias' workshop, Olympia (425–400 BCE) | 82 |
| 3.3. A depiction of a smithy with possible βασκάνιον above the forge at right (520 BCE) | 82 |
| 3.4. Penteskouphia plaque fragments, dedicated by Lokris, showing a βασκάνιον perched on the kiln | 83 |
| 3.5. Depiction on a Penteskouphia plaque of an axe–adze being used to harvest clay | 86 |
| 3.6. Tools from panhellenic sanctuaries: (*a*) Olympia; (*b*) Isthmia | 88 |
| 8.1. Reconstruction of the excavated remains of the *periboloi* of Dexileos (left), Agathon and Sosikrates (middle), and Dionysios (right) along The Street of the Tombs in the Kerameikos | 220 |
| 8.2. Reconstruction of the *peribolos* of Sosikrates and Agathon from Herakleia | 222 |
| 8.3. The grave monument for Nikeratos and his son Polyxenos, excavated at Kallithea | 223 |
| 8.4. The *naiskos* of Korallion | 225 |
| 8.5. Funerary relief for Sosinous from Gortyn, depicted as a copper-smelter | 229 |
| 8.6. Funerary relief for Plangon, daughter of Tolmides, from Plataia | 231 |

# List of Contributors

**Lucia Cecchet** is Senior Lecturer in Greek History at the University of Milan, Italy, https://orcid.org/0000-0001-5983-9765. She is author of *Poverty in Athenian Public Discourse* (2015) and co-author of *Poverty in Ancient Greece and Rome* (2023). Her research focuses on poverty in the Greek world, Greek citizenship from the classical to the imperial period, and the impact of war on ancient communities. She is co-editor of *Citizens in the Graeco-Roman World* (2017) and *The Ancient War's Impact on the Home Front* (2019).

**Anthony T. Edwards** is Professor Emeritus, University of California, San Diego, USA. His research has focused upon historicist analysis of Greek literary texts and exhibits a particular interest in the representation of social space. He has authored the books *Hesiod's Ascra* (2004) and *Achilles in the* Odyssey (1985), as well as a number of articles and book chapters dealing with Homer, Hesiod, Aristophanes, and Solon. He spent a year as a Junior Fellow at the Center for Hellenic Studies in Washington, D.C. and another as a University of California President's Fellow in the Humanities.

**Sara Forsdyke** is Josiah Ober Collegiate Professor of Ancient History at the University of Michigan, Ann Arbor, USA. Her research interests centre on democracy, slavery, and the law, both ancient and modern. Her publications include *Exile, Ostracism and Democracy: The Politics of Expulsion in Ancient Greece* (2005), *Slaves Tell Tales: The Politics of Popular Culture in Ancient Greece* (2012), and *Slaves and Slavery in Ancient Greece* (2021). She is currently working on a book on the ancient Greek jury trial and its lessons for criminal justice reform in the contemporary USA.

**Samuel D. Gartland** is Lecturer in Ancient Greek History and Culture, University of Leeds, UK. His research considers geography and history in the ancient world. He has published articles and chapters on Central Greek history and material culture, and has work forthcoming on Thebes in ancient and modern drama. He currently leads projects on Aristophanes and Greek epichoric history, and is the editor of *Boiotia in the Fourth Century B.C.* (2016) and co-editor (with Robin Osborne) of *Reassessing the Peloponnesian War* (forthcoming).

**Deborah Kamen** is Professor of Classics, University of Washington, Seattle, USA, https://orcid.org/0009-0009-6015-9674. She is the author of *Status in Classical Athens* (2013), *Insults in Classical Athens* (2020), and *Greek Slavery* (2023), has written commentaries on Isaeus 2 & 6 (2000) and Pseudo-Demosthenes' *Against Neaira* (2018), and co-edited (with C. W. Marshall) *Slavery and Sexuality in Classical Antiquity* (2021).

**Rebecca Futo Kennedy** is Associate Professor of Classical Studies at Denison University, Granville, OH, USA. Her research focuses on the political, social, and economic history of ancient Athens, histories of immigration, citizenship, race, ethnicity, women, and gender in the ancient Mediterranean, and the reception of antiquity in modern identity formation.

She is editor of *Brill's Companion to the Reception of Aeschylus* (2019), co-editor of *Race and Ethnicity in the Classical World* (2013) and *Handbook of Identity and the Environment in the Classical and Medieval Worlds* (2016) and author of *Immigrant Women in Athens* (2014) as well as numerous book chapters and articles. She is currently completing a book on race and ethnicity in the ancient world and its modern politics and is beginning a new textbook on understanding race and ethnicity in antiquity with Professor Jackie Murray.

**David M. Lewis** is Senior Lecturer in Greek History and Culture, University of Edinburgh, UK, https://orcid.org/0000-0002-0253-5530. He specializes in the history of labour in Ancient Greece and is co-editor (with E. M. Harris and M. Woolmer) of *The Ancient Greek Economy: Markets, Households and City-States* (2016) and co-editor (with E. Stewart and E. M. Harris) of *Skilled Labour and Professionalism in Ancient Greece and Rome* (2020). His monograph *Greek Slave Systems in their Eastern Mediterranean Context, c.800–146 BC* was published in 2018.

**Sarah C. Murray** is Associate Professor, Department of Classics, University of Toronto, Canada, https://orcid.org/0000-0002-0229-9224. Her research is focused on the archaeology and economy of the Aegean Late Bronze and Early Iron Ages. She has published two monographs, *The Collapse of the Mycenaean Economy* (2017) and *Male Nudity in the Greek Iron Age* (2022), as well as articles in journals including the *Journal of Archaeological Research*, *American Journal of Archaeology*, *Journal of Field Archaeology*, *Hesperia*, *Journal of Archaeological Sciences: Reports*, and *Mouseion*.

**David W. Tandy** is Visiting Research Fellow in Classics, University of Leeds, UK, and Professor Emeritus, Department of Classics, University of Tennessee, Knoxville, USA, http://orcid.org/0000-0002-1343-8509. His books include *Warriors into Traders* (1997); his articles and chapters are on the economies of the Near East and the Aegean; on Paros and Parians; on Homer, Hesiod, lyric poets, Lysias, Skopas, Virgil, and *Beowulf*. Forthcoming are chapters on Homeric slavery; rural/village political and social organization in the Greek archaic period; and the ongoing influence of Karl Polanyi on the study of the economies of the ancient Mediterranean and western Asia.

**Hans van Wees** is Grote Professor of Ancient History, University College London, UK, https://orcid.org/0000-0001-9629-5904. He is the author of three books, including *Ships and Silver, Taxes and Tribute: A Fiscal History of Archaic Athens* (2013), and a forthcoming monograph on *Slave and Free Labour in Early Greece, 750–450 BC* (Bonn Centre for Dependency and Slavery Studies). Among the eight volumes he has (co-)edited is *'Aristocracy' in Antiquity: Redefining Ancient Elites* (with Nick Fisher, 2015), and his most recently published paper is a chapter on the archaic period in S. von Reden (ed.), *The Cambridge Companion to the Ancient Greek Economy* (2022).

**Sara Wijma** is Researcher in Ancient History, University of Groningen, the Netherlands. She is the author of *Embracing the Immigrant: The Participation of Metics in Athenian Polis Religion (5th–4th century BC)* (2014). Her research interest centres on the political culture of classical Athens and in particular on the ways in which status categories are informed by (partial) inclusion and exclusion from a community's defining activities. She is currently working on the articulation of the status of foreigners—as *barbaroi*, *xenoi*, and *metoikoi*—in classical Greece in general.

**Julien Zurbach** is Associate Professor in Greek history, Department of History, École normale supérieure, Paris, France, and Member, UMR 8546 AOROC, Paris. He specializes in Mycenaean epigraphy, particularly on agricultural and fiscal questions, and in the social and economic history of early Greece down to the classical period. He has been leading fieldwork in Kirrha (Phocis) and is now active in Miletus (Ionia). Publications include *Les Hommes, la terre et la dette en Grèce, ca 1400–ca 500 aC* (2017), and *Naissance de la Grèce*, a handbook with C. D'Ercole (2019). He has organized and edited various meetings on ancient Greek society, among which, with St Maillot, *Statuts personnels et main-d'oeuvre en Méditerranée hellénistique* (2021) and with Fr. Lerouxel, *Le Changement dans les économies antiques* (2019). He is currently preparing the publication of recent research in Kirrha and Miletus and the publication of a habilitation on urban craftsmen from Mycenaean palaces to archaic poleis.

# Introduction

## Subordination in Boiotia

*Samuel D. Gartland and David W. Tandy*

It is now conventional to assert that 'the subaltern cannot speak'.[1] This is true for colonialized societies in the modern world, but also for historical ones, the colonizers of recent times being replaced by the combination of specific historical circumstances, the ruthless tyranny of historiography, and the prejudices of modern historians. This project began with an inclination to focus on subalternity in ancient Greece; as more partners joined in, it became recognized that this limited the project by focusing on the conditions under which subaltern groups or individuals lived at the expense of attention on the processes that put them in their positions and on the efforts of the subordinators to keep them there; concentrating on subalternity can also divert us from the efforts of the subordinates to alleviate their conditions or even to escape them. There followed a shift from subalternity to the notion of subordination, focusing on subordinates and subordinators.

In the struggle to define terms and to establish commonality in approaches we recognize that we have been wrestling with many of same issues as the volume *Ancient History from Below* (Courrier and Magalhães de Oliveira 2022). The work is a kindred spirit to this volume, seeking as it does more fully to realize the possibilities of the lived experience of 'the below' in the ancient world, as well as wrestling with the difficulties of the different applications of Gramsci's ideas relating to subaltern experience in different schools of thought and in different parts of the world. We differ from that volume in our more cautious and limited approach to the applicability of 'subalternity' to the ancient Greek world, but we recognize and welcome the important methodological considerations in that volume of *History from Below*, as well as of subordinate agency and experience.[2]

There are subordinators and the subordinated everywhere on the ancient Greek landscape. Individuals are subordinated, but it is possible, even easy, to see that the precarity of an individual's existence is more or less identical for all members of the individual's group/status/class. The chapters in this collection focus on several named subordinators and subordinates, but the lessons we take from

---

[1] Ever since Spivak (1988) asked the question, 'Can the Subaltern Speak?'
[2] Courrier and Magalhães de Oliveira (2022: 8–17).

their experiences provide a better understanding of groups, all of which in one way or another live under a cloud of imminent precarity. The great majority of subordinates in the ancient Greek world cannot speak to us, and will remain invisible: this should only serve to remind us how important it is to recognize commonalities in the experiences of subordinate individuals and groups. If we do not more closely put together the analysis and interpretation of the experiences of subordinates, not only do we miss opportunities for cross-fertilization of approaches, but we will also continue to reconfirm much of the voiceless and invisible condition that they experienced in life.

By way of introduction, we would begin with a brief look at two landscapes that reveal subordination, one each from the beginning and the end of the historical span of the individual contributions in this collection: the world of Hesiod in the early seventh century and the world of Thebes in the fourth, both in Boiotia. The description of Hesiod's world is largely static, more ekphrastic than narrative; the later world of fourth-century Thebes, Thespiai, and other Boiotian *poleis* is more dynamic because historical, more narrative than ekphrastic. Ekphrastic Askra reveals a permanent structure of ranking, with a small number of events or circumstances that show us the precarity of many individuals' lives. The sources for later Boiotia reveal a greater elasticity, allowing us to see the constant pressure that the world brought to bear on *poleis* (and smaller communities) and individuals as they attempt to defend themselves with what weapons they had against those who would subordinate them.

It has long been recognized and generally agreed that Hesiod lives the life of a peasant in Askra, by definition an agriculturalist focused on his household (*oikos*) and committed to reciprocity within his community,[3] as Julien Zurbach describes vividly in his chapter in this volume. His relationship with the Thespiai *polis* is structurally antagonistic and tilted against those in the countryside; this conflict between town and fields is precisely in keeping with our expectations in a landscape of city and peasantry.[4] While it is possible to massage the information that Hesiod and comparative materials make available to us, there is no escaping the conclusion that there is a strong divide between the (proto)urban and the rural in the Valley of the Muses. Hesiod and his fellow villagers are in a subordinated position, not because of individual errors or community flaws or poor judgement or poor stars but because the structure of the political and juridical world of western Boiotia provides this arena of struggle on a field stacked against those in the countryside. The collective of rural persons is structurally subordinated to the urban power of the *polis* and additionally further subordinated or resubordinated

---

[3] The best discussions of the use of the peasant in the analysis of ancient Greek rural producers remain Millett (1984) (with clarifications in Millett 2020: 6–7) and Edwards (2004).

[4] Wolf (1966); Shanin (1971); Kula (1976); Scott (1976, 2013). It should be emphasized that peasant communities are always in conflict with urban centres; the relationship is always a reluctant one for the peasants. But there is no reason why we should expect the playing field always to be so tilted against the peasant side as we see it in the Valley.

with every property alienation such as the one allegedly suffered by Hesiod's brother Perses. Hesiod has between ten and twelve full-time residents on his plot; this requires a property of about 25 acres (10 hectares). Hesiod owns his own farm, his means of production, and he is engaged in extensive surplus-generating agriculture, a system of production that strives to produce as much product as possible for consumption, storage, and exchange.[5] Every single person on the farm is subordinate to Hesiod: all family members, the several nameless unfree persons or slaves (*dmōes Op.* 459, 502, 573, 597, 608, 766), the dependent seasonal workers (a thete and an *erithos* at *Op.* 602-3), even the free independent workers, who work for a wage. All these subordinated persons are voiceless in Askra: Hesiod calls on his neighbours to give orders to their workers—tell your slaves in midsummer: it is time to build huts! (502-3), when the Pleiades rise, get your slaves to work! (572-3), with Orion's rise, urge your slaves to do the winnowing! (597-8)—but the workers do not make answer. Many are these workers, all working for Hesiod, who notoriously urges all around him as he addresses his brother Perses: ὧδ' ἔρδειν, καὶ ἔργον ἐπ' ἔργῳ ἐργάζεσθαι, 'work in this way, and pile work upon work upon work' (*Op.* 382). But even the slightest moment of reflection brings a clear realization: Hesiod does precious little work himself. He is an owner and manager of the means of production and in control of the local labour pool as well. Work is his advice to his subordinates, but his advice to his Askraian peers is quite different: εὐθημοσύνη γὰρ ἀρίστη / θνητοῖς ἀνθρώποις, κακοθημοσύνη δὲ κακίστη, 'good management is best for mortal people, while bad management is worst' (*Op.* 471-2). There is no better comparandus for Hesiod than the *basileus* on Homer's Shield of Achilles, who beams with happiness as he watches his field workers reap the harvest, while his domestic workers prepare a midday meal for all (*Il.* 18: 550-60).[6]

Does Hesiod have peers in Askra? If he had not lost his land, brother Perses might have been one. As we gaze upon the regional topography, there is not enough space for Hesiod to have very many peers, but a few must have been out there, a few men who with their families controlled their own means of production and thus could generate unobligated surpluses. As a member of the community, Hesiod has as his peers all free persons, who share small surpluses in communal mensalities and in small loans (*Op.* 342-54). This is a community of persons with whom Hesiod *qua* Askraian peasant feels comfortable—compare slave, thete, and metic groups at Athens later (as we can see in the chapters by Forsdyke, Cecchet, and Wijma) and also foreign maritime workers allowed to worship in their own

---

[5] Halstead (2014: 60, 121). The greater importance of agriculture than livestock management, as well as the commitment to production maximization on the heroic estates was observed by Hans van Wees (1992: 49-53, 218-48), overturning Finley's presentation in the *World of Odysseus* that emphasized the opposite: the importance of livestock over crops and of self-sufficiency over maximization (Finley 1978: 61-6).

[6] One can compare also the size and labour, both its supply and its make-up, of Hesiod's farm to the farm of former king Laertes on Ithaca at *Odyssey* 24.205 ff.

spaces in fourth-century Athens (RO no. 91. 38–45): these are communities of equals collectively pursuing strategies in defence against those who (would) subordinate them. Other peers would include those who work the docks at Kreusis, where Hesiod brings his surplus;[7] who are the other owners of Hesiod's modest ship (*Op.* 624–9)?[8] Those with whom he interacts at the Gulf are the only persons in the poem who are both peers and at the same time possibly agents of improvement, for the activities that Hesiod undertakes at the Gulf are the only activities that provide Hesiod, *perhaps*, with an unobligated gain/profit, *kerdos* (esp. *Op.* 632, 644; cf. Sol. 13.44). A *kerdos* within a community is called an *epitheke* and is kept within the community by social convention, shared among neighbours in feasts and loans, as mentioned just above; there is little opportunity for investment within small, closed communities—perhaps building terraces to increase production and planting new olive trees and fruit trees, on those very terraces or elsewhere.[9] The only chance for real economic growth is through connections to the outside world. Thus Hesiod takes his exportable surplus into the Gulf of Corinth, in his own ship if he has a destination that is close by; but more likely he is putting it on a big ship[10] that is cabotaging and ferrying passengers[11] in the Gulf. His out-cargo is not specialized manufactured goods (for example, fine ceramics *et sim.*) and so not needed at a great distance, but consumables, which can travel the Gulf looking for markets at which to offload; we have been finding wrecked ships in recent years that were clearly involved in this type of activity.[12]

Numerous are the independent workers in early epic. Hesiod mentions the Askra blacksmith (*Op.* 494, 501); there are potters, carpenters, and singers (*Op.* 25–6). The itinerant specialist workers mentioned in the *Odyssey* are no doubt present in Hesiod's world, too: seers, doctors, carpenters, and singers (17.383–5), and freelance heralds (19.135). In a narrow sense, all these persons are subordinate to no one and thus peers of Hesiod. But, just as Hesiod by his membership in the Askra collective is subordinated to the *polis*, the independent itinerants are subordinated by their isolation from permanent communities.

To return to those who depend on Hesiod for their food and shelter. We might surmise that labour is plentiful and so cheap, since Hesiod makes no mention of any difficulty in finding people, free or slave, to work for him. He is more

---

[7] See Tandy (2018: 48 and references there).

[8] It is often overlooked that Hesiod's ship is a substantial one, for it has a bilge plug (*Op.* 626): this would indicate that it is of a type that would routinely have a deck on it.

[9] On terracing for olive trees and for olive production, see Foxhall (2007). On investment and this early instantiation of western proto-capitalism, see Bresson (2014).

[10] *Op.* 643: νῆ' ὀλίγην αἰνεῖν, μεγάλῃ δ' ἐνὶ φορτία θέσθαι 'praise a small ship, but put your cargo on a big one'.

[11] Often overlooked by historians, this is what Aristotle calls πορθμευτική (Arist. *Pol.* 1291$^b$20); Constantakopoulou (2007: 22–3, 223–6) gives many examples of the phenomenon in the Aegean. In the Homeric epics, 'it is easy to find a ship, if wanted, to sail somewhere' (Knorringa 1926: 7).

[12] Seventh-century ships with just this purpose are emerging from the Aegean (e.g. Leidwanger et al. 2012).

concerned with making sure that he hires and fires his workers at the optimal times (e.g. *Op.* 602-3)—again, everything in its place at the right time (εὐθημοσύνη). This is because the system is structured the way that it is. Land is not easy to come by, to judge by brother Perses' easy loss of his inherited plot and the difficulty he is having acquiring a replacement, but Hesiod has ample land, and, of course, their father had twice the acreage.

Hesiod depends on no one. His reluctant relationship with Thespiai does not actually surface in *Works and Days* (beyond the dastardly treatment of Perses by the *basilēes*), for Hesiod does not bring his production to market there. But, even if Hesiod does not care what the *basilēes* may try to do to him, there is still the fact that his community is subordinated to Thespiai and so he is too. The world of the Valley of the Muses is a hardened structure of social levels that freezes persons and their families in their social rank with no apparent opportunities to improve one's lot. Slaves are not freed in Homer and Hesiod;[13] women are without rights; 'free' workers do not have prospects for self-improvement. It often seems that the only direction up or down for these persons is down. In contrast, Hesiod, manager–owner, has it fairly easy to begin with and also has a chance to move up with hard work and good planning (and good luck): he can get a *kerdos* at home and invest some of it outside the Valley and away from the *polis*. This *kerdos* will raise his position in the Valley, just as the *basilēes* who made off with Perses' land are better off for having done so.

Hesiod's and Homer's society is a slave-holding (not necessarily also a slave-based) society. Some slaves appear to have good life experiences—for example, Dolios' nameless sons on Laertes' farm in *Odyssey* 24. Eumaios, the enslaved foreign swineherd, is quite successful—he has his own slave (but it is Eumaios himself who remind us that 'wide-seeing Zeus takes away half the manliness from a man once the day of slavery takes hold of him'[14]). Eurykleia is the revered nurse and house manager at the palace of Ithaca, but a single error in performance may lead to her execution (Hom. *Od.* 19.482-90). Eumaios and Eurykleia (and several others explicitly or more subtly) are royalty kidnapped and sold into slavery—subordination can be completely unforeseen and nearly instantaneous. Furthermore, there are hierarchies among male and female slaves in the *Odyssey*.[15] Many are the subordinators, many more are the subordinated.

It is not difficult to conclude that the lives of all non-owner–managers in the Valley are discernibly superior to the lives of the enslaved, for, although non-owner–managers have no opportunities for improvement of their lots, like metics

---

[13] Although a circumstantial case can be made for it in the promise of Odysseus to give permission to the enslaved Eumaios and Philoitios to take a wife and to have possessions and a house (*Od.* 21.212-6); see Zanovello (2022). But freedom is not forthcoming to them in the *Odyssey*.

[14] ἥμισυ γάρ τ᾽ ἀρετῆς ἀποαίνυται εὐρύοπα Ζεύς / ἀνέρος, εὖτ᾽ ἄν μιν κατὰ δούλιον ἦμαρ ἕλῃσιν (Hom. *Od.* 17.322-3).

[15] On these hierarchies, see Tandy (forthcoming).

and slaves in classical Athens, dependent labourers of all stripes have the village community to fall back on, for a small loan, part-time work from an owner–manager when needed, a nice feast at a rustic festival (maybe with hexameter accompaniment!). This communitarianism is an excellent strategy against the inescapable structural subordination of their world in the Valley.

This sketch of Hesiod's world contains within it many of the precarities that will surface in the individual studies of subordination in this volume. For every free worker who works for a wage ($\mu\iota\sigma\theta\acute{o}s$) (e.g. *Op.* 370) there are thetes who work for probably a feebler wage (e.g. *Il.* 21.444–5; *Od.* 18.357–8); these workers will reappear later in Athens in the chapters by Murray and Cecchet. The rural disadvantage we see at Askra is recognized easily in the landscapes described by Zurbach and Edwards in their accounts of Hesiod's moral economy and the demotic demands embedded in Solon's verses, respectively. (In Zurbach's discussion of debt in Hesiod's world we can see a point on the road to precarity in the world of Solon's *demos*, the focus of Edwards's paper.[16]) Although the slaves in Hesiod's world are nameless and voiceless, they are nevertheless recognizably present in the accounts by Lewis of the many and varied paths into slavery and by Forsdyke on the struggles for individual improvement through group cooperation.

To conclude by way of repetition from the start of this section: the reason that much of the subordination in Hesiod's world appears to be no different from subalternity is that his world as he shows it to us is largely without narrative. For his readers, in antiquity and today, *Works and Days* is more the perusal of a photo album than a trip to the cinema. There is more action to witness in Boiotia in the fourth century, to which we turn now.

In Hesiod's Askra we have a possible microcosm of archaic Boiotia, allowing us to explore a subsection of a valley in which a variety of subordinate relationships is implied. But there is little opportunity to witness the interaction of Askra as a collective in relationships with other communities. In classical Boiotia, the picture is reversed; we do not have any record that provides the intimacy and colour of the Askra Hesiod presents to us, but we do have a relatively rich documentary record to appreciate state-level processes of political subordination more fully in the same region of the Greek mainland. At this level of interaction there is a tendency, at least in the study of federal states such as 'the Boiotians', to homogenize experience in subordinate communities, and hence sometimes to dehumanize them. But, whenever the effects of community-level interaction and conflict on individuals are visible, their collateral experiences are unexpected and often extraordinary.

We have little information that survives concerning Boiotian history between Hesiod and the late sixth century, by which point the proto-subordination of

---

[16] For one analysis of the trajectory from Hesiod's Askra to Solon's Attic *demos*, see Tandy (1997: 112–38).

smaller communities by *poleis* such as Thespiai had progressed considerably, a level of domination that was recognized in their interactions with their *polis* peers.[17] At the same time, these subordinating communities of Boiotia had already begun to cooperate with one another, and later, in the 440s, a federal structure emerged whereby nearly all major Boiotian *poleis* joined together in a *koinon*. This federal structure attempted to acknowledge, and to represent equitably, the unequal distribution of resources across Boiotia as well as the local subordinations achieved by this date (*Hell. Oxy.* 16.3–4 McKechnie-Kern). The *koinon* was dissolved by the terms of the Peace of Antalkidas in 387/6 and, after a period of Spartan domination, the reunification of the region was achieved by Thebes and Thebans subordinating their fellow Boiotian communities, with varying degrees of violence, from 378 onwards.

When we have enough information to see the processes by which community-level subordination was undertaken, there is a striking variety of ways and means of achieving the goal. The earliest visible action in the fourth century, against Plataia in 373, was a carefully executed trap, in which the Thebans took control of the urban centre of the *polis* while many of the citizens were working in the fields (Paus. 9.1.5–7). Our sources present this as a relatively bloodless coup, with the Plataians allowed to retire to Attica (they had been in alliance relationships with Athens since 519) with just what they could carry (D.S. 15.46.5–6). The Plataians had returned only after 386 from forty years of living as refugees in Athens and Skione, and would not return again until 338 BCE. The membership of the Athenian political community conferred during their exile presented a route towards assimilation for those whose own lack of status made them extremely vulnerable, or for successful opportunists to enrich and aggrandize themselves (such as Eudemos of Plataia, celebrated in the early 320s for benefactions to Athens he had redirected from Plataia).[18]

After the Thebans' stunning victory over Sparta at Leuktra in 371, Orchomenos at first found a way to accommodate the new Theban ascendancy, but in 364 there was an *andrapodismos*: genocide and enslavement (D.S. 15.79.3–6). What enslavement at the hands of Thebans would mean is nowhere clear, and, in general, slaves are strikingly difficult to see in Boiotia in this period.[19] If archaic Askra is a slave-holding society, classical Boiotia is not as easy to define, and slaves here are both nameless *and* invisible.[20] For instance, though it is often assumed that there is a link between the desertion of 'more than twenty thousand' slaves from Dekeleia

---

[17] Ma (2016: 33).
[18] Opportunities and problems faced by the returning Plataians after 338 are discussed in Gartland (2016c: 151–5). Cf. Wijma in this volume that the Plataians in Athens were a group who, even in death, occupied an unusual position somewhere between naturalized Athenians and non-Athenian metics.
[19] See discussion of the fate of Orchomenos in Gartland (2016c: 155–7).
[20] Only in the last moments before Thebes was destroyed by Alexander III in 335 do we see 'enfranchised slaves, refugees, and metics' stationed on the wall as last defenders (Diod. Sic. 17.11.2).

in 413 (Thuc. 7.27.5), and the increased prosperity of Thebes in the period after the Peloponnesian War being fuelled by cheap slave purchases (*Hell.Oxy.* 17.3–4), we cannot see this large slave population in the fourth century. This raises questions about the issues of the opportunities for slaves improving their own conditions. As Forsdyke astutely observes in this volume, the message was clearly heard that Dekeleia offered a route out of Athenian rural slavery (and presumably also away from the threat of attack by marauding raids from the fort), but where did they end up, and can we imagine a situation where their lot *was* improved through this opportunity?

That such a change in policy toward Orchomenos occurred is explained by Pausanias' source as having been caused by the absence of Epameinondas when the decision was taken (Paus. 9.15.3). This is not an untypical apology; despite being the most significant leader in a community that was busy destroying, displacing, and enslaving its neighbours, his reputation is unusually and uniformly positive in surviving ancient historiography.[21] This is in large part because he used the period of greatest Theban influence outside Boiotia to secure a series of reversals of entrenched subordinating processes, most spectacularly at Messene. Epameinondas also supported federalism (particularly the Arkadian *koinon*) rather than imperial subordination. That there was significant variety in the functioning of Greek slave systems (as we see in Lewis's chapter) is made more visible in those rare cases in which they were challenged or (even more rarely) deconstructed. The resilient Messenian defence of their new city in the 360s and after is contrasted with the initial unwillingness of terrified Laconian helots to sing the songs banned by their Spartan masters, even when in the presence of their Theban liberators (Plut. *Lyc.* 28.5). For Plutarch (following Critias) this was evidence that a Spartan slave was the most deeply enslaved of any in the world; for the modern reader it suggests that the Thebans were fascinated (despite centuries of close contact with the Spartans) by the individual experience of this system because it was so alien.

Returning to Boiotia, we note that, compared with Plataia and Orchomenos, a very different approach was taken by Thebes to Thespiai. In 371, after the battle of Leuktra, Thebes used its new ascendancy to enact a *dioikismos* on the *polis*. What this process looked like in practice is not clear, but perhaps it is most likely that many Thespians were permitted to continue living in the area, but broken into smaller communities and without use of their urban centre.[22] From Athenian sources we know that the rebuilding of Thespiai as a *polis* and a political community was a demand made after 371; presumably there were a good number of democratic Thespian exiles in Athens lobbying energetically for the re-establishment of the city in this period. This points to a mixed experience for Thespians, with some

---

[21] Gartland (2016b: 95–6).  [22] Snodgrass (2016: 11–12).

able to remain in Boiotia, and others forced to leave the area until a more favourable political settlement was made. What we are looking at therefore is not an *andrapodismos* as experienced in Orchomenos, nor the widespread dispossession of property and forced exile *en masse* experienced by the Plataians, but instead a variegated experience with a range of measures employed by the dominant local *polis* for their own purposes, with correspondingly varied results for those subordinated.

The closest we can come to understanding the experience of an individual caught in this state-level maelstrom is Mnesarete, more commonly remembered by her nickname as Phryne ('toad'), daughter of Epikles of Thespiai. She was probably a child in the late 370s when Thebans were so energetically remaking Boiotia, and it is possible (and often assumed) that with her family she was a political refugee in Athens following the end of Thespian *polis*-hood in 371. Her life is dated only by rough traditions regarding her career as a *hetaira*, and by her reputed role as the model for some of the sculptures of Praxiteles, including the Aphrodite of Knidos (Ath. 13.591a).[23]

The tradition that has attracted most attention is her trial at Athens on a capital charge. That charge remains unspecified in our sources, but most likely it was for impiety (*asebeia*), and could have been related to her spectacular naked perambulations into the sea at Eleusis and at the Poseidonia in Aegina (Ath. 13.590f–591b). The attention in scholarship on these stories often falls, not on the remarkably successful crafting of a public image, but on whether or not Hyperides won the jury over by having her clothes removed or not.[24] Because of this, Phryne has been a victim as much of modern approaches to subordinates as of those of her contemporaries, and of the ancient sources that remembered very little of what must have been an extraordinary life. Kennedy has been alert to Phryne's situation, and thanks to Kennedy we can look in this volume to the vulnerability of women within the Athenian system being disowned or maltreated by their families and fellow Athenians.[25] The fragility of their wealth and status because of their sex is visible through their experiences in the courts, and the same is true of Phryne, but the system attacks her as a non-citizen and threatens her life rather than her wealth and position. With Kamen and Wijma in this volume we can look to status and rights at different levels of dependency on the *polis*, its laws, and its citizens, but Phryne had neither her home *polis* to support her nor citizenship of Athens. Instead, she was wholly dependent on the networks she had built for

---

[23] An attempt to date Phryne's life is made by Corso (1988: 224–5, n. 904).

[24] Attempts to move beyond the picture of Phryne on trial are made by Rosenmeyer (2001) and Morales (2011). Bremmer (2019: 1020–4) explores Phryne's use of religion in her trial. Her afterlife and modern reception are explored in Cavallini (2006).

[25] Phryne's experience is explored alongside similar cases in the fourth century by Kennedy (2014: 145–8).

herself and her ability to draw on the support, status, and privilege of an Athenian male citizen to prevent her death at the hands of the *polis*.

Throughout her life she seems to have been anything but voiceless and invisible; indeed, in some regards she could be considered among *the* most visible women of the fourth century. This was a result of both her spectacular control of her own presentation, and also her representation in the work of sculptors, painters, and orators. As well as Mnesarete/Phryne as Aphrodite, the statues she erected of herself, at Thespiai as well as at Delphi, were unusual because they represented a living woman and one of low status. Her statue at Delphi was made in gilded bronze, pushing the boundaries of representation of a living Greek individual in terms of sex, achievements, and medium.[26] It was a powerful statement that provoked astonishment from near-contemporaries such as Crates the Cynic (and Theban), and remained unsettling to male viewers such as Plutarch five hundred years later (*Mor.* 336d; 401a; Ath. 13.591b). Phryne's statue was even more remarkable because of its location within the sanctuary, standing just in front of the temple of Apollo between two significant kings of the fourth century, Archidamus III of Sparta and Philip II of Macedon.[27] Philip's actions had a profound effect on the Greek mainland, and Phryne's home *polis* was restored under his protection only after 338. But within the possibilities of her sex and the fate of her family and *polis*, Phryne could perhaps boast no less spectacular achievements than the celebrated Macedonian king.

The life and experience of this fourth-century Thespian exile embody much that the volume explores. Subordinated and precarious in many aspects of her life, she nevertheless raised herself to a position of wealth, power, and perhaps some degree of independence. This peculiar success, alongside the re-formation of Thespiai as a *polis*, permitted at Delphi a unique celebration of her position and legitimacy as a member of her erstwhile home community. On the base of the statue was inscribed 'Phryne, daughter of Epikles, the Thespian' (Paus. 9.27; Ath. 13.591c). The inscription does not survive, but it would have spoken of an individual wishing to be remembered as a member of a citizen family of a home *polis* that had been ruthlessly subordinated most of her life. Another tradition was that she would pay for the rebuilding of the walls of Thebes if they were inscribed 'Alexander destroyed Thebes, but Phryne the *hetaira* rebuilt it' (Athenaeus 13.591d). The parallels with the dedication at Delphi are poignant: Phryne stands shoulder-to-shoulder with Alexander III of Macedon, as she did with his father at Delphi, and, whereas at Delphi she chooses to be identified as simply the daughter of a citizen family of Thespiai, in this (probably apocryphal) offer she is made by Athenaeus and his sources to emphasize the career of sex work forced on her by Theban action.

---

[26] Keesling (2006: 66–71).    [27] Scott (2016: 112–13).

Implied in every subordination at community level are the resultant changed parameters for the individuals dependent to varying degrees on the experience of their group. We see that as clearly in Hesiod's Askra as in Phryne's Thespiai. We should seek to understand Phryne's life as part of the political history of her community, at the same time as we consider the commonalities between her experience and that of Neaira, tried in the 340s for claiming citizenship illegally, and discussed in this volume by Kamen, or of some of the other groups in this volume that share aspects of her precarity: metics, *banausoi*, slaves, and maltreated elite women in Athens.

In Greek history, analysis of macro-subordination frequently dominates: interstate hierarchies, intersections of *poleis* and empires, hegemonies and koinons. It is a product of the surviving materials at our disposal, and scholarship on archaic and classical Boiotian history bears witness to it. But, if we look to find ways of recognizing the intersections of high politics and the experience of individuals, as well as between subordinate groups of different types in different states, we move closer to finding commonalities between the social and political histories of ancient Greece as much as among the voiceless, invisible, and countless individuals affected by membership of or attachment to their groups. The chapters that follow emphasize the precarities that beset individuals who belong to groups that are subject to varied modalities of subordination across the Greek world. That they are all experienced within a few hundred years makes this variety even more remarkable.

Our aim in this volume is to reconsider the varieties of subordination practised and experienced within the Greek world. The *polis* itself is an essential part of this reconsideration, as so much of our awareness of subordination is due to the visibility of the institutional and legal instruments of the *polis*, which created and perpetuated hierarchies. That these occur at all levels of community experience is clear from the examples in this book. With van Wees, we can see that, in Athens, the majority of the population were always in the lowest economic group, and how their relationships to other, elite, citizens were experienced and expressed as a result. This is an example of intra-community subordination resulting in contingent political and social hierarchies, but it is also clear that subordination (and re-subordination) in many cases happens because of a person or a group leaving or being removed from existing communities, through war, high politics, raids, or natural disaster. Simply put, it is no longer sufficient to consider the experience and condition of subordination within a framework in which elite groups are the only or even the principal actors.

Similarly, we need to move beyond the concept of history 'from below', which expresses too static a view of relative status of any actors or groups in the ancient world. Instead, we seek to recognize that, because of the pervasive and ubiquitous precarity in the archaic and classical Greek world, the same individual or group can be both subject to, and agent of, subordination. The processes of subordination are always in motion at different levels, and we need to rethink fundamentally how these processes were formulated and reproduced in different parts of archaic and classical communities from a variety of perspectives. We need also to engage, sensitively and compassionately, with the real people involved in these processes so often full of suffering: *from* below yes, but also *for* below and *with* below.

The necessity of reconsidering the processes of subordination in this way puts the volume in contact with Paulin Ismard's view (2017) of status in Greek societies. This contends that, rather than a gradation of statuses, there are three major polarities open to analysis in Greek society in the oppositions of free/slave, citizen/outside, male/female. This questions the approach to status in ancient Greece as a spectrum of incremental gradations, and instead argues for the importance of practices of honour and dishonour in creating innumerable distinctions in which individuals can hold different statuses when judged against different criteria. This approach emphasizes the instability of status, and the importance of the agency of subordinate individuals and groups in shaping their own experience within the particular framework of their community. We see the instability of status of Athenian women and children demonstrated vividly in Kennedy's chapter. In Forsdyke's chapter, too, we can see both instability and modalities of agency within the heterogeneous community of slaves in classical Athens. Their heterogeneity lay both in their pre-existing status and continuing experience of their subordination, and also in their deeply uneven knowledge of and access to the mechanisms of improving their situation vis-à-vis their citizen subordinators. Recognizing the importance of instability and agency also underscores the need to identify *commonalities of experience* among subordinate groups, rather than to focus only on the relative status or legal position of any one group within any given community.

The importance of the agency of subordinates within Greek communities helps to explain the knotty question of *why groups form*. Littering the inherited historiography of ancient Greece are traditional categories that are employed to conceptualize groups of all types but fail to remain coherent when subjected to sustained analysis or faced with the challenge of new evidence. Many of the chapters in this book demonstrate that, for subordinate groups, these categories do not work, because those whom we might consider members of a particular group do not choose to present themselves as such. This should keep us alert to the long-recognized dangers of the academic investigator reinscribing subordination by not allowing the voices of subordinates to speak for themselves. Wijma's chapter demonstrates that metics in Athens rarely, if ever, present themselves as metics, just as Cecchet's thetes actively avoid that label, and Murray's *banausoi* do not generally choose to identify themselves based on their profession. But where there is value in the label, such as with the Plataians (whose status was different, and in many ways superior to other non-native groups in Athens), Wijma shows that they reinforced their membership of that group by their highly visible and distinctive choices of behaviour and association.

The group that matters most in the *polis* was the citizen body. The energy of new enquiries into citizenship by Duplouy, Blok, Dmitriev, and Duplouy and Brock challenge scholars to think again about this essential aspect of urban life in the Greek world.[28] In different ways, questions surrounding membership of the *polis* are at the heart of the chapters by Kennedy, Wijma, and Cecchet. Similarly, Kamen's chapter compares precisely the difference in how the law of hubris distinguishes in practice the treatment of individuals with different statuses and different histories. Citizenship as a broader issue can be seen as an important constitutive element of one's identity within the *polis* also in the chapters by Zurbach and Edwards, where we see citizens with little access to the 'privileges' of citizenship, and in those of Lewis and Forsdyke, where individuals struggle with lives denied access to those privileges utterly and permanently.

The reassessment of the ancient 'aristocracy' by van Wees and Fisher,[29] rooted as it is in Duplouy's work, successfully redefined our view of ancient elites by challenging inherited orthodoxies regarding the stability of elite groups. This instability also applies to the processes of subordination by which the elite were able to distinguish themselves, and we seek to describe some of those processes here. That work also brings to the fore the permeation of the *polis* and citizenship in the lives of ordinary persons: we see this in the chapters by Kennedy, Cecchet, Wijma, Edwards, and Zurbach, and the career of Phryne—as well as the up-and-down saga of the Plataians—illustrates this different kind of permeation of high politics into the experience of subordinated individuals.

Of course, there is no one more subordinated than a slave. In this collection focused on subordination, we have included two chapters on slaves and slavery: Forsdyke's on the efforts towards agency undertaken by individual slaves acting collectively to improve their lots and Lewis's on the experiences of enslaved groups in different locations in the Greek world. Ancient slavery in the Greek and Roman worlds is deservedly getting a great deal of attention from scholars today because its conclusions have lessons for all of us.[30]

We present this collection as a collective effort at comparative history within the chronological boundaries of 700 and 300 BCE. Traditional comparative history is present in this volume in the chapter by Julien Zurbach on the crowd in seventh-century Boiotia and E. P. Thompson's moral economy of nineteenth-century workers within industrial capitalism; and Forsdyke enhances our appreciation of

---

[28] Duplouy (2006, 2011); Blok (2017); Dmitriev (2018); Duplouy and Brock (2018).
[29] Van Wees and Fisher (2015).
[30] On why we should study ancient slavery and what is the best available current work, see Forsdyke (2021: 247–54).

slave agency by comparing experiences of nineteenth-century slaves in North America. Readers might have preferred more time to have been spent comparing the crowds in the late Republic[31] or in late antiquity[32] or a fuller set of comparisons from the Roman world.[33] But we believe that this collection of studies of subordination and subordinates in archaic and classical Greece is in and of itself comparative. To draw too detailed comparisons with other time periods and places would probably be to minimize, ignore, or deny the variety of subordination that we think this collection demonstrates within our time frame.

Finally, some words about the different approaches to subordination undertaken by our contributors. Van Wees considers the significance of the changing size of the Athenian 'working class'. Kamen's and Kennedy's chapters both reveal the consequences of subordination in the legal sphere. Kamen examines the consequences of status inequality for access to the legal system; Kennedy focuses on the specific example of citizen-women and their children in Athens. A second point of view is found in the four chapters that reveal the limitations of the traditional categories we employ to study groups in the ancient world, categories of elite provenience: Cecchet's thetes do not present themselves as thetes; Wijma's metics did not define themselves as metics so much as people connected to other places; Murray's craftspeople hesitate to assert their identities as such; Lewis's survey of local slave groups demonstrates a need to stop assuming that all chattel slave systems are parallel to that at Athens. Finally, three chapters focus on the ameliorative strategies of subordinate groups: Zurbach on the moral economy of archaic Boiotian peasants; Edwards on the strategy of the *demos* against the state as we can extract it from Solon's verses; and Forsdyke's discussion of slave agency within the Athenian legal system. Together these ten studies highlight the processes that created subordination, how subordination was maintained, and the efforts of the subordinated to alleviate their conditions of precarity.

## Works Cited

Blok, J. (2017). *Citizenship in Ancient Athens*. Cambridge.

Bremmer, J. (2019). 'Religion and the Limits of Individualisation in Ancient Athens: Andocides, Socrates, and the Fair-breasted Phryne', in M. Fuchs, A. Linkenbach, M. Mulsow, B. Otto, R. Parson, and J. Rüpke (eds), *Religious Individualisation*, 1009–32. Berlin and Boston.

Bresson, A. (2014). 'Capitalism and the Ancient Greek Economy', in L. Neal and J. Williamson (eds), *The Cambridge History of Capitalism*, i. *The Rise of Capitalism: From Ancient Origins to 1848*, 43–74. Cambridge.

---

[31] Millar (1998). [32] Magalhães de Oliveira (2020). [33] e.g. Knapp (2011).

Cavallini, E. (2006). 'Phryne: Cnidian Venus to Movie Star', *Conservation Science in Cultural Heritage*, 6/1: 215–36.

Constantakopoulou, C. (2007). *The Dance of the Islands*. Oxford.

Corso, A. (1988). *Prassitele: Fonti epigrafiche e letterarie: Vita e opera*, i (*Xenia-Quaderni* 10). Rome.

Courrier, C., and J. C. Magalhães de Oliveira (2022) (eds). *Ancient History from Below. Subaltern Experiences and Actions in Context*. London.

Dmitriev, S. (2018). *The Birth of the Athenian Community: From Solon to Cleisthenes*. London.

Duplouy, A. (2006). *Le Prestige des élites: Recherches sur les nides de reconnaissance sociale en Grèce entre les $X^e$ en $V^e$ siècles avant J.-C.* Paris.

Duplouy, A. (2011). 'Deux échelons de citoyenneté? En quête de la citoyenneté archaïque', in V. Azouley and P. Ismard (eds), *Clisthène et Lycurge d'Athène:. Autour du politique dans la cité classique*, 89–106. Paris.

Duplouy, A., and R. Brock (2018) (eds). *Defining Citizenship in Archaic Greece*. Oxford.

Edwards, A. T. (2004). *Hesiod's Ascra*. Berkeley and London.

Finley, M. I. (1978 [1954[1]]). *The World of Odysseus*. 2nd rev. edn. Harmondsworth.

Forsdyke, S. (2021). *Slaves and Slavery in Ancient Greece*. Cambridge.

Foxhall, L. (2007). *Olive Cultivation in Ancient Greece: Seeking the Ancient Economy*. Oxford.

Gartland, S. D. (2016a) (ed.). *Boiotia in the Fourth Century* BC. Philadelphia.

Gartland, S. D. (2016b). 'Enchanting History: Pausanias in Fourth-Century Boiotia', in Gartland (2016a: 80–98).

Gartland, S. D. (2016c). 'A New Boiotia? Exiles, Landscapes, and Kings', in Gartland (2016a: 147–64).

Halstead, P. (2014). *Two Oxen Ahead*. Chichester.

Ismard, P. (2017). *Democracy's Slaves: A Political History of Ancient Greece*. Cambridge, MA.

Keesling, C. (2006). 'Heavenly Bodies: Monuments to Prostitutes in Greek Sanctuaries', in C. Faraone (ed.), *Prostitutes and Courtesans In the Ancient World*, 59–76. Madison.

Kennedy, R. (2014). *Immigrant Women in Ancient Athens*. London.

Knapp, R. (2011). *Invisible Romans*. London.

Knorringa, H. (1926). *Emporos*. Amsterdam.

Kula, W. (1976). *An Economic Theory of the Feudal System*. London.

Leidwanger, J., H. Özdaş, and E. Greene (2012). 'Sourcing the Cargos of Three Archaic Shipwrecks: Kekova Adası, Kepçe Burnu, and Caycağız Koyu', *Arkeometri Sonuçları Toplantısı*, 27: 393–409.

Ma, J. (2016). 'The Autonomy of the Boiotian Poleis', in Gartland (2016a: 32–41).

Magalhães de Oliveira, J. C. (2020). 'Late Antiquity: The Age of Crowds?', *Past and Present*, 249: 3–52.

Millar, F. (1998). *The Crowd in Rome in the Late Republic*. Ann Arbor.

Millett, P. (1984). 'Hesiod and his World', *PCPS* 210: 84–115.

Millett, P. (2020). 'Credit where it's Due or Further Reflections on Lending, Borrowing, Banking, and Exchange in Ancient Athens.' Paper posted by author at https://www.repository.cam.ac.uk/bitstream/handle/1810/313106/CreditWhereIt'sDue_Millett,P%20%20-%20Working%20Paper.pdf?sequence=1 (accessed 30 November 2022).

Morales, H. (2011). 'Fantasising Phryne: The Psychology and Ethics of "Ekphrasis"', *Cambridge Classical Journal*, 57: 71–104.

Rosenmeyer, P. (2001). '(In-)Versions of Pygmalion: The Statue Talks back', in A. Lardinois and L. McClure (eds), *Making Silence Speak: Women's Voices in Greek Literature and Society*, 240–60. Princeton.

Scott, J. (1976). *The Moral Economy of the Peasant*. New Haven.

Scott, J. (2013). *Decoding Subaltern Politics*. London.

Scott, M. (2016). 'The Performance of Boiotian Identity at Delphi', in Gartland (2016a: 32–41).

Shanin, T. (1971) (ed.). *Peasants and Peasant Societies*. Harmondsworth.

Snodgrass, A. (2016). 'Thespiai and the Fourth-Century Climax in Boiotia', in Gartland (2016a: 99–120).

Spivak, G. S. (1988). 'Can the Subaltern Speak?', in C. Nelson and L. Grossberg (eds), *Marxism and the Interpretation of Culture*, 271–313. Basingstoke.

Tandy, D. (1997). *Warriors into Traders*. Berkeley and Los Angeles.

Tandy, D. (2018). 'In Hesiod's World', in A. Loney and S. Scully (eds), *The Oxford Handbook of Hesiod*, 43–60. Oxford.

Tandy, D. (forthcoming). 'Slavery, Honour and Ideology in Homer's World', in D. Lewis, M. Canevaro, and D. Cairns (eds), *Slavery and Honour in the Ancient Greek World*. Edinburgh.

van Wees, H. (1992). *Status Warriors: War, Violence and Society in Homer and History*. Amsterdam.

van Wees, H., and N. Fisher (2015). 'The Trouble with "Aristocracy"', in N. Fisher and H. van Wees (eds), *Aristocracy' in Antiquity*, 1–57. Swansea.

Wolf, E. (1966). *Peasants*. Englewood Cliffs, NJ.

Zanovello, S. (2022). 'Homer and the Vocabulary of Manumission', in J. Bernhardt and M. Canevaro (eds), *From Homer to Solon: Continuity and Change in Archaic Greece*, 93–114. Leiden.

# 1

# A Moral Economy of the *Demos* in Early Archaic Greece

*Julien Zurbach*

### Preface

This chapter originates in a larger study on the peasants of archaic Greek societies. Calling them 'peasants' is not universal. This choice originates in a tension between ancient history and other historical fields, particularly medieval and modern history, which is perhaps stronger or more essential in France than elsewhere. Works by Chayanov and others (Boserup, Shanin) towards the definition of a specific type of peasant economy have for a long time been widely read in the long-term, structural history typical of the first age of the Annales school. Calling Hesiod a peasant, in that specific perspective, is an affirmation that ancient history should be written along the same lines as medieval history, for instance. Reading Pierre Ouzoulias and François Menant has been important here. The existence of peasant studies in the economic anthropology of the Anglophone world, and its recent renewal and introduction into history (e.g. Wickham 2005), has, of course, strengthened this line of research.

More specifically, the idea of a 'moral economy' comes also directly from other fields of history, especially modern history and the great article by E. P. Thompson (1971). This notion is perhaps now more often used by anthropologists (e.g. Scott 1976). Here, however, Thompson and the British Marxist historians are more important. The recourse to the notion of moral economy in its Thompsonian definition has been (for me, and surely also for Forsdyke, who uses it as well—see her chapter in this volume) a way out of the riddle of the 'social situation' of Hesiod. Nobody has in fact solved the problem of whether Hesiod may be seen as a 'poor' peasant, a middle-class type, or even a landowner. A solution to this question is to consider *Works and Days* first as a discourse, as the formulation of principles, and at the same time, contrary to those who see it as just a sum of evident *topoi* lacking any originality, specifically to look for the crucible where this discourse originates, for the originalities and coherence it shows, and for the conditions of possibility of such a discourse. This leads to a third area of studies after the Annales/peasant studies and the British Marxist historians: the question of the nature of 'orientalizing' features, and the relation between connectivity and common structures or parallel histories. The moral economy stresses the importance of both factors, whereas the new Mediterranean paradigms developed since 2000 often insist solely on the first element.

Looking at the discourse and seeing it as a moral economy may seem quite postmodern and usher in one more application, not to say invocation, of 'agency'. Especially in modern history, this notion has been at the centre of studies on the subaltern and subordinate, and it seems quite evident that they are to be best examined as individuals or groups looking for some spaces where free action may be possible. This is, of course, quite true, and the 'moral economy' has been coined to avoid mechanical views of popular dissent as mere reactions to food shortage, underlining that the 'crowd' also had views on the functioning of the economy. Nowadays, however, now that the adversaries of Thompson (mechanical, economistic Marxism, and its idealist versions by Althusser) are gone, there is a danger that agency and the accent on popular culture and representations may be exaggerated. Agency, after all, is what makes an agent, and a sociology based on agents cannot be but a liberal one, based on the problems of individual choice. Culture-based readings of Thompson and Bourdieu today clearly go too far in stressing the individual or small groups against class or order, the rational strategies against the collective dynamics of conflict, and the importance of representations against economic, material factors. This is not new, and has been best formulated, to my knowledge, by Sumit Sarkar, one of the leading figures of subaltern studies in India, in the framework of debates internal to this group of Indian historians (see Sarkar 1997: ch. 2, 'The Relevance of E. P. Thompson', and ch. 3, 'The Decline of the Subaltern in *Subaltern Studies*').

## Introduction

The nature of social and political conflicts in Archaic Greece has long been an object of study. However, there are quite diverging views on the significance of those conflicts, taking place at a very crucial moment of the formation of Greek city states and therefore engaging our views on the whole structure of Greek city states. Without going too far in a review of recent works, it is possible to say that a tendency to give more importance to intra-elite conflicts or concurrence, as opposed to the conflicts between rich and poor, has dominated. It is therefore important to examine not only the instances where non-elite groups are involved in conflicts but also the few cases where access may be possible to the views on society and economy expressed by these groups, to the objectives of their political fight.

Drawing on fundamental work that tends to read again the Greek data in the context of studies on popular culture and politics, but also peasant economies,[1] we would like to propose here a new characterization of the peasantry and its political agenda as motivated by a 'moral economy' in Thompson's sense. This is possible only in some cases and, *à tout seigneur tout honneur*, it is necessary to begin with the *Works and Days* attributed to Hesiod.[2]

## *Works and Days*

Defining the nature of the works attributed to Hesiod is almost as difficult a question as their historical significance. If we concentrate only on the *Works and Days* and leave aside the quite similar problems raised by the *Theogony* and the many fragments, a first point is their almost complete isolation in the traditional corpus of what we call ancient Greek literature.[3] At such an early date, the only other work that may echo the quite unusual aspects of the *Works and Days* is the corpus of popular tales transmitted under the name of Aesop, whose most ancient parts are surely archaic.[4] As has long been recognized, however, it is outside Greek literature that the most evident parallels for the *Works and Days* are to be found. Martin West has clearly made this point in his commentary,[5] following earlier studies, notably by Dornseiff and Walcot.[6] Making the case that the work attributed to Hesiod is not 'an early Greek *Georgics*',[7] he establishes a list of works constitutive of what is called sapiential, or wisdom, literature.[8] In doing this, West takes examples very far from Hesiod in time and space;[9] he nevertheless concentrates on a historically coherent group of works from the Ancient Near East and Egypt, which appears to constitute the most pertinent context in which to understand Hesiod's *Works and Days*. The best definition of wisdom literature is probably the domination of what the literary theoretician André Jolles called 'simple forms'[10]—that is, models of short compositions that, like the tale with animal characters or the proverbs, are here integrated into a wider context usually based on a story of human injustice with the main character as the victim.[11] Examples of this literary production[12] include the Egyptian *Instructions of Amenemope*,[13] the Aramaic story of *Ahiqar*, the oldest known version of which is

---

[1] Most notably Gallant (1991); Edwards (2004); Schmitz (2004a); Forsdyke (2005). The thesis presented here is a continuation of Zurbach (2012, 2013, 2017).
[2] The perspective adopted here is focusing on the discourse developed in *Works and Days*. We assume that Hesiod is a peasant, not only because he is neither an aristocrat nor a landless worker, but also in a structural sense, because of the type of economy and community he is advocating. This point is made clear by the fundamental work of Edwards (2004).
[3] See Canfora (1994: 63–82) for an overview.   [4] Luzzato (1996); Kurke (2011).
[5] West (1978).   [6] Dornseiff (1934); Walcot (1962).   [7] West (1978: p. v).
[8] West (1978: 3–25).   [9] See infra.   [10] Jolles 1930.
[11] Zurbach 2012: 182–3.   [12] For an overview, see West (1978: 3–25).
[13] Lichtheim (1976–80); Laisney (2007). The Instructions are a very different genre in ancient Egyptian literature: see West (1978: 10–11), and infra on the contrast between instructions and wisdom or sentence literature. On later texts in this tradition and with an important introduction, see Agut-Labordère and Chauveau (2011).

from fifth-century Elephantine,[14] and of course the different components of the biblical *Book of Proverbs*.[15]

The history of literary forms must be considered at the level of the Eastern Mediterranean,[16] without isolating productions in Greek from productions in other languages. Wisdom literature, however, does not only have formal aspects as common defining features.[17] To put it another way: that it belongs to a wider genre does not mean that there is no point in interpreting historically what Hesiod says—quite the reverse. Certainly, some proverbial material may seem universal, and this has been underlined through precise studies of convergence between proverbs from very different cultural areas.[18] There is, then, an adaptation to context, aiming at producing a coherent, useful discourse in a precise setting, and this opens room for historical interpretation.

It is therefore legitimate to concentrate on the fundamental ideas to be found in the *Works and Days*. The author of this work has a coherent and clear notion of the lines of behaviour he wants to promote in what we call the economy: the production and distribution of goods. The fundamental point in Hesiod's view is the central place of the family.[19] There is almost complete identity of producer and consumer: the product of the work done by the family members is allocated to family members. This has two consequences. The first is that expansion and reduction of work and product follow the life cycle of the family. It is from this point of view that Hesiod may say, for instance, that the more sons you have the more work they do, thus contradicting the advice he has just given, to have only one son to avoid inheritance by division (*Op.* 376–80). The second is the impossibility of a precise compensation for the work done by each individual: family work is collective and consumption as well. Everyone works and gets his or her share of the product, and the rules that govern the allocation of goods may have to do with generation, gender, or the right of the elder (all criteria unknown to Hesiod) but not with the amount of work done by each member of the family.

---

[14] Briquel-Chatonnet (2005) is the best overview of the history of this text; see also Grelot (1972: 427–52).

[15] On *Proverbs*: Buehlmann (2004); Crenshaw (1992, 1993, 1997), with literature; on particular questions, Whybray (1994, 1995).

[16] This, of course, is even more pertinent for the *Theogony* or for some fragmentary works from the Epic cycle, as demonstrated also by West in a masterpiece of erudition: West (1997).

[17] I have argued elsewhere (Zurbach 2012) that the travel of this historically particular mode of arranging composition along the lines of Jolles's 'simple forms' is relevant not only to literary history but also to social history in that it offers a vector to the exchange of common ideas.

[18] Naré (1986) on convergences between Hesiod and traditional wisdom from Congo; parallels with ethnological material from southern France are underlined by Schmitz (2004b), on which see infra. There are other points that deserve attention. When translating from the Egyptian, the writer of *Proverbs* 22–3 does add considerations on the topic of debt; *Ahiqar*, already in the fifth-century version from Elephantine, and Hesiod both offer lengthy treatment of this subject, which is a fundamental problem of the archaic Mediterranean (Zurbach 2012: 182).

[19] Millett (1984) underlines this point; Edwards (2004: 83–9 and ch.. 3 generally); Zurbach (2017: ch. 7).

This fact has nothing to do with ideology or other considerations: it is simply not possible to divide and have accounts of the work because it gets done collectively.[20]

There is only one sphere where Hesiod does mention accounting: exchanges outside the community, under the heading of *emporie*, since it is by definition dependent on seafaring. There, he knows about profit and calculation (*Op.* 617–94). Do not go on *emporie*, he advises, unless you do not have any other possibility; and, if you have to do so, do not take your entire product with you and ensure that you make a good *kerdos*, a gain that is measurable. It should be underlined that this coherent set of principles is not exactly what one usually refers to when referring to Hesiod as an advocate of autarky. On the contrary, it is a structure where the family has the central place and where different channels render external exchanges possible and limit them at the same time, either inside the community or outside it.[21] This type of economy is not only a 'domestic economy'— a quite loose concept; it has essential points in common with a peasant economy, a concept coined by A. V. Chayanov in the 1920s and then adapted to different situations by 'peasant studies' from the 1960s onwards.[22] The advantage in such identification does not lie in the augmentation of the number of 'peasant economies' known from history and ethnography but in the light it may shed on Hesiod's text and principles.[23] It enables the identification of a set of precise economic behaviours at the core of Hesiod's conception of family and community. The nature of the community, in particular, is connected with the domestic economy;[24] it is a sphere where exchange is apparently calculable, but not subject to the quest for profit. Fundamentally it consists of similar families having similar behaviours and principles. It is not an integrated community: Hesiod does not mention common land, commonly organized pasture, or any right or duty of the community regarding the cultivation of land. As such, it is in fact a condition of possibility of the peasant economy at the domestic level, which needs similarly organized family cells around itself—the *geitones*, 'neighbours', so important to Hesiod.[25] On the other hand, the identification of Hesiod's set of principles as peasant economy may serve to underline some originalities of this kind of economy in Early Archaic Greece. Hesiod's ideal peasant family does own slaves, *dmōes*, which obviously do not exist in Chayanov's model and are not a usual feature in peasant studies. Since debt slavery is not mentioned by Hesiod, the *dmōes* are probably bought from outside, an important fact in itself, correcting the

---

[20] Zurbach (2017: ch. 7).
[21] For a discussion on autarky and self-sufficiency, and the distinction between both notions, see Aymard (1983).
[22] Chayanov (1966); Kerblay (1971). For a systematic exploitation of the concept on ancient Greeks sources, see Gallant (1991). A nice example of the use of Chayanov is Kula (1970: 43–54).
[23] Zurbach (2017: ii. 683–90).    [24] Edwards (2004: ch. 3), and Zurbach (2017: i. 311–21).
[25] Schmitz (2004a: 27–104, particularly 52–60).

perspective on the *emporie* as theorized by Hesiod. But on the whole, as far as the precise type of domestic peasant economy advocated by Hesiod is concerned, the presence of slaves does not change the fundamental pattern of the economy: the number of slaves could modify the connection of family work to family consumption, but we are not in a position to make any calculation on those points. Instead, it is important that Hesiod, even considering the presence of slaves as an advantage, does not want it to modify anything; he never lets one think that exploiting land with slaves could, for instance, allow one to have more sons; he just says that more sons do more work.[26]

## A Moral Economy of the *Demos*

In Greek, *Works and Days* was probably not isolated but part of a wider literature, which survives only in a very fragmentary state, and to which we can add the Aesopic tales. They probably were not alone, therefore, in presenting both as desirable and at the same time as real a precise type of economy, as opposed to cataloguing a set of loosely integrated principles. Are we in a position to trace these ideas in the development of Greek societies in the Archaic age? Megara may offer a good case study.[27] Two texts are of interest here. The first is on the way to power, followed by the tyrant Theagenes, probably in the second half of the seventh century. It keeps memory of a particular event, without very close parallels in the literature on tyrants and therefore surely worthy of attention. Theagenes, it is said, came to power using a popular uprising during which the poor slaughtered the animals of the rich at a river.

> Πάντες δὲ τοῦτο ἔδρων ὑπὸ τοῦ δήμου πιστευθέντες, ἡ δὲ πίστις ἦν ἡ ἀπέχθεια ἡ πρὸς τοὺς πλουσίους, οἷον Ἀθήνῃσί τε Πεισίστρατος στασιάσας πρὸς τοὺς πεδιακούς, καὶ Θεαγένης ἐν Μεγάροις τῶν εὐπόρων τὰ κτήνη ἀποσφάξας, λαβὼν παρὰ τὸν ποταμὸν ἐπινέμοντας. (Arist. *Pol.*, 1305ᵃ21–6)

And they all used to do this when they had acquired the confidence of the people, and their pledge of confidence was their enmity towards the rich, as at Athens Pisistratus made himself tyrant by raising up a party against the men of the plain, and Theagenes at Megara by slaughtering the cattle of the well-to-do which he captured grazing by the river.   (trans. Rackham)

---

[26] This illustrates that Hesiod's world is self-contained, production and consumption for the most part isolated. In this sense, Hesiod and his neighbours resemble other groups of subordinates in this collection, especially manual labourers (Murray), slaves (Forsdyke, Lewis), and the agricultural producers at Athens (Edwards).

[27] On Archaic Megara, in addition to Robu (2014) and the earlier collection of papers in Figueira and Nagy (1985), see now Beck (2018) and Stein-Hölkeskamp (2018).

There has been a lot of discussion on the meaning of this event: why were the cattle at a river? Why did the poor slaughter them?[28] Probably the river is only a strategically chosen location, since we would not expect much pastureland along a river of the Megarid, which was most probably a seasonal river. The animals were then on their way—but to where? Maybe it was for a sacrifice or for another occasion of meat consumption, and here we are reminded of the other important text on Megara, from Plutarch.[29]

> Τίς ἡ παλιντοκία; Μεγαρεῖς Θεαγένη τὸν τύραννον ἐκβαλόντες, ὀλίγον χρόνον ἐσωφρόνησαν κατὰ τὴν πολιτείαν· εἶτα πολλὴν κατὰ Πλάτωνα καὶ ἄκρατον αὐτοῖς ἐλευθερίαν τῶν δημαγωγῶν οἰνοχοούντων, διαφθαρέντες παντάπασι τά τ' ἄλλα τοῖς πλουσίοις ἀσελγῶς προσεφέροντο, καὶ παριόντες εἰς τὰς οἰκίας αὐτῶν οἱ πένητες ἠξίουν ἑστιᾶσθαι καὶ δειπνεῖν πολυτελῶς· εἰ δὲ μὴ τυγχάνοιεν, πρὸς βίαν καὶ μεθ' ὕβρεως ἐχρῶντο πᾶσι. Τέλος δὲ δόγμα θέμενοι, τοὺς τόκους ἀνεπράττοντο παρὰ τῶν δανειστῶν οὓς δεδωκότες ἐτύγχανον, παλιντοκίαν τὸ γιγνόμενον προσαγορεύσαντες. (Plut. *Quaes. Gr.* 18 = *Mor.* 295C–D)

What is 'return-interest'? When the Megarians had expelled Theagenes, their despot, for a short time, they were sober and sensible in their government. But later, when the popular leaders poured a full and heady draught of freedom for them, as Plato says, they were completely corrupted and, among their shocking acts of misconduct towards the wealthy, the poor would enter their homes and insist upon being entertained and banqueted sumptuously. But, if they did not receive what they demanded, they would treat all the household with violence and insult. Finally, they enacted a decree whereby they received back again the interest that they happened to have paid to their creditors, calling the measure 'return-interest'. (trans. Babbitt, adapted)

Here we learn about two very particular events in the radical democracy of the early sixth century in Megara. First, the *demos* had the wealthy reimburse the interest on the loans; secondly, they came to the houses of the wealthy to take part in the meals. Here again we are faced with traits without exact parallels and an otherwise unattested word, the *palintokia*, for the return of the interest. Much discussion has centred on that word; much less on the question of the meals. There may, however, be a connection between the slaughter of the cattle and the forced participation in the meals of the wealthy: both actions seem to allude to some precise claim on the organization of the allocation of the product from the

---

[28] Among others, Oost (1973) and Link (1991: 129–31).
[29] For those concerned about the passage of time undercutting Plutarch's reliability, Hans Beck has fashioned a clear exposition on why we should be comfortable with Plutarch's allusions to and discussion of Megarian events and sentiments (Beck 2018: 37–41). Theagenes as a historical figure was alive in the Athenian public imagination in 421 when Aristophanes mentions him in a joke about meat (*Pax* 925–8).

land. But, even without this connection, it is quite clear that here we are facing some quite interesting facts. In the second half of the seventh century, the poor of Megara, among whom the peasants must have been the most numerous, attack the rich by seizing one of the most evident and symbolic parts of their wealth. Given the role of cattle in elite wealth in Iron Age and archaic Greece, it is probably not necessary to suppose that there was a turn to pastoralism imposed by the wealthy as a mean of wealth accumulation, and a conflict on land rights as a consequence. It cannot be excluded, but we cannot affirm that the cattle were a cause of the conflict; in the state of our knowledge, they are only victims of it. This kind of violent action, however, has long been recognized, notably by Hobsbawm, as a typical feature of peasant revolutionary action.[30] Since it is probable that the meat from the slaughter was consumed on the spot, the main contention may be the distribution of the products of agriculture and husbandry.

The second episode may take us further. A source for scepticism among historians lies in the surprisingly moderate measure of the 'return of interest'. A generation later in Athens, Solon would abolish all debts, and now we are faced with a supposedly radical democracy abolishing only the interest! The first answer is that there are forms of debt servitude where the interest, not the principal, is to be reimbursed through the work of the debtor, since interest can be so heavy that it becomes the problem much more than the principal. A second one, not exclusive of the first, is that here, as well as with the slaughter of the cattle and the forced participation in the meals of the wealthy, we see the practical application of a corpus of precise ideas about the organization of the economy.[31]

The similarities with the views expressed in *Works and Days* should be highlighted. Hesiod knows about lending and borrowing. Loans known to Hesiod seem, however, to consist of loans in kind, and are limited to food in the period when it is scarce, before harvest, and to oxen or tools according to the period of the year when they are most needed. Hesiod's advice is to avoid loans and to have enough stored food and enough oxen not to rely on any one else. In any case, it is a matter between neighbours and equals. Hesiod says that we should pay back well, 'even more' (καὶ λώιον: *Op*. 350), in order to find again someone to make a

---

[30] Hobsbawm (1974; again in 1998: 223–55); Zurbach (2017: ii. 738–40). The British historian, during the analysis of Peruvian land occupation in the middle of the twentieth century, a very different yet quite similar context, defines a typical peasant form of direct action through its strategic use of the means of production whose use and control lie at the very heart of the bigger economic problem. Peruvian peasants occupied precisely the land they wanted to redistribute. In that perspective, the attack on the Megarian livestock takes on a new dimension.

[31] S. Forsdyke has proposed another interpretation of this text. In a fundamental article (Forsdyke 2005; see below on the notion of moral economy), she interprets this text as an instance of ritual reversal as known in modern Europe and in some other instances in ancient Greece–for instance, among the Cretan cities for the slaves (Ath. 263f, for Kydonia). Certainly, there is a very important point here. It is perfectly reconcilable with the views developed here, particularly because the frontier between those rituals and riots may be unclear, and in times of tensions rituals may turn into violent uprisings (Forsdyke 2005: 84–90). The main difference in fact is that I believe that Plutarch's texts are to be taken at face value, whatever their ideological content, and that there must have been some kind of popular government in Megara in the sixth century.

loan in the future (*Op.* 349–60). But this is not interest in the strict sense, since it is not connected to time. The quantity over the principal, the 'even more' that we have to add, may refer in such a context to a full measure as opposed to a flat one. In any case, there is no connection with the duration of the loan, and accordingly Hesiod does not use the word *tokos*. In Hesiod, the concept of the loan is present, but that of the calculation of interest connected with time is not.[32]

There is another point of importance here: Hesiod does mention the allocation of the product inside the family, but, as is widely known, he condemns payments to the *basilēes* made in the agora. His brother did win in court only because he paid the *basilēes*. There is an ongoing discussion on the nature of this payment, but the fact is clear.[33] Hesiod does not mention any levy that he might consider legitimate. This is an original perspective, in a world where levies are indeed well-attested. The Homeric epics do not lack instances where a member of the elite is exacting wealth from the *demos*.[34] Telemachus in one instance regrets that the suitors are powerful men, because, he says, were they from the people, he would gather again with force all that he has lost, without a problem (*Od.* 2.74–8)! When the king of the Phaiacians tells his fellow *basilēes* to add to the gifts for Odysseus, he simply says that they will each take it back from the *demos* (*Od.* 13.14–15). In all instances—there are others—levies on the *demos* look natural and evident, but also linked to the use of force, so that Carlier could write that everyone having the necessary force could make a levy, and that this appears an important criterion to distinguish *demos* from elite 'quiconque a la force et l'impunité peut extorquer des dons'.[35] This reality underlies also Hesiod's discourse on the unjust leaders (*Op.* 238–47), which, as opposed to those who give 'straight judgments' and lead their city to peace and prosperity, 'practise violence' and can be assumed to be identical with the gift-eating, *dorophagoi* leaders just mentioned (*Op.* 220–1).[36] Hesiod, however, seems to construct a world whose actors are equals, where differences in wealth are visible but remain on a modest level between those who have oxen and those who do not, those who have to borrow food before harvest and those who do not need to. *Basilēes* eating gifts seem to be outside the community of Askra. To possess more livestock than is necessary for agriculture, to exact levies on poorer members of the community, to calculate interests on loans, all this is condemned by Hesiod as well as by the Megarian democrats.[37]

---

[32] On lending in Hesiod, quite different views expressed by Will (1957) (beginning of peasant indebtedness leading to pre-Solonian *hektemeroi*); Millett (1984: 99–103) (embedded in reciprocity); Millett (1991: 46); Edwards (2004: 92–102) (accent on reciprocity as well); Zurbach (2017: i. 311–17).
[33] Edwards (2004: notably 63–4); Zurbach (2017: ii. 308–10).
[34] Carlier (1984: 160–2); see also Zurbach (2010).    [35] Carlier (984: 162).
[36] On Hesiodic *basilēes*, see Tandy (2018: 52–3).
[37] As with several other subordinate groups in his volume, Hesiod and his neighbours are affected by decisions made by others: there is no civic life beyond their small group of neighbours in Askra, which begs for comparison with Athenian women (Kennedy) and slaves (Forsdyke, Kamen, Lewis) and metics (Wijma). All subordinate groups suffer from this same frustration.

This negative side of Hesiod's ideas may be characteristic of what we called a peasant economy. But there is something more. *Works and Days* certainly is a prescriptive work throughout. However, there is something more in the condemnation of inequality and violence from above than there is in practical advice on the way to open a storage jar or the right moment to sharpen iron sickles—there is something militant even more than just prescriptive. This dimension of Hesiod's work is best described as a kind of moral economy.

## The Archaic Greek Moral Economy

The notion of 'moral economy' was coined by the British Marxist historian E. P. Thompson,[38] then borrowed by the anthropologist James Scott,[39] and it has since been used in many areas. Thompson's aim was to go against a 'spasmodic view of popular history',[40] a mechanical understanding of popular uprising in eighteenth-century Britain as spontaneous and reactive movements, to be explained as pure reactions to a food shortage. He argued that there was a corpus of definite ideas beyond such uprisings, giving them some sort of coherence from one episode to the following. Thompson writes about a time of changes towards the free market. For Scott, who analyses peasant movements in twentieth-century Burma and Vietnam, the moral economy lies with the food producer, not the food consumer. Since that time, the notion has had a particular fortune in African studies, but in very diverse forms. J. Siméant[41] has described the fate of the notion and has made constructive proposals to clarify the situation. She distinguishes very loose uses of 'moral economy', as various forms of embeddedness, with or without real economic dimensions of the set of values (what she calls ME2 and ME3). She argues for a return to earlier definitions by Thompson and Scott—her ME1—to restore a clear dimension of social conflict and ideas 'at work' in a context of social tensions.[42]

A proposal for the use of this notion to analyse elements of popular behaviour in ancient Greece has been put forward by S. Forsdyke in a quite different but complementary perspective.[43] She also relies on Thompson's strict definition of the notion. Taken in that sense, the moral economy is a corpus of ideas and values about the relationship between social groups, with food allocation as its main object. It is most often studied in periods of radical transformation, since that is

---

[38] Thompson (1971). The notion already appears in Thompson (1963: 68, 222), as underlined by Siméant (2015: 164).
[39] Scott (1976).
[40] Thompson (1971: 76). It is perhaps no wonder that this article begins with a quote from *Proverbs* XI.26!
[41] Siméant (2010 [2014], 2015).
[42] Siméant (2015: 168–71).  [43] Forsdyke (2005), on which see already supra.

the occasion for it to grow in coherence and make its appearance in the sources; it may show a conservative or even reactionary side. It may be a way to re-enact older shared values about a paternalist protection from the wealthy and turn it against them.[44] Siméant has elaborated a very detailed definition of this notion.[45]

The most common reference nowadays as far as ideological and political conflicts in archaic Greece are concerned is to the opposition between 'elitist' and 'middling' ideologies, as defined by I. Morris in the 1990s. It has been widely discussed.[46] Its great advantage is that it tries to define a conflict of discourses linked to different groups. Certainly, part of its success lies in this: the opposition defined by Morris was able to make sense of the inner struggles dividing the archaic city states. There are, however, also some critics, and some shortcomings. The 'middling' ideology is defined by Morris as follows:

> The core of the middling philosophy was the idea that all local men were more or less the same, and that all others—foreigners, women, slaves—were utterly different. The only legitimate authority came from within the local male community. Appeals to ties with gods, eastern monarchs, and ancient heroes were worthless. Elitists claimed precisely the opposite: their divine, oriental, and heroic connections set them above the rabble, and they alone should rule.[47]

The social group constructing a middling ideology may be quite easy to define, but the problem is with the content of this ideology. In the definition just quoted, it seems that it has been drawn from a general notion of what an Athenian of the fifth century would consider important. On the other side, the contrast of the ideologies has probably been much influenced by the funerary record from the early Iron Age onwards, as shown in a lengthy discussion by Kistler.[48] This is certainly legitimate in some sense, but the result is a very abstract and general definition of the content of this complex of values. Another danger is the teleological one: since the very core of the archaic middling ideology coincides so well with classical views held by Athenian citizen, we should certainly conclude that the middling ideology has won, and the other one has disappeared. The advantages of the notion of 'moral economy' are clear on both points: first, it is a genuine archaic ideology; second, it did not succeed, or only in a restricted way, in some places and for some time. Let us seek when and where.

---

[44] 'While [the] moral economy [of the poor] cannot be described as "political" in any advanced sense, nevertheless it cannot be described as unpolitical either, since it supposed definite, and passionately held, notions of the common weal—notions which, indeed, found some support in the paternalist tradition of the authorities; notions which the people re-echoed so loudly in their turn that the authorities were, in some measure, the prisoners' (Thompson 1971: 79), quite pertinently quoted by Forsdyke (2005: 89).
[45] See Siméant (2015: 168–9).    [46] See especially Kistler (2004).
[47] Morris (2005: 12); see also Morris (2000: 155–91).    [48] Kistler (2004).

## The Moral Economy as a Historical Factor

In our view, the main interest of the notion of 'moral economy' is to refer to ideas at work in social conflicts. Is it possible to go further than the Megarian case? Probably the best element to begin with is a quite astonishing Spartan use mentioned by Xenophon in his *Constitution of the Lacedaemonians* (VI 3). According to him, any Spartan, if in need, is allowed to use the helots of a fellow Spartan; we can turn this the other way round: for anyone who is asked, it is forbidden or at least very bad form to refuse the loan of a helot. This does not make very much sense in the context of Xenophon's praise of Sparta. He could certainly have elaborated on Spartan generosity without this precise element. Aristotle confirms this point (Arist. *Pol.* 1263ª35–7). This is probably not directly linked to the rewriting of Spartan history from the fourth century onwards, since, as underlined by Ducat and Hodkinson, helots being private property is a presupposition of the obligation to agree to lend them.[49] The origin of such communal use of individual property is usually seen in military life, 'typical soldierly sharing with comrades'.[50] But there is certainly another possibility, which lies in the fear expressed many times by Hesiod of being in a situation where there is no possibility of borrowing something essential, be it an ox, some tools, or food. Xenophon adds sharing practices about horses and food reserves, and Aristotle speaks of horses, dogs, and food. This may point to a peasant more than a military context. The main element, however, in favour of peasant context is the integration of a series of limitations of private property characterizing archaic Greek legislation and practices, which may be traced back, it will be argued, to the moral economy linked to Hesiod, into a coherent set of measures.

Let us first go back to an old, vexed question. Did there exist something like inalienability of the land in early Greece? This was once a widespread belief, but it was widely refuted in the second half of the twentieth century. Earlier theories wanted it to be a general state of things among the earliest Greek communities.[51] Nowadays the opposite position, symmetrically extreme, seems to be in favour: land was generally, simply, and directly alienable. This position may well be disqualified for its oversimplification.[52] It is too far-fetched, and ignores the possibility that different categories of land may have existed. If we turn to the data again, it may seem that there is no general rule of inalienability in early Greece, but instead

---

[49] Ducat (1990: 21–2). Detailed discussion in Hodkinson (2000: 199–201). Hodkinson points out that Aristotle's report is coherent with Xenophon's but not dependent on it.
[50] Hodkinson (2000: 200). [51] Zurbach (2017: ii. 699–704), with literature.
[52] For instance, Mackil (2017: 83, n. 52) tends to consider that, if one Cretan text says that one plot should be protected against pledge, this means that there was no inalienability. The conceptual frame of this judgement, that private property and state building go together hand in hand, may be characterized as a kind of naive modernistic liberal view (see notably Mackil 2017: 79–80).

many tentative regulations to restrict the alienation.[53] In Elis, a law existed that forbade loans collateralized by half the land of any citizen (Arist. *Pol.* 1319$^a$10–14). In Epizephyrian Locroi, a law stated that selling part of the land was restricted to those able to prove they had suffered a reversal of fortune (Arist. *Pol.* 1266$^b$17–21). Pheidon of Corinth had established, when the Bacchiads were still in power, a law stating that the *kleroi* should not vary in size (Arist. *Pol.* 1265$^b$12–16); Philolaos, another Bacchiad, exiled in Thebes, introduced a law on adoption with the aim of stabilizing the number of *kleroi* (Arist. *Pol.* 1274$^b$2–5). At some time around the end of the seventh century, it is possible that the inalienability of the allotments included in the first division in foundations planned by the Corinthian tyrants became a part of a Corinthian-type constitution for new cities, like the situation in Leucas (Arist. *Pol.* 1266$^b$21–4) and which the many analogies between Leucas and other foundations seem to indicate.[54]

It is then possible to trace the development of a set of analogous measures, not to re-establish the idea of an old inherited practice of inalienability but rather to consider it typical of archaic legislations—a set of related but not equivalent regulations that aimed at stopping the consequences of alienation, which in many cases might have been concentration of land, as is most clear in Solon's law establishing a maximum for land possession (Arist. *Pol.* 1266$^b$16–18).[55] This seems to be the reality behind the generalizing statements by Aristotle (e.g. *Pol.* 1319$^a$10–11), that in 'many cities' there were laws forbidding sale of the first *kleroi*.

A second element here is the very status of helotic groups. Here as well, the older views hold that these groups were of very ancient creation, and they were considered as consequences of the conquest through new populations and subsequent enslavement of earlier populations, at the end of the Bronze Age.[56] H. van Wees has shown in a ground-breaking study that these groups were mostly creations of the archaic period,[57] which best explains their widespread but poorly documented presence in new foundations. He also showed that the presence of such groups was very common in the city states of that period, not a Spartan exception but something like a general rule. Now the status of helots and other groups has also been revised. Ducat, and then Hodkinson, clearly and forcefully argued that the 'communitarian dependence' or the like was a phantom, and that helots were nothing but slaves.[58] They are normally called *douloi* in classical sources, written before the speculations by Hellenistic philologists creating a series of groups supposedly 'between freedom and slavery', as the famous phrase

---

[53] I refrain here from discussing the Spartan case, which is probably the most difficult of all; see Hodkinson (2000: 85–90, and the whole of his ch. 3).
[54] Zurbach (2017: ii. 564–5).  [55] Zurbach (2017: ii. 699–703).
[56] Notably by Lotze (1959), whose book remains an excellent study, even if this point of view is probably outdated.
[57] Van Wees (2003).  [58] Ducat (1990: ch. 3); Hodkinson (2000: 113–31); Lewis (2018: ch. 6).

holds it.[59] Helots, *penestai*, and others are distinguished through the limitations to the exercise of private property imposed on them by their individual master. An example is the use of helots by other Spartans mentioned above, and the most clearly established restriction is the impossibility to of selling these slaves abroad.[60] Here again there is clearly a case of limitation of private property rights through the city state. It stands in close parallel to the inalienability of land, as interpreted above, and it seems that the limitation of private property rights on land and workforce can be seen as a fundamental aspect of archaic legislation.

A third case of manipulation of private property rights may be seen in the evolution of common meals from elite symposia to common meals including all citizens, which may be seen as a rupture with past arrangements. This has been discussed above. It is an element of a global redrawing of the entitlement system, based again on a collective control on the allocation of resources from the land.[61]

Is there a link between these phenomena and the moral economy of the peasantry as championed by Hesiod? It may seem at first sight that these limitations are exactly the opposite of the obsession with private property rights and peasant independence characterizing Hesiod's discourse. 'Work, Perses, in order that you may buy another's land, not the reverse,' runs the famous verse (*Op.* 341). But this would be to overlook the dynamic, creative part of the moral economy, underlined by Thompson, perhaps also its reactive part. Hesiod does not speak of any of the problems of the late seventh century in Attica or Megara; he does not speak of debt slavery or servitude, land concentration, or even loan interests. If we take a dynamic look at these facts, another process comes to light. The late seventh century sees the development of levellers, the poorest members of the community arguing for a complete redistribution of the land. The Athenian case is the most obvious, but there are hints at a similar situation at Megara and Sparta.[62] This echoes Hesiod in a negative sense: it is not to negate private property rights in the sense of Hesiod; it is to re-establish them, as the basis of peasant independence. In a context of expansion of indentured labour or debt slavery, of concentration of land, a new element had to be introduced into the 'moral economy'. It was not enough to recall the elite to their ancient duties. It was the community, quite loose and weak in Hesiod, who had to establish the limits and give protection to the peasant households. In many cases this was done as the result of a compromise, as in Athens.

The comparison between good and bad government in *Works and Days* may indicate the beginning of this shift (*Op.* 225–47). For those who give justice to their people in the right way, prosperity is designed for the entire community; for those who give crooked decisions and injustice, pest and famine are the result (*limos* and *loimos* at one time, *Op.* 243). It is clear from the context that those who

---

[59] See Lewis, this volume.　[60] Ducat (1990: 21–2).
[61] Zurbach (2013: 988–9).　[62] See Arist. *Pol.* 1306$^b$37–1307$^a$1.

give straight sentences and observe justice are the exact opposite of the gift-eating kings, the *dorophagoi* (*Op.* 221), who had been bribed by Hesiod's brother. The central question between the two then appears to be the levy exercised on the peasantry. As a matter of fact, the gifts to the kings are the only kind of payment to an authority or group mentioned by Hesiod. It has to be seen in a continuum leading from the irregular, sometimes violent levies exercised by Homeric elites, to the traditional 'gifts' from the cities—or more probably villages—offered by Agamemnon to Achilles, and the 'gifts' to powerful local members of the elite mentioned in Naxos in one fragment of Aristotle (fr. 558 Rose = 566 Gigon = Athenaeus 8.348$^b$).[63] This early form of levy made way to more systematic levies long before Solon, so that at some point it became simply not enough to recall an old idealized practice, as Hesiod still seems to do, and other means were necessary. But the aims remained identical: the peasant independence, based on private property rights on land and the workforce.[64]

This does not mean that the moral economy 'won'. There was no redistribution of land in Athens, and the Megarian popular government did not last. The results of those struggles differed from city state to city state, and we are not in a position to reconstruct them in detail. But this moral economy was a vector of popular action. In Thompson's words:

> It is of course true that riots were triggered off by soaring prices, by malpractices among dealers, or by hunger. But these grievances operated within a popular consensus as to what were legitimate and what were illegitimate practices in marketing, milling, baking, etc. This in its turn was grounded upon a consistent traditional view of social norms and obligations, of the proper economic functions of several parties within the community, which, taken together, can be said to constitute the moral economy of the poor.[65]

## Conclusions

The main advantage of considering popular movements in the archaic period linked to a corpus of ideas, itself in evolution, which we may call 'moral economy', is that it constitutes this very complex, and the nature of such movements, as a historical problem. This is the very essence of the introduction of the notion by Thompson: the rupture with the 'spasmodic view of popular history' and the recognition of 'the crowd' as a rational historical agent. The importance of ideology is certainly not enough to reduce the formation of city states to a conflict of meanings: as was clear for Thompson, and from the evolution from Hesiod to the

---

[63] Zurbach (2017: ii. 447–9). [64] See Edwards, this volume.
[65] Thompson (1971: 78–9).

Athenian levellers, it should never be forgotten that the concrete and material struggles are determinant.

In that sense, a line of future research will be to trace down the aspects of classical city states where this moral economy has left some traces. The many aspects of the protection of the household, for instance, could be read again in this perspective. The cases examined here may allow one to conclude that the moral economy had more bearing on the city states usually seen as conservative than on the ones we consider innovative (probably inaccurately). There are other aspects where the moral economy barely left any trace. One of them is the military. There is nothing military in Hesiod or among the Athenian levellers, so that the idea that the city state should protect the modest households to have enough soldiers is probably not pertinent. On the contrary: there is here a quite interesting connection with recent reinterpretations of archaic military history, setting the origin of hoplite warfare in the elite more than among the modest citizenry.[66] Here the city states would have been influenced more by elite innovations than by the moral economy of the crowd.

In the context of the social history of early Greece, this seems an urgent objective to attain. In recent decades there has been quite a separation between the history of slavery or economic history, on the one hand, and the general paradigms of archaic Greek history, on the other. These paradigms were based on elite culture and its transition towards a citizen culture. From this perspective, the analysis of archaic history as a struggle between groups—whether they may be called classes or status groups is another question—is essential. It may allow us to identify the importance of reinterpretations of elite practices, as in the case of common meals; it may also allow us simply to introduce the people back into archaic social history, which would not be a pity.

All this may seem quite obvious for a social historian working on other periods and places. From a general point of view, perhaps, the most striking element of this moral economy is its incorporation in works showing intense connections to other parts of the Mediterranean basin. This may mean that the 'orientalizing' phenomenon is not only a story of goldsmiths and luxuries used by the elite, but that there are things travelling at deeper levels as well. The space of the travel of literary objects described here has much in common with the regional-based diversity recently identified by Lewis.[67] We have made the case above that the question of social, economic, and ideological implications of the transfers of wisdom literature should remain an open question.[68] It is, in my view, a critical question for future research, a possible opening on a common history of the Mediterranean.

---

[66] Van Wees (2013).   [67] Lewis (2018).
[68] A theoretical framework beyond strict comparison or one-way transfer may be found in Espagne (2013).

## Works Cited

Agut-Labordère, D., and M. Chauveau (2011). *Héros, magiciens et sages oubliés de l'Egypte ancienne: Une anthologie de la littérature en égyptien démotique*. Paris.

Aymard, A. (1983). 'Autoconsommation et marchés: Chayanov, Labrousse ou Le Roy Ladurie?', *Annales: Economies, sociétés, civilisations*, 38: 1392–1410.

Beck, H. (2018). '"If I am from Megara": Introduction to the Local Discourse Environment of an Ancient Greek City-State', in Beck and Smith (2018: 15–45).

Beck, H., and P. Smith (2018) (eds). *Megarian Moments: The Local World of an Ancient Greek City-State*. Tiresias Supplements Online. Münster.

Briquel Chatonnet, F. (2005). 'L'Histoire et la sagesse d'Ahiqar: Fortune littéraire de l'histoire d'un dignitaire araméen à la cour assyrienne', in J.-L. Bacqué-Grammont, A. Pino, and S. Khoury (eds), *D'un Orient l'autre*, 17–40. Leuven.

Buehlmann, A. (2004). 'Proverbes', in T. Römer, J.-D. Macchi, and C. Nihan (eds), *Introduction à l'Ancien Testament*, 511–22. Geneva.

Canfora, L. (1994). *Histoire de la littérature grecque d'Homère à Aristote*, trans. D. Fourgous. Paris.

Carlier, P. (1984). *La Royauté en Grèce avant Alexandre*. Strasbourg.

Chayanov, A. (1966). *The Theory of Peasant Economy*, trans. R. E. F. Smith. Homewood, IL.

Crenshaw, J. (1992). 'Proverbs, Book of', in D. Freeman (ed.), *The Anchor Bible Dictionary*, 513–20. New York.

Crenshaw, J. (1993). 'Wisdom Literature: Retrospect and Prospect', in H. McKay and D. Clines (eds), *Of Prophets' Visions and the Wisdom of Sages: Essays in Honour of R. Norman Whybray on his Seventieth Birthday*, 161–78. Sheffield.

Crenshaw, J. (1997). *Old Testament Wisdom: An Introduction*. Atlanta.

Dornseiff, F. (1934). 'Hesiods *Werke und Tage* und das alte Morgenland', *Philologus*, 89: 397–415. (Reprint in E. Heitsch (ed.), *Hesiod. Wege der Forschung 44, 131–50*. Darmstadt, 1966.)

Ducat, J. (1990). *Les Hilotes*, Bulletin de correspondance hellenique supplément 20. Paris.

Edwards, A. (2004). *Hesiod's Ascra*. Berkeley and Los Angeles.

Espagne, M. (2013). 'Comparison and Transfer: A Question of Method', in M. Middell and L. Roura (eds), *Transnational Challenges to National History Writing*, 36–53. New York.

Figueira, T., and G. Nagy (1985) (eds). *Theognis of Megara: Poetry and the Polis*. Baltimore.

Forsdyke, S. (2005). 'Revelry and Riot in Archaic Megara: Democratic Disorder or Ritual Reversal?', *Journal of Hellenic Studies*, 125: 73–92.

Gallant, T. W. (1991). *Risk and Survival in Ancient Greece: Reconstructing the Rural Domestic Economy*. Cambridge.

Grelot, P. (1972). *Documents araméens d'Egypte*. Paris.

Hobsbawm, E. (1974). 'Peasant Land Occupations', *Past and Present*, 62: 120–52 (repr. in Hobsbawm 1998: 223–55).

Hobsbawm, E. (1998). *Uncommon People: Resistance, Rebellion and Jazz*. London.

Hodkinson, S. (2000). *Property and Wealth in Classical Sparta*. London.

Jolles, A. (1930). *Einfache Formen: Legende, Sage, Mythe, Rätsel, Spruch, Kasus, Memorabile, Märchen, Witz*. Halle.

Kerblay, B. (1971). 'Chayanov and the Theory of Peasantry as a Specific Type of Economy', in T. Shanin (ed.), *Peasants and Peasant Societies*, 150–60. Harmondsworth.

Kistler, E. (2004). '"Kampf der Mentalitäten": Ian Morris' "Elitist-" versus "Middling-Ideology"', in Rollinger and Ulf (2004: 145–75).

Kula, W. (1970). *Théorie économique du système féodal: Pour un modèle de l'économie polonaise, 16e–18e s*. Paris.

Kurke. L. (2011). *Aesopic Conversations: Popular Tradition, Cultural Dialogue, and the Invention of Greek Prose*. Princeton.

Laisney, V. (2007). *L'Enseignement d'Aménémopé*, Studia Pohl 19. Rome.

Lewis, D. (2018). *Greek Slave Systems in their Eastern Mediterranean Context, c.800–146 BC*. Oxford.

Lichtheim, M. (1976–80). *Ancient Egyptian Literature*. 3 vols. Los Angeles.

Link, S. (1991). *Landverteilung und sozialer Frieden im archaischen Griechenland*. Historia Einzelschriften 69. Stuttgart.

Lotze, D. (1959). Μεταξὺ ἐλευθέρων καὶ δούλων. *Studien zur Rechtsstellung unfreier Landbevölkerungen in Griechenland bis zum 4. Jahrhundert v. Chr*. Berlin.

Luzzato, M. (1996). 'Esopo', in S. Settis (ed.), *I Greci: storia, cultura, arte, societ*à, 1307–24. Turin.

Mackil, E. (2017). 'Property Claims and State Formation in the Archaic Greek World', in C. Ando and S. Richardson (eds), *Ancient States and Infrastructural Power*, 63–90. Philadelphia.

Millett, P. (1984). 'Hesiod and his World', *Proceedings of the Cambridge Philological Society*, 30: 84–115.

Millett, P. (1991). *Lending and Borrowing in Ancient Athens*. Cambridge.

Morris, I. (2000). *Archaeology as Cultural History*. Oxford.

Morris, I. (2005). 'The Eighth-Century Revolution', version 1.0: https://www.princeton.edu/~pswpc/pdfs/morris/120507.

Naré, L. (1986). *Proverbes salomoniens et proverbes mossi: Étude comparative à partir d'une nouvelle analyse de Pr 25–29*. Frankfort.

Oost, S. (1973). 'The Megara of Theagenes and Theognis', *Classical Philology*, 68: 186–96.

Robu. A. (2014). *Mégare et les établissements mégariens de Sicile, de Propontide et du Pont-Euxin: Histoire et institutions*. Berne.

Rollinger, R., and C. Ulf (2004) (eds). *Griechische Archaik. Interne Entwicklungen— Externe Impulse.* MELAMMU 3. Berlin.

Sarkar, Sumit (1997). *Writing Social History*. Oxford.

Schmitz, W. (2004a). *Nachbarschaft und Dorfgemeinschaft im archaischen und klassischen Griechenland.* Klio Beiheft 7. Berlin.

Schmitz, W. (2004b). 'Griechische und nahöstliche Spruchweisheit: Die *Erga kai Hemerai* Hesiods und nahöstliche Weisheitsliteratur', in Rollinger and Ulf (2004: 311–33). Berlin.

Scott, J. (1976.) *The Moral Economy of the Peasant: Rebellion and Subsistence in Southeast Asia.* New Haven.

Siméant, J. (2010 [2014]). 'Économie morale et protestation: détours africains', *Genèses*, 81: 142–60.

Siméant, J. (2015). 'Three Bodies of Moral Economy: The Diffusion of a Concept', *Journal of Global Ethics*, 11: 163–75.

Stein-Hölkeskamp. E. (2018). 'Theognis and the Ambivalence of Aristocracy', in Beck and Smith (2018: 129–38).

Tandy, D. (2018). 'In Hesiod's World', in A. Loney and S. Scully (eds), *The Oxford Handbook of Hesiod*, 43–60. Oxford.

Thompson, E. P. (1963). *The Making of the English Working Class.* London.

Thompson, E. P. (1971). 'The Moral Economy of the English Crowd in the Eighteenth Century', *Past and Present*, 50: 76–136.

van Wees, H. (2003). 'Conquerors and Serfs: Wars of Conquest and Forced Labour in Archaic Greece', in S. Alcock and N. Luraghi (eds), *Helots and their Masters in Laconia and Messenia: Histories, Ideologies, Structures*, 33–80. Cambridge.

van Wees, H. (2013). 'Farmers and Hoplites: Models of Historical Development', in D. Kagan and G. Viggiano (eds), *Men of Bronze: Hoplite Warfare in Ancient Greece*, 222–55. Princeton

Walcot, P. (1962). 'Hesiod and the Didactic Literature of the Near East', *Revue des études grecques*, 75: 13–36.

West, M. L. (1978). *Hesiod. Works and Days.* Oxford.

West, M. L. (1997). *The East Face of Helicon: West Asiatic Elements in Greek Poetry and Myth.* Oxford.

Whybray, R. (1994). *The Composition of the Book of Proverbs.* Journal for the Study of the Old Testament Supplement 168. Sheffield.

Whybray, R. (1995). *The Book of Proverbs: A Survey of Modern Study.* History of Biblical Interpretation Series 1. Leiden.

Wickham, C. (2005). *Framing the Early Middle Ages: Europe and the Mediterranean, 400–800.* Oxford.

Will, É. (1957). 'Aux origines du régime foncier grec: Homère, Hésiode et l'arrière-plan mycénien', *Revue des études anciennes*, 59: 5–50.

Zurbach, J. (2010). 'La 'Société homérique' et le don', *Gaia*, 13: 57–79.

Zurbach, J. (2012). 'Hésiode oriental, ou le discours sur l'économie avant le *logos oikonomikos*', in K. Konuk (ed.), *Stéphanéphoros. De l'économie antique à l'Asie mineure: Hommages à Raymond Descat*, 179–91. Bordeaux.

Zurbach, J. (2013). 'La Formation des cités grecques: Statuts, classes et systèmes fonciers', *Annales: Histoire, sciences sociales*, 68: 957–98.

Zurbach, J. (2017). *Les Hommes, la terre et la dette en Grèce c.1400–c.500 a.C.* 2 vols. Bordeaux.

# 2
# Solon and the *Demos* in his Poetry

*Anthony T. Edwards*

## Preface

In this chapter I centre the *demos* within the political process of Solon's archonship. Along with women, craftsmen, or the enslaved, rural inhabitants, engaged in agricultural labour and dwelling amidst the fields they cultivate, constitute one of the subordinated and silenced groups that have attracted the attention of both historians and literary scholars working on ancient Greece. I imagine that in many Greek cities the rural *demos* might have been identified as the most exploited and oppressed class. For Solon, it is the *demos* who are the other that shadows his speech, and I attempt here to disentangle a demotic voice from Solon's. I set myself a similar task in an essay I wrote on the *Odyssey* now many years ago (Edwards 1993). In that case, the *Odyssey*'s contrast between the rural zone and the *polis* was central to my argument. Solon, of course, says nothing in his poetry about habitation patterns or the spatial organization of his city and its territory, but what can we reasonably assume?

In my argument I rely upon the fragments of Solon's poetry to answer a historical question: what did the *demos* expect from Solon? Certain assumptions must precede any attempt at a solution. I mention in the introduction my suspicions of the accounts of Solon's Athens offered in the *Athenaion Politeia* and by Plutarch. The question of social complexity—how far had the *poleis* of archaic Greece, Athens in particular, advanced towards mature statehood—underlies doubts about these two sources for Athens at the time of Solon's archonship. I follow the recent work of a number of scholars in the view that these sources overstate the complexity of Athenian institutions at the beginning of the sixth century. I regard the Athenian *demos* as a subordinated group under increasing pressure to supply labour to the *polis*'s elite in support of their unfinished state-building project. This assumption is in line with recent work on unfree labour in archaic Greece, notably, with the contributions of Lewis and of Zurbach in this volume. The social and political dimensions of such economic oppression are analysed in this volume by Cecchet, though she focuses upon the classical period.

The strategy I adopt for analysing Solon's fragments assumes that his discourse is fundamentally dialogical, inhabited not only by his own thoughts and intentions but also by those of others. Theorists of language's radical intersubjectivity regard this as a property of language generally. In this line I maintain that political speech in particular, even when it makes no explicit reference to an adversary, nevertheless overtly incorporates within itself that opposing discourse, if only to distort or subvert it. This quality of Solon's political fragments offers the possibility of separating out strands of demotic discourse from the fabric of Solon's own words. Sara Forsdyke (2012) has completed a similar analysis of what I consider more challenging texts, as have I in that earlier study of the *Odyssey* noted above. If I have succeeded with this approach, then I have excavated from Solon's verses demotic speech that he has subordinated to the logic of his own political rhetoric in his effort to subordinate the *demos* itself.

## Introduction

The Athenian *demos* serves as a frequent variable in Solon's political calculations, one whose agency he wished to influence and before whom he felt compelled to justify himself. Although the *demos* may have wielded slight political leverage at the beginning of the sixth century, it appears nevertheless to have been capable of political action. We do not have from Solon's time any sources directly expressing the viewpoint of the *demos*. Indeed, to the extent that a demotic voice can be heard at all in Greek literature, generally it must emerge through the filter of literary conventions and the distorting ideologies of elite authors. So it should not be controversial to acknowledge that our sole documentary source from the period for the Athenian *demos*, Solon's poetry, cannot give us unmediated access to the aspirations and motives of the *demos* but only to his representation of that.

Granting that limitation, however, the premise of my argument is that political discourse in particular, in which a speaker must at minimum refute the arguments of his adversaries and will often attempt to misrepresent, appropriate, or reinterpret them to fashion his own case, necessarily, therefore, bears embedded in its own body the arguments that it opposes. If the Athenian *demos* constituted a coherent political force through shared legal, social, political, and economic conditions—that is, through shared exclusion from the privileges of elite status—then any expectations they entertained for Solon's archonship would have left their traces in the fragments from his poems that discuss or address the *demos*.[1] Such citations of demotic discourse in his poetry must, of course, remain recognizable as such for his audience—even if in a distorted form—in order for Solon to exploit them effectively in appeals directed to different audiences. So, although Solon may aim to misrepresent and exploit demotic aspirations in his poetry, the voice of the *demos* should nevertheless become audible for us precisely in such

---

[1] I discuss Solon's use of the word δῆμος in Appendix I.

dialogical interactions with Solon's own voice.[2] Plutarch, in fact, tells us that Solon himself attributed the sentiment expressed at 33.5–7, discussed in detail below, to 'the many' (τοὺς πολλοὺς καὶ φαύλους: *Sol.* 15.1), the Athenian *demos*. Either, therefore, Solon acknowledged his own citation of demotic discourse in poetry known to Plutarch or, at a minimum, no less a student of Greek literature than Plutarch found the report of Solon's borrowing completely credible.[3]

As Solon struggled to reform Athens' laws and institutions in order to forestall a violent upheaval, he confronted an elite that was factionalized, engaged in intense competition for wealth, status, and prestige, whose membership was in a continuous state of churning, and for whom personal influence was a more significant factor than political institutions. Duplouy as well as van Wees and Fisher have argued accordingly that terms such as 'aristocracy' or 'nobility' are misleading for such an unstable elite.[4] Those Athenians outside the circle of the city's elite, whom Solon refers to in his poetry as the *demos*, were no more homogeneous or unified than the elite. One can confidently conjecture that variables such as locality, disparities in access to land and in levels of prosperity, and the idiosyncrasies of local elite and demotic leaders would shape perceptions of self-interest and of community. The Athenian population, moreover, was distributed across a variety of voluntary associations that would have further channelled relations of cooperation and rivalry. The picture is further complicated by continuities between elite and demotic culture in the common ethic of competition for status

---

[2] It is, of course, well established that Solon also responds to his peers in the Athenian elite. See Irwin (2005: 91–111) and Balot (2001: 79–98). Werlings (2010) focuses upon demotic demands in ch. 5, ¶¶21–30 (references to chapter and paragraph numbers of electronic edition). See also Wallace (2007: 50–1, 59, 65–8) regarding the demands of the *demos* and the article as a whole for Solon's accommodation of the *demos* in his reforms. Murray in this volume enumerates the pitfalls of relying upon literary texts as sources for a demotic perspective. Forsdyke (2012: 4–18), however, clearly analyses the complexities of reading ancient Greek literature from below and lays out a method for doing so. I think, though, that Solon's poems differ from the texts that Forsdyke treats in their connection to a specific, known historical context. Additionally, although Solon may wish to distort demotic views in his poems, he does not wish to disguise them as such. These characteristics diminish, even if they do not eliminate, the usefulness for my argument of 'indirect methods' of analysis (Forsdyke 2012: 14–7). Note as well Rose's sharp observation (2012: 209–10) on the complexity of determining the authenticity of elite representations of subordinated voices.

[3] I refer to Solon's poems by the fragment and line numbers in West (1989). I rely as much as possible in what follows upon evidence from Solon's poetry, assigning less importance to the accounts of the *Athenaion Politeia* and Plutarch's *Solon*, the sources for most of Solon's fragments. See the summary discussions of the trustworthiness of the *Athenaion Politeia* and Plutarch in Bintliff (2006), Forsdyke (2006), and Lewis (2017), as well as the longer consideration presented by Almeida (2003: 2–19, 119–74).

[4] Gehrke (2009) assigns the appearance of state institutions in Athens to the sixth century. Foxhall (1997: 115–22), van Wees (2000; 2013: 237–40), and Ismard (2018: 146–51) support the view that, as a state, Athens was at this point very much in the process of formation. See also Hammer's analysis (2005) of the instability of the archaic *polis*. Duplouy (2014, 2015, 2018) and van Wees and Fisher (2015) demonstrate the instability of archaic Greek elites and the role of competitive performance to establish claims to citizenship and relative status. I regret that I have not been able to see Duplouy's *Le Prestige des élites: Récherches sur les modes de reconnaissance sociale en Grèce entre les Xe et Ve siècles avant J.-C.* (Paris, 2006).

through performance of public roles, in membership in voluntary associations open to the elite and the *demos* alike, and in the very permeability of the boundary between the two groups.[5]

Solon's poetry, however, does not shed much light on specific factions within either elite or *demos*, though I make some suggestions on this topic, especially regarding the *demos*, in what follows. In so far as the *demos* intrude upon his concerns, Solon is preoccupied with the fundamental contrast between the elite and the *demos*, the wealthy and the poor. The basic distinction between those able to command the labour of others and those who, reciprocally, must under various forms of compulsion supply a share of their labour to others, or, put otherwise, between those with land exceeding their own labour for working it and those whose labour supply exceeds the land they possess, this distinction underlies all of Solon's concern with the *demos*, and it serves as the foundation for any unity of purpose and shared identity of the Athenian *demos*, as it does likewise for the city's elite.[6] Labour, land, and the power to control them lie at the heart of what the *demos* demands from Solon.

## Restoration of Citizens

Under this heading I refer to Solon's restoration and repatriation of enslaved Athenians, a topic treated in 36.

>πολλοὺς δ' Ἀθήνας πατρίδ' ἐς θεόκτιτον
>ἀνήγαγον πραθέντας, ἄλλον ἐκδίκως,
>ἄλλον δικαίως, τοὺς δ' ἀναγκαίης ὑπὸ
>χρειοῦς φυγόντας, γλῶσσαν οὐκέτ' Ἀττικὴν
>ἱέντας, ὡς δὴ πολλαχῆι πλανωμένους·
>τοὺς δ' ἐνθάδ' αὐτοῦ δουλίην ἀεικέα
>ἔχοντας, ἤθη δεσποτέων τρομεομένους,
>ἐλευθέρους ἔθηκα....

(36.8–15)

---

[5] See Ismard (2010: ch. 1 (pp. 44–83), ¶¶49–51 (references to chapter and paragraph numbers of electronic edition)) regarding membership in associations from across the Athenian census classes and Ismard (2010: ¶¶1–79) regarding such associations generally in archaic Athens. See Duplouy (2014: 68–71) and van Wees and Fisher (2015: 15–33) regarding the sharing of common values, especially that of competition, by elite and *demos*.

[6] Foxhall (1997: 129–32) and van Wees (2006: 67; 2013: 229–33; Chapter 5, this volume) propose a stark division between the rich and the poor—i.e. the thetes, the census group corresponding to Solon's *demos*, characterized as 'dependent smallholders and landless men' (van Wees: 2006: 365) and estimated to make up 80–85% of the population of archaic Athens. Cecchet in this volume details the more complex relationship between the *demos* and the thetic census class in the classical period. Mülke (2002: 181) and Werlings (2010: ch. 5, ¶¶7–14, 47) maintain that Solon regards the *demos* as a distinct and self-aware class.

>And I brought back many men to Athens, our divine fatherland,
>men sold as slaves—one illegally,
>another legally—and others fleeing under dire
>necessity, no longer speaking in Attic,
>like those who wander far and wide.
>And those enduring unseemly slavery right here
>and trembling at the moods of their masters,
>I set free....

Solon introduces slavery here through a three-way distinction. First, he contrasts Athenians abroad with those at home. The former group he further subdivides into those sold abroad into slavery (9: πραθέντας; cf. πραθέντες at 4.25) and those who, rather, fled abroad hoping to escape 'dire necessity' (10–11: τοὺς δ' ἀναγκαίης ὑπὸ / χρειοῦς φυγόντας). Then, in lines 13–15 Solon returns to the Athenian homeland to describe the plight of the latter group enduring slavery there (13: δουλίην ἀεικέα). The fact that Solon groups slaves at home and those sold overseas with men who remain free even if under conditions of exile implies that all three groups owe their predicament to a common set of circumstances, to the same ἀναγκαίη χρειώ, 'dire necessity'. This context may suggest that those who fled (11: φυγόντας) with their freedom intact were anticipating seizure and enslavement. By qualifying this slavery, moreover, with modifiers that question its legitimacy—ἐκδίκως (9: 'unjustly'), δικαίως (10: 'justly'), and ἀεικέα (36.13: 'unseemly')—Solon narrows his focus even further.[7] Solon claims to have liberated only a specific group of slaves, those who have passed, in some cases through an illegal process, from status as free Athenian citizens to that of enslaved as a result of the same circumstances that drove others into exile. Without more detailed information about the forms of unfree labour in Athens of the early sixth century and the percentage of the labour force composed of enslaved workers, one cannot avoid speculating, but such a limited manumission must seem more likely than that Solon executed a one-time emancipation of all the enslaved or that he abolished slavery altogether.

Solon's claim in 36 to have repatriated individuals sold abroad illegally and others who fled abroad in advance, presumably, of the same fate entails that there remained free members of the *demos* yet unenslaved, contradicting the assertion of the *Athenaion Politeia* that 'the many were enslaved to the few' (5.1: τῶν πολλῶν δουλευόντων τοῖς ὀλίγοις). At 4.17–31 he sketches out the consequences for

---

[7] Lewis (2004: 26–9) argues that 'unjust' and 'unseemly' enslavement boils down to abduction by force, against which there was no legal recourse for the *demos*. See also Harris (1997: 105–6) and Noussia-Fantuzzi (2010: 471). The interpretation of Solon's references to slavery as debt slavery that is offered by the *Athenaion Politeia* (2.2) and Plutarch (*Sol.* 13.2–3) is no longer tenable. See the summary discussions with bibliographic references in Mülke (2002: 140–1) and Noussia-Fantuzzi (2010: 29–41). Kroll (1998: esp. 228–9) seems to me to exaggerate the pace at which lending at interest would have penetrated all sectors of the Athenian economy.

Athens of its present regime of δυσνομίη, foreseeing for the poor that many (τῶν δὲ πενιχρῶν...πολλοί) will arrive in foreign lands sold and in bonds (4.23–5). Solon casts as a prophecy here the fulfilment of a process already underway but still incomplete. As Solon's probably partial emancipation attests, the enslavement of the Athenian poor, the *demos*, should be understood as incomplete, contested, and subject to shifting social and economic conditions. Morris and Scheidel provide valuable analyses of, respectively, the economic forces precipitating the demise of Athenian hectemorage in Solon's time and of those propelling the subsequent rise of chattel slavery at Athens.[8] Zurbach (2013) contextualizes this development within the history of status hierarchies in the archaic city states, Athens in particular, and within the related evolution of the land tenure system. He argues that the crisis faced by Solon arose from the progressive enslavement of Athenians as chattel, which precipitated in turn a transition to an unfree labour force of enslaved foreigners: Athenians could no longer be enslaved in their own homeland.[9]

Van Wees has argued convincingly that it was during the seventh century that whole populations such as the Messenian and Laconian helots or the Thessalian *penestai* were reduced to the status of epichoric slaves.[10] The pattern outlined by van Wees does not correspond in all respects to the situation confronted in Athens by Solon, whom he does not discuss in this connection, but it offers an illuminating context for Solon's references to the ongoing enslavement of residents of Athens and Attica. David Lewis's contribution to the present volume, though his purpose is precisely not to discuss Athens further, demonstrates the variety of such systems of agricultural production utilizing enslaved labourers tied to the soil they cultivate. A frequent feature of the systems of this type is that although the enslaved are subject to sale, they cannot be sold abroad. Lewis regards this restriction on the treatment of private property as a recognition of the need to protect enslaved families as the source of new enslaved workers. Zurbach, again in this volume, argues that this ban on the external sale of such epichoric slaves originates in a 'moral economy' of mutual obligation between the enslaved and their enslavers.[11] The Athenian *hektemoroi* mentioned both in the *Athenaion Politeia* and by Plutarch remain poorly understood.[12] If, however, as Athens emerged from the seventh century, these *hektemoroi* originated in the

---

[8] Morris (2002: 31–42); Scheidel (2008: 107–26).

[9] Zurbach (2013: 971–84, 993–7).

[10] Van Wees (2003: esp. 48–61, with passing notice of Solon and Athens at 68–9). Social and political hierarchy may have persisted in the Greek world from the Mycenean collapse through the Dark Age, as Foxhall (1995: 244–7) and Bintliff (2006: 327–9) have argued. But such relations of inequality lacked the institutional force and geographical reach enjoyed by those analysed by van Wees for the seventh and sixth centuries.

[11] Van Wees (2003: 70); Zurbach, Chapter 1, this volume; Lewis, Chapter 6, this volume.

[12] Noussia-Fantuzzi (2010: 32–40) provides an excellent summary of modern accounts. Cassola's framing of the question (1964: 26–34) remains fundamental.

Athenian elite's still incomplete project to secure their own population of epichoric slaves, then their sale abroad, which Solon mentions, might have violated the established terms under which they served their masters and provoked predictable popular outrage.

Even if we remain ignorant of many specifics, there can be little doubt that the Athenian elite by the time of Solon's archonship had long relied upon enslaved labourers. Such labourers do impose considerable overhead costs on their enslavers: they run away, they revolt, they steal and sabotage, and they require constant oversight, care, and surveillance. Yet in Athens and other cities an elite could not exist apart from unfree labour. The consumption of luxuries, military obligations, contributions to civic and religious initiatives, maintenance of clients, especially an armed retinue, and so forth by the former can only be financed by reduced consumption and inflated labour contributions on the part of the latter. No one, however, would regard this as a labour regime free either of risks for the elite or of resentments for the enslaved.[13]

As noted, Solon reports that it is the poor, the *demos*, who have suffered enslavement. Such slaves would still have felt connected to community and kin, who were no doubt aggrieved by the enslavement of a relative or neighbour.[14] It is difficult to imagine the specifics of tracing, purchasing in the case of the enslaved, and repatriating Athenians from overseas, but the task seems inherently formidable. Evidence for the question of tracing and repatriating captives sold into slavery is regrettably thin, but those intended for ransoming by their captors would, obviously enough, be more likely to be redeemed by their kin or city than those simply sold at auction.[15] Apart from not only the participation of kin and friends with some idea of who should be sought and where but their insistent pressure as well, it seems unlikely that such a task would even have been considered. So this element of Solon's programme is probably directed not only at rehabilitating the

---

[13] Scott (2017: 150–82 and *passim*) documents the necessity for an elite of securing an exploitable labour force and the reciprocal resistance of those exploited as fundamental characteristics of early states. See also in the present volume Forsdyke's analysis of indirect forms of resistance adopted by the enslaved in classical Athens.

[14] Welwei (2005: 36) argues that smallholders forced into dependent status prior to Solon's archonship would nonetheless have remained integrated in their tribes, phratries, and the emergent citizen community. Ismard (2018: 146–51) enumerates forms of voluntary association in place before Solon's archonship that would have linked even the poorest Athenians into broader networks. We remain uncertain of the specific forms of unfree labour in Solon's Athens, though we can reasonably assume that they differed in some respects from those of the later classical period and from Aristotle's time in particular.

[15] Both modes of disposing of captives are found in Homer: ransom (e.g. *Il.* 6.45–51, 10.378–81) and sale (e.g. *Il.* 24.751–3, *Od.* 15.449–53). Otherwise, evidence for monetizing captives is mostly from the classical and hellenistic periods. Primary sources are collected by Mulliez (1992) and Bielman (1994). Near Eastern material is presented by Blok and Krul (2017: 624–37). See Lewis (2019: esp. 96–98) regarding pirates, who employed both methods. In such cases the fortuitous intervention of a benefactor, a *euergetes*, who ransoms a known person from slavery on the spot, is a common motif. Dem. 57.18 is exemplary. Sosin (2017: 132–41) lays out the complexity and expense of ransoming individuals who have already been sold as slaves.

individuals deprived of their citizenship but equally at making families and communities deprived of their members whole. But, even if Solon succeeded in liberating primarily the enslaved who remained in Athenian territory, such an effort would certainly have met with resistance from the enslavers of these Athenians. The families, moreover, of any individuals who were not repatriated from abroad would have remained embittered over Solon's perceived betrayal. Consequently, Solon might not have regarded this emancipation as a promising enterprise and would have undertaken it only under pressure from the demotic families affected.

This conjecture, that Solon may have achieved less to restore freedom and homeland to enslaved members of the Athenian *demos* than he declares in 36, implies, of course, that the lines in question are principally intended to dampen continuing demotic criticism of Solon's failure to deliver on a promise or else to misrepresent to an elite audience the continuing discontent of the *demos* as unjustified—or possibly both. The occurrence of δουλίην (36.13), 'slavery', and occurrences of πραθέντας / -ες (36.9 and 4.25), 'sold', clearly refer to a form of labour resembling chattel slavery, a condition that has befallen members of the *demos* exclusively. Yet three additional references to slavery, δουλοσύνη, in Solon's fragments remain, whose connotation is in fact at odds with those attestations just considered.[16]

> τοῦτ' ἤδη πάσηι πόλει ἔρχεται ἕλκος ἄφυκτον,
> ἐς δὲ κακὴν ταχέως ἤλυθε δουλοσύνην,
> ἣ στάσιν ἔμφυλον πόλεμόν θ' εὕδοντ' ἐπεγείρει,
> ὃς πολλῶν ἐρατὴν ὤλεσεν ἡλικίην.
>
> (4.17–20)

This inescapable wound arrives soon for the whole city,
    and it falls quickly into vile slavery,
    which wakens civil strife and slumbering war,
    which destroys the sweet youth of many.

Solon describes at 4.17–20 the 'inescapable wound' that comes upon the entire city (17: πάσηι πόλει), followed by successive stages of civic disintegration: vile slavery (18: κακὴν...δουλοσύνην), civil war (19: ἔμφυλον πόλεμον), and the loss of many lives (20: πολλῶν ἐρατὴν...ἡλικίην). In this context of the entire city, the best interpretation of κακὴν...δουλοσύνην, 'vile...slavery', is subjection of the city to a tyrant's rule, the outcome of the lawlessness detailed in the preceding lines

---

[16] Earlier in 36, ll. 5–7, Solon describes the Γῆ μέλαινα ('black Earth'), from which he has removed the ὅροι ('markers'), as δουλεύουσα, 'enslaved', prefiguring the circumstances of the men working the land. The noun δοῦλος does not appear in Solon's extant fragments; Solon uses words formed on the stem δουλ- five times.

9–16 and the cause in turn of civil war and slaughter.[17] Additionally, at 9.3–4 Solon describes a tyranny as δουλοσύνη to a μόναρχος, 'slavery' to a 'sole ruler', and at 11.4 he again refers to a tyranny as κακὴν...δουλοσύνην.[18] Δουλίη and δουλοσύνη, then, are used by Solon both as a metaphor for the oppressive regime established by a tyrant and to refer directly to actual enslavement.

A tyrant's control of the distribution of civic offices, of the prerogatives of civic institutions such as council and courts, of military service, of opportunities to enrich oneself, and so forth no doubt seemed like the power of a master over his slaves to members of a city's elite, who gauged their personal standing by such pursuits. But, if for the elite slavery was a tyrant's intolerable monopolization of the political process, for the *demos*, whose objective living conditions might even improve under a tyrant, slavery was slavery: the forced labour—hectemorage, chattel slavery, and so on—that they endured at the hands of an elite more engaged with slavery as a metaphor than as lived fact.[19] Solon's rhetoric nevertheless manages to present himself and his elite peers as the victims of slavery just as much as the *demos*, perhaps in an effort to obfuscate the force and urgency of demotic demands for relief from this particular form of oppression.

## Subsistence

For the *demos*, subsistence depends upon access to land. To focus specifically upon the relationship of the cultivators to the land, it is surprising that the two words most closely associated with this aspect of Solon's programme by Aristotle and Plutarch, ἑκτήμοροι and σεισάχθεια, do not appear in the extant fragments of his poetry. The term ἰσομοιρίη, 'equal share', likewise neither a common nor a poetic word, does, however, appear at the end of 34, where Solon vehemently rejects such an 'equal distribution':

> ἁνδάνει...        οὐδὲ πιεί[ρ]ης χθονὸς
> πατρίδος κακοῖσιν ἐσθλοὺς ἰσομοιρίην ἔχειν.
>
> (34.8–9)
>
> nor does it suit me...that of the fatherland's fertile earth
> the nobles have an equal share with the base.

If, as I think, the terms κακοί and ἐσθλοί refer to members of the *demos* and of the elite, respectively, Solon asserts here that he refused demands that

---

[17] Regarding the rendering of πάσηι πόλει as 'the whole city' rather than 'every city', see Mülke (2002: 129–30) and Noussia-Fantuzzi (2010: 245). Linforth (1919: 201), Mülke (2002: 131–2), and Noussia-Fantuzzi (2010: 247) take δουλοσύνην at 4.18 to refer to a tyranny.
[18] See Mülke (2002: 208–9, 131–2) and Noussia-Fantuzzi (2010: 315, 333).
[19] I return to this topic of tyranny and the *demos* in my final section ('Politics').

commoners and members of the elite should have an equal share of the fatherland's fertile earth.[20]

Such demotic initiatives for land reform were far from unprecedented. Cecchet, in her survey of land redistributions proposed or carried out by cities in the archaic period, mentions Tyrtaeus' reference to a demand for a redistribution of land (Tyrtaeus 1 [West] = Arist. Pol. 1306$^b$37–1307$^a$2).[21] Diodorus (7.13.2) notes an uprising against the Argive Temenid dynasty over the distribution of land probably occurring in the mid-sixth century.[22] The uprising against the Pythagorean rulers of Croton at the end of the sixth century also resulted in a redistribution of land among the *demos*.[23] Exemplary of the circumstances that might lead to such conflicts is the fierce competition for land waged within the Athenian elite over the seventh and sixth centuries, a rivalry that reduced proportionally the land available for the remaining non-elite 85 per cent of the population.[24] Zurbach in this volume discusses legislation enacted in archaic cities designed to forestall such a concentration of land into large holdings. The same author, in another place, argues in detail that it is precisely the question of land, who can own it and how much, that shapes the social statuses of the archaic city—not only slave versus free or citizen versus non-citizen but also such status hierarchies as Solon's census classes.[25] Control of land lies at the heart of much of the civil conflict of the archaic period. The demand for ἰσομοιρίη confronting Solon is not exceptional.[26]

Solon, however, does not specify the frame of reference for ἰσομοιρίη. Does this slogan demand an equal distribution among all citizens of all the arable of the plain of Athens? Is a redistribution of land formerly held in common for cultivation and foraging but now gobbled up by the elite for exclusive use as pasture at stake? Perhaps the break-up of elite holdings swollen by fields seized from demotic farmers is demanded or a remedy for some other contested form of land tenure.[27] Solon's reference to ἰσομοιρίη does not permit us to answer these

---

[20] See my discussion of ἐσθλός, κακός and equivalents in Solon's fragments and in this passage in particular in Appendix II below. I use the word 'commoner' as a convenience and do not imply by it a corresponding elite organized as an aristocracy or nobility.

[21] Cecchet (2009: 191–8, esp. 194–5). Raaflaub and Wallace (2007: 36–9) discuss the context of this redistribution.

[22] Robinson (1997: 82–3) and Wallace (2007: 73–4).    [23] Robinson (1997: 76–8).

[24] Van Wees (2013: 237–40). See also Foxhall (1992: 155–9) and Rose (2012: 211–13, 224–5) regarding the skewed distribution of land in archaic and classical Athens, respectively.

[25] Zurbach (2013: 984–93 and *passim*).

[26] Raaflaub and Wallace (2007: 44) note the movement of this idea from the colonial outposts to the metropoles of Greece. Welwei (1992: 158–61) summarizes precedents for the demand of ἰσομοιρίη that Solon confronts. Werlings (2010: ch. 5, ¶¶23–30) takes 34.8–9 to refer to a demand by the *demos* for a general redistribution of land. Noussia-Fantuzzi's argument (2010: 453–4) that χθονός at 34.8 refers to political rights rather than land is adequately answered by Mülke (2002: 358).

[27] See Link's discussion (1991: 15–25) of the uncertainties and contradictions in the *Athenaion Politeia*'s and Plutarch's presentations of the land crisis faced by Solon. Almeida (2003: 19–69) and Faraguna (2012) provide very useful reviews of scholarly discussions of land and labour at the time of Solon's archonship.

questions. But, the fragment may testify that the importance to the *demos* of the particular land in question or of the process of its acquisition is great enough to unify the *demos* around its loss in spite of any variance in the amount of land owned by individual demotic families. Either that or these lines perhaps preserve Solon's effort to misrepresent the view of one demotic faction as the demand of the *demos* as a whole in order to inflame the passions of his elite audience. Certainly, though, the fragment does at least inform us that land is at stake whose possession separates κακοί from ἐσθλοί and that would require a redistribution, a γῆς ἀναδασμός, to achieve some level of parity between the two groups. Cecchet (2009) has shown that there is little evidence from the archaic or even the classical period for such redistributions undertaken solely to establish equality among citizens, but redistributions of property by cities were familiar from other contexts such as founding new settlements abroad, confiscations of property, and admissions of new citizens. So, it seems to me that in the context of an ongoing grievance over land, it would be a small step for some demotic firebrand to adapt a familiar procedure to a new context and to name it with a slogan contesting elite oppression: ἰσομοιρίη.[28]

Solon uses ἰσομοιρίη in an unqualified statement about the disposition of Athenian land: 'nor does it suit me...that of the fatherland's fertile earth the nobles have an equal share with the base' (34.8–9). These lines suggest that between ἐσθλοί and κακοί the former insist on preserving the existing unequal distribution of land while the latter demand ἰσομοιρίη—which Solon assures his peers he has refused. If this demand is viewed in the historical context of Athens at the beginning of the sixth century, when its elite were defending themselves as a distinct group, moving Athens in the direction of a more hierarchized state, engaging in intense competition for status, pressing for control over the community's best land, and exploiting forms of unfree labour, ἰσομοιρίη effectively rejects the evolving organization and institutions of the community. Even if it is understood to apply only to a limited class of land, Solon confronts in ἰσομοιρίη a demotic slogan of surprising implications. As a principle of equal distribution across the population, ἰσομοιρίη questions both the status of Athenian land as either public resource or private property and likewise, therefore, the nature of the relationship among citizens as either fundamentally egalitarian or hierarchical.[29]

The meaning of the compound ἰσομοιρίη in reference to land can express the viewpoint only of the *demos*, those whose access to land has been obstructed.[30]

---

[28] Contra, Mülke (2002: 359).
[29] Cecchet (2009: 185) notes the ambivalence of γῆς ἀναδασμός as simultaneously a principle of equality among citizens and a policy destroying the social order.
[30] See points 1 and 2 in my discussion of fragment 34 in Appendix II below. The semantics of σεισάχθεια likewise can express the viewpoint solely of the *demos*, since the idea of *shaking off* a burden of oppression, as opposed to 'lifting' or 'abolishing' it, is necessarily reflexive or middle-voiced (*LSJ* s.v. σείω III), something that the subject does for himself. That rare word may also preserve a

Does ἰσομοιρίη as a political demand imply an extensive political theory, a conception of an ideal state that the *demos* would like to implement? Does it imply some level of organization and leadership among free, semi-free, and unfree members of the *demos*? Even if we imagine leaders of elite factions courting the *demos* as an ally in rivalries with other factions in the expectation that they would themselves assume the role of leader of the *demos* (cf. δήμου θ' ἡγεμόνων at 4.7, discussed in Appendix I), there would nevertheless be little motive for the *demos* to stick out their collective neck by taking sides in elite clashes unless they were already nursing serious grievances against the status quo. For such an alliance between the *demos* and an elite champion, the obvious model would have been that of client and patron. In fact, the *demos* were harbouring shared grievances, which presuppose if not a full-blown political theory at least a critical orientation towards the status quo and a concept of social justice. Presumably such grievances were being discussed with adequate intensity to produce vocal advocates for various courses of action. I believe, though, that the *demos* and any leaders they may have followed would have been pragmatists, focused upon resolving the specific challenges at hand, rather than upon constructing an ideal state.[31] In a setting of growing exploitation of the *demos* by the Athenian elite as a whole, I expect that leadership would have emerged from among the *demos* themselves— either to find a patron and protector among the city's elite or to become targets for kidnapping and sale abroad by a hostile member of that same class (cf. 36.8–10).

So, Solon insists that he did not grant ἰσομοιρίη of the fatherland's fertile earth, since he did not think that the κακοί should be equal to the ἐσθλοί in this (34.8–9). Solon's rejection of ἰσομοιρίη in 34 limits what we can make of his boast in 36 that he removed the mysterious ὅροι, 'markers', from the black Earth:

> ...Γῆ μέλαινα, τῆς ἐγώ ποτε
> ὅρους ἀνεῖλον πολλαχῆι πεπηγότας.
>
> (36.5–6)
>
> ...black Earth, from whom I once
> removed the markers fixed far and wide.

Solon connects the removal of the ὅροι to his emancipation of enslaved Athenians (36.5–12), presenting it, apparently, as a land reform measure: he freed the land

---

demotic slogan. Rhodes (1993: 128), indeed, infers from the plural number of the verb in the phrase ἃς σεισάχθειαν καλοῦσιν (*Ath. Pol.* 6.1: 'which *they* call *seisachtheia*') that it is not Solon's own term.

[31] If Foxhall's picture (1997: 131–2) of a prosperous and self-sufficient upper tier among the class of thetes, or the *demos*, is accurate, then the hypothesis of a native demotic leadership appears more likely still. Rosivach (1992: 154–5) and Noussia-Fantuzzi (2010: 445) are both sceptical that leadership informed by a social or political theory could have emerged from the *demos* in Solon's day. From a comparative perspective, however, Magalhaes de Oliveira's analysis (2020) of the crowd in the cities of the late Roman Empire outlines how collective demotic action might have unfolded in the archaic Greek city. Phratries, religious cults, and other voluntary associations (as catalogued by Ismard 2010: 44–83), and even reciprocities among neighbours, would have been adequate to support collective identity and action for the *demos*.

itself and those who worked it. But, whether the ὅροι signalled claims against smallholders' parcels, the privatization of formerly communally held land, or some other hindrance to usufruct, certainly Solon's own words entail that removal of the ὅροι added up to less than the radical redistribution of farmland envisioned under the banner of ἰσομοιρίη. He boasts of accomplishing the one in the interest of the *demos* and of denying the other in the interest of the ἐσθλοί. Solon rejects a demand for ἰσομοιρίη, since it brings the *demos* into too direct a confrontation with the interests of the elite. Instead, he emancipates the land held in bondage by the ὅροι.

Solon discusses these two agrarian initiatives in separate poems, fragments 34 and 36, where he presents them in contrasting terms. Though 36 closes with a sop for members of Solon's own class (36.20–7), the poem otherwise enumerates benefits he bestowed upon the *demos*. In the opening lines he summons as a witness for the defence μήτηρ μεγίστη δαιμόνων Ὀλυμπίων / ἄριστα, Γῆ μέλαινα (36.4–5). As Solon describes how he restored to 'the greatest and best mother of the Olympian gods, black Earth' her freedom (πρόσθεν δὲ δουλεύουσα, νῦν ἐλευθέρη: 36.7) by pulling up the marker stones, all in rather formal language, he links the goddess to those Athenians whom he likewise freed from δουλίην ἀεικέα (36.13: 'unseemly slavery'). Solon opens 4 with similar high diction to contrast immortals (4.1–4) with mortals (4.5–8), but in that poem the juxtaposition serves to reveal the self-destructive depravity of men when set against the steady philanthropy of the gods.[32] But, in 36 Solon flatters his demotic audience by representing the deity as enslaved and abused just as they are and by linking her freedom to theirs. Solon, moreover, implicitly flatters himself as emancipator not only of the *demos* but of the goddess herself.

The treatment of the land question in 34 differs dramatically from that found in 36.

> οἱ δ' ἐφ' ἁρπαγῆισιν ἦλθον· ἐλπίδ' εἶχον ἀφνεήν,
> κἀδόκ[ε]ον ἕκαστος αὐτῶν ὄλβον εὑρήσειν πολύν,
> καί με κωτίλλοντα λείως τραχὺν ἐκφανεῖν νόον.
> χαῦνα μὲν τότ' ἐφράσαντο, νῦν δέ μοι χολούμενοι
> λοξὸν ὀφθαλμοῖς ὁρῶσι πάντες ὥστε δήϊον.
>
> (34.1–5)

Others came for loot; they hoped to be wealthy.
Each expected to find great riches
And that I, though coaxing sweetly, would reveal my ruthless intent.
Their planning was futile then, but now they're angry at me.
They all gaze at me warily, like an enemy.

In the final lines of this fragment (34.7–9) Solon goes on to reject vehemently ἰσομοιρίη, an 'equal distribution' of land between κακοί and ἐσθλοί, as we have

---

[32] Cf. 11.1–4, 13.1–17, and 14 for similar formulations of this topos.

seen, and in the opening lines quoted here he contemptuously dismisses the planned 'looting' (1: ἁρπαγῇσιν), the 'hope for wealth' (1: ἐλπίδ'... ἀφνεήν), and anticipation of 'great riches' (2: ὄλβον... πολύν) entertained by the *demos*. Solon prepares us for his principled rejection of an equal redistribution of land with accusations against the *demos* of greed (34.1–2) as well as of underhanded politics (34.3–5). Solon thus defends the elite's accumulation of land by accusing the *demos* of rapacity and of violating the social order in seeking to acquire a share of land for itself. The difference between these two treatments of demotic demands for land is stark. In 36 Solon is celebratory and self-congratulatory. He draws the divine realm into contact with the human in a picture of cosmic order restored. The *demos* have reason to be grateful, as the fragment's opening couplet suggests. But in 34 this same *demos* seeking the same source of subsistence security are censured for their avarice and summarily rejected.

Solon characterizes himself as caught between conflicting and mutually exclusive demands, turning his shield back and forth to protect either side against the other (5.5–6), spinning like a wolf surrounded by hounds (36.26–7), or a marker stone in the no man's land between two battle lines (37.9–10). This is the picture of a politician calculating what he must give up to opposing interests not only to save himself but to preserve his *polis*. Tearing the ὅροι up out of the earth (36.5–7) may constitute Solon's programme to free the *demos* of economic and legal dependency, or it may be an inconsequential measure advertised here in a gambit to frame the *demos* as ingrates before an elite audience. But the defensive question that opens 36—'which of the things I promised the *demos* did I leave undone?' (ἐγὼ δὲ τῶν μὲν οὕνεκα ξυνήγαγον / δῆμον, τί τούτων πρὶν τυχεῖν ἐπαυσάμην)— acknowledges from the outset the dissatisfaction of the *demos* with what his reforms have brought it. The *demos* were not the constituency in Athens whose influence was the greatest or whose contentment weighed most heavily on Solon's mind. So, he might well have calculated that amid conflicting demands he could get away with offering the *demos* less than the πιεί[ρ]ης χθονὸς / πατρίδος... ἰσομοιρίην (34.8–9), 'equal share of the fatherland's fertile earth', that they sought.[33]

The view I am offering of Solon's relationship to the Athenian *demos* is supported by his condescension towards them and their dissatisfaction with him. The first line of 5, δήμωι μὲν γὰρ ἔδωκα τόσον γέρας ὅσσον ἐπαρκεῖν ('to the *demos* I granted such a boon, enough to suffice'), sets a low bar for the satisfaction of demotic aspirations, just enough to get by. A grant of ὅσσον ἐπαρκεῖν for the *demos*, Solon's guarantee to the powerful and rich (5.3: οἳ δ' εἶχον δύναμιν καὶ χρήμασιν ἦσαν ἀγητοί, 'those who were wielding power and were magnificent in their wealth') that he contrived 'nothing insulting' (5.4: μηδὲν ἀεικές) for them, followed by his summary declaration that he did not permit either side to 'conquer unjustly' (5.6: νικᾶν... ἀδίκως), provide a revealing perspective on his objection to

---

[33] Nemeth's failure (2005) to consider the *demos* as a political constituency limits his analysis of Solon's treatment of the land. Cf. Link's more nuanced account (1991: 24–41) of Solon's intentions.

ἰσομοιρίη between κακοί and ἐσθλοί (34.8–9): enough to get by for the one and nothing to disturb the other in their wealth and power is Solon's justice.[34] In 5 Solon acknowledges that he did not offer much to the *demos* in his reforms. In 37.1–3 he coolly advises the *demos* that they are lucky to have what they got:

> δήμωι μὲν εἰ χρὴ διαφάδην ὀνειδίσαι,
> ἃ νῦν ἔχουσιν οὔποτ' ὀφθαλμοῖσιν ἂν
> εὕδοντες εἶδον...
>
> (37.1–3)
>
> If I must openly fault the *demos*,
> what they now possess they would never have set eyes on
> in their dreams...

But, if, thanks to Solon, the *demos* now possess what formerly they would not have dreamed of, what could provoke this defensive assertion of his generosity if not discontent from the *demos* in place of the gratitude he suggests that he deserves? With this complacent yet patronizing formulation, Solon must intend to dispose of a prior accusation by the *demos* that what he has provided does not satisfy their expectation for a more equitable distribution of wealth, a reform possibly justified as a restoration of resources formerly held either communally or individually by members of the *demos*.

Solon's criticism of the *demos* at 34.1–5, his self-justifying claim at 37.1–3, and his unequivocal rejection of ἰσομοιρίη as an affront to the social order taken together suggest that the *demos* demanded not only a degree of prosperity beyond what would barely suffice (5.1) but so much that it threatened to drain resources claimed for themselves by Athens' wealthy. Solon caps his catalogue of all that he achieved for the *demos* (36.4–20)—removal of the ὅροι, freeing of the enslaved and repatriation of Athenians abroad, written laws and straight justice for commoners and nobles alike (τῶι κακῶι τε κἀγαθῶι: 36.18)—with the claim that another man taking up the goad (κέντρον: 36.20), some demagogue, would not have kept back the *demos* (οὐκ ἂν κατέσχε δῆμον: 36.22) as he had. Solon implies that his demotic initiatives were aimed, in fact, at restraining the *demos*. What Solon did for the *demos* was only enough to get by, enough to neutralize them as parties to civil war. In the face of a social ideology that rationalized an unequal distribution of the community's wealth and a political leadership consequently unwilling and probably unable to deliver fundamental reforms, the *demos* sought, as I will now argue, a solution beyond the bounds of what Solon considered conventional politics.

---

[34] In view of how little Solon credits to the *demos* in 5, I am inclined to detect a note of sarcasm in his use of such common elements of epic diction as γέρας and τιμή (5.1–2) to describe his dealing with it. See Noussia-Fantuzzi (2010: 286–7) on usage. Also, in so far as ὅσσον ἐπαρκεῖν can be understood as an evaluation of his services to the *demos* listed at 36. 5–20, Solon does not thereby make much of having removed the ὅροι.

## Politics

In the archaic period, tyranny as a form of government had not yet acquired the negative reputation that it possessed by the classical period.[35] Cawkwell, moreover, maintains that tyrants of the seventh and sixth centuries did not rely upon either demotic or hoplite support but rather upon their own wealth. Anderson advances Cawkwell's account of tyranny, arguing that archaic tyrants were legitimate aristocratic leaders rather than extra-constitutional strongmen relying on the support of the rabble.[36] As Anderson acknowledges, though, Solon's hostility to tyranny makes him an exceptional case.[37] Tyrannies emerged in the archaic *polis* from a political context animated not by conflict between rich and poor so much as by intra-elite competition. This is certainly the sort of crisis confronted by Solon, who undoubtedly had among his elite followers men hoping he would establish himself as tyrant. Yet, even if one concedes that the Athenian *demos* was neither a principal nor a perennial player in the city's politics before the fifth century, still it is the commoners whom Solon identifies as the primary support for a tyrant. Solon must have worried that rival elite factions were not above attempting to recruit the support of the *demos* in order to gain a competitive edge.[38] I suggest that Solon's effort to placate the *demos* resulted from his fear of tyranny. As one element of his effort to stabilize the Athenian state, he wished to neutralize the *demos* as a political actor. Certainly, if the *demos* felt dissatisfied, even betrayed, with the reforms that Solon promulgated, he must have earlier made promises to the *demos* in an effort to bind them to him politically. From their side, then, the *demos* no doubt understood that in a moment of heightened conflict within the city's elite, when *stasis* threatened, they wielded greater political leverage than at other times and might be able to extract concessions from an otherwise unaccountable leadership.

Solon is obsessed by the possibility of a tyrant coming to power in Athens. He uses the terms τυραννίς or τυραννεύω ('tyranny', 'rule as tyrant') on three occasions, once each in fragments 32, 33, and 34, and he refers to tyranny implicitly, I believe, in fragments 9, 11, and 36. Tyranny weighs so heavily on his mind that he defines the character of his own archonship by opposition to it, as not a tyranny (32.1–4, 34.7–8). In fragments 32, 33, 34, and 36, Solon denounces tyranny but

---

[35] De Libero (1996: 37–8); Anderson (2005); Noussia-Fantuzzi (2010: 416–17, 429); Sagstetter (2013: 12–19).
[36] Cawkwell (1995); Anderson (2005).    [37] Anderson (2005: 207–8).
[38] Regarding intra-elite competition and recruitment of the *demos* by elite factions, see Ellis and Stanton (1968: 95–9), Stahl (1987: 60–6, 98–104), Link (1991: 35–41), Foxhall (1997: 118–22), Balot (2001: 73–9), Anderson (2005: 186–9), and Noussia-Fantuzzi (2010: 248); cf. van Wees (2000). Hammer (2005: esp. 117–26) argues along new lines for the intimate relationship between tyrants and *demos* in Athens and elsewhere, and Rose (2012: esp. 201–6) offers a compelling defence of the central role of the *demos* and the class conflict between rich and poor in the rise of tyrants in the archaic period.

simultaneously acknowledges that at least some of his followers had expected him to seize power as a tyrant. The persona of 33 reproaches Solon by name for not making himself tyrant (τυραννεύσας: 33.6) when he had the chance (33.1–4) in a speech that then evolves into an unwitting, comic self-accusation. In the fragment's three remaining lines Solon puts in his character's mouth words meant to reveal indirectly Solon's own critique of this speaker's accusation: he asserts that if he could be tyrant of Athens for only a day, claiming power and boundless wealth, he would not mind thereafter being flayed alive and seeing his entire family wiped out. With this self-contradictory speech Solon defends his choice not to seek to rule as a tyrant, but against what critics? Plutarch (*Sol.* 14.6–15.1) characterizes this attack voiced by Solon's fictive critic as an opinion circulating among the *demos*: ταῦτα τοὺς πολλοὺς καὶ φαύλους περὶ αὐτοῦ πεποίηκε λέγοντας (Plut. *Sol.* 15.1), 'he reports that the lower classes spoke these things about himself'. Solon ventriloquizes his demotic critic to present the elite take on the commoner's lack of understanding of how wealth is acquired, accumulated, and enjoyed, knowledge and practices over which the elite protects its monopoly.[39]

In 32 Solon gives an explicit response to the critic of 33 by representing his rejection of a tyranny in the language of heroic patriotism but tyranny itself in the language of shame.[40]

> εἰ δὲ γῆς (φησιν) ἐφεισάμην
> πατρίδος, τυραννίδος δὲ καὶ βίης ἀμειλίχου
> οὐ καθηψάμην μιάνας καὶ καταισχύνας κλέος,
> οὐδὲν αἰδέομαι· πλέον γὰρ ὧδε νικήσειν δοκέω
> πάντας ἀνθρώπους.

> If I spared (he says) the soil
> of my fatherland and I did not lay hold of a tyranny
> and relentless violence, staining and disgracing my name,
> I am not ashamed. For in that way I expect to surpass
> all men the more.

The poem's moral logic lines up γῆς πατρίδος, 'soil of my fatherland', κλέος, 'name', 'reputation', οὐδὲν αἰδέομαι, 'I am not ashamed', and νικήσειν, 'surpass'

---

[39] Fragment 33 thus corresponds to 4c, in which Solon again adopts a demotic voice to criticize the elite, but in that case he seriously censures the addressee. Linforth (1919: 217) hears the voice of the 'common man' in 33. Mülke (2002: 338) and Noussia-Fantuzzi (2010: 433–4) rather detect an elite speaker pursuing aristocratic values to an illogical extreme. Ll. 9–22 of 4, beginning with bad manners at a banquet and culminating in civil war, better exemplify Solon's critique of the destructive results of elite competition. Fragment 33's persona strikes me rather as a demotic Lord of Misrule than as an Achilles or Harry Hotspur.

[40] It is quite possible that fragments 32 and 33 belong to the same, single poem. See Noussia-Fantuzzi's discussion (2010: 420–2) of this question. The two fragments are in any case clearly in dialogue with one another.

against βίης ἀμειλίχου, 'relentless violence', μιάνας, 'staining', and καταισχύνας, 'disgracing.' Lodged amid the list of shameful things, moreover, is τυραννίδος, 'tyranny', which, along with 'relentless violence', Solon rejects in order to protect his reputation from stain and disgrace.[41] Solon responds in these two fragments to a constituency—in my view, the *demos*—that had supported him in the expectation that he would set himself up as a tyrant.[42]

Corresponding to indications in 32 and 33 that the *demos* were disappointed in Solon's failure to make himself tyrant in Athens, other fragments give evidence for Solon's view that the *demos* needed to be actively restrained in order to forestall their support for some charlatan on the path to tyranny. As I have already discussed, in 36 Solon provides a catalogue of his achievements specifically for the *demos*, culminating in his writing laws and imposing justice (36.15–20). He then surprisingly caps his list off by comparing himself to an imaginary alternative:

> ... κέντρον δ' ἄλλος ὡς ἐγὼ λαβών,
> κακοφραδής τε καὶ φιλοκτήμων ἀνήρ,
> οὐκ ἂν κατέσχε δῆμον· ...
>
> (36.20–2)
>
> ... but another, taking up the goad as I did,
> an ill-counselled and greedy man,
> would not have restrained the *demos*...

It is as if Solon fears that his good service to the *demos*, summarized in the lines preceding, will invite accusations from other quarters that he has corrupted the people's character or worse. Similarly, in the first couplet of 6, Solon advises explicitly that the *demos* will best follow their leaders when neither too liberated nor too oppressed (μήτε λίην ἀνεθεὶς μήτε βιαζόμενος: 6.2). Leaders who wish to manage the *demos* successfully would err to give them too much or too little. The characterization of this alternative wielder of the κέντρον, this ἄλλος, in 36 as κακοφραδής and φιλοκτήμων, 'ill-counselled' and 'greedy', links him to a group of tyrannical figures in other fragments: the αἱμύλος ἀνήρ, 'scheming man', whose words dissemble his deeds (11.7–8); the μόναρχος, 'dictator', who emerges from the *polis*-destroying ἄνδρες μεγάλοι (9.3–4), 'big men'; and the rogue of 37.8, who steals the butter from the milk.[43] This butter thief of 37, a leader whom Solon contrasts with himself (ἐγὼ δέ, 37.9), attracts the same phrase that Solon uses to describe his κακοφραδής and φιλοκτήμων alternative at 36.22: οὐκ ἂν κατέσχε

---

[41] Noussia-Fantuzzi (2010: 430) answers Anderson's argument (2005: 206, n. 82) that μιάνας and καταισχύνας (32.3) describe the consequence of Solon *not* making himself tyrant.

[42] Noussia-Fantuzzi (2010: 415–17), noting that, 'in fact, [Solon] did more than the rich and advantaged hoped, and less than the poor and disadvantaged hoped' (p. 415), discusses the necessity that Solon defend himself in this way.

[43] See Noussia-Fantuzzi's explanation (2010: 492–4) of the problematic phrase at 37.7–8: οὐδ' ἐπαύσατο / πρὶν ἀνταράξας πῖαρ ἐξεῖλεν γάλα.

δῆμον (37.7), 'he would not have restrained the *demos*'.[44] The *demos* in Solon's judgement needs restraining. With the phrase ἄλλος ὡς ἐγὼ in line 20 of 36, Solon separates himself from the κακοφραδής and φιλοκτήμων would-be tyrant solely by the latter's reluctance and his own willingness to put the goad to the *demos*—to restrain them, redirect them, and perhaps to renege on promises made to them to win their support.

In 9 and 11, both quoted by Diodorus, Solon blames the *demos* for their own misfortune, namely, a tyrant.[45] Fragment 9 opens with a couplet illustrating, if not cause and effect, at least a normative sequence: from a cloud come snow and hail, from lightning there is thunder. Juxtaposed to suggest equal regularity are lines 3–4:

ἀνδρῶν δ' ἐκ μεγάλων πόλις ὄλλυται, ἐς δὲ μονάρχου
δῆμος ἀϊδρίηι δουλοσύνην ἔπεσεν.

By its big men a city perishes, and into a sole ruler's slavery the *demos* falls in their witlessness.

Solon's ἄνδρες μεγάλοι refers, I believe, to members of the elite—'big men', with weapons, lands, a retinue, and an extended family to rely on—whose destructive competition and infighting lead to the emergence from their midst of a μόναρχος, a tyrant, to rule the city.[46] The *demos*, the commoners in this context, become slaves to a μόναρχος, moreover, through their own ignorance and gullibility. Fragment 11 echoes 9, though it does not mention the *demos* explicitly: owing to your own depravity (ὑμετέρην κακότητα: 11.1), namely, providing support to 'these men' (τούτους: 11.3), you endure harsh slavery (δουλοσύνην: 11.4). You have been taken in by a deceiver's flattery (ἔπη αἱμύλου ἀνδρός: 11.7).[47] Solon makes explicit in this fragment what is assumed in 9, that support by the *demos* for certain leaders has led to their own oppression: αὐτοὶ γὰρ τούτους ηὐξήσατε ῥύματα δόντες (11.3), 'you yourselves strengthened these men by giving them support'.[48]

In both 9 and 11 the movement from plural (9.3: ἀνδρῶν δ' ἐκ μεγάλων, 11.3: τούτους) to singular (9.3: μονάρχου, 11.7: αἱμύλου ἀνδρός) shows Solon is thinking

---

[44] This same theme of restraining the *demos* may be present at 9.5 (λίην δ' ἐξάραντ' <οὐ> ῥᾴδιόν ἐστι κατασχεῖν), if it means 'it is not easy to restrain [the *demos*: l. 4] when they raise up too insistently [a *monarchos*: l. 3]'. So Linforth (1919: 206) takes it. See Noussia-Fantuzzi's discussion (2010: 317–18).

[45] Diodorus presents both fragments as commentary by Solon on Pisistratus, but Mülke (2002: 202, 217) and Noussia-Fantuzzi (2010: 309–10) are sceptical of this claim on chronological grounds and owing to the fragments' surprising generality, following in this Linforth (1919: 303–7).

[46] See Noussia-Fantuzzi (2010: 315) regarding the word μόναρχος. I discuss the connotation of 'commoners' for δῆμος at 9.4 in Appendix I.

[47] Both Linforth (1919: 207) and Noussia-Fantuzzi (2010: 328) understand the addressee (ὑμετέρην: 11.1) to be the *demos*; Mülke (2002: 217–18) regards the *demos* as an unlikely addressee but concludes that the reference is uncertain. For the reading of ῥύματα δόντες in l. 3 and the interpretation that it refers to granting support to τούτους, i.e. the same as the μεγάλοι ἄνδρες of 9.3, see Noussia-Fantuzzi (2010: 332–3).

[48] Similarly, δι' ὑμετέρην κακότητα: 11.1 and διὰ ταῦτα: 11.4.

of the emergence of a single leader for the city, a tyrant, out of the ranks of elite citizens competing for power and status. Yet, even if the political power of the Athenian *demos* was in Solon's time far less than in the fifth century, the passages quoted in our sources demonstrate nonetheless that the *demos* did support establishing a tyranny and even expected Solon to do so. We consequently find Solon engaged in an effort simultaneously to placate the *demos*, probably with minimal concessions, and to restrain them from offering their support to a leader whom Solon regarded as a danger to collective elite rule. As I suggested above regarding Solon's emancipation of enslaved Athenians, the same figure whom the *demos* anticipated as their liberator Solon feared as an enslaver of the elite.

To return to 34, in its final lines Solon pairs up his rejection of ἰσομοιρίη with his rejection of a τυραννίς:

> ...οὐδέ μοι τυραννίδος
> ἁνδάνει βίηι τι[..], ε[ι]ν, οὐδὲ πιεί[ρ]ης χθονὸς
> πατρίδος κακοῖσιν ἐσθλοὺς ἰσομοιρίην ἔχειν.
>
> (34.7–9)
>
> ...neither does it suit me
> to [do anything][49] with the violence of a tyrant,
> nor that of the fatherland's fertile earth
> the nobles have an equal share with the base.

The two branches of the sentence marked by the correlative occurrences of οὐδέ could be understood antithetically, placing Solon between opposing groups: I neither made myself tyrant as my elite supporters demanded, nor did I redistribute land as expected by the *demos*. But the poem's consistent aim at a single target and the sudden forcefulness of the final lines argue, I think, against this view. The fragment's ending, as we have it at any rate, does not, moreover, offer one of the familiar images of Solon isolated amid opposing sides (cf. 5.5–6, 36.26–7, 37.9–10), as we might expect if the poem contrasted two groups that each want something from Solon. After he has exposed in 34.1–6 the selfish motives of his critics, their dishonest expectations, their irrational sense of betrayal, and then lamented the futility of it all, Solon bluntly denies in the final verses that either tyranny or land redistribution was ever on his agenda. The strength and conviction of Solon's closing assertion as well as its abrupt specificity in comparison to the preceding lines suggest again that the *demos* expected him to establish a tyranny as a platform for a land reform programme. Solon's τυραννίς was anticipated as the means of achieving ἰσομοιρίη. At a minimum, when Solon refers to the ἀϊδρίη (9.4) of the *demos*, and their susceptibility to the αἱμύλος (11.7), κακοφραδής τε καὶ φιλοκτήμων (36.21), and butter-snatching (37.8) ἀνήρ, he may in fact allude

---

[49] Kenyon's τι ῥέζειν (1920: 9) is generally accepted as the most plausible supplement for l. 8.

to explicit threats from the *demos* that if their demands were not met, they would seek out a leader prepared to fulfil them.

The evidence that the *demos* demanded a tyrant to lead them is Solon's repeated expressions of fear that a tyrant will seize power with demotic support, even if a tyranny relying in part upon demotic support is atypical for the archaic period.[50] It may be that the demands for land reform and emancipation exceeded what the *demos* could expect even from a reform-minded archon were he to remain within the boundaries of political traditions and what Athens' elite would tolerate, a circumstance that would have pushed the *demos* towards supporting a tyranny. If, however, we allow that the *demos* might have been prepared to follow such a reformist archon, or that Solon's halfway programme attracted enough demotic supporters to leave their erstwhile, perhaps more desperate, comrades too weak to act, then what of Solon's denunciations of the *demos*'s gullibility and his claims to have turned them back from their destructive course? What Solon has to say about tyrants is certainly addressed as a warning to the *demos*. But it is addressed equally to members of his own class to raise a warning, again, but also to present himself as their defender. If his repeated admonitions about a tyrant should, rather, misrepresent the intentions of the *demos*, the fragments we have considered would serve, then, to pander to the anxieties of individuals for whom any leadership indebted to the *demos* would be cause for alarm. To misrepresent the *demos* in this way would simultaneously undermine their credibility before the city's elite and inflate Solon's reputation for protecting elite interests. Although I find the direct interpretation—that the *demos* expected Solon to make himself tyrant—the more persuasive, the alternative considered here adds nothing to Solon's reputation as benefactor of the *demos*.

Notwithstanding the admiration in which tyrants may have been held during the archaic period, Solon appears adamantly opposed to the possibility of a tyrant for Athens. Solon elaborates in his poetry a political ideology able to accommodate tyranny only within the category of the irrational, as the product of a self-destructive wish fuelled by greed and violence, by the ἀϊδρίη (9.4) and κακότης (11.1), the 'witlessness' and 'wickedness', of the *demos*. Solon's understanding of tyranny illuminates the threat it presents to the city, but it conceals from him what the *demos* might nevertheless expect to gain from such a leader. Solon's solution to the riddle of tyranny blinds him to the source of his solution's inevitable collapse. The regime that Solon foresaw as violence and chaos (4.17–29)

---

[50] That the *demos* support tyrants is precisely Aristotle's position (*Pol.* 1310$^b$9–16, quoted by Cawkwell 1995: 73), the very theory that Cawkwell (1995) sets out to refute. It is also, however, what Solon states repeatedly in the passages just examined and perhaps preserved to begin with, admittedly, on account of their agreement with Aristotle. Rose's discussion (2012: 211–13, 223–5) of the nexus of tyranny, land, wealth, and exploitation of the *demos* illuminates Solon's archonship, whether one accepts the role Rose assigns to a 'money-form' or not.

may well have been anticipated by the *demos*, confronted with enslavement and expropriation by wealthy neighbours, as a restoration of customary protections and social order. Demotic support for a tyrant can in context, then, be understood as the product of a rational calculation of how the *demos* might best defend itself from the depredations of the same elite whom Solon struggles to preserve.[51]

## Conclusion

Clues for what the Athenian *demos* hoped to achieve in the midst of the social upheaval surrounding Solon's archonship emerge from Solon's poetry, as we would expect, at those points where his own discourse meets the voice of the *demos*. We are able to discern the outlines of what the demos wanted through the maze of Solon's boasts about what he provided, declarations of what he refused, and recommendations for what served the interest of the *demos*. It is also evident both from Solon's ideas about how best to manage the *demos* and from his defensive justifications for how he served it, that what he delivered fell short of what the *demos* had hoped for from him.

In the case of slavery, the evidence supplied by Solon leaves us uncertain what specific class of enslaved Athenians were freed and how far Solon might have actually got with that initiative. But he does seize on the metaphor of slavery to cast the Athenian elite as potential victim of the *demos*. Likewise in the case of land, we remain in the dark regarding precisely what land is at issue, what is demanded by the slogan ἰσομοιρίη, and how the *demos* benefited by Solon's removal of the ὅροι. Solon, however, exploits that slogan to defame the *demos* for unrestrained greed in their pursuit of some share of the land accumulated in the hands of the elite. In spite of all uncertainty, it appears nevertheless that the *demos* did indeed win some benefits from Solon with respect to land and labour.

With regard to tyranny, however, Solon pointedly rejected this form of leadership that lay outside the existing set of institutions devised to rotate elite power among many hands. Solon claimed to have improved conditions for the *demos*, but he was motivated to emancipate slaves and remove the marker stones from the fields, I believe, out of a desire to limit elite access to the fundamental forms of wealth, land, and labour that could be devoted to the destructive intra-elite competition such as he describes at 4.5–31.[52] The outcome that Solon most wished to forestall was the rise of a tyrant, the form that a complete victory of one elite

---

[51] I have approached the fragments of Solon's poetry as the site of a rhetorical struggle in which radically opposed discourses are joined side by side as Solon strives to win mastery for the one over the other. Such opposed rhetorics, however, only instantiate opposed ideologies. Rose (2012: 201–66) offers a valuable discussion of the ideological conflicts and contradictions animating Solon's poetry in its specific historical conjuncture.

[52] See Ellis and Stanton (1968: 99–104) regarding Solon's use of such a strategy.

faction or another would take. The reforms he drafted to rein in elite excess, moreover, and to regulate their political life made the *demos* for their part more directly dependent upon the authority and legitimacy of Athenian political and legal institutions by, for example, ensuring free status for those formerly enslaved, providing written laws, and distributing political and judicial rights solely on the basis of wealth. Perhaps this approach should be understood as a movement in the direction of citizenship as a legal status, which became so important for the Athenian *demos* in the fifth century.[53]

If, however, we view the period around Solon's archonship from the perspective of the *demos* and in terms of existing forms of social relationships, we can perhaps understand the *demos*'s disappointment with Solon. A relationship of reciprocity between the *demos* and Solon by which the former provided political support in exchange for a larger share of the city's wealth from the latter should be understood as a bid by the *demos* to become a dependent in a patron–client relationship with Athens' pre-eminent patron, the city's new tyrant.[54] But I infer that what Solon finally provided to the *demos* amounted to less in material benefits than a tyrant might have been willing to bestow on a valued client and that at the same time Solon's constitutional reform pointedly preserved, perhaps even reinforced, the social, political, and economic hierarchy against which the *demos* struggled. If so, in spite of any gains it won from Solon, the *demos* was bound to be dissatisfied.

## Appendix I: Solon's Use of the Word Δῆμος

The noun δῆμος occurs nine times in Solon's extant fragments. Solon's usage falls within the range of the principal meanings offered by Homer: 1. a territory; 2. all the inhabitants of a territory, or a citizen body; 3. the citizen body minus the elite, or the commoners. Solon uses the word in senses 2 and 3, and it is not always possible to distinguish one from the other with certainty.

1. At 5.1 δήμωι is placed in opposition to the phrase in 5.3 οἳ δ' εἶχον δύναμιν καὶ χρήμασιν ἦσαν ἀγητοί, the elite, and must refer to the commoners. See Linforth (1919: 180), Mülke (2002: 181–3), and Noussia-Fantuzzi (2010: 283–5).
2. The same contrast appears at 6.1 between δῆμος and ἡγεμόνεσσιν, requiring likewise a meaning of 'commoners' for δῆμος. See Mülke (2002: 194–5) and Noussia-Fantuzzi (2010: 289–90).

---

[53] See Balot (2001: 73–5) and Ismard (2010: ¶26).
[54] Tandy (1997: 112–38) offers a detailed analysis of the historical process that might have led Solon and the *demos* to such divergent expectations and solutions. Zurbach's concept of a 'moral economy', as developed in this volume, can also provide a broader context for the sense of mutual obligation that I suggest obtains between a tyrant and his demotic supporters.

3. This pattern repeats itself a third time in the contrast between δήμωι at 37.1 and ὅσοι δὲ μείζους καὶ βίην ἀμείνονες of 37.4, arguing again for a meaning of 'commoners'. See Mülke (2002: 397–400) and Noussia-Fantuzzi (2010: 387–9).

4–5. Solon twice describes an opportunist who might have gained power in his stead with the phrase οὐκ ἂν κατέσχε δῆμον (37.7 = 36.22). In both of these passages Solon establishes a context that signals a need to keep a firm hand on the *demos*, so I assign these two attestations as well to meaning 3, 'commoners'. See Linforth (1919: 188-9), Mülke (2002: 390-1, 406), and Noussia-Fantuzzi (2010: 455, 479-80, 488-9, 493-4).

6. δῆμος at 9.4 may repeat the idea of πόλις in the line preceding, giving meaning 2. But, the attribute of ἀϊδρίη assigned to δῆμος (9.4, cf. 9.6) suggests that Solon instead has in mind the 'commoners'. So, I prefer meaning 3 as more likely. Mülke (2002: 209) understands meaning 2, but Noussia-Fantuzzi (2010: 309-11) appears to prefer meaning 3 for δῆμος.

7. δήμου at 4.7 occurs in the phrase δήμου θ' ἡγεμόνων, either 'the leaders of the commoners' (meaning 3) or 'the leaders of the city' (meaning 2). Linforth (1919: 196-8) adopts 'commoners', meaning 3, as does Mülke (2002: 110-12), reasoning that the ἡγεμόνες compose a leadership class distinct from those who are led. The first portion of the fragment (4.1-31), moreover, devoted to the reign of δυσνομίη, catalogues the moral failings and abuses of the Athenian elite, to which the ἡγεμόνες of 4.7 certainly belong. This specificity is underlined by the separate fate, distinct from that of the elite (4.17-23), that is reserved for the poor (τῶν δὲ πενιχρῶν: 4.23-5), who comprise the *demos* in the restricted sense of meaning 3. The occurrences, however, of πόλις (4.1), πόλιν (4.5), and ἀστοί (4.6), δημοσίων (4.12), πόλει (4.17), ἄστυ (4.21), δήμωι (4.23), δημόσιον (4.26), and Ἀθηναίους (4.30), in so far as they refer to the totality of the city's residents, provide a context suggesting meaning 2. See Noussia-Fantuzzi (2010: 228). I cannot discern clear grounds for deciding between meaning 2 and meaning 3 here.

8. At 36.1-2 the phrase ξυνήγαγον / δῆμον might refer to a city-wide assembly, meaning 2. Considering, though, that 36 is devoted to enumerating Solon's services to the commoners, it is also a likely possibility that the phrase refers to a convocation of them alone, meaning 3. Linforth (1919: 185) assumes 'commoners'; Mülke (2002: 370) insists on the citizenry as a whole. I incline to meaning 3.

9. δήμωι at 4.23, ταῦτα μὲν ἐν δήμωι στρέφεται κακά, appears in a passage (4.17-26) focused on the effects of civil war upon the city's inhabitants, so that πόλει in l. 17 and ἄστυ in l. 21 refer to the populace rather than places. Meaning 2 therefore seems best here, but meaning 1 is possible. See Mülke (2002: 140) and Noussia-Fantuzzi (2010: 252-3).

## Appendix II: *Κακοί* and *Ἐσθλοί* in Fragment 34

The markers of social status and moral quality ἀγαθός, καλός, and ἐσθλός are used by Solon as animate substantives only in explicit opposition to either δειλός or κακός. There are five passages in which such combinations occur: 13.33, 13.39, 15.1, 34.9, and 36.18. Καλός at

13.40 contrasts with the litotes οὐ χαρίεσσαν, completing a sixth pair. At 13.33 (ἀγαθός τε κακός τε) and 36.18 (τῶι κακῶι τε κἀγαθῶι) the contrasting pairs simply express the idea 'everyone'. In these two passages ἀγαθός must refer to the elite and κακός to everyone else, the δῆμος in sense 3 of 'commoners'. The same contrast in social status organizes 13.39 and 13.40. In 15, however, Solon expresses his frustration that wealth and poverty do not necessarily line up with the corresponding social statuses of the καλός and the κακός as they ought: πολλοὶ γὰρ πλουτέουσι κακοί, ἀγαθοὶ δὲ πένονται (15.1).[55] In the final lines of 34 Solon asserts that he did not permit the κακοί to gain an equal share of land with the city's ἐσθλοί, preserving this natural asymmetry of wealth between the two. There is no dispute over the identity of the ἀγαθοί–ἐσθλοί in fragments 15 and 34, Athens' elite, but there is regarding the identity of the κακοί.

Noussia-Fantuzzi (2010: 279–80) argues that the κακοί of 15 are members of a prosperous mercantile class whose rise in Athens threatens the established nobility with a 'new economic order'. Of course, trade is not the only economic mechanism able to move elite families into poverty and poor families into wealth. Processes such as marriages, inheritances, and land transfers may in fact offer the wider path into and out of wealth for Athens of the early sixth century.[56] Indeed, the final line of 15—χρήματα δ᾽ ἀνθρώπων ἄλλοτε ἄλλος ἔχει—describes a situation closer to the latter scenario than to a one-time transformation of society by an expansion of trade. Either way, Solon refers to a group whose roots in the demotic poor are still remembered.

This same group of wealthy, non-aristocratic merchants invoked to explain 15 are likewise identified as the κακοί of 34.9: μοι.../ ἀνδάνει...οὐδὲ πιεί[ρ]ης χθονὸς / πατρίδος κακοῖσιν ἐσθλοὺς ἰσομοιρίην ἔχειν (34.7–9).[57] This line of reasoning rejects the hypothesis that the Athenian masses of Solon's day were demanding a redistribution of land on an equal basis, though there can be no doubt that it is the *demos* who would have benefited the most from land reform at the time of Solon's archonship. Fragment 34, moreover, appears in the *Athenaion Politeia* (12.3), third in a series of five quotations meant to illustrate Solon's hard-nosed approach to the *demos*.

The argument that the κακοί in question are wealthy non-aristocrats, the same κακοί proposed for 15, seems to me to run into trouble precisely with the term ἰσομοιρίη.

1. Since many of these *nouveaux riches* κακοί would, according to this account, be wealthier than many elite families, it seems unlikely that they would consider an equal redistribution of land across the entire population as something particularly beneficial to themselves. A demand for a redistribution of land on the principle of

---

[55] See Rosivach (1992: 155 with nn. 14 and 15) regarding this fragment specifically and the connotations of κακός and καλός generally in Solon.

[56] See the summaries of how the poor might rise to wealth without engaging in trade provided by Rosivach (1992: 156–7 with n. 23) and by Stahl (1987: 90). A wealthy mercantile class shut out of political rights by an entrenched aristocracy is, in fact, an unlikely scenario, since archaic trade was organized for and by the elite itself. See Tandy (1997: 4, 59–83) and Reed (2003: 62–8). Additionally, van Wees and Fisher (2015: 7–15) offer a forceful refutation of the established account in which there arose in the archaic period a mercantile or military class excluded from elite status and induced as a result to challenge the privilege of an entrenched aristocracy.

[57] Mülke (2002: 358–60); Welwei (2005: 35–7); Noussia-Fantuzzi (2010: 445–7).

ἰσομοιρίη within the restricted pool of only *nouveaux riches* κακοί and the ἐσθλοί, eliminating the poor from participation, also strikes me as improbable for the same reason: κακοί whose landed wealth rivalled the fortunes of the ἐσθλοί would not have uniformly expected to benefit from such a redistribution.

2. If, however, as Noussia-Fantuzzi (2010: 453–4) and Mülke (2002: 358–9) propose, ἰσομοιρίη in 34 refers to a demand by the wealthy of non-aristocratic families, the κακοί of l. 9, for equal political rights with aristocratic, Eupatrid families, then it must be acknowledged that that is precisely what Solon provided to them with his census classes: political rights distributed on the basis of wealth without reference to family heritage. But, or course, Solon denies that he granted to the κακοί ἰσομοιρίη with the ἐσθλοί. In any case, these wealthy κακοί would certainly have acquired the land whose productivity determined a family's census class. On the one hand, loss of wealth for the elite families can mean only the transfer of land into other hands, and, on the other, for a society like archaic Athens, the only form that the stable accumulation of wealth can take is acquisition of land. Again, see Rosivach (1992: 156). If we imagine that such *nouveaux riches* κακοί were somehow prevented from acquiring land, it would make more sense for them to demand removal of that prohibition than to demand ἰσομοιρίη of either political rights or land.

3. The phrases ἐλπίδ'...ἀφνεήν and ὄλβον...πολύν in the first two verses of 34 have been argued to be both unlikely and unrealizable goals for so impoverished and numerous a group as the Athenian *demos*. So, it is argued, Solon must refer to a smaller group here, ex-supporters of his, most likely merchants or impoverished aristocrats, the same men whom Solon later labels κακοί at 34.9.[58] But, the appropriateness of these terms to a demotic expectation of help from Solon is entirely a matter of perspective. Solon addresses his peers from an elite outlook in this fragment and refers to the intended booty, property remaining, thanks to Solon, safe in the hands of its elite proprietors, in terms expressing its value to that class rather than to myriad smallholders, each hoping to own a small fraction of the total.

## Acknowledgements

I wish to thank my fellow authors Lucia Cecchet and Julien Zurbach as well as the anonymous reviewers at OUP for their valuable comments and suggestions. I also express here my gratitude to David Tandy and Samuel Gartland not only for their comments and suggestions but also for the enormous effort it took to see this project to its end.

## Works Cited

Almeida, J. A. (2003). *Justice as an Aspect of the Polis Idea in Solon's Political Poems: A Reading of the Fragments in Light of the Research of New Classical Archaeology.* Mnemosyne Supplement 243. Leiden.

---

[58] Regarding these phrases in 34's opening lines, see Rosivach (1992: 154), Mülke (2002: 350–1), and Noussia-Fantuzzi (2010: 446), the latter two with additional bibliography.

Anderson, G. (2005). 'Before Turannoi Were Tyrants: Rethinking a Chapter of Early Greek History', *Classical Antiquity*, 24: 173–222.

Balot, R. K. (2001). *Greed and Injustice in Classical Athens*. Princeton.

Bielman, A. (1994). *Rétour à la Liberté: Libération et sauvetage des prisonniers en Grèce Ancienne*. Athens.

Bintliff, J. (2006). 'Solon's Reforms: An Archaeological Perspective', in Blok and Lardinois (2006: 321–33).

Blok, J., and J. Krul (2017). 'Debt and its Aftermath: The Near Eastern Background to Solon's *Seisachtheia*', *Hesperia*, 86: 607–43.

Blok, J., and A. P. M. H. Lardinois (2006) (eds). *Solon of Athens: New Historical and Philological Approaches*. Leiden.

Cassola, F. (1964). 'Solone, la terra e gli ectemori', *La Parola del passato*, 19: 26–68.

Cawkwell, G. L. (1995). 'Early Greek Tyranny and the People', *Classical Quarterly*, 45: 73–86.

Cecchet, L. (2009). '$Γῆς\ ἀναδασμός$: A Real Issue in the Archaic and Classical Poleis?', *Athenaeum*, 55: 185–98.

de Libero, L. (1996). *Die Archaische Tyrannis*. Stuttgart.

Duplouy, A. (2014). 'Le Prestige des citoyens: *Agôn* et citoyenneté dans la Grèce archaïque', in F. Hurlet, I. Rivoal, and I. Sidéra (eds), *Le Prestige, autour des formes de la différenciation sociale*, 67–76. Lyons.

Duplouy, A. (2015). 'Genealogical and Dynastic Behaviour in Archaic and Classical Greece: Two Gentilician Strategies', in Fisher and van Wees (2015: 59–84).

Duplouy, A. (2018). 'Citizenship as Performance', in Duplouy and Brock (2018: 250–75).

Duplouy, A., and R. Brock (2018) (eds). *Defining Citizenship in Archaic Greece*. Oxford.

Edwards, A. T. (1993). 'Homer's Ethical Geography: Country and City in the Odyssey', *Transactions of the American Philological Association*, 123: 27–78.

Ellis, J. R., and G. R. Stanton (1968). 'Factional Conflict and Solon's Reforms', *Phoenix*, 22: 95–110.

Faraguna, M. (2012). 'Hektemoroi, isomoirie, seisachtheia: ricerche recenti sulla riforme economiche di Solone', *Dike*, 15: 171–93.

Fisher, N., and H. van Wees (2015) (eds). *'Aristocracy' in Antiquity: Redefining Greek and Roman Elites*. Swansea.

Forsdyke, S. (2006). 'Land, Labor, and Economy in Solonian Athens: Breaking the Impasse between Archaeology and History', in Blok and Lardinois (2006: 334–50).

Forsdyke, S. (2012). *Slaves Tell Tales and Other Episodes in the Politics of Popular Culture in Ancient Greece*. Princeton.

Foxhall, L. (1992). 'The Control of the Attic Landscape', in B. Wells (ed.), *Agriculture in Ancient Greece*, 155–9. Stockholm.

Foxhall, L. (1995). 'Bronze Age to Iron: Agricultural Systems and Political Structures in Late Bronze Age and Early Iron Age Greece', *Annual of the British School at Athens*, 90: 239–50.

Foxhall, L. (1997). 'A View from the Top: Evaluating the Solonian Property Classes', in Mitchell and Rhodes (1997: 113–36).

Gehrke, H.-J. (2009). 'States', in K. A. Raaflaub and H. van Wees (eds), *A Companion to Archaic Greece*, 395–410. Oxford.

Hammer, D. (2005). 'Plebiscitary Politics in Archaic Greece', *Historia*, 54: 108–31.

Harris, E. M. (1997). 'A New Solution to the Riddle of the *seisachtheia*', in Mitchell and Rhodes (1997: 103–12).

Irwin, E. (2005). *Solon and Early Greek Poetry: The Politics of Exhortation*. Cambridge.

Ismard, P. (2010). *La Cité des réseaux: Athènes et ses associations VIe–Ier siècle av. J.-C.* Paris. Open Edition Books https://books.openedition.org/psorbonne/10202 (30 January 2023).

Ismard, P. (2018). 'Associations and Citizenship in Attica from Solon to Cleisthenes', in Duplouy and Brock (2018: 146–60).

Kenyon, F. G. (1920). *Aristotelis atheniensium respublica*. Oxford.

Kroll, J. H. (1998). 'Silver in Solon's Laws', in R. Ashton and S. Hunter (eds), *Studies in Greek Numismatics in Memory of Martin Jessop Price*, 225–32. London.

Lewis, D. (2017). 'Making Law Grip: Inequality, Justice, And Legal Remedy in Solonian Attica and Ancient Israel', in I. K. Xydopoulos, K. Vlassopoulos, and E. Tounta (eds), *Violence and Community: Law, Space and Identity in the Ancient Eastern Mediterranean World*, 28–49. London.

Lewis, D. (2019). 'Piracy and Slave Trading in Action in Classical and Hellenistic Greece', *Mare Nostrum*, 10: 79–108.

Lewis, J. (2004). 'Slavery and Lawlessness in Solonian Athens', *Dike*, 7: 19–40.

Linforth, I. M. (1919). *Solon the Athenian*. Berkeley and Los Angeles.

Link, S. (1991). *Landverteilung und sozialer Frieden im archaischen Griechenland*. Stuttgart.

Magalhães de Oliveira, J. C. (2020). 'Late Antiquity: The Age of Crowds?', *Past and Present*, 249: 3–52.

Mitchell, L., and P. J. Rhodes (1997) (eds), *The Development of the Polis in Archaic Greece*. London.

Morris, I. (2002). 'Hard Surfaces', in P. Cartledge, E. E. Cohen, and L. Foxhall (eds), *Money, Labour, and Land: Approaches to the Economies of Ancient Greece*, 8–43. London.

Mülke, C. (2002) *Solons politische Elegien und Iamben: Einleitung, Text, Übersetzung, Kommentar*. Munich.

Mulliez, D. (1992). 'Les Actes d'affranchissement delphiques', *Cahiers du Centre Gustave Glotz*, 3: 31–44.

Nemeth, G. (2005). 'On Solon's Land Reform', *Acta antiqua Academiae Scientiarum Hungaricae*, 45: 321–8.

Noussia-Fantuzzi, M. (2010). *Solon the Athenian, the Poetic Fragments*. Leiden.

Raaflaub, K. A. and R. W. Wallace (2007). '"People's Power" and Egalitarian Trends in Archaic Greece', in Raaflaub et al. (2007: 22–48).

Raaflaub, K. A., J. Ober, and R. W. Wallace (2007) (eds). *Origins of Democracy in Ancient Greece*. Berkeley and Los Angeles.

Reed, C. M. (2003). *Maritime Traders in the Ancient Greek World*. Cambridge.

Rhodes, P. J. (1993). *A Commentary on the Aristotelian* Athenaion Politeia. Oxford.

Robinson, E. W. (1997). *The First Democracies. Early Popular Government outside Athens*. Stuttgart.

Rose, P. W. (2012). *Class in Archaic Greece*. Cambridge.

Rosivach, V. J. (1992). 'Redistribution of Land in Solon, Fragment 34 West', *Journal of Hellenic Studies*, 112: 153–7.

Sagstetter, K. S. (2013). 'Solon of Athens: The Man, the Myth, the Tyrant?' Ph.D. dissertation. Philadelphia.

Scheidel, W. (2008). 'The Comparative Economics of Slavery in the Greco-Roman World', in E. Dal Lago and C. Katsari (eds), *Slave Systems Ancient and Modern*, 105–26. Cambridge.

Scott, J. C. (2017). *Against the Grain: A Deep History of the Earliest States*. New Haven.

Sosin, J. D. (2017). 'Ransom at Athens ([Dem.] 53.11)', *Historia*, 66: 130–46.

Stahl, M. (1987). *Aristokraten und Tyrannen im archaischen Athen: Untersuchungen zur Überlieferung, zur Sozialstruktur und zur Entstehung des Staates*. Stuttgart.

Tandy, D. (1997). *Warriors into Traders*. Berkeley and Los Angeles.

van Wees, H. (2000). 'Megara's Mafiosi: Timocracy and Violence in Theognis', in R. Brock and S. Hodkinson (eds), *Alternatives to Athens: Varieties of Political Organization and Community in Ancient Greece*, 52–67. Oxford.

van Wees, H. (2003). 'Conquerors and Serfs: Wars of Conquest and Forced Labour in Archaic Greece', in N. Luraghi and S. Alcock (eds), *Helots and their Masters in Laconia and Messenia: Histories, Ideologies, Structures*, 33–80. Washington.

van Wees, H. (2006). 'Mass and Elite in Solon's Athens: The Property Classes Revisited', in Blok and Lardinois (2006: 351–89).

van Wees, H. (2013). 'Farmers and Hoplites: Models of Historical Development', in D. Kagan and G. Viggiano (eds), *Men of Bronze*, 222–55. Princeton.

van Wees, H., and N. Fisher (2015). 'The Trouble with "Aristocracy"', in N. Fisher and H. van Wees (2015: 1–57).

Wallace, R. W. (2007). 'Revolutions and a New Order in Solonian Athens and Archaic Greece', in Raaflaub et al. (2007: 49–82).

Welwei, K.-W. (1992). *Athen: Vom neolithischen Siedlungsplatz zur archaischen Großpolis*. Darmstadt.

Welwei, K.-W. (2005). 'Ursachen und Ausmaß der Verschuldung attischer Bauern um 600 v. Chr, *Hermes*, 133: 29–43.

Werlings, M.-J. (2010). *Le Dèmos avant la démocratie: Mots, concepts, réalités historiques*. Nanterre. Electronic edn: Open Edition Books https://books.openedition.org/pupo/2355 (30 January 2023).

West, M. L. (1989). *Iambi et elegi Graeci ante Alexandrum cantati*. 2nd edn. Oxford.

Zurbach, J. (2013). 'La Formation des cités grecques: Statuts, classes et systèmes fonciers'. *Annales: Histoire, Sciences Sociales*, 68: 957–98.

# 3

# Reconstructing the Lives of Urban Craftspeople in Archaic and Classical Greece

Sarah C. Murray

## Preface

A welcome development in the study of the ancient world in the last several decades has been a vigorous turning of attention to groups of people outside the circumscribed sphere of elite male authors who had previously dominated much discourse. One of the groups that has merited new attention comprises people who had to work for a living, including socio-economically subordinate individuals who engaged in industrial or craft activities to make that living. While a general interest in art, and thus artistic production, in the earlier twentieth century led some pioneering scholars to investigate the lives of urban workers, the pace of investigation on this topic has increased remarkably since the 1980s.

The timing of this development is difficult to situate with precision. It seems most likely that it is related to several factors. First, since Bernal's publication of *Black Athena* and the ensuing controversy in the 1980s, Classicists have generally become more aware of the discipline's elitist and racial biases and sought to correct them through exploration of material and points of view beyond the canon. At the same time, practitioners of Classics have themselves become a more diverse group, including members of the working class and scholars of different racial and ideological backgrounds. This diversification of the field has fostered an interest in reconstructing a concomitantly more inclusive picture of life in the ancient world. In the realm of Mediterranean archaeological practice, large-scale excavations designed to bring major monuments and aesthetic masterpieces to light have been joined by survey projects investigating the countryside and day-to-day life. Mediterranean surveys have produced much new data from which to reconstruct the lives of a socio-economically broader swathe of the population than was possible in the middle of the twentieth century. The post-processual movement of the late 1980s and 1990s also encouraged archaeologists to think carefully about individual experiences of living in the world rather than the top-down organization and progression of political structures and great empires.

In this chapter, I try to build upon these trends through an interdisciplinary approach aimed at reconstructing a kind of cultural history of the urban worker in Archaic and Classical Greece. From the point of view of method, I suggest that thoughtful interpretation of material evidence, especially the archaeological and epigraphic records, offers the most promising route to such a cultural history. In reflecting on what is and is not accomplished in the chapter, it is clear there remains much work to be done on ancient workers, and several exciting paths forward seem open. While archaeological contexts can provide insight into living and working conditions, study of human remains aimed at identifying chronic injuries and traumas could add a great deal to the study of the embodied experience of workers in ancient Greece. The study of tools in their contexts has often been neglected, because these objects are not visually prepossessing; revisiting the analytical possibilities of such objects might yield new insights into the history and role of working people in the production and dedication Greece's wonderful material culture. Finally, comparative work drawing on the ethnographic record, with its rich documentation of pre-industrial craft production (technology, workshop organization, gendering of production, and so on), might allow more insight into the likely ancient correlates of these topics in a Greco-Roman context.

## Introduction

An abundance of fine craft products and artistic creations surviving in the archaeological record demonstrates that artisans and craftspeople made up a significant population within ancient urban environments.[1] Indeed, many scholars of antiquity were originally drawn to the field because of the arresting quality of ancient art and craft. For much of the twentieth century, however, little effort was applied to enlightening the life experiences or social strategies of the artisans responsible for creating the material fabric of the ancient world. In part, a longstanding neglect of the craftsperson in ancient history relates to the character of ancient texts. Extant textual evidence concerning artisans is not particularly voluminous, and that which does exist must be approached with interpretative caution, because it is often written from an elite point of view according to which non-agricultural work was an undesirable way to make a living.[2] But it is also true that investigating the picayune banalities of life in workshops and factories was once not a central interest of ancient history, with its traditional focus on

---

[1] On the probable proliferation of craftspeople in an ancient Greek city, see Xen. *Cyr.* 8.2.5. On modern attempts to calculate the size of the population of potters in ancient Athens, see Sapirstein (2013). Acton (2014: 6–7) discusses the scale of the manufacturing sector in Athens, which he sees as rather large.

[2] Verboven and Laes (2016: 1); Sapirstein (2018a: 95–6).

political and military affairs.[3] The discipline, however, has developed greater interest in social history since the late twentieth century. The study of craft practices and people is, concomitantly, now a thriving subfield within archaeology and ancient history.[4]

Craftspeople of the archaic and classical periods fit comfortably under the heading of subordinate/voiceless that ties together the people considered in this volume. While probably often literate, they did not leave behind extensive autographical accounts of their own lives or ideas. While authors of extant texts do speak for and about them, it is plausible that these accounts might mischaracterize rather than clarify matters concerning ancient artisans and craftspeople. It is not possible to generalize about the social status of those who made things in the ancient Greek world, because there was a great deal of diversity within the category of ancient craftspeople, but in general it seems many were seen as leading undesirable or dishonourable lives and were thus likely to have been of low to middle status. Craftspeople have traditionally been an archaeological subaltern as well as a textual one. Artisans are the people that built or made things analysed by classical archaeologists, but their lives have been relatively understudied.[5] Thus, this seems a category worthy of consideration in the context of this project's goals, which concentrate on reviving an understanding of the life experiences of and commonalities among ancient groups who are unable to speak to modern scholars directly in their own voices and who have thus been treated cursorily in scholarship to date.

In this chapter I consider whether and how we might be able to understand the voices or views of ancient Greek craftspeople. I begin by reviewing the textual evidence for the role of craftworkers in Greek society, which shows an interesting historical trajectory. I then consider some possible vectors along which we might explore a social history of artisans. I suggest that focusing on creative interpretation of material cultural contexts where craftspeople probably once trod may offer a productive path forward. Finally, I reflect on persistent problems with reconstructing the voices of the non-agricultural working class in the ancient

---

[3] Morley (2018: 13–34). Exceptions include monographs by Glotz (1920), Mossé (1966), and Burford (1972).

[4] Scholarly interest in work and workers in the Greek and Roman world has increased dramatically in the last several decades. Recent publications on the topic include Malacrino (2010); Brisart (2011); Sapirstein (2013); Acton (2014); Bourriot (2015); Hurwit (2015); Hedreen (2016); chapters in Eschbach and Schmidt (2016); chapters in Verboven and Laes (2016); chapters in Lytle et al. (2018).

[5] Artisans have long been of great interest to archaeologists, anthropologists, and ethnographers because their skills and daily routines tend to be exceptional within premodern agro-pastoral economies and because the products of their work effectively comprise the 'cultures' upon which many mid-twentieth-century culture–historical archaeologies were based. An example of a publication arising from fascination with extraordinary skills and routines is Vossen's study (1975) of Spanish tinajamakers in twentieth-century Villarrobledo. Hodder's work critiques the traditional connections archaeologists have tended to draw between the style of craft products and culture–historical groups (e.g. Hodder 1982).

Greek world, and how these workers relate to other voiceless members of the ancient world.

## Defining Ancient Craftworkers as a Group

Modern studies of ancient work have identified four kinds and groups of workers in pre-industrial Europe: peasants, merchants, artisans, and wage labourers. All of these groups can be detected in ancient Greece.[6] Here I focus on artisans and craftworkers, which I define as individuals in the non-agricultural sphere who worked producing things by hand for a living. In Greek texts, the term used to describe people who made art or craft objects in a full-time, specialist manner was *banausoi*. *Banausoi* is a useful term to use here, because it seems to distinguish serial producers of ordinary, low-cost goods from both aristocratic, extraordinary craftspeople who generated exquisite unique high-cost goods (these would include famous craftsmen such as Pheidias and Praxiteles) and professional architects. The latter two groups were respected among aristocrats and are thus not clearly definable as subordinates.[7]

I therefore draw a preliminary analytical circle around *banausoi* in this chapter. The validity of this category, however, is worth considering with some scepticism, at least in part because it seems apparent that the cohort included significant internal diversity. In ancient Athens, *banausic* professions were evidently occupied by a mixture of citizens, metics, women, slaves, and non-citizens.[8] This is intriguing from the point of view of a subaltern perspective, because it implies that careful study of *banausoi* could potentially help us to understand the lives of many kinds of individuals whose viewpoints are not represented clearly in extant texts. On the other hand, it calls into question whether the investigative topic of *banausoi* coheres in a meaningful way. The experiences of builders, potters, painters, smiths, founders, carpenters, weavers, and cobblers were likely to be different both from one profession to the next and across individual workers and workshops. *Banausic* tasks were probably performed by people of diverse social statuses, genders, and economic means. Some *banausoi* are probably best defined as specialists, who devoted their labour to full-time work in a single industrial context, but much craft production was probably accomplished by multitasking individuals, seasonal workers, or collective labour shared along the spectrum of the production process, a situation that is commonly observed in ethnographic studies of craft production.[9]

---

[6] Lis and Soly (2012: 12–14).      [7] Seaman (2017); Sapirstein (2018a: 101).

[8] Randall's examination (1953) of the workers mentioned in the Erechtheion building accounts shows a mixed workforce of 24 citizens, 42 metics, 20 slaves, and 21 individuals who could not be confidently attributed to one of these categories. See also Acton (2014: 271–88).

[9] Wright (1991: 198). Sapirstein's quantitative study (2013) of attribution rates among Attic vase-painters demonstrated a bimodal pattern of productivity, indicating that some painters were non-specialists who may have dedicated much of their labour to other tasks—such as potting—while others specialized in painting exclusively.

In parallel with a point Wijma (this volume) raises in her discussion of metics, we may expect that lumping *banausoi* together as a collective risks unintentionally silencing diverse voices through categorical homogeneity.

There is not sufficient space to explore fully the complex evidence for differentiation among craftspeople in the current context, but it is apparent that the diversity of life experiences within such populations could have been dramatic, even inside of a single 'profession'.[10] Given the limited space available, it seems optimal to address the categorical integrity of Greek craftspeople piecemeal, in light of specific evidence that illuminates archaic and classical craft producers presented in the body of the chapter. In pondering the dilemma of subordinate categorization, I emphasize two questions that may be useful to keep in mind throughout, and to which I return in the final discussion below. First, does an analytical framing of *banausoi* gain analytical credibility by virtue of the term's existence as an ancient category? Or might the ancient term represent an essentializing categorization that was in fact intended to marginalize and subordinate in its original context? Second, to what extent does the category circumscribe a group that is collectively characterized by attributes that seem generalizable to the notion of subordinates overall?

## Greek Attitudes towards *Banausoi*: Diachronic Trends

Stating that the lives of *banausoi* are of interest and worth reconstructing is an easier task than getting a concrete sense of the experience of life as an ancient Greek artisan based on current evidence. We do not possess direct textual records from archaic and classical Greece that describe the life of ancient Greek *banausoi* in their own words. Although artisans like potters did produce writing in the form of signatures and annotations on their works, they do not speak directly to us in eloquent ways that reveal their perspectives.[11] Extant textual evidence about craftspeople is largely part of a literary tradition that was written by and for elites. Moreover, this tradition was ideologically impacted by an apparent elite view, shared by some influential early ancient historians, that having to work as a *banausos* was oppressive, and that those who worked in such professions were inferior.[12] Thus, the textual evidence available for accessing the lives and voices of ancient craftspeople is less than ideal. But, while it is often stated that the textual evidence from ancient Greece, and the premodern world in general, reflects a persistent and consistent bias against craftworkers, and even against work in general, the reality is quite complex. There are interesting diachronic trends, as well

---

[10] Feyel (2006).  [11] On signatures, see, e.g., Hurwit (2015) and Hedreen (2016).
[12] On the ancient sources, see below. For some modern sources taking ancient sentiment at face value, see, e.g., Burckhardt (1929: 45–6); Mitford (1822–1823: iii. 6). On Burckhardt's view of *banausoi* and the downfall of Hellenic ideals, see also Bourriot (2015: 24–36).

as many relevant and revealing texts, that we should not overlook in our attempt to locate the craftworker in ancient Greek society. In what follows I briefly review the general diachronic trend in apparent social attitudes towards craftspeople in Greek literature, before turning to a discussion of some textual evidence that, taken together with material contexts, may go some way towards providing a view of craftspeople's experiences.

Greek texts recorded in Linear B script recovered from Late Bronze Age sites show that makers of crafts, especially smiths, occupied a prominent role in the bureaucratic apparatus of Mycenaean palatial society, and should be classified as elites within that society. The texts attest that individual craftspeople sometimes possessed dependent labourers and played an active role in many state-organized economic transactions. It is therefore clear that categorizing Bronze Age producers as subalterns is not consistent with the evidence.[13] An early tradition of esteem for makers, and the lack of a bifurcation between working with one's hands and aristocratic virtue, is likewise apparent in early Greek literature. In Homeric epic, heroes and gods alike take pride in work, including artisanal or *banausic* work, when it is done well. The gods in the *Iliad* envy the fine craftsmanship exhibited by the Achaeans when they are building the wall around their camp in the Trojan plain (Hom. *Il.* 7.435–53). Hephaestus' work at the anvil is treated at length and is a source of awe (Hom. *Il.* 18.468–82). Odysseus speaks of making his own home and bed near the end of the *Odyssey* (Hom. *Od.* 23.189–204), describes himself as a *chalkeus* in the Cyclops episode of book 9 (Hom. *Od.* 9.391), and elsewhere Homer provides a lengthy description of his skill in boatbuilding (Hom. *Od.* 5.228–61).[14] He knows how to build a raft to escape Kalypso's island, and, in some traditions, he built the Trojan Horse.[15] In general, Homer's discussions of production indicate that he performed for an audience among whom finely crafted objects and buildings were revered, even fawned over, and who had no obvious bias against the performance of craftwork.[16]

A different, but also positive, ideological approach to work is apparent in Hesiod's *Works and Days* (422–9, 493–5).[17] According to Hesiod, work is generally an important and good endeavour. There is no indication in the poem that the average farmer had negative views of craftwork or craftworkers. Hesiod is knowledgeable about how to go about selecting wood and executing the tasks of a carpenter, including building carts and ploughs. His admonition to pass by the metalworker's bench in the winter suggests that farmers were friendly enough with the smith to make this a tempting distraction from the work waiting at

---

[13] Nakassis (2013: 89).   [14] On Odysseus as a craftsman, see Newton (1987: 13–14).
[15] More commonly, Epeios, a Daidalos-esque figure, is credited with the horse's construction (Zachos 2013).
[16] Porter (2011: 7). On the ideology of work in Homeric poetry, see Ndoye (2010).
[17] Lis and Soly (2012: 18).

home.[18] There is likewise evidence from the archaic period that labour was considered important and noble, the key to building a strong city and having a stable economic basis. According to the tradition transmitted by Plutarch (*Sol.* 22.1), Solon promoted craftwork as a boon to the community. Although Plutarch should not be considered a reliable source for archaic Greece, there is corroborating evidence that builders and makers were relatively prosperous in the form of fine dedications by craftsmen at sanctuaries and depictions of craftspeople at work on figured Athenian pottery dating to the sixth and early fifth centuries BCE.[19]

Beginning in the fifth century, on the other hand, literary texts witness the rise of an attitude that those who worked full-time at non-agricultural tasks ought to be despised, as Herodotus states they were by most Greeks (Hdt. 2.167.2). There are indications throughout the existing *corpus* of classical texts that some professions, and even having to work for a living at all, were considered unsuitable for citizen males of a certain standing. Classical authors often express the attitude that work was humiliating because it was something done by slaves. Male citizens, in turn, should not have to work, devoting their attentions to politics and to self-improvement instead. Philosophical, historical, and dramatic texts of all genres explicitly state that a life free from labour is to be highly preferred over a life of toil and that artisanal occupations should be viewed with scorn.[20] When work is viewed positively in classical texts, it is usually agricultural in nature, probably reflecting the fact that most citizens derived their wealth from agricultural holdings.[21]

Given the date that such attitudes seem to gain prominence in extant texts, we should consider the somewhat dissonant idea that democratic governance engendered a thoroughgoing distaste for working people among elite citizens within the Athenian state in the fifth and fourth centuries.[22] Such attitudes towards work might have arisen because Athenian democracy's institutions demanded intense participation, which in turn required citizens to devote large quantities of free time to the consideration of policy, serving in the law courts, training together in the gymnasium, and other non-work activities.[23] Or, it could be that

---

[18] Hes. *Op.* 493.
[19] On dedications by craftspeople at sanctuaries, see below. For depictions of craftspeople at work in Greek pottery and in Greek art, see Bundrick (2008), Lewis (2010), Haug (2011), Chatzidimitriou (2014), and Sapirstein (2018b).
[20] Examples include but are not limited to Xen. *Oec.* 4.2–3; Xen. *Mem.* 3.7.5–6; Ar. *Eq.* 733–40; Ar. *Plut.* 507–26; Lucian, *Somn.* 22; Andoc. 1.146; Dem. 25.38; Dem. 57.30–6. See also Ober (1989: 274–7, 310–11).
[21] Mossé (1966: 28–9).
[22] There is no consensus regarding the socio-political position of artisans in democratic Athens. For discussions positing a low status of artisans under the democracy, see de Ste. Croix (1981: 274–5); Gill and Vickers (1990: 6–8); Vickers and Gill (1994: 93–6). Feyel (2006), on the other hand, argues that artisans were always a mixed group in terms of background and socio-economic status.
[23] See, e.g., Arist. *Pol.* 7.1328$^b$–1329$^a$: 'It is therefore clear from these considerations that in the most nobly constituted state, and the one that possesses men that are absolutely just, not merely just relatively to the principle that is the basis of the constitution, the citizens must not live a mechanic or a

democracy increased the social role of lower-class citizens like *banausoi* by enfranchising them politically, thereby raising the elite's hackles against them.[24] In general, it is important to bear in mind that the social role of artisans and workers in society and attitudes towards craftwork seem to have been variable depending on the craft involved and highly dynamic even within the confines of Greek history. Such attitudes were probably bound together with social and political developments in complicated ways that are not yet clearly understood.

## Reconstructing the Lives of Workers: Archaeological Contexts

Within the limited view that can be derived from Greek literature, it is apparent that artisans, who seem to have been respected, well-off, and even successful members of communities in the archaic period, were increasingly considered to be undesirable members of the community by elites during the later fifth and fourth centuries. Thus, while we certainly may read about these individuals in the classical textual sources, the views on artisanal work expressed in most historical and literary texts are unlikely to represent the lives or voices of craftspeople in a straightforward way. This, of course, is a common evidentiary dilemma, one that scholars investigating all the subordinate groups and individuals discussed in this volume share in confronting.

The contributions in this volume aim to think through and around the limitations of available evidence to access a deeper, or at least alternative, view of ancient subordinates using a variety of methods. I focus on archaeological remains here, in part because I am an archaeologist by training, but equally because it is generally acknowledged that material remains may offer a view of the ancient world that is distinct from those presented in canonical authors. In some cases, it seems apparent that archaeological contexts can provide strikingly granular views of the lives of voiceless groups.[25] Along these lines, an opportunity seems available in the form of ample quantities of workshops and workers' tools that exist in the Greek archaeological record, but that have yet to be fully put into the service of social and cultural history. Of course, as do texts, such contexts and objects require creative interpretation if they are to provide compelling analytical traction. For archaic and classical Greece, a spatiotemporal context

---

mercantile life (for such a life is ignoble and inimical to virtue), nor yet must those who are to be citizens in the best state be tillers of the soil (for leisure is needed both for the development of virtue and for active participation in politics)' (trans. Rackham).

[24] Raubitschek (1949: 465) suggested that the presence of dedications by artisans on the acropolis, which all postdate 525 BCE, should be read as evidence that these individuals 'gained social standing when the democracy was established'. See also Williams (1990: 36), Wagner (2000: 386-7), and Neer (2002: 87-134). A similar dynamic may be apparent in the case of the thetes who served as rowers in the fleet (Arist. *Pol.* 1304ª; 1327ª).

[25] See, e.g., Bowes (2021) on archaeological evidence for the lives of Roman peasants.

from which both texts and archaeological contexts are available in considerable abundance, it seems best to interpret the two together in arriving at a social history of craftspeople. Just as examining the physical scene alongside verbal testimony is a better way to go about solving a crime than relying on eyewitness reports alone, assessing the material spaces and objects involved in craft production together with contemporary written sources is necessary if we are to gain a clearer view of craftworkers' experiences in premodern contexts.

In what follows I present several examples of such contexts and consider what they can tell us about the lives of *banausoi* in classical Greece. I investigate what material evidence can tell us about the kinds of spaces where *banausoi* worked and the kinds of objects that surrounded them. In addition, I consider ritual practices that may be associated with artisans in particular, based on the material and epigraphic evidence we can gather. Finally, I assess how and whether archaeological evidence might be utilized to reconstruct the mortuary behaviour of artisans.

## The Archaeology of Workplaces

One obvious source for reconstructing the experience of craftworkers can be found in the archaeological contexts that have been identified as workshops because of the tools and detritus found in them. These kinds of contexts have long been a sort of archaeological subaltern in receiving less attention than deposits associated with civic buildings or sanctuaries. More recently, however, they are being leveraged to provide original insight into the lived experience of ancient artisans.[26] In what follows I discuss two such workshops, both from the Athenian agora.

The so-called House of Mikion and Menon is located to the south-west of the Athenian Agora, near the edge of the NW slope of the Areopagos.[27] Partly excavated over two seasons, first in 1932 and again in 1968, the house has an irregular layout, centred on a courtyard containing two cisterns.[28] It was probably in use from the mid-fifth century to the third century, when it was apparently demolished. Five rooms to the south of the courtyard have been explored, while the northern part of the house has not been excavated. The excavators found that the interior of most of the rooms was coated in a thick layer of marble dust and marble chips.[29] The discovery of pieces of unfinished marble sculpture in nearby

---

[26] E.g. Van Oyen et al. (2022).
[27] Both names are commonly attested in Attica (45 Mikions and 70 Menons are attested in Osborne and Byrne 1996).
[28] Burr (1933); Shear (1969). The name of the house is derived from two objects: a bone stylus inscribed with the name Mikion from the workshop area (5th c. BCE) and several ceramic vessels inscribed with the name Menon that were excavated from a cistern near the house (3rd c. BCE).
[29] Burr (1933: 87).

cisterns, along with the presence of marble workers' tools among the debris in the building, made the identification of this house with a workshop of marble workers relatively firm.[30] Some of the tools, recently re-examined by Tsakirgis, are lead strips, bent at one end, perhaps so that they could be tied to a string around one's neck.[31] These tools are not hard enough for working marble and may have been used to shape wax or clay models that served as reference for sculptors hoping to avoid mistakes while working marble blocks.[32] The conspicuous absence of any of the iron tools like chisels that we might expect to find in a sculptor's workshop may indicate that even used or old iron tools were carefully gathered and sold by the artists when they moved or retired. Two large stone pounders, pumice lumps for polishing finished works, and one bone stylus, inscribed "Ὁ Μικίων ἐποίε[σε]" (Mikion made [me]), came from the same shop (Figure 3.1).[33]

It is possible to use these tools themselves and the debris left behind in the workshop to reconstruct some aspects of the day-to-day lives and priorities of the sculptors that would otherwise have remained obscure to us. The presence of the inscribed tool, 'Mikion's' stylus, perhaps used for drawing designs on a wax tablet, is perplexing. Why would Mikion bother to express his manufacture of what appears to be a completely unexceptional bone tool of a type that is 'ubiquitous' in the ancient world?[34] It is, of course, impossible to provide a definite answer to such a question. *Epoiesen* inscriptions are often taken to indicate pride in a job well done.[35] However, this is such a simple artefact that such pride seems at least

**Figure 3.1** Mikion's stylus (Agora excavations, image 2008.01.0052 (art. BI 818)). (Ephorate of Antiquities of Athens City, Ancient Agora, ASCSA: Agora Excavations. Copyright © Hellenic Ministry of Culture and Sports/Hellenic Organization of Cultural Resources Development (HOCRED).)

---

[30] On the excavation of the cisterns, see Thompson (1934: 87–107), Miller (1974), and Rotroff (1997: 451). On the tools from the house of Mikion and Menon, see Tsakirgis (2015: 10–12).
[31] Tsakirgis (2015: 12–13).
[32] As suggested by Tsakirgis (2015: 13). Comparanda come from possible workshop contexts in Greek sanctuaries, including Olympia (Schiering 1991), Aphaia on Aegina (Furtwängler 1906: 424; Bankel 1984), Isthmia (Rostoker and Gebhard 1980: IM 458, IM 459), Rhamnous (Petrakos 1999: 267–9), and Nemea (Miller 1979).
[33] Tsakirgis (2015: 11, catalogue no. BI 819).    [34] Tsakirgis (2015: 14).
[35] Lazzarini (1976: 73).

somewhat oddly placed. The name may have been inscribed to verify the tool's rightful owner instead, which might indicate that craftspeople were anxious that their tools not be stolen by others (in which case we may surmise that such tools were hard to come by or hard to afford among sculptors). Alternatively, it might be that tools were sometimes shared among workers, so that a label was required to ensure their return to a rightful owner. At a basic level, the presence of the labelled stylus indicates that someone near the workshop, or even Mikion himself, was sufficiently literate to write the inscription. Such artisanal literacy, along with playful and often perplexing use of the written word among archaic and classical craftspeople, is well attested in the signatures and texts that appear on decorated ceramic vessels.[36]

The location of the house, near the acropolis, the Kerameikos, and the urban centre, indicates that these artisans, who probably worked in the same house as they lived in,[37] could have easily walked to building sites and heavily sculpted neighbourhoods, either to admire their own work or to gain inspiration. Their proximity to a major thoroughfare also facilitated sales, because it allowed them to advertise their wares to passers-by.[38] Finally, the abundance of marble dust, chips of old sculptures, and debris in the workshop allows us to envision a daily environment of work that may not have been particularly comfortable, pleasant, or safe. Lucian's description (*Somn*.1.6) of what a stonemason looked like while working helps enliven this reconstruction of a dusty workshop full of sharp bits of marble: 'One was like a workman, masculine, with unkempt hair, hands full of callous places, clothing tucked up, and a heavy layer of marble-dust upon her, just as my uncle looked when he cut stone' (trans. Harmon). This is not a complimentary description—in context the purpose of the anecdote is to describe the unappealing look of a woman Lucian encounters in his dream. A passage from Plutarch's *Moralia* (*De Genio Socratis*) likewise enlivens our imaginations regarding what this area of the Agora, the zone of the sculpture-makers, might have been like: billowing with marble dust, open drains, and herds of pigs running amok.[39]

A similarly compelling vision of the life of an ancient craftsman can be glimpsed in House D, also near the agora, which appears to have hosted a shop and residence of fourth-century metalworkers. The house is located in a

---

[36] The topic is sufficiently complex that I do not treat it extensively here. For expansive discussions of artists' signatures and the use of writing on vases, see, e.g., Sapirstein (2013), Hurwit (2015), and Hedreen (2016).
[37] Bettalli (1985).   [38] Tsakirgis (2015: 15).
[39] Plut. *Mor.* 580e–f: 'As they were walking along the street of the statuaries past the law-courts, they were met by a drove of swine, covered with mud and so numerous that they pressed against one another; and as there was nowhere to step aside, the swine ran into some and knocked them down, and befouled the rest' (trans. de Lacy and Einarson).

neighbourhood that is generally associated with smiths.[40] An inscription from the area (*IG* i³ 370-1) mentions some metalworkers buying copper, tin, lead, wood, and charcoal in order to make cult statues here in the neighbourhood of the Hephaisteion, and there are some other literary sources mentioning bronze working taking place in the vicinity.[41]

Once again, however, our best evidence for what these *banausoi* might have been doing comes from the material record. House D was excavated in the final years of the 1940s.[42] Compared to the houses nearby, it was a small, cramped structure, with four rooms arranged around a courtyard, about 4 × 5 m in size. Taking up most of the courtyard was what excavators describe as a 'great hearth,' 3 × 1 m long, paved with tiles that had been cracked and flaked by what was apparently very hot, frequent conflagration.[43] The hearth was full of ashes and charcoal, and surrounded by slags of bronze and iron, which suggested to the excavators that this building was the home and workplace of metalsmiths. No doubt, like the marble workers, they toiled in uncomfortable surroundings: their lives were filled with soot, and the smoke and the crackling heat of the fire would have often been an oppressive presence, especially during the sweltering Attic summers. Given that the location of the house, probably in the deme of Kollytos or Melite, was in a neighbourhood full of artisan metics that has been dubbed an 'industrial quarter', we may imagine the artisans working in House D as residents of a bustling, chaotic neighbourhood, with collaborators and competition nowhere in short supply. This vision is supported, in the case of House D, by the presence of a lead curse tablet in the house's floor.[44] The curse tablet reads as follows:

Καταδέω Ἀρίσται[χ]μ<ο>ν τὸ(ν) χαλκέα
πρὸς τοὺς κάτω καὶ Πυρρίαν τὸν χαλκέα
καὶ τὴν ἐργασίαν αὐτοῦ καὶ τὰς ψυχὰς
αὐτῶν καὶ Σωσία(ν) τὸν Λάμιον
καὶ τὴν ἐργασία(ν) καὶ τὴν ψυχὴν αὐτο[ῦ]

---

[40] Mattusch (1977: 341). Wilamowitz (1887: 117-28) lists metic artisans in this area of Athens as including 'goldsmith, worker in encaustic, cabinet maker, mason, sculptor, carver of ornamental stone work, gilder, lead merchant, brick-layer, and odd-jobber'.

[41] Andoc. *De Mysteriis* 40: 'On his return to Athens he found a commission already appointed to investigate, and a reward of one hundred minae offered for information; so seeing Euphemus, the brother of Callias, son of Telocles, sitting in his smithy, he took him to the temple of Hephaestus' (trans. Maidment); *Anecd. Bekk.* I, 316.23-4: 'Chalko: a placename, where the bronze is sold, and where the Hephaisteion is' (trans. author).

[42] The excavation of House D is mentioned at Thompson (1949: 217). See full publication at Young (1951: 217-26), and also discussion in Mattusch (1977: 341-2, 377).

[43] Young (1951: 222).

[44] Thompson (1949: 217); Young (1951: 223); Mattusch (1977: 341-2). The text is still in dispute. I quote the text as printed by Young (1951: 223), although there are several misspellings on the tablet, an intentional feature of curses.

καὶ *ΑΛΗΓΟΣΙ* καὶ ἁδρῶς {καὶ ἁδρῶς}
καὶ Ἀγήσι(ον) τὴν Βοιωτ[ί]α[ν].

I bind Aristaichmos the bronze worker
to those below and also Purrias the bronze worker
and his work as well as their spirits,
and Sosias of Lamia,
and his work and his soul
and Alegosi[45] and firmly {and firmly}
and Agesion the Boiotian Lady.

Such evidence encourages the reconstruction of burning rivalries and competitiveness among fourth-century metalworkers in the Agora.[46] The tablet from House D is one of a large group of curse tablets from ancient Athens that speak to the rivalries, ritual concerns, and conflicts among workers, which taken together form an unusually rich basis of information about ritual belief and practice among urban working communities.[47] As Eidinow's analysis has shown, a surprising quantity of such *defixiones* deal with marginal urban workers.[48] Tavern-keepers are particularly common figures in the curse tablets, which may suggest that taverns were a focus or nexus of competitive commercial and social life. On the other hand, artisans are not so regularly mentioned in the *corpus*. This may indicate that craftspeople were less liable to resort to curses than tavern owners, in which case the tablet from House D should be seen as an exception rather than the rule.[49]

To return to the archaeological context, the final feature of House D relevant to discussion here is a small burnt pyre in the centre of the courtyard.[50] Susan Rotroff has produced a masterful and highly insightful study of this variety of pyre, the saucer pyre.[51] Saucer pyres consist of small burnt deposits containing miniature drinking vessels and a distinctive kind of saucer along with burnt animal bones. Though saucer pyres were originally interpreted as child cremations, Rotroff argued that these deposits were probably associated with a cleansing ritual feast undertaken when a new owner took over a building, or when renovations took place

---

[45] This incomprehensible set of letters may be an intentional misspelling.
[46] Gager (1992: 151–3).
[47] Other examples include *IG* iii appendix 87 (a tablet from an unknown context in fourth-century BCE Attica); *IG* iii appendix 55 (a tablet from an unknown context in fourth-century BCE Attica); Peek 1941: Fluchtafeln no. 1, Taf. 23.4 (a tablet from fifth-century BCE Kerameikos). See also Gager (1992: nos 60, 62, 64, 68, 70, 72) for additional *defixiones* dealing with individuals practising artisanal or commercial trades.
[48] Eidinow (2007: 191).
[49] Eidinow (2007: 195). Eidinow raises the possibility that the *chalkea* in the Agora tablet might refer to someone from Chalkis or Chalke in Larisa instead of a bronzeworker.
[50] Young (1951: 218–19).      [51] Rotroff (2013).

in order to cleanse a space after something unfortunate had happened there.[52] Such pyres are concentrated in industrial facilities, like House D. Rotroff suggests that the affiliation of the saucer pyres with the locations of industrial work could reflect one of two things: the frequent turnover of workshop ownership[53] or the unusual frequency of accidents in workshops.[54] Craftsmen in the ancient world often worked in proximity to extremely hot fires, transported heavy loads, and dealt with sharp implements, perhaps making their work particularly prone to horrible disasters, never mind economically disastrous failures of production. According to Plutarch (*Per.* 13.7–8), Pericles dedicated a statue to Athena Hygieia in thanks for the miraculous survival of a workman grievously hurt during the construction of the Propylaia (*IG* i² 395). A dedicatory *stele* from Epidauros (*IG* ii² 4356; *CEG* 764) likewise might depict a carter who was saved from falling rocks, perhaps a result of catastrophic toppling from an over- or badly loaded cart.[55] Although such accidents are only occasionally mentioned in surviving textual accounts, we must imagine that casualty rates among ancient workers were not insignificant.

The pyre in House D and the curse tablet that went along with it, taken together, help us to sketch a vision of the ritual belief systems that may have played a defining or at least important part in the lives of artisans in classical Greece. In general, it seems apparent that they may have engaged in chthonic, aspirationally manipulative, extraordinary ritual practices more commonly than non-artisans. Such a view is highlighted by the wonderful Κάμινος poem, which survives in the *Suda* and in the Pseudo-Herodotean *Life of Homer* and is thought to have been composed in fifth-century Athens. The poem describes the story of a poet who offers to sell a poem beseeching Athena's protection to a group of potters. Lest they hesitate to leap at the opportunity, the poet adds a threat: if the potters fail to pay, he will perform a curse instead. The text reads as follows:

εἰ μὲν δώσετε μισθὸν ἀοιδῆς, ὦ κεραμῆες,
δεῦρ' ἄγ' Ἀθηναίη, καὶ ὑπέρσχεθε χεῖρα καμίνου,
εὖ δὲ μελανθεῖεν κότυλοι καὶ πάντα κάναστρα,
φρυχθῆναί τε καλῶς καὶ τιμῆς ὦνον ἀρέσθαι,

---

[52] For interpretation of the pyres as child cremations, see Young (1951: 218–19). Shear later suggested that the pyres might represent the remains of a purification ritual (Shear 1984: 46). Rotroff (2013: 75–80) ultimately argues that saucer pyres were related to industrial ritual specifically.

[53] Rotroff (2013: 80–1); see also Aeschin. *In Tim.* 1.124, on frequent change in the identity and ownership of shops in the Agora.

[54] Rotroff (2013: 81).

[55] The reading of the inscription is uncertain. Hansen (*CEG* 764) suggests that the carter was saved *ek polemon*, but Güntner (1994: 39) amends this to *ek petron*. Both readings are restored on the basis of a terminal ν, so are equally hypothetical. For a warning against just such an incident, Hes. *Op.* 692–3.

πολλὰ μὲν εἰν ἀγορῆι πωλεύμενα, πολλὰ δ'ἀγυιαῖς,     5
πολλὰ δὲ κερδῆναι, ἡμᾶς δὲ δὴ ὥς σφας ὀνῆσαι.
ἢν δ'ἐπ'ἀναιδείην τρεφθέντες ψεύδε'ἄρησθε,
συγκαλέω δῆπειτα καμίνων δηλητῆρας,
Σύντριβ'ὁμῶς Σμάραγόν τε καὶ Ἄσβετον ἠδὲ Σαβάκτην
Ὠμόδαμόν θ', ὃς τῆιδε τέχνηι κακὰ πολλὰ πορίζει·     10

If you are going to pay for my singing, O potters,
then come, Athena, and hold your hand over the kiln:
may the cups turn a fine black, and all the dishes,
and be thoroughly baked, and earn the price they are worth
as they sell in quantity in the market and the streets,
and make good profits, and benefit me as it does them.
But if you turn to shamelessness and deceit,
then I will invoke all of the kiln gremlins,
Smasher and Crasher, Overblaze and Shakeapart
and Underbake, who does this craft much harm.[56]

The curse evokes five gremlins: the Σύντριψ ('Smasher'), Σμάραγος ('Crasher'), Ἄσβετος ('Overblaze'),[57] Σαβάκτης ('Shakeapart'), and, finally, Ὠμόδαμος ('Underbake').[58] The poem goes on to envision a true crafter's nightmare, with wailing potters and a kiln alternately chewing up pots 'as a horse's jaw munches' (ll. 13–14) and collapsing in on itself (l. 19). Papadopoulos has argued that a gremlin of the type summoned in the poem appears on a roughly incised sherd from Pheidias' workshop at Olympia (Figure 3.2).[59] Likewise, two textual fragments attest to the fact that *banausoi* believed in the power of a charm called the βασκάνιον, an apotropaic creature, mostly human but somewhat grotesque in nature, that kept things from going wrong in the workshops, probably especially at very dangerous moments of firing or forging.[60] The *baskanion* may appear in a black-figure vase painting from the late sixth century and in a painting on one of the Penteskouphia plaques, a collection of votive plaques created by and often depicting potters from a ritual deposit near Corinth (Figures 3.3 and 3.4; see discussion of the Penteskouphia plaques below).[61] In general it seems that belief in

---

[56] The text and translation are taken from West (2003: 390–3).
[57] The manuscript tradition is not consistent regarding the name of this gremlin. Ἄσβετον is printed by West in the Loeb edition (2003) reproduced here, but elsewhere the same editor has chosen Ἄσβολον (Merkelbach and West 1967: no. 302), while other editions reconstruct the metrically problematic Ἄσβεστον (*Suda* s.v. Ὅμηρος (ο 251)). The precise name of the gremlin does not have a direct implication on the discussion in the current context.
[58] See discussion in Papadopoulos (2003: 191–6) and Rotroff (2013: 82 and n. 130).
[59] Papadopoulos (2003: 193–5).     [60] Aristophanes fr. 592 K–A.; Pollux 7.108.
[61] Mallwitz and Schiering (1964: 237–47, fig. 68, pl. 79); Papadopoulos (2003: 192, fig. 3.1 (Athens NM 1114-2624 [442]); 193–5, fig. 3.4 (Munich Glyptotek inv. 1717, *c*.520 BCE); Berlin Antikenmuseum F 683/757/829/822).

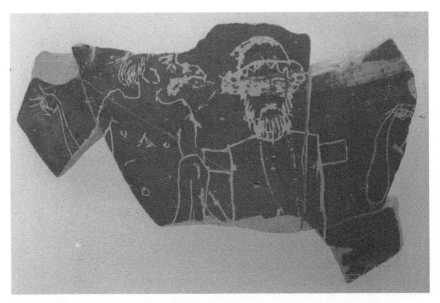

**Figure 3.2** Possible depiction of a goblin on a sherd from Phidias' workshop, Olympia (425–400 BCE). (Copyright © Hellenic Ministry of Culture and Sports (L.4858/2021.) Image courtesy of the Ephorate of Antiquities of Illias DAI-Athen. Photograph by Eva-Maria Czakó.

**Figure 3.3** A depiction of a smithy with possible βασκάνιον above the forge at right (520 BCE). (Munich, Glyptotek und Museum antiker Kleinkunst, inv. 1717.) Courtesy of the State Collection of Antiquities and Glyptothek Munich. Photograph by Renate Kühling.

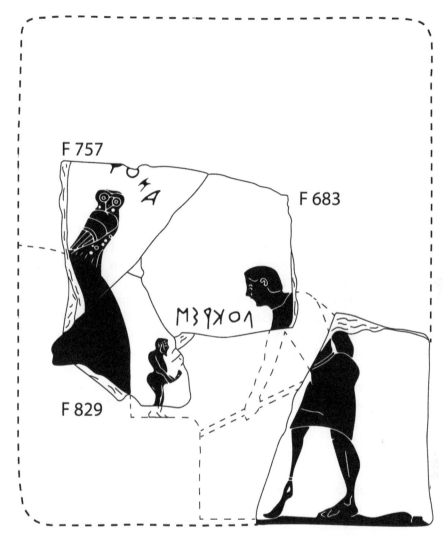

**Figure 3.4** Penteskouphia plaque fragments, dedicated by Lokris, showing a βασκάνιον perched on the kiln. (Berlin Antikenmuseum F 683/757/829/822.) Drawing by Y. Nakas (Hasaki 2021, fig. 4.54 (B41)), used with courtesy of the Trustees of the American School of Classical Studies at Athens.

supernatural forces that could impact the safety and productivity of crafting was a powerful force operating under the surface of the ancient artisan's world.

While it is difficult to discern the precise role of ritual practice in artisanal lives, Rotroff's suggestion that artisans' predilection for religious practices related to preventing disasters arose from the dangerous or precarious conditions in which they worked is appealing.[62] Surely the risks of daily exposure to extreme

---

[62] Rotroff (2013: 81).

temperatures at a forge or kiln and a multiplicity of sharp and heavy objects could have contributed to a culture committed to the active pursuit of luck through supernatural means. Likewise, given that craftspeople depended on success in an apparently competitive and precarious market for survival, we might see the practice of curses and cursing as a sort of coping mechanism that assuaged the anxieties of everyday life as a subordinated member of society. But both of these interpretations rely on a relatively negative reading of craftspeople within the fabric of society, not as actors but as reactors only able to respond to conditions to which they were subjected because of their socio-political marginalization. This viewpoint seems somewhat problematic, in that it reifies the suppression of agency among craftsmen that is already embedded in the elitist nature of most ancient written sources.

Instead of apotropaic ritual practice among workers as a reaction to difficult and dangerous conditions, these practices may have comprised an active strategy for cultivating a particular impression among the consumers and competitors workers engaged with in their pursuit of economic success. The experience of watching any metalworker at the forge or kiln-operator transforming elements from one state to another is fraught with a sense of magic and wonder. Therefore, it may be that craftsmen consciously engaged in obscure, mysterious rituals to enhance outsiders' awe at the extraordinary nature and mystical characteristics of their work, and in so doing to increase their own status.[63] From this point of view, we may glimpse the craftsman as a strategic, wily manipulator of the social and economic environment, not just a reactive victim of frequent accidents and fierce competition.

## Dedications and Votives

We can reconstruct some of the private beliefs, anxieties, and ritual strategies of artisans from the epigraphic and archaeological records. There is likewise abundant epigraphic evidence for artisans' participation in various kinds of public dedicatory practices. Dedicatory *stelai* and other votive offerings from Athens are known from cobblers (*SEG* 55.307),[64] potters (*IG* i³ 620, 628, 633, 824), fullers

---

[63] Greek philosophers frequently use analogies drawn from craft production in order to frame discussions of essential concepts, from the elemental nature of man and the universe to notions of beauty, utility, and the good (e.g. Empedocles frs. B23, B71, B73, B75; Plato *Grg.* 514c; Plato *Euthphr.* 13a–14b; Aristotle *Eth. Nic.* 1106ᵇ5–14; Xen. *Mem.* 3.10). The consistent use of such craft analogy indicates that philosophers often observed craftspeople at work. It seems likely that such frequent observation was related to a real fascination with the transformative characteristics of craft production. If such a fascination did exist, it would not be surprising to find that craft producers, although somewhat marginalized politically, sought to manipulate outsiders' perceptions of the skill and mystery of their work for some kind of social or economic gain.

[64] Taylor (2017: 1–2) begins her recent study with this *stele*. For publication of the relief in its archaeological context (Agora excavation object I 7396), see Lawton (2017: 89, no. 89, figs 2–3, pl. 27).

(*IG* i³ 554, 616, 905), tanners (*IG* i³ 646), and an architect (*IG* i³ 606).⁶⁵ The existence of these *stelai* demonstrates that artisans could afford to purchase such dedications, at least in the case of particular windfalls.⁶⁶ The texts also offer an occasional glimpse into artisans' ambitions, successes, and hopes for life.⁶⁷ Bacchios, a potter, brags of winning contests and being the first among his group of craftsmen,⁶⁸ the cobbler Dionysios asks for wealth and health for himself and his family, and most dedications express some degree of pride in the dedicant's work.⁶⁹ Considering the diachronic developments in textually apparent attitudes towards *banausoi* discussed above, it is interesting to note that dedications explicitly mentioning craftspeople come primarily from the archaic period, when texts do not yet betray a negative view of craftwork and craftworkers. Perhaps the chronology of these dedications provides additional support for the notion that the social status of craftworkers declined over the course of the fifth and fourth centuries.

Hasaki's recent comprehensive publication of the archaic dedicatory plaques from Penteskouphia, near Corinth, provides additional evidence for change over time in the circumstances encountered by craftworkers.⁷⁰ The site of Penteskouphia is located west of Corinth. It is not mentioned in ancient texts and preserves no architecture. Significant activity at the site is not evident prior to or following the archaic period. A local farmer unearthed a large corpus of dedicatory plaques at Penteskouphia in 1879, and additional examples were found by American excavators in 1905; about 1,200 pieces or plaques were recovered in total. The plaques date to the first half of the sixth century BCE. Many of the plaques depict stages of the ceramic production process (Figures 3.4 and 3.5), and it is generally thought that they represent the material outcome of ritual behaviour by a group of potters who occupied a workshop somewhere in the general area. Hasaki's analysis highlights the extent to which this remarkable assemblage constitutes evidence for a short-lived episode of ritual practice by Corinthian potters. Based on chronological alignment between the dedications' timing and an apparent crisis in the Corinthian potters' industry owing to competition from Athens, Hasaki argues that the phenomenon of the Penteskouphia plaques may represent an instance of desperate behaviour by a collective of artisans 'in distress' hoping to stave off economic disaster.⁷¹ If Hasaki's argument is correct, the plaques could be interpreted as evidence of collective agency among a group of artisans seeking to control their material conditions through extraordinary ritual action.

---

⁶⁵ See further discussion in Beazley (1944: 21–5); Raubitschek (1949); van Straten (1981: 92–5); Wagner (2000: 383–7); Keesling (2002: 69–75); Jim (2014: 168–75); Hurwit (2015: 94–6); Taylor (2017: 207–11); Sapirstein (2018a: 98–100). Note, however, that Raubitschek often associated dedications with potters based on tenuous or circumstantial evidence.
⁶⁶ Jim (2014: 166–7). On the idea that dedications were often made at particularly lucrative moments for groups or individuals, see Stissi (2002).
⁶⁷ Jim (2014: 174).   ⁶⁸ *IG* ii² 6320.   ⁶⁹ *IG* i³ 1361, *IG* ii² 8883, 10051.
⁷⁰ Hasaki (2021).   ⁷¹ Hasaki (2021: 279–300).

**Figure 3.5** Depiction on a Penteskouphia plaque of an axe–adze being used to harvest clay. (Berlin Antinkensammlung F 831 (P303)). Drawing by Y. Nakas (Hasaki 2021: fig. 4.23 (B5)), used with courtesy of the Trustees of the American School of Classical Studies at Athens.

Beyond the dedication of votive *stelai* and the use of special-purpose ritual sites seemingly visited exclusively by artisanal groups, is there evidence that craftspeople participated in mainstream religious festivals, including festivals at the major *periodos* sites of Olympia, Delphi, Nemea, and Isthmia? Given that participation in most games was limited to citizen males, any artisans who were not citizens or males would not have been able to enter the competitions.[72] Other craftspeople probably would not have been able to afford the luxury of time and transportation to attend games far from home.[73] Some objects dedicated at major sanctuaries, however, bear inscriptions that refer to craftworkers. A representative

---

[72] On rules circumscribing participation in sport to those with citizen status, and the likely exclusion of the poor and other social groups through indirect measures, see Nielsen (2018: 89, 92); Murray (2020: 105–6).

[73] Some evidence for manufacturing at sanctuaries indicates that craftspeople may have travelled to festivals in order to produce and sell votives, although it may instead be that there were resident workers that had a more permanent relationship with sanctuary administrators. On evidence for manufacturing in sanctuaries, see Kilian (1983) (Philia); Felsch (1983) (Kalapodi); Kyrieleis (2002) (Olympia); Rolley (1977: 131–46) (Delphi); Verdan (2013: 145–53) (Eretria); on craftspeople operating at sanctuaries, see Morgan (1990: 35–9). On the difficulties confronting people with limited means who wished to travel to panhellenic festivals, see Kampakoglou (2014: 16–22). On restrictions regarding the entry of non-citizens to the games, see Pleket (1992).

example is the strigil dedicated by Dikon the bronzeworker in the fifth century BCE: [τάν]δὲ Δίκον Διὶ δῶρον ἀπ' [ca. 3]ας | ἀνέθεκεν αὐτὸς ποιέ[σ]ας [ca. 6] ἔ[χ]ει σοφίαν ('Dikon dedicated this, a gift to Zeus from (his work?); he himself made it, for he has the skill').[74] At the sanctuary of Apollo at Kamiros on Rhodes, a smith dedicated an inscribed bronze wheel to the god in the mid-sixth century. The inscription reads: Ὄνησός με ἀνέθεκε τὀπόλονι ὁ χαλκότυπος τροχὸν ἅρματος ('Onesos the bronzeworker dedicated me, a chariot wheel, to Apollo').[75] One notable aspect of both inscriptions is that they do not include patronymics, which sets them apart from normal formulaic dedicatory inscriptions that tend to specify the dedicant's father's name.[76] The use of the simple names Dikon and Onesos, without even an indication of ethnic or regional affiliation, could be interpreted in a variety of ways, including as an indicator of lower social status.

Aside from the epigraphic record, there is indirect evidence of the presence of workers at Greek sanctuaries in the form of their tools. Given the quantity of more aesthetically impressive finds at sanctuaries, and the relatively unappealing appearance and poor preservation of corroded iron tools, it is not surprising that the archaeological record of iron age to classical tool deposition has not been a particularly popular area of research.[77] A wide variety of tools, however, from pruning hooks to chisels and hammers, have been identified in assemblages at Isthmia, Delos, and Olympia (Figure 3.6a–c).[78] What are the tools, and perhaps their owners, doing in these sanctuaries? Since the tools that have been uncovered at sanctuaries do not retain inscriptions, we can only speculate as to their function. Were these dedications by hardworking *banausoi* proffered to the god, or simply dropped and forgotten or broken and abandoned implements left over from what must have been frequent episodes of construction, reconstruction, and manufacture required by the infrastructural and dedicatory needs of the visitors to and organizers of panhellenic festivals? The jury seems to be out: publications of finds from the different sanctuaries express different opinions. Kilian-Dirlmeier suggested that some of the iron tools found in the north-western area of the Olympia sanctuary must be recycled dedications to the god, because they were so abundant. She deemed it plausible to associate the dedications with the altar of Athena Ergane near the Zeus temple.[79] On the other hand, Baitinger and Völling concluded that none of the tools in the sanctuary (the vast majority of which were for working wood, metal, or stone) could be considered dedications, because there were no discernible concentrations of tools near altars and because the tools

---

[74] Olympia Museum Inv. B 5703, *CEG* 387; see discussion at van Straten (1981: 93); Hurwit (2015: 149). The strigil was found together with bronze fire tongs and an iron spit.
[75] Kontis (1949–51: 347 (Rhodos 14464)). [76] Lazzarini (1976: 62–5).
[77] Blackwell (2020: 532).
[78] For Isthmia, Raubitschek (1998: 119); on Delos, Deonna (1938); on Olympia, Baitinger and Völling (2007).
[79] Kilian-Dirlmeier (2002). See also Hampe and Jantzen (1936–7: 46). On Athena Ergane at Olympia, see Dörpfeld (1935: i. 83, no. 6).

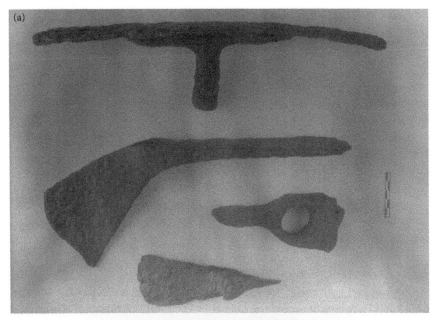

**Figure 3.6** Tools from panhellenic sanctuaries: (*a*) Olympia (Baitinger and Völling 203, Kat. Nr. 811, Taf. 72. 79; Copyright © Hellenic Ministry of Culture and Sports) (L.4858/2021) and Ephorate of Antiquities of Illias. Image courtesy of DAI-Athen. Photograph by Hermann Wagner. (*b*) Isthmia (Raubitschek 1998: pl. 66, no. 425), used with courtesy of the Trustees of the American School of Classical Studies at Athens.

did not bear inscriptions.[80] They conclude that the discarded tools' presence in the sanctuary attests to the frequent activities of masons, metallurgists, and carpenters on the grounds, probably in between festivals, to construct and repair monuments.

---

[80] Baitinger and Völling (2007: 215–16).

While Baitinger and Völling are conservative in their interpretation of the tools at Olympia, a more expansive view of the life cycle of utilitarian metal tools could account for multiple functions that are not necessarily mutually exclusive. One obvious possibility is that tools served both as functional tools and as dedications, since workers in sanctuaries might have dedicated their tools once they were worn out or broken. Tools used in sanctuaries may have been conceived of as possessions of the gods already, and we can easily imagine that special rules governed their disposal. In terms of inscriptions, an old tool is unlikely to have borne an engraving, since the text had would have to be cut into a big adze or chisel before casting—for example, before the useful life of the tool began. Painted inscriptions might have been preferable in such a circumstance, since they could have been added once a tool was marked out for discard through dedication, but the paint would obviously not survive. Thus, utilitarian objects dedicated by those who could not afford custom-made dedications might simply be less visible in the archaeological record than custom-made dedications, exacerbating the problem of the voicelessness of craftspeople in the archaeological and epigraphic record of ancient Greece.

Supporting the notion that workers in sanctuaries would have been among worshippers and dedicants, Raubitschek has argued that at least some implements excavated at the sanctuary of Poseidon at Isthmia were gifts to the gods.[81] This argument is largely based on the spatial distribution of tools in the sanctuary. Among the dedications are a bronze compass (probably used by a ceramicist) and iron axe-adzes of the sort used by smiths in the classical period, but also useful for digging in clay beds, as evident in imagery on the Penteskouphia plaques, discussed above (see Figure 3.5).[82] As Raubitschek points out, it may not be coincidental that a sanctuary close to Corinth, which Herodotus specifies as least inimicable to craftspeople among Greek cities, preserves the best examples of craftspeople's dedications.[83] However we want to interpret these finds from sanctuaries, their presence, again, allows us some glimpse into the experiences of the craftspeople—they certainly spent time working in sanctuaries and probably participated in the normal Greek rituals of *aparche* in their cities of residence and in rural sanctuaries frequented more famously by athletes and elites.[84]

## Mortuary Evidence for *Banausoi*

Another category of archaeological context that might be productively mined for enhanced understandings of the lives and identities of craftworkers is the

---

[81] Raubitschek (1998: 119).
[82] Raubitschek (1998: 119–20). For the Penteskouphia plaques, see Hasaki (2021), with comprehensive references.
[83] Hdt. 2.167.2: Corinthians despise least those who work with their hands (ἥκιστα δὲ Κορίνθιοι ὄνονται τοὺς χειροτέχνας).
[84] e.g. *Anth. Pal.* 6.205, the dedication of carpentry tools to Athena by Leontichos upon his retirement. On *aparche* in Greece generally, see Jim (2014).

mortuary record. Although reading identity from mortuary deposits is always a fraught undertaking, the presence of tools in mortuary contexts might indicate that the deceased was someone whose relatives identified them strongly enough with a tool or set of tools to include these in the funerary ritual.

In reality, tools are rare in burials from the archaic and classical periods. A fragmentary knife comes from a sixth-century tomb in the Kerameikos,[85] and a few tombs of women from rural Attica contained agricultural tools.[86] Such artefacts are unusual in the rather large corpus of tomb assemblages from archaic and classical Greece. This is particularly striking, because tools do occur with some regularity in Mycenaean tombs,[87] in some post-palatial tombs (for example, those at Perati, which contain chisels for shipbuilding and knives for leatherworking),[88] and in protogeometric tombs at Lefkandi,[89] in the Athenian Agora,[90] and at other sites ranging from Central Greece to Epirus.[91] The paucity of burials with tools from the archaic and classical periods might be interpreted in a number of ways. Perhaps artisans were buried in extra-urban locations that are not well documented in the archaeological record. Perhaps elite attitudes against manual labour among elites in classical culture precluded individuals from identifying strongly with their tools in the aspirational arena of mortuary display. Alternatively, perhaps the tools were considered so valuable to artisans that they were passed on to relatives or apprentices rather than being removed from circulation through mortuary deposition.[92] In any case, the contrast between

---

[85] Kerameikos grave 243.

[86] An interesting exception is the presence of agricultural tools in the fifth-century burials of women in the Attic deme of Oa (near modern Paiania) (Kakavogianni 2000: 133–4; Kakavogianni and Galiatsatou 2009: 406–7).

[87] The tools often include things that could be used by artisans, including chisels and awls (Cavanagh and Mee 1998: 51, 55, 73; Kilian-Dirlmeier 2009).

[88] Murray (2018: 50–2).

[89] e.g. Popham and Lemos (1996: pl. 148); discussion of tools at Catling and Catling (1980: 256). The tools found in the cemetery are limited to axes, which are suggested to have been used for chopping wood for fires lit to cook meat. During the protogeometric period, such axes are often discovered in association with metal spits and firedogs, which are probably part of an ensemble belonging to aristocrats partaking in elite feasts (see Tandy 1997: 155–65). Therefore, it is probably a mistake to associate these tools with artisans or workers; but it may be observed that the presence of tools in these contexts corroborates the observation that work and aristocracy were not easily separable in the early iron age.

[90] Papadopoulos and Smithson (2017: 963–6): the tools from early iron age tombs in Athens include all-purpose knives and one axe. The knives come from both male and female tombs and may have been suspended from a belt with a band or strap that does not survive archaeologically. The all-purpose nature of small knives precludes us from confidently associating them with craftworkers. One chisel was found in Athens agora grave XXII, dated to c.900 BCE, for which see Blegen (1952: 281–2, figs 3 and 7).

[91] Early iron age sites with knives in tombs include but are not limited to Kyme in Euboia (Sapouna-Sakellaraki 1998: 104, fig. 44, nos 31–43), Marmariani and Theotokou in Thessaly (Heurtley and Skeat 1930-1: 36–8, fig. 15, no. 23; Wace and Thompson 1912: 212, fig. 147), Elateia in Lokris (Dakoronia 1987), and Vitsa Zagoriou in Epirus (Vokotopoulou 1986: 297).

[92] The fact that metal tools were regularly recycled and reused is suggested by the quantitative mismatch between the number of tools we know must have been used in daily life and those that have appeared in the archaeological record. For example, ploughshares must have been present in Greek households, but no iron ploughshares dated to the archaic or classical periods have been recovered by archaeologists. For a few bronze age ploughshares, see Blackwell (2020: 526–8).

earlier and later traditions concerning the deposition of tools in burials is intriguing and may be worth further attention.

## Conclusions

In this chapter I have sought to establish that, although the voices of *banausic* workers are heard only obliquely in the canon of Greek historical and literary sources, we can tentatively reconstruct some aspects of their lives through creative engagement with the written and material records. Workers probably faced dangerous or uncomfortable conditions on a regular basis. Their livelihoods were subject to the whims of the market, where agonism abounded and rivalries among peers undoubtedly flourished. *Banausoi* probably occupied a world of uncertainty, risk, and competition. To some extent, these conditions were present in the lives of all ancient people. At least some categories of ancient craftspeople, however, encountered risks that were extraordinarily large in magnitude, exceptional in material intensity, and more frequently confronted than others. For example, metallurgists and potters regularly engaged in pyrotechnics requiring encounters with temperatures of 1000–1300° C, where the risk of catastrophic explosion was high. Sculptors, builders, and their assistants had to quarry, move and lift monumental stone objects weighing many tonnes in precarious situations where a minor mistake could mean both sudden, serious injury and the loss of months if not years of labour should a block or statue be smashed or cracked. Perhaps unsurprisingly, then, Greek craftspeople developed ritual practices aimed at avoiding disaster or bringing it down upon their competition as part of complex, distinct cultural systems, and built bespoke ritual stages into the production process. Such practices served to assuage anxieties about danger and risks, in addition to reinforcing a sense of belonging within an exclusive community in possession of elaborate knowledge that was difficult for outsiders to penetrate. Furthermore, rituals practiced within industrial contexts may have been intended to effect a collective manipulation of outsiders' views of *banausic* work, increasing public perception of the mystique associated with transformative processes. While epigraphic evidence makes it clear that craftspeople participated in regular dedicatory practice at sanctuaries, especially in the archaic period, the extent to which they were more active as clients of sanctuaries, accepting contracts to build or repair temples or producing votives for pilgrims, rather than devotees themselves, remains unclear. More studies of artisans' tools in the archaeological record might help to flesh out the relationship between artisans and Greek religious and mortuary practices.

Before closing I return briefly to the question of categorization. While it is convenient to discuss craftspeople together as a group, does the classical *banausos* constitute a satisfactory analytical category based on the evidence reviewed in this chapter? The answer appears to be mainly negative. There are certain aspects that bind the evidence discussed above together—artisans probably all faced certain physical risks because of their specializations. The existence of economic competition probably drove many craftspeople's strategies. At the same time, there is reason to envision a situation in which so-called *banausic* professionals did not see themselves as a coherent group. Archaic dedicatory inscriptions naming craftspeople as dedicators never use this term, nor is an internal sense of technical craft producers as a collective ever expressed. Rather, the vocabulary in texts produced by craftspeople indicates strong individual identification with specific craft practices. Curse tablets mention a number of artisanal professionals as targets (potters, carpenter, silver-worker, helmet-maker, and so on), but a collective term for such workers is never used.[93] We might, therefore, deduce that smiths, sculptors, painters, potters, and so on identified as such rather than as *banausoi*.

The term *banausoi* seems, then, most likely to constitute an external grouping imposed on craftspeople by authors of fifth-century and later texts (the earliest appearances are in the second half of the fifth century) rather than a term that craftspeople would have chosen for themselves.[94] The etymology of the word is somewhat obscure, but it perhaps derives from a compound from βαῦνος, 'furnace', and αὔω, 'scoop'.[95] This provides some insight into how artisans were envisioned beginning in the fifth century. A person who spent their time scooping around furnaces was probably often filthy in appearance and laboured in dangerous and unpleasant conditions. The name does not seem very complimentary, rather calling to mind a vivid image of exactly the sort of dirty work that classical sources deride. It may be reasonable to conclude, then, that craftspeople did not themselves consider the collective label useful or accurate. Instead, the evidence encourages us to reconstruct a range of scenarios for craftspeople's lives and perspectives. Some craftspeople were prosperous and economically independent, while others probably struggled in obscurest penury; others probably experienced changes of fortune that altered their socio-economic position through the course of a lifetime. The identity and experience of craftworkers was neither fixed through time nor generalizable in any given period.

Are there connections between craftspeople and other groups treated in this volume? Two points of contact stand out. First, craftspeople called *banausoi* were characterized by a lack of leisure, which compounds their obscurity in the literary and historical record. Unlike wealthy individuals whose livelihood arose from the labour of others, *banausoi* probably lacked the free time to indulge in the pursuits that shaped elite culture—for example, philosophizing, athletics, and writing—and

---

[93] Eidinow (2007: 196–9).   [94] Soph. *Aj.* 1121; Hdt. 2.165.6.
[95] For an extended discussion of the etymology of the word *banausos* and its historiography, see Bourriot (2015: 5–22, 243–5). Chantraine (1968: 164) and Beekes (2010: 199–200) provide the compound explanation, though it may be that the word is simply non-Greek in origin.

that in turn both engendered a sense of solidarity among elites and allowed ample opportunity to generate the discourses that determine modern conceptions of antiquity.

Second, as is true for many other members of the ancient world, the lives of craftspeople in ancient Greece are obscured by the categorizations imposed upon them by ancient elite authors, a problem compounded by scholarly tendency to follow those categorizations. But breaking down such categories into constituent parts that might bear more verisimilitude to the internal logic of ancient subordinate communities is challenging. Even when we look beyond elite texts and seek to build such categories up from the archaeological and textual records, we face difficult interpretative problems: we cannot see invisible aspects of the performativity and multivalence of status;[96] we have a hard time distinguishing between poor workmen and wealthy craftsmen in the archaeological record;[97] the rural, rather than the urban, craftsman remains elusive in the material record; the gender of craftspeople is not usually possible to discern from archaeological remains, and female contributions to craft production have generally not been considered by scholars.[98] Overall, there seems quite a lot of work yet to be done in reconstructing ancient craftspeople's ideas, priorities, and voices. Nonetheless, I hope that the material presented in this chapter demonstrates that careful contextual study of workshops, tools, and the epigraphic record may create opportunities for an improved understanding of craftspeople's lives in ancient Greece.

## Works Cited

Acton, P. (2014). *Poiesis: Manufacturing in Classical Athens*. Oxford.

Baitinger, H., and T. Völling (2007). *Werkzeug und Gerät aus Olympia*. Berlin.

Bankel, H. (1984). 'Griechische Bleistifte', *Archäologischer Anzeiger*, 1984: 409–11.

Beazley, J. (1944). *Potter and Painter in Ancient Athens*. London.

Beekes, R. (2010). *Etymological Dictionary of Greek*. Leiden.

Bettalli, M. (1985). 'Case, Botteghe, *Ergasteria*: Note sui luoghi di produzione di vendità nell' Atene classica', *Opus*, 4: 29–42.

Blackwell, N. (2020). 'Tools', in I. Lemos and A. Kotsonas (eds), *A Companion to the Archaeology of Early Greece and the Mediterranean*, 523–37. Hoboken.

Blegen, C. (1952). 'Two Athenian Grave Groups of about 900 BC', *Hesperia*, 21: 279–94.

---

[96] See Davies (2017) for a compelling discussion of the many vectors of status and social roles liable to have been operating all at once in ancient Greece.
[97] See Molloy (2016: 1–2) on the inability of the archaeological record to capture the full range of craftspeople's experiences.
[98] Murray et al. (2020).

Bourriot, F. (2015). *Banausos-Banausia et la situation des artisans en Grèce classique*. Zurich.

Bowes, K. (2021) (ed.). *The Roman Peasant Project, 2009–2014: Excavating the Roman Rural Poor*. Philadelphia.

Brisart, T. (2011). *Un art citoyen: Recherches sur l'orientalisation des artisanats en Grèce proto-archaïque*. Brussels.

Bundrick, S. (2008). 'The Fabric of the City: Imaging Textile Production in Classical Athens', *Hesperia*, 77: 283–334.

Burford, A. (1972). *Craftsmen in Greek and Roman Society*. Oxford.

Burckhardt, J. (1929). *Griechische Kulturgeschichte*. Berlin.

Burr, D. (1933). 'A Geometric House and a Proto-Attic Votive Deposit', *Hesperia*, 2: 542–640.

Catling, H., and E. A. Catling (1980). 'Objects in Bronze, Iron, and Lead', in M. Popham, L. Sackett, and P. Themelis (eds), *Lefkandi I: The Iron Age*, 231–64. London.

Cavanagh, W., and C. Mee (1998). *A Private Place: Death in Prehistoric Greece*. Jonsered.

Chantraine, P. (1968). *Dictionnaire étymologique de la langue grecque: Histoire des mots*. Paris.

Chatzidimitriou, A. (2014). 'Craftsmen and Manual Workers in Attic Vase-Painting of the Archaic and Classical Period', in A.-C. Gillis (ed.), *Corps, travail et statut social: L'Apport de la paléoanthropologie funéraire aux sciences historiques*, 63–93. Villeneuve d'Ascq.

Dakoronia, F. (1987). 'Αταλάντη· Οδός Δημοτική (οικόπεδο Αχ. Γκούρα)', *Archaiologikon Deltion*, 42/B'1: 226–8.

Davies, P. (2017). 'Articulating Status in Ancient Greece: Status (In)consistency as a New Approach', *Cambridge Classical Journal*, 63: 29–52.

Deonna, W. (1938). *Le Mobilier délien*. Délos XVIII. Paris.

de Ste. Croix, G. E. M. (1981). *The Class Struggle in the Ancient Greek World*. Oxford.

Dörpfeld, W. (1935). *Alt-Olympia: Untersuchungen und Ausgrabungen zur Geschichte des ältesten Heiligtums von Olympia und der älteren griechischen Kunst*. 2 vols. Berlin.

Eidinow, E. (2007). *Oracles, Curses, and Risk among the Ancient Greeks*. Oxford.

Eschbach, N., and S. Schmidt (2016). *Töpfer, Maler, Werkstatt: Zuschreibungen in der griechischen Vasenmalerei und die Organisation antiker Keramikproduktion*. Munich.

Felsch, R. (1983). 'Zur Chronologie und zum Stil geometrischen Bronzen aus Kalapodi', in Hägg (1983: 123–9).

Feyel, C. (2006). *Les Artisans dans les sanctuaires grecs aux époques classiques et hellénistiques à travers la documentation financière en Grèce*. Athens.

Furtwängler, A. (1906). *Aegina: Das Heiligtum der Aphaia*. Munich.

Gager, J. (1992). *Curse Tablets and Binding Spells from the Ancient World*. Oxford.

Gill, D., and M. Vickers (1990). 'Reflected Glory: Pottery and Precious Metal in Classical Greece', *Jahrbuch des Deutschen Archäologischen Instituts*, 105: 1–30.

Glotz, G. (1920). *Ancient Greece at Work: An Economic History of Greece.* New York.

Güntner, G. (1994). *Göttervereine und Götterversammlungen auf attischen Weihreliefs: Untersuchungen zur Typologie und Bedeutung.* Würzburg.

Hägg, R. (1983) (ed.). *The Greek Renaissance of the Eighth Century BC: Tradition and Innovation.* Stockholm.

Hampe, R., and U. Jantzen (1936-7). 'Die Grabung im Frühjahr 1937', *Bericht über die Ausgrabungen in Olympia,* 1: 25-97.

Hasaki, E. (2021). *Potters at Work in Ancient Corinth: Industry, Religion, and the Penteskouphia Plaques.* Princeton.

Haug, A. (2011). 'Handwerkerszenen auf attischen Vasen des 6. und 5. Jhs. v. Chr. berufliches Selbstbewusstein und sozialer Status', *Jahrbuch des Deutschen Archäologischen Instituts,* 126: 1-31.

Hedreen, G. (2016). *The Image of the Artist in Archaic and Classical Greece: Art, Poetry, and Subjectivity.* Cambridge.

Heurtley, W., and T. Skeat (1930-1). 'The Tholos Tombs of Marmariane', *Annual of the British School at Athens,* 31: 1-55.

Hodder, I. (1982). *Symbols in Action: Ethnological Studies of Material Culture.* Cambridge.

Hurwit, J. (2015). *Artists and Signatures in Ancient Greece.* Cambridge.

Jim, T. (2014). *Sharing with the Gods: Aparchai and Dekatai in Ancient Greece.* Oxford.

Kakavogianni, O. (2000) 'Ἀττική οδός.' *Archaiologikon Deltion,* 55: 133-6.

Kakavogianni, O., and P. Galiatsatou (2009). 'Ἀπό τα αρχαία νεκροταφεία στα Μεσόγεια. Ο αρχαίος δήμος της Ὄης', in V. Vasilopoulou and S. Katsarou-Tzeveleke (eds), *Ἀπό τα Μεσόγεια στον Αργοσαρωνικό: Β' Εφορεία Προϊστορικών και Κλασικών Αρχαιοτήτων. Το έργο μιας δεκαετίας, 1994-2003,* 399-422. Markopoulo.

Kampakoglou, A. (2014). 'Cowherd or Athlete: Aegon's Ambiguous Status and the Erotics of Genre in Theocritus *Idyll* 4', *Phoenix,* 68: 1-26.

Keesling, C. (2002). *The Votive Statues of the Athenian Acropolis.* Cambridge.

Kilian, K. (1983). 'Weihungen aus Eisen und Eisenverarbeitung im Heiligtum zu Philia (Thessalien)', in Hägg (1983: 131-46).

Kilian-Dirlmeier, I. (2002). *Kleinfunde aus dem Athena Itonia-Heiligtum bei Philia (Thessalien).* Römisch-Germanisches Zentralmuseum Monographien 48. Paris.

Kilian-Dirlmeier, I. (2009). 'Burials with Tools: Evidence for Aegean Craftspeople', in D. Danilidou (ed.), *Δ'ΩPON: Τιμητικός Τόμος για τον Σπύρο Ιακωβίδη,* 383-90. Athens.

Kontis, I. D (1949-51). 'Δύο ἀρκαικαι ἐπιγραφαὶ ἐκ Καμίρου', *Annuario della Scuola archeologica di Atene e delle Missioni italiane in Oriente,* 27-29: 347-9.

Kyrieleis, H. (2002). 'Zu den Anfängen des Heiligtums von Olympia', in H. Kyrieleis (ed.), *Olympia 1875-2000: 125 Jahre deutsche Ausgrabungen,* 213-20. Mainz.

Lawton, C. (2017). *The Athenian Agora XXXVIII: Votive Reliefs.* Princeton.

Lazzarini, M. (1976). 'Le formule delle dediche votive nella Grecia arcaica', *Memorie: Atti della Accademia nazionale dei Lincei, Classe di scienze morali, storiche e filologiche,* 19: 47-354.

Lewis, S. (2010). 'Images of Craft on Athenian Pottery: Context and Interpretation', *Bolletino di Archeologia On Line*, 1: 12–26.

Lis, C., and H. Soly (2012). *Worthy Efforts: Attitudes to Work and Workers in Pre-Industrial Europe*. Boston.

Lytle, E., A. Montenach, and D. Simpson (2018) (eds). *A Cultural History of Work in Antiquity*. London.

Malacrino, C. (2010). *Constructing the Ancient World*. Princeton.

Mallwitz, A., and W. Schiering (1964). *Die Werkstatt des Pheidias in Olympia*. Olympische Forschungen 5. Berlin.

Mattusch, C. (1977). 'Bronze- and Iron-Working in the Area of the Athenian Agora', *Hesperia*, 46: 340–79.

Merkelbach, R., and M. L. West (1967). *Fragmenta Hesiodea*. Oxford.

Miller, S. (1974). 'Menon's Cistern', *Hesperia*, 43: 194–245.

Miller, S. (1979). 'Excavations at Nemea', *Hesperia*, 48: 73–103.

Mitford, G. (1822–1823). *The History of Greece*. 5 vols. London.

Molloy, B. (2016). 'Introduction: Thinking of Scales and Modes of Interaction in Prehistory', in B. Malloy (ed.), *Of Odysseys and Oddities*, 1–23. Oxford.

Morgan, C. (1990). *Athletes and Oracles: The Transformation of Olympia and Delphi in the Eighth Century BC*. Cambridge.

Morley, N. (2018). *Classics: Why it Matters*. Cambridge.

Mossé, C. (1966). *Le Travail en Grèce et à Rome*. Paris.

Murray, S. (2018). 'Imported Exotica and Mortuary Ritual at Perati in Late Helladic IIIC East Attica', *American Journal of Archaeology*, 122: 33–64.

Murray, S. (2020). 'Rules and Order', in P. Christesen and C. Stocking (eds), *A Cultural History of Sport in Antiquity*, 95–120. London.

Murray, S., I. Chorghay, and J. MacPherson (2020). 'The Dipylon Mistress: Social and Economic Complexity, the Gendering of Craft Production, and Early Greek Ceramic Material Culture', *American Journal of Archaeology*, 124: 215–44.

Nakassis, D. (2013). *Individuals and Society in Mycenaean Pylos*. Leiden.

Ndoye, M. (2010). *Groupes sociaux et idéologie du travail dans les mondes homérique et hésiodique*. Besançon.

Neer, R. (2002). *Style and Politics in Athenian Vase-Painting: The Craft of Democracy, ca. 530–460 BCE*. Cambridge.

Newton, R. (1987). 'Odysseus and Hephaestus in the *Odyssey*', *Classical Journal*, 83: 12–20.

Nielsen, T. (2018). *Two Studies in the History of Ancient Greek Athletics*. Copenhagen.

Ober, J. (1989). *Mass and Elite in Democratic Athens: Rhetoric, Ideology, and the Power of the People*. Princeton.

Osborne, M., and S. Byrne (1996). *Lexicon of Greek Personal Names II: Attica*. Oxford.

Papadopoulos, J. (2003). *Ceramicus Redidivus: The Early Iron Age Potters' Field in the Area of the Classical Athenian Agora*. Hesperia Supplement 31. Princeton.

Papadopoulos, J., and E. Smithson (2017). *The Early Iron Age: The Cemeteries*. Athenian Agora XXXVI. Princeton.

Peek, W. (1941). *Kerameikos III: Inschriften Ostraka Fluchtafeln*. Berlin.

Petrakos, B. (1999). *Ο Δῆμος τοῦ Ραμνοῦντος*. Athens.

Pleket, H. W. (1992). 'The Participants in the Ancient Olympic Games: Social Background and Mentality', in W. Cousen and H. Kyrieleis (eds), *Proceedings of an International Symposium on the Olympic Games, 5–9 September 1988*, 147–52. Athens.

Popham, M., and I. Lemos (1996). *Lefkandi III: The Toumba Cemetery: the Excavations of 1981, 1984, 1986, and 1992–4: Plates*. Athens.

Porter, J. (2011). 'Making and Unmaking: The Achaean Wall and the Limits of Fictionality in Homeric Criticism', *Transactions of the American Philological Association*, 141: 1–36.

Randall, R. (1953). 'The Erechtheum Workmen', *American Journal of Archaeology*, 57: 199–210.

Raubitschek, A. (1949). *Dedications from the Athenian Acropolis*. Cambridge, MA.

Raubitschek, I. (1998). *The Metal Objects (1952–1989)*. Isthmia VII. Princeton.

Rolley, C. (1977). *Fouilles de Delphes III: Les Trépieds à Cuve Clouée*. Paris.

Rostoker, W., and E. Gebhard (1980). 'The Sanctuary of Poseidon at Isthmia: Techniques of Metal Manufacture', *Hesperia*, 49: 347–63.

Rotroff, S. (1997). *The Athenian Agora, XXIX. Hellenistic Pottery, Athenian and Imported Wheelmade Tableware and Related Material*. Princeton.

Rotroff, S. (2013). *Industrial Religion: The Saucer Pyres of the Athenian Agora*. Hesperia Supplement 47. Princeton.

Sapirstein, P. (2013). 'Painters, Potters, and the Scale of the Attic Vase-Painting Industry', *American Journal of Archaeology*, 117: 493–510.

Sapirstein, P. (2018a). 'Work, Skill, and Technology', in Lytle et al. (2018: 95–111, 187–90).

Sapirstein, P. (2018b). 'Picturing Work', in Lytle et al. (2018: 33–56, 177–83).

Sapouna-Sakellaraki, E. (1998). 'Geometric Kyme: The Excavation at Viglatouri, Kyme, on Euboea', in M. Bats and B. A'Agostino (eds), *Euboica: L'Eubea e la presenza euboica in Calcidica e in Occidente*, 59–104. Naples.

Schiering, W. (1991). *Die Werkstatt des Phidias in Olympia, zweite Teil: Wekstattfunde*. Olympische Forschungen XVIII. Berlin.

Seaman, K. (2017). 'The Social and Educational Background of Elite Greek Artists', in K. Seaman and P. Schultz (eds), *Artists and Artistic Production in Ancient Greece*, 12–22. Cambridge.

Shear, T. L. (1969). 'The Athenian Agora: Excavations of 1968', *Hesperia*, 52: 257–97.

Shear, T. L. (1984). 'The Athenian Agora: Excavations of 1980–1982', *Hesperia*, 53: 1–57.

Stissi, V. (2002). 'Pottery to the People: The Production, Distribution, and Consumption of Decorated Pottery in the Greek World in the Archaic Period (650–480 BC)'. Ph.D. dissertation. Amsterdam.

Tandy, D. (1997). *Warriors into Traders*. Berkeley and Los Angeles.

Taylor, C. (2017). *Poverty, Wealth, and Well-Being: Experiencing* Penia *in Democratic Athens*. Cambridge.

Thompson, H. (1934). 'Two Centuries of Hellenistic Pottery', *Hesperia*, 4: 311–476.

Thompson, H. (1949). 'Excavations in the Athenian Agora: 1948', *Hesperia*, 18: 211–29.

Tsakirgis, B. (2015). 'Tools from the House of Mikion and Menon', in M. Miles (ed.), *Autopsy in Athens: Recent Archaeological Research on Athens and Attica*, 9–17. Oxford.

Van Oyen, A., G. Tol, R. Vennarucci, A. Agostini, V. Serneels, A. M. Mercuri, E. Rattighieri, and A. Benatti (2022). 'Forging the Roman Rural Economy: A Blacksmithing Workshop and its Tool Set at Marzuolo (Tuscany)', *American Journal of Archaeology*, 126: 53–77.

Van Straten, F. (1981). 'Gifts for the Gods', in H. S. Versnel (ed.), *Faith, Hope and Worship: Aspects of Religious Mentality in the Ancient World*, 65–151. Leiden.

Verboven, K., and C. Laes (2016). 'Work, Labour, and Professions: What's in a Name', in K. Verboven and C. Laes (eds), *Work, Labour, and Professions in the Roman World*, 1–19. Leiden.

Verdan, S. (2013). *Le Sanctuaire d'Apollon Daphnéphoros à l'époque géometrique*. Eretria XXII. Bern.

Vickers, M., and D. Gill (1994). *Artful Crafts: Ancient Greek Silverware and Pottery*. Oxford.

Vokotopoulou, I. (1986). *Βίτσα· Τα νεκροταφεία μίας Μολοσσκής κώμης*. Athens.

Vossen, R. (1975). *Guía de los Alfares de España*. Madrid.

Wace, A., and M. Thompson (1912). *Prehistoric Thessaly*. Cambridge.

Wagner, C. (2000). 'The Potters of Athena: Dedications on the Athenian Acropolis', in G. Tsetskhladze, A. Prag, and A. Snodgrass (eds), *Periplous: Papers on Classical Art and Archaeology Presented to Sir John Boardman*, 383–7. London.

West, M. L. (2003). *Homeric Hymns, Homeric Apocrypha, Lives of Homer*. Cambridge, MA.

Wilamowitz, U. (1887). 'Demotika der Attischen Metoeken I', *Hermes*, 22: 107–28.

Williams, D. (1990). 'Euphronios: Du peintre au potier', in A. Pasquier and M. Denoyelle (eds), *Euphronios: Peintre à Athènes au Vie siècle avant J.-C.*, 33–7. Paris.

Wright, R. (1991). 'Women's Labour and Pottery Production', in J. Gero and M. Conkey (eds), *Engendering Archaeology: Women and Prehistory*, 194–223. Oxford.

Young, R. (1951). 'An Industrial District of Ancient Athens', *Hesperia*, 20: 135–288.

Zachos, G. (2013). 'Epeios in Greece and Italy: Two Different Traditions in One Person', *Athenaeum*, 101: 5–23.

# 4
# 'Don't tell anybody you are a thete!'
## Athenian Thetes: Identity and Visibility

*Lucia Cecchet*

### Preface

As other chapters in this book point out, subordinated groups in the ancient cities were a diverse category, including ethnic minorities (Lewis and Wijma), women (Kennedy), unfree people (Forsdyke and Kamen), and people from the working classes (Edwards, Murray, Zurbach). Each of these groups experienced different kinds of subordination, ranging from limitation of rights, physical exploitation, and political exclusion. This chapter deals with the barely audible voices from within the group of the Athenian citizens, namely, voices of working-class citizens, which in the Solonic order were identified as the fourth census class, the 'thetes'. Unlike those from slaves and metics, manifestations of pride for professional achievements appear to be rare from Athenian thetes. This makes it more difficult to identify thetes in the material (epigraphic) record, a fact that characterizes them as mostly 'voiceless' in our sources.

In the case of thetes, a more subtle and less apparent form of subordination was at play as compared to the subordination experienced by other groups: formally, thetes were a part of the citizen body. In fact, however, their access to offices was limited by specific rules, whether or not they were observed, and their activity as manual labourers had to face the prejudices of the Athenian elites, which are reiterated in Athenian public discourse. In antiquity, no one seems to admit that he or she is a thete. Literary sources bear very limited testimonies of the use of this word. Its few occurrences show close association to servile status. Despite the large amount of material evidence for the life of the working classes at Athens (such as, manufactures, tombstones, traces of workshops, and so on), we have little material we can attribute with confidence to thetes.

This chapter also aims at contributing to the recent trend of studies on poverty in Greek antiquity. Much work has been done recently on poverty in the Greek world and in classical Athens, focusing on a number of topics, including social, political and economic aspects of poverty,[1] literary representations of the poor,[2] analysis of poverty discourses,[3] the experience of *penia* in classical Athens,[4] and social and cultural aspects related to begging.[5] These works, drawing on advances made in the social sciences, have highlighted that poverty is not simply an economic phenomenon. This is very clear in the case of Athenian thetes, who were not necessarily poor in financial terms, but are labelled as such in public discourse. This chapter explores their position in classical Athens and discusses the consequences that subordination imposed by elite-shaped views on manual labour had in terms of the visibility of thetes in the source material.

## The 'Thetic Ban': A Paradox of Athenian Democracy?

There is a sort of paradox in Athenian democracy, albeit a paradox that seems to have troubled scholars much more than the Athenians themselves. Athenian democrats praised democracy for its participatory and inclusive character—namely, for the fact that every citizen, with no distinction as to wealth or poverty, could take part in political and public life. We read in the famous funerary speech of Perikles for the dead in the first year of Peloponnesian War, as 'reconstructed' by Thucydides, that in Athens poverty is no obstacle to public life (Thuc. 2.37.1), nor is it a shame for the citizen, while it is shameful not to fight against it (Thuc. 2.40.1).[6] From the tragic stage, Theseus in Euripides' *Supplices* observes that in Athens people rule in turn, changing every year, and that both the rich and the poor have equal share (Eur. *Supp.* 406–8). Xenophon claims that in Athens the assembly is filled with fullers, leather-workers, joiners, smiths, farmers, and merchants (Xen. *Mem.* 3.7.6). Along the same lines, Socrates, in Plato's *Protagoras*, affirms that, in the assembly, anyone, from the carpenter to the bronze-worker and the shoemaker, the merchant and the shop owner, can partake in deliberations (Pl. *Prot.* 319c–d). For the very same reason, oligarchic and conservative voices, such as that of the Old Oligarch, strongly criticized the democratic system, pointing to the detrimental role of the demos in politics and to the effect of *penia* in promoting evil actions and ignorance ([Xen.] *Ath. Pol.* 1.5). Yet, the paradox consists in the fact that, despite praises and criticism of Athenian democracy as a system in which even the 'poor' can partake in political life, in reality there were specific limitations to their role in politics. The thetes—the lowest stratum of the citizen body—were not allowed to take up magistracies.

---

[1] Articles in *Ktèma* 38 (2013), Galbois and Rougier-Blanc (2014), and Carlà-Uhink et al. (2023, part 1—Greece).
[2] Coin-Longeray (2014).   [3] Cecchet (2015).   [4] Taylor (2017).
[5] Chapters in Helmer (2020).
[6] On Perikles' view on 'active poverty', see Cecchet (2015: 28–30). Cf. Lenfant (2013: 42–4).

The standard reference for our knowledge of this limitation is a passage of the Aristotelian *Constitution of the Athenians*, in which the author explains that Solon divided Athenian citizens into four classes (*tele*), according to specific amounts of agricultural produce: 500 measures qualified the members of the first class, 300 measures (or alternatively the capability of keeping a horse) those of the second class, 200 measures the third class, and all those Athenians who fell below this threshold belonged in the fourth class, called 'thetes'.[7] He further explains that only members of the first three classes can hold offices. The treasurers of Athena were appointed from the first class only,[8] and before 457 BCE the members of the third class (the *zeugitai*) could not access the archonship ([Arist.] *Ath. Pol.* 26.2) (Rhodes 1993: 328–1). Thetes were granted access to the assembly and to the jury courts alone; they could not hold offices or sit in the boule, nor could they be treasurers. How effective these limitations were, and for how long they were observed, we do not know: Pseudo-Aristotle adds that, in his own day, during the allotment of offices, no one would reveal he was a thete: 'if a candidate for office is asked what *telos* he belongs to, no one would say the thetic class' (οὐδ' ἂν εἷς εἴποι θητικόν: [Arist.] *Ath. Pol.* 7.4).[9] This shows, on the one hand, that Athenians were aware that thetes had limited access to offices, but, on the other, that they avoided the problem by simply lying or avoiding answering the question.

Now, one could say that, in comparison with oligarchic constitutions, in which political participation was regulated by timocratic criteria and the landless were excluded from the citizen body, the Athenian system did at least recognize important rights for the 'poor'. They could in fact sit in the assembly, propose and vote for common decisions, and serve as jurors. These facts alone gave thetes a considerable role in political life. But the formal ban to hold offices struck a blow against political equality.

When thinking of the major differences between ancient and modern democracy in terms of equality and rights, we usually point to the exclusion of women from the political community and to the institution of slavery. Both these facts, repellent as they are to a contemporary eye, remained a constant aspect of both democratic and oligarchic regimes until the modern era. Notably, Aristotle was a theorist both of slavery and of male supremacy over women.[10] Needless to say, no ancient author ever argues in favour of extending political participation to these groups. But we often tend to forget that, as Kurt Raaflaub reminds us, in Athens

---

[7] [Arist.] *Ath. Pol.* 7.2–4 with Rhodes (1993: 136–46). Cf. Rosivach (2002).
[8] [Arist.] *Ath. Pol.* 47.1 with Rhodes (1993: 551).
[9] Cf. [Arist.] *Ath. Pol.* 26.2. There seems to have been some room for individual choice: ordinary citizens preferred to take up magistracies that required no particular expertise, whereas more demanding offices, such as the *strategia*, were allowed only to skilled candidates; see [Xen.] *Ath. Pol.* 1.3.
[10] See Arist. *Pol.* 1254$^b$. See the commentary to Aristotle's *Politics*, book I, by Curnis and Besso (2011: ad loc.).

there were forms of political exclusion even within the citizen group.[11] The formal limitation to the political participation of thetes was clearly at odds with the very root of democratic pride, which is the idea that everybody—among male citizens—can rule in turn. Thus, one cannot avoid regarding the 'thetic ban' as an intrinsic contradiction of Athenian democratic ideology.

It is worth noting further that we have very little information on thetes in Athenian classical sources, and no attestations of individuals openly calling themselves 'thetes' either in private speeches or in inscriptions. It is therefore legitimate to ask whether the 'thetic ban' had some impact on the public perception of thetes as part of the citizen body and on their own self-perception as citizens, and whether thetes simply complied with the rules of their political exclusion or whether they employed strategies to overcome the barriers set by institutions. This chapter will discuss these questions, in an attempt to dig out voices of thetes from literary and epigraphic sources.

## Thetes as Wage Labourers

Who were the thetes in the archaic and classical world? The word has been attested in literary sources since the archaic period, starting with the epics.[12] While its etymology is obscure, its meaning, as the meaning of the denominative verb θητεύειν, i.e. 'to serve' or 'to work' for a reward, seems to be clear: in the *Iliad*, in the *Odyssey*, and in Hesiod's *Works and Days*, thetes are day or seasonal labourers or domestic servants of free status, working for a reward (Hom. *Il*. 21.444–52; *Od*. 11.488–91, 18.357–61; Hes. *Op*. 602). In the archaic world, the reward for their service is generally provided in kind—for example, as food and shelter for the duration of their activity.[13] Thetes are not bound to a master, as slaves are, and they are free to move anywhere in search of employment opportunities. However, in the epics they seem to be generally stationary. Wandering professionals are referred to with another word, *demioergoi*. These were professionals such as artists, artisans, or even physicians, who travelled to different places, settling down only temporarily where their services were required. The characteristic feature of *demioergoi*, as they are described by Eumaeus in *Odyssey* 17, is their high degree of specialization in fields other than manual work, such as medicine

---

[11] Raaflaub (1996: 139–74, esp. 154–9) in response to Ober (1996), arguing that ordinary Athenians gained power with the revolution of 509/8 BCE. On the stages of the integration of the thetes into the political community, see also Raaflaub (1997); on their isolation, see Jacquemin (2013). On the scanty political participation of the Athenian demos, see now Giangiulio (2016). On limitation of political rights based on census in Athens, see also Schmitz (1995) and Blösel (2014).

[12] For an overview of the history of the Greek word *thes* (θής), see Bravo (1992).

[13] See the reward (*misthos*) that Eurymachus offers Odysseus, in exchange for a year's work, at *Od*. 18.357–61; on wage labourers in the archaic world, see Dreizehnter (1981).

(Hom. *Od.* 17.381–7). Thetes, by contrast, are mostly construction workers or land-tillers or, in the case of women, housemaids.

Plutarch, drawing to a good extent on the Aristotelian *Ath. Pol.*, uses the noun 'thetes' to designate the peasants within the system of obligations to the wealthy that led to the outbreak of the crisis in sixth-century Attica (Plut. *Sol.* 13.2).[14] In the fourth-century narrative of the crisis—and in Plutarch's account later on— Solon liberated the land-tillers from their obligation to pay, enfranchising those who had lost their freedom and prohibiting slavery for debts, though debt bondage continued to exist, as Edward Harris has shown (Harris 2002a: 415–30). It is, of course, tempting to believe that the four census classes of the Solonic constitution were reshaped shortly after the 'cancellation of debts' and that the liberated peasants ended up in the fourth class, the thetes. But we must be wary about making assumptions based on later accounts of the Solonian crisis. According to *Ath. Pol.* 7.3, the census classes existed even before Solon, even though the text is rather unclear on this point, and it is debated whether the classes were three, rather than four, in the pre-Solonian order.[15]

The word *thes* and the verb *theteuein* do not change their meaning in the classical period, but in classical sources 'thetes' is only rarely used for designating the working class in general. For this, Attic Greek rather deploys words such as *hoi penetes* ('the poor'), *ho demos* ('the people'), or *hoi polloi* ('the many'). *Theteuein* and *theteia* remain closely associated with—though not limited to—agricultural work and husbandry. So, in Herodotus (8.137.2), the verb *theteuein* describes the work of Perdiccas and his brothers as shepherds; similarly, in Sophocles' *Oedipus Tyrannus* (1027–9), the noun *theteia* refers to the activity of a shepherd. In Plato's *Euthyphro*, *theteuein* designates the activity of a hired servant, tilling land in Naxos (Pl. *Euthyphr.* 4c). Despite its ties with the rural world, however, the word 'thetes' in the urban world of the classical period also designates wage labourers— that is, those working for a *misthos*. In Athens, the wage labourers in search of a job met daily at a spot in the Athenian Agora called Kolonos Agoraios—also known as Kolonos Ergatikos and Kolonos Misthios or, simply, *misthoterion*— which has been identified with the hill west of the Agora. The adjective Agoraios is obviously topographical, while the other adjectives refer to the manual workers (*ergatai*) and wage labourers (*misthotoi* or *mistharnountes*) who gathered there in the hope of employment. The spot was a meeting point for labour exchange— namely, a place where jobseekers and employers made short-term arrangements.[16] Indeed, not all those gathering were thetes; a good proportion of them were certainly metics or manumitted slaves. However, since the number of landless

---

[14] For discussion of sources and literature, see Edwards, this volume. See also Faraguna (2012a).
[15] See Rhodes (1993: 137–8) for the possibility that Solon just divided the first class into the very rich (*pentakosiomedimnoi*—the nomenclature suggests a later addition) and the *hippeis*, creating thereby four classes from the existing three classes.
[16] See Fuks (1984 [1951]).

citizens in Athens increased after the loss of Athenian assets overseas in 404 BCE, it is plausible that places like the Kolonos Agoraios might have become increasingly attended by Athenian citizens in the fourth century.

Aristotle in the *Politics* maintains a distinction between the categories of thetes and *banausoi* (artisans), and, within the category of the *banausoi*, he distinguishes between specialized ones (*technitai*) and non-specialized (*atechnitai*: Arist. *Pol.* 1258$^b$26–7).[17] He does not explain, however, the difference between *banausoi* and thetes. As mentioned above, it seems that thetes were mostly confined to land-tilling and construction work. Professionals such as potters, goldsmiths, butchers, and so on were more likely to fall into the category of artisans (*banausoi*).

Aristotle notes that in oligarchies, in which wealth requirements are strictly relevant to citizenship, thetes are excluded from the citizen body, while artisans—having in mind the specialized ones (*technitai*)—are admitted because they can be wealthy. By contrast, in aristocracies neither artisans nor thetes are admitted to the civic body, because they cannot pursue virtue and merit (Arist. *Pol.* 1278$^a$11–25).[18] In democracies they are both part of the civic body, but not all democracies are the same. Aristotle classifies democracies according to the composition of the demos. The best kind, in his view, is the form of democracy in which the demos consists mainly of farmers, because they have little time for politics and are not prone to attending the assembly and holding offices (Arist. *Pol.* 1318$^b$10–16). The worst kinds of democracy are, by contrast, those in which the demos consists mainly of artisans and wage-labourers, who live in the city and have time to attend the assembly (Arist. *Pol.* 1319$^a$26–31). In several places in the *Politics*, he compares both categories to slaves (*Pol.* 1277$^b$1; 1337$^b$21).[19]

The link between thetic status and servile status was not an idea peculiar to Aristotle. In Euripides' *Cyclops*, the chorus laments the condition of the servant of Polyphemus by using the verb *theteuein* and directly comparing his condition to that of a slave (Eur. *Cyc.* 78: *doulos*). The negative connotation of *theteia* as 'serfdom' and 'slavery' survives also in Isocrates' *Busiris* 38. Such a negative connotation in classical sources might be a legacy from an earlier period. In the archaic period, in fact, though thetes were workers of free status, the fact that their service was usually rewarded with food and shelter did assimilate them to slaves. Notably, in *Odyssey* 11.488–91, Achilles, in the underworld, says that he would prefer to serve as a thete of a landless man rather than rule over the dead. He shows thereby the two extremities of the social ladder: on the one hand, the ruler; on the other, the servant/slave. A further aspect that contributed to assimilate thetes to slaves in common perception may have been their limited autonomy

---

[17] See the commentary to Aristotle's *Politics*, book I, by Curnis and Besso (2011: ad loc.). Nagle (2006: 119–20) considers *banausoi* at a lower level than thetes in Aristotle's view. However, *Pol.* 1278$^a$11–25 seems to imply the contrary.

[18] Accattino and Curnis (2013: ad loc.).

[19] See Curnis et al. (2016: ad loc.) and Bertelli et al. (2022: ad loc.).

in professional activities and their low level of technical specialization. While *banausoi* performed highly skilled work and they often owned their own workshop, thetes, in the socio-economic meaning of the word, were hirelings working for an employer. All this comes as no surprise: as Walter Scheidel has pointed out, the association between hireling and slave survives for a long time even after antiquity.[20] On this note, this fact is worth of our attention: in fourth-century Attic speeches, speakers often depicted themselves as poor—*penetes*, or, in some cases, even as *ptochoi*, 'destitute'—as part of rhetorical strategies to evoke the pity of the jurors.[21] But not one of them ever says he is a thete. We will return to this point in due course.

## Thetes between Census Class and Military Function

So what about thetes with reference to the fourth census class? In general, it must be noted that we have very few references for the census classes apart from the sources attesting Solon's timocratic reform. In the inscription bearing the text of the foundation decree of Brea, we read that only *zeugitai* and *thetes* will take part in the colonizing expedition (*IG* i$^3$ 46.43–6 = OR no. 142). This is, so far, the only occurrence of the word 'thetes' in the epigraphic record. In the *Ath. Pol.* Pseudo-Aristotle refers to a votive inscription, which he vaguely places in a distant time, dedicated on the Acropolis by a certain Anthemion, son of Diphilos, to celebrate his passage from the thetic to the hippic class ([Arist.] *Ath. Pol.* 7.4). This would have been, had it survived, a further piece of evidence for the use of thetes as referring to the census class. (We will return to this passage below.)

Scholars generally point to Thucydides 6.43—a description of the preparation for the Sicilian expedition in 415 BCE—as evidence for the thetes as census class. Thucydides says that, among all hoplites who took part in the expedition, 1,500 were from the *katalogos* and 700 were thetes who participated as *epibatai*—the rest being allies and mercenaries. Geoffrey de Ste. Croix interpreted the word 'thetes' in this text as a reference to the census class.[22] David Pritchard and Vincent Rosivach have rejected this view in favour of the idea that the word is used in its socio-economic meaning referring to the wage labourers among the citizens, and not to the *telos*.[23] However, if this was the case, it would be an *unicum* in Thucydides' work, as the historian never uses the word 'thetes' to indicate ordinary Athenians. He usually reverts to other expressions, such as *demos*,

---

[20] Scheidel (2002). [21] Cecchet (2013; 2015: 194–226). [22] De Ste. Croix (2004: 21).
[23] Pritchard (1998 and 2010: 24–5); Rosivach (2012). A generic meaning as ordinary citizens also seems to be preferred by Gomme (1970: 310) and Hornblower (2008: 1062).

*plethos*, *hoi polloi*, or *ochlos*.[24] Moreover, the fact that he uses 'thetes' in the context of the description of the organization of a military operation, showing those who are not on the *katalogos* of the hoplites, makes it likely that he refers to the census class: a parallel case occurs also at 3.16.1, where Thucydides says that the two wealthiest *tele*, the *hippeis* and the *pentakosiomedimnoi*, were granted exemption from the naval levy in 427 BCE.

Returning to Thucydides' description of the Sicilian expedition (6.43), we should note that the historian says hoplites were recruited from the official list (*katalogos*), while the thetes serving as marines seem to have participated in the expedition as volunteers.[25] Commenting on this passage, Kurt Raaflaub has argued that no official register may have existed for the thetes.[26] Long before, Antony Raubitschek suggested that thetes were not even recorded on the casualty lists.[27] Those who are more sceptical about the equality of Athenian democracy have gone so far as to doubt whether thetes were ever registered on the civic lists—the *lexiarchika grammateia*.[28] However, the evidence is mostly based on *argumenta ex silentio*. These are the missing references to a thetic catalogue and the fact that Thucydides is vague about casualties among light-armed troops and oarsmen, while he is more precise about hoplite casualties. Notably, speaking about the plague at the beginning of the Peloponnesian War, the historian provides the exact number of casualties among heavy infantry and cavalrymen, but he admits that the number of the dead among the multitude (*ochlos*) 'cannot be determined' (Thuc. 3.87.3).[29] This question is far from being settled,[30] and this is indeed not the place for a thorough discussion. I will limit myself to note that, while it is plausible that a thetic *katalogos* was not the usual way of conscripting sailors, as thetes mainly served in the fleet on a voluntary base for the *misthos*, it is very unlikely that they were not registered in the civic lists. Civic lists were in fact the formal proof of Athenian citizenship,

---

[24] The word *demos* in Thucydides indicates the Athenian people in general without any explicit class distinction (see Athenagoras' definition of *demos* at 6.39.1). However, he often uses this word with reference to the supporters of democracy—the majority of which were ordinary citizens—and in opposition to the oligarchs, who were likely to come from the wealthier strata. See, e.g., Thuc. 6.60.1 and 4 (cf. the use of *plethos* at 6.60.4); 6.35.2 and 6.39 (Athenagoras is the leader of the *demos* and of *hoi polloi* against the oligarchic faction); 8.68.4 (Athenian *demos* as opposed to the oligarchs of Theramenes). On Thucydides' use of *demos*, see Moggi (2005: 15–17). *Hoi polloi* is used by Athenagoras at 6.38.4 in opposition to oligarchic factions. *Ochlos* indicates the mass of the common people, however, not exclusively citizens: see 6.20.4, where Nicias calls the people manning the ships ὄχλος ὁ πληρώσων. This group included also metics and slaves. Cf. also Thuc. 3.87.3.

[25] Recently, Van Wees (2018: 135), commenting on this passage of Thucydides, has noted that volunteering probably applied also to those thetes who could afford hoplite armour. On the mechanism of conscription of hoplites, see Christ (2001).

[26] Raaflaub (1996: 155–6).

[27] Raubitschek (1943: 48, n. 102 (quoted also by Raaflaub 1996: 156)).

[28] Hignett (1952: 132–42). On civic lists in Athens, see now Faraguna (2021: 155–63).

[29] τοῦ δὲ ἄλλου ὄχλου ἀνεξεύρετος ἀριθμός. Cf. Thuc. 4.101.2.

[30] See, e.g., Christ (2001: 415), who maintains there were conscription lists for the sailor-thetes and points to Ps.-Dem. 50.6 and 50.16 on the conscription of sailors in 362; cf. Guìa and Gallego (2010: 260).

they were periodically scrutinized, and disputes about citizenship were settled before the court, as Demosthenes' *Against Euboulides* (Dem. 57) shows. To exclude the thetes from such lists would entail formal exclusion from the citizen body. Moreover, the evidence from *IG* I³ 1032 clearly shows that citizen rowers were an important component of naval crews and, as such, of the citizen body as a military force. The inscription—which consists of twelve fragments found on the Acropolis, and probably originally located in the Erechtheion—lists the complements of four triremes.[31] As well as the names of trierarchs, other high officers, and marines, the text also contains the names of sailors. These are listed with a clear distinction between citizen rowers, foreign rowers, and slaves. The proportion of these three groups varies from trireme to trireme. The number of citizens is far from negligible: their proportion is about 17 per cent in trireme I and 30 per cent in trireme IV.[32] Citizen rowers were likely to be members of the thetic *telos*, but it should be noted that the text shows no differentiation according to the census.

Apart from military contexts, we find a reference to the thetic class in Pseudo-Demosthenes' *Against Makartatos*, in which the speaker refers to the allegedly Solonian law about thetic *epikleroi*, the female heiresses of thetic census ([Dem.] 43.54). The law prescribed that *epikleroi*-thetes should either get married to their nearest of kin or be provided by him with a dowry, in an amount fixed according to his own census class. We do not know if this law was genuinely Solonic.[33] But the fact that the speaker refers to this law shows that, as late as 370–365 BCE, census classes could still come into play for regulating private issues, such as inheritance. Did they matter to anything else?

There has been a discussion as to whether the Solonic *tele* mattered to the levy of the *eisphora*. Pollux refers to different quotas of payment varying from *telos* to *telos*, and he affirms that thetes did not pay anything (Poll. 8.130). Hans van Wees noted that he probably refers to the levy of the *eisphora* before 378 BCE, when a reform of the system was carried out and 100 taxation units (the *symmoriai*) were created (van Wees 2006: 369). If this was the case, it means that, at least until 378 BCE, the Solonic classes were still considered valid criteria for defining individual wealth for the purpose of levying taxes. But this is unlikely: the quotas of agricultural produce introduced by Solon may already have been well out of date by the fifth century. It was de Ste. Croix's view that neither *hippeis* nor *zeugitai*, let alone the *pentakosiomedimnoi*, were ever qualified by the measures indicated by

---

[31] IG i³ 1032 = OR no. 190 (part of the *stele*) = AIO 965).

[32] Trireme I: *c*.30 citizens (16 names preserved); 28 foreigners; more than 120 slaves. Trireme II: at least 39 citizens, no. of foreigners unknown; slightly above 40 slaves. Trireme III: 14 names of citizens preserved, but total no. unknown; no. of foreigners unknown; 79 slave names preserved, but total no. of slaves unknown. Trireme IV: about 55 citizens (4 names preserved); 40 foreigners (33 names preserved); 85 slaves (35 names preserved). See RO 190: 544–6.

[33] Canevaro's studies (starting with Canevaro 2013) have made a strong case against the authenticity of the laws and documents quoted by orators. See Leão and Rhodes (2015) for a recent review of Solon's laws.

Aristotle, not even in Solon's constitution. He maintained that it was rather a military status—that is, the capability of keeping a horse or of acquiring hoplite armour—that would qualify individuals in a census class.[34] By contrast, Hans van Wees believes that census classes were assessed in terms of agricultural produce as early as Solon's time, but, since criteria were never formally changed and land was no longer the only source of wealth in the classical period, the census classes gradually lost their currency.[35]

Thetes are the clearest example of the fact that Solon's criteria of agricultural produce had become meaningless for defining wealth in the classical period. The fourth *telos*, as we understand from *Ath. Pol.* 7.4, included those citizens who possessed small plots or no land at all. But in the fourth century one could have no land and still be rich by means of trade, banking, crafts, or industry. And, vice versa, citizens who had for generations belonged in the highest census classes may have lost considerable parts of their wealth by the mid-fourth century. At *Ath. Pol.* 47.1, Pseudo-Aristotle says that it was possible to become treasurer of Athena only if ranked with the *pentakosiomedimnoi*, but he adds being 'very poor' (*panu penes*) did not in fact matter. This note is interesting. By the time the *Ath. Pol.* was written, Athenians could become impoverished for several reasons. The practice of the partition of land among heirs, which repeated itself through generations, could cause the size of plots to be reduced dramatically, though factors such as dowries and deaths of landowners did, on the other hand, counterbalance this phenomenon.[36] The most important factor causing loss of land—in Attica or overseas—did indeed remain war. We can think, for example, of the story of the family of Aristarchos, mentioned in Xenophon's *Memorabilia* 2.7.1–14. This family lost its land during the civil war of 404/3 BCE, and many female relatives, having become widows or orphans, moved to Aristarchos' house. In order to survive, they had to convert their source of income from land to wool working.[37] This family did not become poor. A business of wool-working, performed by women, proved to be a success. But it is clear that, in terms of the Solonic census, they would no longer be able to provide the agricultural produce required to qualify for the highest classes. Thus, we can assume that membership in a *telos* remained a feature of family history, something passed on from generation to generation, but it no longer functioned as a valid indicator of economic standing.

Let us return to the definition of the census class in terms of military role. This idea solves some problems, but it poses new ones. For a long time, the common view was that thetes could not afford hoplite armour and that they mainly volunteered as crews on the ships or as light-armed soldiers. Hans Van Wees, however,

---

[34] De Ste. Croix (2004: 54–5); cf. Rosivach (2002).
[35] Van Wees (2006: 375); cf. Duplouy (2014).
[36] See, now, Humphreys (2019: 109) for marriages within the kindred as a strategy to preserve family estates; on other strategies to limit fragmentation of landholdings among heirs, see pp. 147–50.
[37] For discussion, see Taylor (2016: 267–9).

has observed that hoplites did not need a full panoply to fight in the phalanx, and the minimum equipment required was not very expensive, so that even citizens of modest means could afford it.[38] In the light of this, it may well be that, from the military point of view, thetes were split up between an upper layer, able to acquire armour and to fight as hoplites, and a bottom layer, serving as oarsmen in the fleet.[39] Changes in individual wealth could obviously also bring about the opposite situation—namely a 'downgrade' towards a lower military function in the event that individuals were no longer able to afford the upkeep of a horse, to buy armour, or to devote time to military training. This might have brought about cases of former hoplites serving as oarsmen together with thetes, metics, and slaves. Among the citizen oarsmen listed in IG I³ 1032, there may well have been also citizens of a former hoplite census who were no longer able to afford hoplite armour. Since the text of the inscription does not differentiate between census classes, however, this is impossible to determine.

In the absence of regular public assessments of individual wealth, however, Athenians would have advertised a formal change in their *telos* only in the event they could rank in a higher one and only, as it seems, as a matter of personal prestige. This seems to have happened fairly rarely. Beyond the Anthemion's inscription attested in the *Ath. Pol.*, we have no evidence for individuals advertising a change in their *telos*-membership. This is easily explained by the fact that, since the *tele* had lost importance in the classical period, Athenians would not have bothered to register any change. Beyond military capacity and wealth, it is likely that what mattered for assigning individuals to the *tele* in terms of public perception was professional occupation. No matter how wealthy a skilled artisan could be, his profession would always have shown him as belonging in the census of the thetes. But, just as it was easy to lie about membership in the thetic census, loss of wealth would not be a problem when it came to accessing the magistracies reserved for the *pentakosiomedimnoi*. In all likelihood, no Athenian aiming at becoming treasurer would be asked to show that his estate did still produce 500 measures.

## Thetes, *Penia*, and the Importance of Work

The question whether thetes were the 'poor' in Athenian society brings us onto slippery ground. On the one hand, the fact that in the classical period the census classes no longer reflected actual economic conditions, and that even the landless could acquire considerable wealth, points to the fact that thetes were not

---

[38] Van Wees (2006; cf. 2018: 135–6).
[39] Cf. Van Wees (2018: 136) speaks of 'leisure-class hoplites', i.e. *zeugitai*, who were liable for conscription, and 'working-class hoplites', i.e. the wealthiest stratum of the thetes, who could afford a panoply but served in the army as volunteers. On *zeugitai* and their military function as hoplites, see also Foxhall (1997) and Van Wees (2001).

necessarily poor in economic terms. On the other hand, it has long been acknowledged in the social sciences that poverty is not simply a concept that can be understood in economic terms. To define a quantitative threshold for poverty would only answer questions concerning subsistence and survival, but it would fail to address the broader context of poverty in its social and cultural meaning.[40] When we try to establish a threshold for poverty and wealth in contemporary societies, we inevitably face the problem of deciding what we want to classify as valuable things, as commodities. In other words, we inevitably resort to subjective criteria. The difficulty entailed in defining poverty was well known to Athenian thinkers: notably, in Xenophon's *Memorabilia* 4.2.37–8, Socrates asks Euthydemus to define who the poor and the rich are. He answers that the *penetes* are those who do not have enough to pay for what they want, whereas the rich (*plousioi*) have more than enough. But this is not a good answer. Socrates notes that 'not having enough' is a relative concept, as some who have very little find it enough, whereas some others, though having large means, cannot live within them.[41]

In the attempt to provide an alternative to the absolute and quantitative approach, research in the social sciences has developed, especially from the 1960s onwards, several ways of exploring poverty. The so-called relative approach is based on observing what society itself holds to be a decent standard of life, and what it maintains to be fundamental for individual well-being beyond economic commodities.[42] More recently, the so-called capability approach puts the accent on what individuals are capable of achieving, in terms not only of economic goods but also of social relations—that is, of 'social' and 'symbolic capital' to express it in Bourdieu's terms.[43]

When it comes to classical Athens, one of the main problems ancient historians have to tackle is looking for traces of 'the poor'. Literary texts are authored by members of the elite, and elite voices reflect their own perception of what a decent life is and who the poor are. Indeed, literary texts are not the only type of evidence historians need to look at for evidence of poverty: private inscriptions provide valuable information on the values and self-perception of the working classes. However, as we will see later, inscriptions also present some problems when it comes to providing information specifically on citizen workers.

From an elite perspective, the word *penetes* indicates all those who earn their living by working, which includes the majority of the polis inhabitants. Thetes were indeed reckoned as *penetes*, but this does not mean they were poor, either in

---

[40] For an overview of the debate in the social sciences and its impact on the study of poverty in the Greek world, see Cecchet (2015: 13–31); on the Graeco-Roman world, see now Carlà-Uhink et al. (2023: 1–6). For a comparison of four different approaches to poverty, see Ruggeri Laderchi et al. (2003). For the difficulties of defining and representing poverty, see Green (2007).

[41] For discussion see Cecchet (2015: 21); Taylor (2017: 31–2).

[42] For the relative approach to poverty, see the pioneering works of Townsend (1962, 1970, 1974).

[43] For discussion of the capability approach and its application to classical Athens, see now Taylor (2017: 19–22 and *passim*), drawing from Sen (1987). On Bourdieu's forms of capital, see Bourdieu (1986).

economic terms—judging from a modern middle-class perspective—or in terms of social relations, professional life, and individual capacity to conduct a satisfactory life. The studies on wealth distribution in classical Athens carried out by Robin Osborne, Lin Foxhall, Hans van Wees, Geoffrey Kron, and Josiah Ober have convincingly shown that, in the fourth century, land in Attica was concentrated in the hands of a rather small elite, though Kron and Ober maintain Athens was quite an egalitarian society, as compared to other ancient societies.[44] Many citizens were likely to earn their living in activities outside the agricultural sector.[45] Edward Harris estimated the figures of citizen workers (presumably citizens who owned no land or plots too small for sustaining large families) at around 10,000 in the fourth century, so at about a third of the citizen population.[46] In his exploration of the non-agricultural sector in classical Athens, he identified a variety of about 170 technical specializations (not professions) that citizens, together with slaves and metics, did perform; recently, David Lewis has shown that their number was even higher.[47] The building accounts of the Erechtheion (IG I$^3$ 475–6) show a significant proportion of Athenian workers among slaves and metics.[48] The study of Peter Acton on manufacturing in classical Athens has highlighted the large involvement of male and female citizens in crafts, industry, and manufacture.[49] Similarly, Leslie Shear has pointed to the evidence for an Athenian workforce in construction works even outside Athens in the classical period, though sources are not always conclusive on the status of workers.[50]

Did the Athenians involved in manufacture and building activities regard themselves as 'poor'? Evidence from private oratory suggests that working-class Athenians shared the upper-class perspective in defining themselves as *penetes*. But the fact that they depict themselves as poor or even destitute in private speeches is often a rhetorical strategy, as cases of inheritance litigation show.[51]

---

[44] Osborne (1992: 24): 7.5% of Athenians owned c.30% of land; Foxhall (1992: 157–8): 9% owned 35% and controlled a further 10% by leasing (cf. Foxhall 2002); van Wees (2011): 4–7% (the wealthy) owned 27–43%, and 25% (the poor) owned 1–2%. On wealth and income distribution: Kron (2011: 135): 1–10% owned 31–60% of wealth; Ober (2010): 1% owned 16–18% of income (including non-citizens); cf. Ober (2015: 71–100): 23–9% owned 49–51% of income (citizens only). For recent discussion of these models, see Taylor (2017: 80–96).

[45] See the many successful examples in Acton (2014: esp. 272–3).

[46] Harris (2002b: 70). For the view that thetes owned land and that a thetic plot was sufficient to maintain a nuclear family, see Burford (1993: 186–209).

[47] Harris (2002b); Lewis (2020). Cf. also Harris and Lewis (2016: 24–5, n. 123).

[48] Erechtheion accounts (IG i$^3$ 475, 476) attest, among workers whose status is clear, the following distribution: 24 citizens, 42 metics and 20 slaves. See Harris (2002b: 70); Shear (2016: 10); Carusi (2020: 499–500); on the fact that this distribution reflects the usual structure of the building industry and not a special case, see Carusi (2020: 502).

[49] Acton (2014: 299–317).

[50] Shear (2016: 10) refers to the recruitment of Athenian labour for construction works at Epidauros (IG iv$^2$ 103. 158–61) and at Argos (Thuc. 5.82.6). However, these texts do not contain clear information about the status of the workers.

[51] See, e.g., Lys. 32.17; Is. 5.10, 11, 39; [Dem.] 44.3–4. Cecchet (2015: 218–24). On elite culture versus popular culture in democratic Athens, see Canevaro (2016).

In public forensic oratory, and in particular in the speeches delivered in the years of the Corinthian War (395–387 BCE) and in the aftermath of the Social War (357–355 BCE), speakers often resort to hyperbolic depiction of poverty. This entailed designating Athenian politicians as originally *penetes*, 'poor' and even *ptochoi* 'destitute persons, beggars' before becoming rich through 'robbery of the demos'.[52] This may explain why, in a famous passage of Aristophanes' *Plutus* of 388 BCE, the personified character of Poverty (Penia) reminds the audience that Penia is a completely different condition from Ptocheia. Differently from the *ptochos*, the *penes* does not lack the necessaries of life (Ar. *Pl.* 550-4). So, she explains, if *penia* disappeared and everyone were rich, no one would perform crafts and trades any longer. This situation would ultimately lead the city to financial ruin (Ar. *Pl.* 510-16).[53] Penia mentions activities such as hammering iron, building ships, cutting up leather, and baking bricks. The impression is that, as well as launching a warning against the public misuse of the concept of poverty, Penia also reminds the Athenians that their work is beneficial to the entire polis. It provides an encouragement to citizen workers to be proud of their technical specialism, in contrast with the dominating idea promoted in public discourse that manual work is a degrading activity.

## Voices of the Thetes

This last aspect brings us straight to the question of the self-perception of thetes—and in broader terms of Athenians—as citizen workers. It is well known that it was a common practice in the Roman world to highlight professional activity and membership in professional associations (*collegia*), both on tombstones and in votive inscriptions. It was certainly not limited to *liberti* or slaves, but a habit that Roman citizens largely shared. Catharina Lis and Hugo Soly have pointed to several attestations of Romans citizens taking pride in having improved their financial conditions and accessed the equestrian census and highest offices by means of their labour.[54] In the same volume, Nicolas Tran has identified the aspects of their professions that helped generate pride.[55] In comparison with the Roman world, such evidence in classical Athens is much less visible.[56]

---

[52] Athenian politicians as originally *penetes*: Lys. 27.9; 28.1–2; as *ptochoi*: Dem. 3.29; 8.66; 23.209, and, implicitly, Lys. 27.10. Cf. ordinary Athenians begging in Isoc. 7.83. Robbery of the demos: Lys. 27.3, 6 and 11. For discussion, see Cecchet (2015: 144–62; 2017).

[53] Orfanos (2014) interprets Penia's words as the viewpoint of the poor, after they acquired more power in the fourth century (p. 213). However, evidence for the increase in the power of ordinary Athenians in fourth-century politics is problematic; see Cecchet (2015: 133–8).

[54] Lis and Soly (2016).   [55] Tran (2016: 246–61).

[56] Indeed, the epigraphic record of Athens attests several kinds of associations and networks (Taylor 2015; 2017: 167–77). To a limited extent, the so-called *eranistai*-associations (Faraguna 2012b; Thomsen 2015) can be compared to Roman professional *collegia*. *Eranistai*-associations were

When looking for 'voices' of the thetes, we obviously turn to private inscriptions, mainly votive and funerary. The (lost) Anthemion inscription of *Ath. Pol.* 7.4, mentioned above, attests a change in *telos*, but it makes no reference to how the dedicator improved his financial condition. The text contained an epigram of two pentameters, which is quoted by the author of the *Ath. Pol.*:

Διφίλου Ἀνθεμίων τήνδ᾽ ἀνέθηκε θεοῖς,
θητικοῦ ἀντὶ τέλους ἱππάδ᾽ ἀμειψάμενος.

According to the traditional reading, this translates: 'Anthemion son of Diphilos dedicated this statue to the gods, having changed membership in the thetic census for the *telos* of the *hippeis*.' Geoffrey de Ste. Croix noted that 'it is very strange to find an Athenian gratuitously advertising his former thetic condition in commemorating his elevation to the status of Hippeus'.[57] Following a suggestion by L. H. Jeffery, he proposed an alternative reading of the text, as follows: 'having exchanged membership of the hippad *telos* for the thetic.' However, this reading of the text—which has found no followers so far—is based on an interpretation of the syntactic construction and meaning of *ameibein* that has no known parallel in Greek classical texts.[58] Anthemion is here advertising not his former thetic condition, but rather the fact that he has climbed up the social ladder and became a *hippeus*, which was probably made possible by an improvement in his economic condition. Iconography confirms this reading: the inscription was accompanied by a statue (*eikon*) of a man with a horse beside him, a powerful way of underlining the new status of cavalryman.[59] Another good example of socio-economic climbing is that of Apollodorus, the son of the freedman Pasion, who is proud of

---

not profession-based associations. Joint-dedications by professionals, such as the 'washers' relief', a mid-fourth-century dedication to the Nymphs (IG ii² 2934), can hardly be taken as a testament to the professional pride of Athenian citizens: the list of names shows the washers were mainly metics and slaves.

[57] De Ste. Croix (2004: 71). For the several problems concerning the inscription, including the fact that consecutive pentameters are very rare and the possibility that the second is a graffito added later, see Rhodes (1993: 144).

[58] De Ste. Croix (2004: 71). Cf. the syntactic construction in Hom. *Il.* 6.235–6, in which the active form of *ameibein* occurs, with the meaning of giving up something (in the accusative) to receive something (in the genitive). However, this Homeric passage is no equivalent to the Anthemion inscription, in which we have the medio-passive form of *ameibein* and the preposition *anti* accompanying the genitive. De Ste. Croix suggested other texts, which he considered parallels to this inscription: for objections, see Rhodes (1993: 144–5). Jeffery's suggestion was never published according to discussion in Rhodes (1993: 144–5) and de Ste. Croix (2004: 70–1).

[59] Following Jeffery, Geoffrey de Ste. Croix claimed that Plut. *Cim.* 5.2–3 attests a voluntary change towards a lower position in the military rank (from cavalryman to thete)—in his view a parallel case to Anthemion. As the story goes, Cimon dedicated the bridle of his horse to Athena on the Acropolis, took a shield from those dedicated to Athena, and left to serve as an *epibates* on the fleet, in order to encourage Athenians to fight at sea. However, Plutarch's story does not attest to a change of *telos*: it is in all probability an anecdote connected to Cimon's plea for a more effective maritime policy.

having achieved a high position as a wealthy Athenian undertaking liturgies for the city.[60]

Before turning to evidence for the work activities of the thetes, it should be noted that, in the face of an abundance of references—both literary and iconographic—to the role of hoplites on the battlefield, there are fewer attestations to the role of Athenian rowers in our sources. Though, as we saw, it is not possible to articulate a univocal connection between census classes and military functions, the majority of the Athenians who served as rowers, together with metics and slaves, were indeed thetes. This is not to say that the fleet itself is absent from the Athenian war discourse: Barry Strauss has collected and discussed positive mentions of it in literary texts, arguing that the fleet served as a 'school of democracy' that shaped belonging in the political community.[61] Ryan K. Balot has pointed to (lost) monuments for the victory of Salamis, attested by literary sources, which, in his view, provide 'an important indication of public recognition of the thetic contribution to the city's military success'.[62]

However, two facts should be noted: first, this evidence is fairly scanty as compared to the eulogies of hoplite–farmers, which dominate the discourse of war in public rhetoric, drama, and visual arts.[63] Second, when it comes to the fleet, praise focuses mainly on the collective entity—that is, the navy as part of the Athenian army—or historical events—such as the victory of Salamis—but we rarely have an explicit eulogy of the thete-rower, nothing remotely comparable to the eulogy of the hoplite–farmer.[64] What about voices of the thetes themselves?

Funerary inscriptions, especially beginning in the mid-fourth century, often do attest the profession of the deceased. Indeed, as Claire Taylor has pointed out,[65] this can be taken as a statement of pride in individual work or professional skills and, in broader terms, as a clue to the self-awareness of one's role in society. But who are these people? An assessment of the evidence is difficult, because it is not always possible clearly to distinguish Athenians from non-Athenians in

---

[60] In [Dem.] 45.78, Apollodorus boasts of having been more generous towards the polis than those who are citizens by birth, thereby putting emphasis on his non-Athenian origins. On Apollodorus and status anxiety, see Lape (2010: 216–19).

[61] Strauss (1996).

[62] Balot (2014: 190–1). Cf. his reading of Lyc. 1.69–71 as a celebration of the sailors' role in the battle of Salamis (p. 193).

[63] Similarly, representations of triremes are fairly rare in sculpture, with the exception of the famous Lenormant Relief (Athens, Acropolis Museum 1339, c.410 BCE). They are more common in vascular painting, but scenes of hoplitic combats are far more frequent. On the absence of representations of the navy in the iconography of the Athenian state burial, see Stupperich (1994: 97). On the ideological treatment of lower-class citizens in war commemoration, see also Pritchard (2010: 36–8) and Balot (2014).

[64] See, e.g., the eulogy of the hoplite–farmer in Eur. Or. 917–22. In some cases, as Ar. Eq. 595–610, we can presume an elites' appropriation of 'thetic pride' to the credit of their own class: the chorus of cavalrymen proudly recalls how their horses eagerly leaped aboard the triremes and rowed to Corinth. I wish to thank Tony Edwards for drawing my attention to this passage.

[65] Taylor (2017: 206; for discussion of funerary inscriptions, see pp. 202–11).

private inscriptions, while, as Michele Faraguna has pointed out, this distinction is much clearer in public documents.[66] Despite lack of uniformity in onomastic practice, however, in private inscriptions too citizens are often identified by the presence of the patronymic or the demotic. But evidence for citizens openly advertising their profession as artisans on tombstones is scanty. There are indeed some cases: one is the fourth-century funerary stele of Bacchios son of Amphis(—?) (*IG* ii² 6320). Bacchios' workshop produced Panathenaic amphorae. The inscription, two awkward elegiac couplets, reads: 'Of those who blend earth, water, fire into one by art, Bacchios was judged by all Hellas first, for natural gifts; and in every contest appointed by the city he won the crown.'[67] Indeed, we have here no average artisan. Bacchios was a high-profile professional: his workshop received a public commission from the city to produce objects of significant religious, symbolic—and certainly economic—value. The deceased recalls his victories in all the public competitions—further proof of the special recognition of his talent granted by the community. Recently, Edward Harris has made a strong case for the fact that professionals such as sculptors and doctors were granted recognition in the Greek *poleis*, but he also pointed to the fact that they were somewhat exceptional cases, which stood apart from ordinary craftsmen.[68]

Among dedications, we have more cases of citizens mentioning (or representing with a relief) their activity as professionals. Some of them are women: a significant case is provided by a votive inscription from the Acropolis, dating to the period of the Persian Wars, issued by the washerwoman Smikythe (*IG* I³ 794). Some scholars maintain Smikythe was Athenian,[69] but the absence of patronymic makes this assumption not certain. Smikythe was a πλύντρια, she laundered clothes for her clients. One other case is represented by a tombstone found in the deme of Acharnae, dating to the first half of the fourth century, representing the Athenian Phanostrate, daughter (?) of a man from the deme of Melite (*IG* II² 6873).[70] Phanostrate was a midwife and a doctor (μαῖα καὶ ἰατρὸς). One famous case is that of Dionysios and his children, who, in the early fourth century, dedicate an inscription with the relief of their workshop—or, at least, the workshop in which they worked as cobblers—to the hero Kallistephanos (Agora I 7396). Moreover, among the famous potters and painters of the late sixth and early fifth centuries, who left signatures on vases and dedications to the gods, we do have some cases of Athenian citizens: the famous painter Euphronios, who, in the first half of the fifth century, dedicated an inscription to Athena in which he clearly

---

[66] See Faraguna (2014: 165–83; on tombstones, p. 168). For example, Smikros, the tanner (Akr. 6972, *IG* I³ 646), Polyxenos (EM 6535, *IG* I³ 905) and Simon (EM 6248, *IG* I³ 616), both fullers, and the shoemaker Xanthippos (British Museum 628 1805.7-3.183) were perhaps Athenian citizens, but there is no conclusive evidence since patronymics are not provided.
[67] Trans. Sparkes (1991: 67–8).
[68] Harris (2020: 29–67, esp. 50).
[69] Brock 1994, Hochscheid 2020.
[70] However, see Kosmopoulou (2001: 299) for the possibility that Phanostrate was a slave.

identifies himself as a vase painter (*kerameus*, IG I³ 824), was probably an Athenian citizen; certainly Athenian was the potter Nikias, son of Hermokles.[71] Some craftsmen's signatures on Attic pottery found outside Attica attest the ethnic *Athenaios* as a complement of the painter's name.[72] These cases belong generally to the group of craftsmen and artists also known as 'the Pioneers' whose fame reached well beyond the borders of Attica. But in the major part of the inscriptions attesting to professions—of any kind—we rarely have clear identifiers of citizen status. Attic names alone are not conclusive evidence: children of metics and slaves were often given Athenian names, as a means of integration. The absence of any patronymic or demotic, however, is likely to be an indicator of non-citizen status.[73]

We do have, by contrast, abundant evidence for foreigners (metics and slaves) showing pride in their profession: so, we read in *IG* i³ 1361, from the second half of the fifth century BCE: 'This is the beautiful tomb of Manes, the son of Orymas, the best of Phrygians in spacious Athens. "By Zeus, I never saw any woodcutter better than I." He died in the war.' Manes is proud of his skills as a *hylotomos*, woodcutter, to the point of mentioning his professional talent on his gravestone.[74] But we should note that he also makes it clear he was no Athenian. He proudly stresses his ethnic origin—he is a Phrygian, and, as he says, one of the best among them. In a fourth-century votive inscription to Athena Ergane (*IG* ii² 4334), a woman, Melinna, appears to be proud to have raised her children by virtue of her labour. The name is not attested elsewhere in Attica; the absence of a patronymic suggests that Melinna was probably not a citizen.

In her examination of Attic funerary stelai of female professionals, Angeliki Kosmopoulou noted that, in most funerary carved stelae of wet nurses (*titthai*), the deceased women are represented without clear iconographic signs of servile status. They are often wearing a chiton and a mantle, which are also worn by female citizens (*astai*) on other memorials.[75] But some features of their tombstones often reveal foreign origins. In some cases, we find references to foreign geographic provenance (ethnics), and the recurring word *chreste* on many of these stelae suggests they were slaves. There are, of course, some exceptions. In the funerary reliefs representing female wool-workers we do find some cases of *astai*—that is, women of citizen status. Athenian origin is shown by their patronymics, in association with iconographic details, such as clothing. Such is the case with *IG* ii² 7315, from the mid-fourth century BCE, in which Kleonike, daughter of Diagoras, from the deme Prospalta is represented sitting at a loom. Kleonike was

---

[71] Williams et al. (2009: 309–10).  [72] Williams et al. (2009: 310).
[73] On this, see Faraguna (2014: 172).
[74] Cf. the woman Phrygia, breadseller (ἀρτόπολ[ις]) in IG i³ 546. On the identity of Manes, see Vlassopoulos (forthcoming).
[75] Kosmopoulou (2001: 289). For some important corrections to Kosmopoulou's discussion of the evidence, see Kennedy (2014: 157, n. 61).

an Athenian, as indicated by the name of the father and the demotic: *Κλεωνίκη Διαγόρου Προσπαλτίου*. She was probably conducting wool-working mostly as a domestic activity for her family. We cannot rule out the possibility that she might also have worked upon commission, as in the case of the women of the family of Aristarchos described in Xenophon's *Memorabilia*.

Nonetheless, we should be wary about generalizing from a small number of cases. We should be wary too about assuming that, within the working classes, citizens and non-citizens alike shared the same attitude towards work, manual labour, and free time. Kostas Vlassopoulos has pointed to the existence of 'free spaces' in the polis—namely, spaces such as the agora, the workshop, and the ship, where several groups (citizens, metics, slaves) lived and worked side by side. These spaces contributed to blurring the boundaries between status groups and to creating fluid identities.[76] This perspective has been pushed further: Deborah Kamen has argued that it was the Greek binary thought system that stressed the dichotomy between citizen and non-citizen, while, in fact, the boundaries between status groups were fluid.[77] Rebecca Kennedy has reminded us that, among the female non-citizen population, it is often impossible to distinguish between metics and slaves.[78] However, while it is certainly true that the reality was more complex than a binary system, the boundary between citizens and non-citizens did indeed matter in many respects, including access to ruling bodies, landownership, public pay, and other rights. The notion of citizenship itself, together with aspects such as autochthony, ethnic origin, and political participation in the government of the polis, remained important factors defining Athenian identity.[79] Different status groups (citizens, metics, slaves) in Athens may well have defined and perceived their role and position in the polis in different ways. Private speeches provide us with clues that the attitude to manual labour and the social and psychological impact of *penia* were not the same for citizens and non-citizens. In Demosthenes' speech *Against Euboulides* (Dem. 57), Euxitheus defends himself against the accusation that he is not a citizen. The context is the scrutiny of the civic lists conducted in 346/5 BCE.[80] A fellow-demesman, named Euboulides, accused Euxitheus of being the son of a non-Athenian woman, thus of being illegally inscribed in the list of the citizens.[81] Apparently, the only evidence that Euboulides produced was the fact that Nikarete, mother of Euxitheus, had recently worked as a ribbon-seller and, in the past, as a wet nurse. These

---

[76] Vlassopoulos (2007: 33–52). Along the same line, Sobak (2015: 669–712). For the place of metics (including women) in polis-religion, see Wijma (2014).
[77] Kamen (2013: 113–14 and *passim*).  [78] Kennedy (2014: 3).
[79] See Lape (2010) on race ideology as a foundation of citizen identity at Athens. For a discussion of Athenian citizenship, see Blok (2017). On the construction of identity (not only civic identity) in the Attic orators, see Filonik et al. (2019).
[80] About the scrutiny introduced by the decree of Demophilus, see Aeschin. 1.77, 1.86.
[81] On the fact that the legal status of women was often contested because they were not registered in the demes, see Kennedy, this volume.

activities were usually performed by slaves, and for Euboulides they were sufficient proof of non-citizen status. So Euxitheus explains to the jurors that his mother was indeed Athenian, and that she had married a poor man (*penes*). Nikarete had had a difficult life: her husband was captured and sold into slavery during the Dekeleian War (Dem. 57.18). Being away from Athens for what was probably a long period of time before joining Thrasyboulos (Dem. 57.42), he lost his Athenian accent, a detail that probably contributed to making it more difficult for him and his wife to integrate socially. While the husband was away at war, Nikarete was compelled to work as a wet nurse and, more recently, as a seller in the Agora. Euxitheus notes that in his own day many Athenian women were still working as nurses.[82] The fact that one has to work, he claims, is not *per se* evidence of a servile status.

It is clear that Euxitheus' appeal to the jurors is not a statement of pride—very different from Bacchios' and Manes' references to their profession, and from Melinna's pride in having raised her children alone. Euxitheus' appeal is almost an *excusatio*. His perspective on labour lines up with the elite discourse that we find in authors such as Plato, Aristotle, and Xenophon. Euxitheus does not present a counterargument to the elite's view on labour; rather he attempts to adjust it to the reality of life: Athenians must resort to 'humble jobs' when they have no choice.

As we know, private speeches do not directly preserve voices of the working classes. Even in the case of speeches such as *Against Euboulides*, what we have is the literary and published version of the speech that a professional speechwriter produced for his client. And a client such as Euxitheus was, after all, well off enough to hire a speechwriter. Poorer Athenians delivered their own speeches themselves. We do not know what arguments they used, though the surviving examples of successful speeches suggest they might have deployed similar strategies for eliciting the pity of the jurors. When references to work activities occur, they are usually part of the accusation strategy, or they are made in reply to an accusation. For example, the speaker of Lysias 24, the invalid who claims his right to a state pension, runs a business in (or near) the Agora. The plaintiff has claimed that this business is very successful and that the invalid is neither disabled—as he is able to sit on a horse—nor poor. The defendant makes only a few short references to his *techne*, and he never makes it clear what it is.[83] He explains that, having no inheritance from his father, this trade is his only source of income, and that he cannot afford to own a slave. Rebutting the allegation that his workplace is the meeting point of bad people (24.19: *ponerous anthropous*), he notes that it is

---

[82] Dem. 57.35. On Euxitheus' rhetoric strategy, see Lape (2010: 203–15) and, now, Kasimis (2018: 148–67). On female work in classical Athens, see Brock (1994) and Kennedy (2014) (on metic women).

[83] The invalid mentions his trade as *techne* at 24.4–6, and at 24.19–20 he seems to imply he has a shop in the Agora.

not unusual for Athenians to pay a call at a perfumer's, barber's, or shoemaker's shop, especially those near the Agora. Addressing the *bouleutai* who are judging the case—this is a *dokimasia*-speech—he claims that even they may well have been among the Athenians attending such places (Lys. 24.20). From this, we can presume the speaker owns a shop. But this is all we can guess about his work. The vague character of the references to his profession is, in part, explained by the necessity of minimizing the success of his business, and convincing the court that he is poor. At the same time, however, his choice also speaks to the fact that he has no interest in putting much emphasis on his work as a remedy against poverty. Or, at least, that he did not consider it a good argument for eliciting the sympathy of the audience.

One last case: in the Pseudo-Demosthenic *Against Leochares* we read about inheritance litigation. In order to highlight that his family is poor and to add some pathos to the argument, the speaker points to his father, who is also before the court, and on whose behalf the speech is made. He describes him as a clear example of a poor man and a private citizen, claiming that the jurors can see the 'manifests signs' (*phaneras tas marturias*) of poverty (*tes penias*) and of being a private citizen (*tou idiotes einai*) ([Dem.] 44.4). This is probably an invitation to consider his poor clothing, together with the broader picture: Aristodemus is a *kerux*, a public crier, working at the Piraeus and in the Agora. Yet again, as in the case of Euxitheus' mother Nikarete and the invalid of Lysias 24, Aristodemus' profession is described as something the jurors should pity, rather than admire or appreciate.

## Conclusion

In the classical period there was no correlation between membership in a census class, wealth, and military function. By the fourth century, the Solonic *tele* had become obsolete, and this is the reason Athenians disregarded the thetic ban in politics. The word 'thete' itself is only sporadically attested. Some hints in sources, however, suggest that the word evoked proximity with servile status.

Court speakers referring to their own condition as 'poor' never describe themselves as 'thetes', but they rather prefer to depict themselves as *penetes* or even, hyperbolically, *ptochoi*. This might be because the word 'thetes' was evocative of servile status or of restrictions in access to offices, but it was also probably related to the fact that thetes were not poor in economic terms. Especially in the vivid economic life of fourth-century Athens, they could acquire wealth in a variety of professions, from trade to industry, crafts and banking. Thus, given the large number of Athenians working in these sectors, and following Perikles' positive words on poverty in Thucydides' *epitaphios logos*, one would expect to have several attestations in private oratory and inscriptions of working-class Athenians taking pride in their status as workers. But such expectations do not match reality. No doubt, a skilled Athenian artisan could take pride in his successful business, as Bacchios' inscription shows. But where, in the epigraphic record, are all the shoemakers, carpenters and other craftsmen that, according to Plato and Xenophon, filled the Athenian assembly? Manifestations of professional pride specifically from Athenian citizens are fairly rare. The arguments of court speakers about their own and their relatives' work can hardly be taken as manifestos of pride. Similarly, in funerary inscriptions, the majority of the deceased who mention their professions are metics and slaves. There are some exceptions, but only a very few stressed professional pride together with Athenian identity.

In light of this, we can possibly read Penia's appeal in Aristophanes' *Plutus* not only as a warning against utopian ideas about wealth but also as an appeal to 'thetic pride', encouraging Athenians to raise their voices against the negative view of banausic and manual work that dominated public discourse. This appeal to the audience attests indeed to the existence of a counter-discourse on *penia* and labour, a discourse alternative to the elite perspective. But it also suggests that this discourse was flowing underground, and that it needed encouragement to be spoken out aloud. While we can comprehend the reason for which 'thete' is a word that remains in the shadow, we will remain wondering about the silence of Athenian thetes in the broader context.

## Acknowledgements

I would like to thank the editors of this book for their useful comments on the several drafts of this chapter and the anonymous reviewers of OUP for their suggestions. This chapter is the improved version of the paper delivered in 2017 in Oxford: my thanks go to the participants in the workshop *Subordinated Voices in Archaic and Classical Greece* organized by S. Gartland and D. Tandy, who provided lively discussion and helpful critiques. My friends and colleagues at the University of Milan also gave precious feedback: I am particularly grateful to Michele Faraguna.

## Works Cited

Accattino, P., and M. Curnis (2013) (eds). *Aristotele, la Politica. Libro III*. Rome.

Acton, P. (2014). *Poiesis:. Manufacturing in Classical Athens*. Oxford.

Balot, R. K. (2014). *Courage in the Democratic Polis: Ideology and Critique in Classical Athens*. Oxford.

Bertelli, L., M. Canevaro, and M. Curnis (2022) (eds). *Aristotele, la Politica, Libri VII–VIII*. Rome.

Blok, J. (2017). *Citizenship in Classical Athens*. Cambridge.

Blösel, W. (2014). 'Zensusgrenzen für die Ämterbekleidung im klassischen Griechenland: Wie groß war der verfassungsrechtliche Abstand gemäßigter Oligarchien von der athenischen Demokratie?', in W. Blösel, W. Schmitz, G. Seelentag, and J. Timmer (eds), *Grenzen politischer Partizipation im klassischen Griechenland*, 71–93. Stuttgart.

Bourdieu, P. (1986). 'The Forms of Capital', in J. Richardson (ed.), *Handbook of Theory and Research for the Sociology of Education*. New York.

Bravo, B. (1992). 'I *Thetes* ateniesi e la storia della parola *thes*', *Annali della Facoltà di Lettere e Filosofia di Perugia. 1. Studi classici*, 15–16: 69–97.

Brock, R. (1994). 'The Labour of Women in Classical Athens', *Classical Quarterly*, 44: 336–46.

Burford, A. (1993). *Land and Labour in the Greek World*. Baltimore.

Canevaro, M. (2013). *The Documents in the Attic Orators: Laws and Decrees in the Public Speeches of the Demosthenic Corpus*. Oxford.

Canevaro, M. (2016). 'The Popular Culture of the Athenian Institutions: "Authorized" Popular Culture and "Unauthorized" Elite Culture in Classical Athens', in L. Grig (ed.), *Popular Culture in the Ancient World*, 39–65. Cambridge.

Carlà-Uhink, F., L. Cecchet, and C. Machado (2023) (eds). *Poverty in Ancient Greece and Rome: Realities and Discourses*. London.

Cartledge, P., E. Cohen, and L. Foxhall (2002) (eds). *Money, Labour and Land: Approaches to the Economies of Ancient Greece*. London.

Carusi, C. (2020). 'L'organizzazione dell'industria delle costruzioni nell'Atene di età classica', *Annali della Scuola Normale Superiore di Pisa*, 12: 485–517.

Cecchet, L. (2013). 'Poverty as Argument in Athenian Forensic Speeches', *Ktèma*, 38: 53–65.

Cecchet, L. (2015). *Poverty in Athenian Public Discourse: From the Eve of the Peloponnesian War to the Rise of Macedonia*. Historia Einzelschriften 239. Stuttgart.

Cecchet, L. (2017). 'The Use and Abuse of Poverty: Aristophanes, *Plutus* 415–610 and the Public Speeches of the Corinthian War', *Hormos*, 9: 100–25.

Christ, M. R. (2001). 'Conscription of Hoplites in Classical Athens', *Classical Quarterly*, 51: 398–422.

Coin-Longeray, S. (2014). *Poésie de la richesse et de la pauvreté: Étude du vocabulaire de la richesse et de la pauvreté dans la poésie grecque antique, d'Homère à Aristophane*: ἄφενος, ὄλβος, πλοῦτος, πενία, πτωχός. Mémoires du Centre Jean Palerne, 38. Saint-Etienne.

Curnis M., and G. Besso (2011). *Aristotele, la Politica, Libro I*. Rome.

Curnis, M., M. E. De Luna, and C. Zizza (2016) (eds). *Aristotele, la Politica, Libri V–VI*. Rome.

de Ste. Croix, G. E. M. (2004). *Athenian Democratic Origins and Other Essays*, ed. D. Harvey and R. Parker with the assistance of P. Thonemann. Oxford.

Dreizehnter, A. (1981). 'Zur Entstehung der Lohnarbeit und deren Terminologie im Altgriechischen', in E. Welskopf (ed.), *Soziale Typenbegriffe im alten Griechenland und ihr Fortleben in den Sprachen der Welt*, 269–81. Berlin.

Duplouy, A. (2014). 'Les Prétendues classes censitaires soloniennes: À propos de la citoyenneté athénienne archaïque', *Annales HSS*, 69/3: 957–98.

Faraguna, M. (2012a). '*Hektemoroi, isomoiria, seisachtheia*: Ricerche recenti sulle riforme economiche di Solone', *Dike*, 15: 171–93.

Faraguna, M. (2012b). 'Diritto, economia, società: Riflessioni su *eranos* tra età omerica e mondo ellenistico', in *Transferts culturels et droits dans le monde grecque et hellénistique. Publications de la Sorbonne*, 129–53. Paris.

Faraguna, M. (2014). 'Citizens, Non-Citizens, and Slaves: Identification Methods in Classical Greece', in M. Depauw and S. Coussement (eds), *Identifiers and Identification Methods in the Ancient World*, 165–83. Leuven.

Faraguna, M. (2021). 'I registri dei cittadini', in L. Boffo and M. Faraguna (eds), *Le poleis e i loro archivi: Studi su pratiche documentarie, istituzioni e società nell'antichità greca*, 151–75. Trieste.

Filonik, J., B. Griffith-Williams, and J. Kucharski (2019) (eds). *The Making of Identities in Athenian Oratory*. London.

Foxhall, L. (1992). 'The Control of the Attica Landscape', in Wells (1992: 155–60).

Foxhall, L. (1997). 'A View from the Top: Evaluating the Solonian Property Classes', in L. Mitchel and P. J. Rhodes (eds), *The Development of the Polis in Archaic Greece*, 113–36. London.

Foxhall, L. (2002). 'Access to Resources in Classical Greece: The Egalitarianism of the Polis in Practice', in Cartledge et al. (2002: 209–20).

Fuks A. (1984 [1951]). '*Kolonos Misthios*. Labour Exchange in Classical Athens', *Eranos*, 49 (1951): 171–3; repr. in A. Fuks, *Social Conflict in Ancient Greece* (Jerusalem, 1984), 303–5.

Galbois E., and S. Rougier-Blanc (2014) (eds). *La Pauvreté en Grèce ancienne: Formes, représentations, enjeux*, Scripta Antica 57. Bordeaux.

Giangiulio, M. (2016). 'Due paradossi della democrazia di Atene', in F. De Luise (ed.), *Legittimazione del potere, autorità della legge: un dibattito antico. Atti del seminario (Trento, 30 settembre–1 ottobre 2015)*, 35–51. Trento.

Gomme, A. W. (1970). *A Historical Commentary on Thucydides. Vol. IV: Books V. 25–VII.* Oxford.

Green, M. (2007). 'Representing Poverty and Attacking Representations: Perspectives on Poverty from Social Anthropology', in D. Hulme and L. Toye (eds), *Understanding Poverty and Well-Being*, 24–45. London.

Guía, M. V., and J. Gallego (2010). 'Athenian Zeugitai and the Solonian Census Classes: New Reflections and Perspectives', *Historia*, 59: 257–81.

Harris, E. M. (2002a). 'Did Solon Abolish Debt-Bondage?', *Classical Quarterly*, 52: 415–30.

Harris, E. M. (2002b). 'Workshop, Marketplace and Household: The Nature of Technical Specialisation in Classical Athens and its Influence on Economy and Society', in Cartledge et al. (2002: 67–99).

Harris, E. M. (2020). 'Many Ancient Greek Occupations, but Few Professions', in Stewart et al. (2020: 29–67).

Harris, E. M., and D. M. Lewis (2016). 'Introduction: Markets in Classical and Hellenistic Greece', in E. M. Harris, D. M. Lewis, and M. Woolmer (eds), *The Ancient Greek Economy: Markets, Households and City-States*, 1–37. Cambridge.

Helmer, É. (2020). (ed.). *Mendiants et mendicité en Grèce ancienne*. Paris.

Hignett, C. (1952). *A History of the Athenian Constitution to the End of the Fifth Century BC*. Oxford.

Hochscheid, H. (2020). 'Professionalism in Archaic and Classical Sculpture in Athens: The Price of *Technē*', in E. Stewart, E. Harris, and D. Lewis (eds), *Skilled Labour and Professionalism in Ancient Greece and Rome*, 205–29. Cambridge.

Hornblower, S. (2008). *A Commentary on Thucydides: Volume III: Books 5.25–8.109*. Oxford.

Humphreys, S. (2019). *Kinship in Ancient Athens: An Anthropological Analysis*. Oxford.

Jacquemin, A. (2013). 'D'une condition sociale à un statut politique, les ambiguïtés du thète', *Ktèma*, 38: 7–13.

Kamen, D. (2013). *Status in Classical Athens*. Princeton.

Kasimis, D. (2018). *The Perpetual Immigrant and the Limits of Athenian Democracy*. Cambridge.

Kennedy, R. F. (2014). *Immigrant Women in Athens: Gender, Ethnicity, and Citizenship in the Classical City*. London.

Kosmopoulou, A. (2001). 'Working Women: Female Professionals on Classical Attic Gravestones', *Annual of the British School at Athens*, 96: 281–319.

Kron, G. (2011). 'The Distribution of Wealth in Athens in Comparative Perspective', *Zeitschrift für Papyrologie und Epigrafik*, 179: 129–38.

Lape, S. (2010). *Race and Citizen Identity in the Classical Athenian Democracy*. Cambridge.

Leão, D., and P. J. Rhodes (2015). *The Laws of Solon: A New Edition with Introduction, Translation and Commentary*. London.

Lenfant, D. (2013). 'Intégrés ou dénoncés: la place faite aux pauvres dans les discours grecs sur la démocratie', *Ktèma*, 38: 37–51.

Lewis, D. (2020). 'Labour Specialization in the Athenian Economy: Occupational Hazards', in Stewart et al. (2020: 129–74).

Lis, C., and H. Soly (2016). 'Work, Identity and Self-Representation in the Roman Empire and the West-European Middle Ages: Different Interplays between the Social and the Cultural', in Verboven and Laes (2016: 262–90).

Moggi, M. (2005). 'Demos in Erodoto e Tucidide', in G. Urso (ed.), *Popolo e potere nel mondo antico*, 11–24. Pisa.

Nagle, B. (2006). *The Household as the Foundation of Aristotle's Polis*. Cambridge.

Ober, J. (1996). *The Athenian Revolution: Essays on Ancient Greek Democracy and Political Theory*. Princeton.

Ober, J. (2010). 'Wealthy Hellas', *Transactions of the American Philological Association*, 140: 241–86.

Ober, J. (2015). *The Rise and Fall of Classical Greece*. Princeton.

Ober, J., and C. Hedrick (1996) (eds). *Dēmokratia: A Converstion on Democracies, Ancient and Modern*. Princeton.

Orfanos, Ch. (2014). 'Le Ploutos d'Aristophane: Un éloge de la pauvreté?', in E. Galbois and S. Rougier-Blanc (eds), *La Pauvreté en Grèce ancienne: Formes, représentations, enjeux*, Scripta Antica 57, 213–22. Bordeaux.

Osborne, R. (1992). 'Is it a Farm? The Definition of Agricultural Sites and Settlements in Ancient Greece', in Wells (1992: 21–8).

Osborne, R., and P. J. Rhodes (2017). *Greek Historical Inscriptions 478–404 BC*. Oxford (OR).

Pritchard, D. M. (1998). 'Thetes, Hoplites and the Athenian Imaginary', in T. Hillard, R. Kearsley, C. Nixon, and A. Nobles (eds), *Ancient History in a Modern University*, i. *The Ancient Near East, Greece and Rome*, 121–7. Grand Rapids, MI.

Pritchard, D. M. (2010). *War, Democracy and Culture in Classical Athens*. Cambridge.

Raaflaub, K. (1996). 'Equalities and Inequalities in Athenian Democracy', in Ober and Hedrick (1996: 139–74).

Raaflaub, K. (1997). 'The Thetes and Democracy', in I. Morros and K. Raaflaub (eds), *Democracy 2500? Questions and Challenges*, 87–104. Dubuque, IA.

Raubitschek, A. (1943). 'Greek Inscriptions: Note on the Epistatai of the Athena Promachos Statue', *Hesperia*, 2: 12–88.

Rhodes, P. J. (1993). *A Commentary on the Aristotelian Athenaion Politeia*, 2nd edn. Oxford.

Rosivach, V. (2002). 'The Requirements for the Solonic Classes in Aristotle AP. 7.4', *Hermes*, 130: 36–47.

Rosivach, V. (2012). 'The Thetes in Thucydides 6.43.1', *Hermes*, 140: 131–9.

Ruggeri Laderchi, C., R. Saith, and F. Stewart (2003). 'Does it Matter that We do not Agree on the Definition of Poverty? A Comparison of Four Approaches', *Oxford Development Studies*, 31: 243–74.

Scheidel, W. (2002). 'The Hireling and the Slave: A Transatlantic Perspective', in Cartledge et al. (2002: 175–84).

Schmitz, W. (1995). 'Reiche und Gleiche: Timokratische Gliederung und demokratische Gleichheit der athenischen Bürger im 4. Jahrhundert v. Chr.', in W. Eder (ed.), *Die athenische Demokratie im 4. Jahrhundert v. Chr. Vollendung oder Verfall einer Verfassungsform? Akten eines Symposiums 3.–7. August 1992 in Bellagio*, 573–97. Stuttgart.

Sen, A. (1987). *The Standard of Living*. Cambridge.

Shear, T. L., Jr (2016). *Trophies of Victory: Public Building in Periklean Athens*. Princeton.

Sobak, R. (2015). 'Sokrates among the Shoemakers', *Hesperia*, 84: 669–712.

Sparkes, B. A. (1991). *Greek Pottery: An Introduction*. Manchester.

Stewart, E., E. Harris, and D. Lewis (2020) (eds). *Skilled Labour and Professionalism in Ancient Greece and Rome*. Cambridge.

Strauss, B. (1996). 'The Athenian Trireme, School of Democracy', in Ober and Hedrick (1996: 313–25).

Stupperich, R. (1994). 'The Iconography of the Athenian State Burials in the Classical Period', in W. Coulsen (ed.), *The Archaeology of Athens and Attica under the Democracy*, 93–103. Oxford.

Taylor, C. (2015). 'Social Networks and Social Mobility in Fourth-Century Athens', in C. Taylor and K. Vlassopoulos (eds), *Communities and Networks in the Ancient Greek World*, 35–53. Oxford.

Taylor, C. (2016). 'Social Dynamics in Fourth-Century Athens: Poverty and Standards of Living', in C. Tiersch (ed.), *Die Athenische Demokratie im 4. Jahrhundert. Zwischen Modernisierung und Tradition*, 261–77. Stuttgart.

Taylor, C. (2017). *Poverty, Wealth and Well-Being: Experiencing* Penia *in Democratic Athens*. Oxford.

Thomsen, Ch. A. (2015). 'The *Eranistai* of Classical Athens', *Greek, Roman and Byzantine Studies*, 55: 154–75.

Townsend, P. (1962). 'The Meaning of Poverty', *British Journal of Sociology*, 13: 210–27.

Townsend, P. (1970). *The Concept of Poverty: Working Papers on Methods of Investigation and Life-Styles of the Poor in Different Countries*. London.

Townsend, P. (1974). 'Poverty as Relative Deprivation: Resources and Style of Living', in D. Wedderburn (ed.), *Poverty, Inequality and Class Structure*, 15–42. Cambridge.

Tran, N. (2016). 'Ars and Doctrina: The Socioeconomic Identity of Roman Skilled Workers (First Century BC–Third Century AD)', in Verboven and Laes (2016: 246–61).

van Wees, H. (2001). 'The Myth of the Middle-Class Army: Military and Social Status in Ancient Athens', in T. Bekker Nielsen and L. Hannestad (eds), *War as Cultural and Social Force*, 45–71. Copenhagen.

van Wees, H. (2006). 'Mass and Elite in Solon's Athens: The Property Classes Revisited', in J. Blok and A. Lardinois (eds), *Solon of Athens: New Historical and Philological Approaches*, 351–89. Leiden.

van Wees, H. (2011). 'Demetrius and Draco: Athens' Property Classes and Population in and before 317 BC', *Journal of Hellenic Studies*, 131: 95–114.

van Wees, H. (2018). 'Citizens and Soldiers in Archaic Athens', in A. Duplouy and R. Brock (eds), *Defining Citizenship in Archaic Greece*, 103–43. Oxford.

Verboven, K., and Laes, Ch. (2016) (eds). *Work, Labour, and Professions in the Roman World*. Leiden.

Vlassopoulos, K. (2007). 'Free Spaces: Identity, Experience and Democracy in Classical Athens', *Classical Quarterly*, 57: 33–52.

Vlassopoulos, K. (forthcoming). 'An entangled history of the Peloponnesian War', In S. Gartland and R. Osborne (eds), *Reassessing the Peloponnesian War*.

Wells, B. (1992) (ed.). *Agriculture in Ancient Greece*. Stockholm.

Wijma, S. (2014). *Embracing the Immigrant: The Participation of Metics in Athenian Polis Religion (5th–4th century BC)*. Historia Einzelschriften 233. Stuttgart.

Williams, D., J. Oakley, and O. Palagia (2009) (eds). 'Picturing Potters and Painters', in *Athenian Potters and Painters*, ii. 306–17. Oxford.

# 5
# The Athenian Working Class
## Scale, Nature, and Development

*Hans van Wees*

## Preface

'Working class' is a term rarely used with reference to ancient Athens, and for most people probably evokes a class of small but independent working farmers, who are commonly imagined as the majority, or at any rate the largest single group, in any ancient Greek community.[1] This seems to me a profoundly mistaken image of Athenian society. The single largest group of free Athenians were those who did not have enough land or other assets to make an independent living and therefore relied partly or wholly on wage labour. It is this majority that should be called the 'working class', and I believe I can show that it formed some 90 per cent of the free population around 600 BCE and probably not much less than 50 per cent in 322 BCE.

Importantly, this chapter shows that most of the Athenian working class experienced highly exploitative conditions for a wage of only one-sixth of the crops they cultivated on their employers' farms. Economic growth and social reform in the sixth century meant that a substantial 'middle class' of independent working producers emerged and that in classical Athens only about 50 per cent of citizens were still reliant on wages, now earned from casual or seasonal labour. Contrary to recent claims that wage labour was exceptionally well rewarded in classical Athens, this chapter argues that the Athenian working class continued to earn only a bare subsistence.

Crucial evidence is provided by the Athenian property–class system, which is well attested in literary texts and some inscriptions but has been curiously sidelined in most work on the distribution of wealth at Athens, at least in part presumably because it points to a social structure quite different from the common model. Here, I venture to suggest simply that the common model is derived from

---

[1] E.g. de Ste. Croix (1981: 114, 209): 'peasants and other independent producers...formed the actual majority of the total population'; Hanson (1995: e.g. 208, 406): one-third to half of population are 'yeoman farmers', with *c*.4 ha (10 acres of land); Hanson (2013: 260): 'nearly 20,000 middling farm owners'. By contrast, Ober (1989: 129–30) accepts that 'some' of the poorest 21,000 citizens (70%) in fourth-century Athens made a living from wage labour.

elite sources with a narrow view of the world in which the lowest classes barely register, whereas the property–class system, together with a few other quantitative data, provides us with the bigger picture and reveals that a large section of society fell below the radar of most of our sources.[2]

## 'Wage Labourers' as a Property Class

In Athens, the highest of the four property classes was called *pentakosiomedimnoi* and was named in at least one Solonian law (frs 74/3ab L–R = *Ath. Pol.* 8.1; 47.1). The name itself spelled out their property qualification: 'five-hundred-*medimnoi* men.' One *medimnos* of barley—Attica's major grain crop—weighed 1 talent, i.e. 27.5 kg,[3] and 500 *medimnoi* accordingly amounted to 13,750 kg. Modern records show that between 1911 and 1950 the average barley yield in Attica was 800 kg per hectare (ha), and since in the latter half of that period the figures were climbing because of the use of chemical fertilizer, this seems the highest conceivable average for ancient Attica.[4] To produce 500 *medimnoi*, therefore, one needed at least 17.2 ha under cultivation, and, assuming biennial fallowing (a practice regarded as the norm by our sources),[5] an estate of 34.4 ha (85 acres), or 378 *plethra*, to use the ancient measure. The lowest land price we know from classical Athens was 50 drachmas per *plethron*,[6] so that in fourth-century Attica the minimum value of the minimum amount of land needed to produce 500 *medimnoi* of barley was 18,900 drachmas. Adding the value of a house and slaves, this corresponds closely to the property value indicated by classical sources as the threshold for inclusion in the 'liturgical class', the richest of the rich, *c*.18,000–24,000 drachmas (3–4 talents).[7] While using different criteria, Solon thus set the boundary for the highest socio-economic group at the same level as it stood in fourth-century Athens.

---

[2] As in previous discussion of the subject, I build on the insights of Foxhall (1997).

[3] As shown by the Grain Tax Law of 374/3 BCE (RO no. 26.21–5, with pp. 124–5); notably lower than the previously accepted weight of 33.55 kg (Foxhall and Forbes 1982, used in, e.g., van Wees 2001: 49).

[4] Gallant (1991: 77). It is important that Gallant's statistics show a much higher barley yield (793.7 kg/ha) than wheat yield (629.1 kg/ha) in Attica. Assumed grain yields of 600–650 kg/ha (e.g. Sallares 1991: 79; Moreno 2007: 26–8; Bissa 2009: 175) may be plausible in general but very probably underestimate Attic barley yields.

[5] Hom. *Il.* 10.351–3; 13.703–7; 18.541–9; *Od.* 5.127; 13.31–3; Hesiod, *Op.* 464; Xen. *Oec.* 16.10–15; common in Attic leases: Osborne (1987: 41–3); Moreno (2007: 327–9).

[6] Lambert (1997: 229–33, 257–65 (esp. 262: 12.5 dr. per land unit (assumed to be a quarter-*plethron*) as minimum price).

[7] See Davies (1971: pp. xxiii–xxiv). Most informative sources: Isaios 7.32, 42 (30,000 dr. estate 'obviously able to undertake trierarchies'); 11.44–7, 49–50 (19,000 dr. estate may become liable for trierarchies when 3,000 dr. are added); Dem. 27.64 (6,000 or 12,000 dr. estates become liable for trierarchies when value doubles or trebles).

Scholars have plausibly argued that this class was a new creation by Solon, while the other three classes, with the less artificial-sounding names of 'horsemen' (*hippeis*), 'yoke-owners' (*zeugitai*), and 'wage labourers' (*thetes*), existed even before his day as informal social and economic groups.[8] Some have further suggested that these other classes remained informal categories even after Solon and that the quantitative definitions reported by our sources were later inventions,[9] but this is highly unlikely. Solon's legislation fixed numbers for everything: the level of fines; days and nights in the stocks; the cost of sacrificial animals; bonuses for athletes and killers of wolves; distances and depths in feet to be observed in farming; even the length in cubits of the pole to which 'a biting dog' should be tied.[10] In this context, and while creating a quantitatively defined top class, Solon must surely also have defined precise qualifications in a matter as important as eligibility for the political rights that came with membership in the 'horseman' and 'yoke-owner' classes.[11]

Moreover, the thresholds set for these classes represented meaningful distinctions in wealth and again corresponded closely to fourth-century counterparts. The boundary between the *hippeis* and the *zeugitai* was drawn at an annual production of 300 *medimnoi* of barley. This would require 10.5 ha under cultivation and 21 ha (52 acres) including biennial fallow, worth 11,550 drachmas, *c*.2 talents.[12] Comparative evidence from the modern Mediterranean suggests that 8–10 ha is the maximum a single span of oxen with a single ploughman can cover, and the use of multiple labourers would allow a rather larger area to be ploughed.[13] The Roman agricultural writer Columella thought that a single span was enough to cover 6.3 ha under wheat plus a similar area under legumes—that is, about 12 ha in all.[14] Solon's 'yoke-owners' were thus probably so named because they could manage with a single yoke of oxen, while his 'horsemen' were landowners who kept more than a single span of oxen and could also afford to keep one or two horses.

The boundary between *zeugitai* and *thetes* was set at 200 measures of produce *per annum*, which on the same calculations as above requires at least 7 ha under cultivation and an estate of 14 ha (34 acres), including biennial fallow, worth at

---

[8] Rhodes (1981: 137); Schmitz (1995: 576); Duplouy (2014: 427–34).
[9] De Ste. Croix (2004: 46–51); Raaflaub (2006: 404–23); Duplouy (2014: 425).
[10] e.g. frs 26, 30a, 32a L–R (fines); 23cd (stocks), 35 (dog), 60–2 (distances in farming), 80/2 (sacrifices), 81, 92 (wolves), 89 (prizes).
[11] Rhodes (1981: 137, 143); Schmitz (1995: 576).
[12] Cf. the 10,000-dr. census for the highest military offices in the spurious constitution of Draco (*Ath. Pol.* 4.2), which, as Valdes Guia (2022: 66) suggests, might be intended to reflect the lower boundary of the *hippeis* property class.
[13] Halstead (2014: 42–4 (8–10 ha max., assuming a single ploughman doing all the work); 36–9 (0.2–0.3 ha daily)); cf. Foxhall (2003: 80–3); van Wees (2006: 382–5).
[14] Columella *RR* 2.12.8 (25 *iugera* = 6.3 ha under wheat), 2.12.7 (125 *modii* of seed grain, at 5 *modii* per *iugerum* [2.9.1, 15], plus 125 *modii* of legumes). He assumes that barley requires less ploughing time than wheat (2.12.2).

least 7,750 drachmas plus the value of a house and slaves. This number is significant, because it corresponds to modern estimates of the minimum property required in classical Athens to join the 'leisure class' of those who could afford to live off the labour of others. The ancient evidence here consists of a single text in which someone claims that he inherited a property worth only 4,500 drachmas, 'on which it is not easy to live', but made his fortune in silver-mining 'by my own physical toil' (Dem. 42.20, 22). Evidently, the leisure-class threshold lay well above 4,500 drachmas, and this is the basis for the modern figures of 6,000 or 9,000 drachmas.[15] I would argue that the latter is confirmed by the threshold for the *zeugitai* class, and that the threshold was set at this level precisely because it was the leisure-class minimum.

The reason for setting a boundary here was that the property–class system made *zeugitai* eligible for holding political office and membership of the Council,[16] functions that made great demands on one's time and could be taken on only by those who were wealthy enough to live lives of leisure. Not until pay for office was introduced in the fifth century did this situation change. Further confirmation, if it were needed, of a high threshold is Aristotle's statement that the property requirements set by Solon meant that only the 'notables' (*gnorimoi*) and 'well-off' (*euporoi*) could serve as magistrates and Councillors (*Pol.* 1274a18 22).[17]

Many a modern study gives the impression that our information about the property classes is hopelessly muddled,[18] but our sources are clear and unanimous on the boundaries, with the partial exception of the *hippeis* qualification insofar as 'some said' that it had originally been the ability to keep horses while others thought it 'more logical' that it had always been 300 measures of annual produce (*Ath. Pol.* 7.4).[19] There is not a hint of debate about the crucial qualification for the *zeugitai* class, which divided the office-holding classes from the disenfranchised rest of the community. All agree that the threshold stood at 200 measures. Plutarch claims to have read many accounts of Solon's reforms (e.g. *Sol.*15.4-5)—which must have been covered by every single local history of Attica—but he gives the same figure as (Pseudo-)Aristotle's *Athenaion Politeia*. Pollux's *Lexicon* provides details of the property classes that do not appear in

---

[15] 6,000 dr.: Davies (1981: 28–9); followed by, e.g., Ober (1989: 128–30); van Wees (2001: 51). 9,000 dr.: Kron (2011: 129, n. 4).

[16] *Ath. Pol.* 7.3 does not explicitly mention membership of the Council (of 400) but implies it in the statement that the *thetes* were confined to assembly and law court.

[17] Schmitz (1995: 577). Cf. Isoc. 7.26: office-holding under Solon and Kleisthenes was only for 'those who had the means to be at leisure and had a sufficient livelihood'.

[18] A striking example is Taylor (2017: 13–15), the most detailed discussion to date of the distribution of wealth at Athens, which mentions the property classes only to list the supposed inconsistencies in the sources.

[19] That *Ath. Pol.* refers to the original Solonian qualification is clear from the use of the perfect tense: 'it had been divided [διῃρῆσθαι] by measures.'

either Aristotle or Plutarch and must come from another source, but he too reports the same property threshold.[20]

Such unanimity about what the thresholds were, in combination with the hint of uncertainty about what they might have been in the past, strongly suggests that Aristotle and his predecessors cited the property thresholds that were in use in their own time. Although the property classes had lost most of their roles by Aristotle's day, they remained a valid legal category.[21] Candidates for office were still obliged to state their property class, even if no one checked any longer whether their estate truly met the threshold,[22] while a law on heiresses still required higher property classes to provide larger dowries (see below). One may object that a definition of wealth in terms of agricultural produce was anachronistic in the fifth and fourth centuries, when a great deal of revenue came from non-agricultural sources and wealth was normally expressed in terms of the monetary value of property rather than income in kind. However, this need not have posed a problem for the continued functioning of the property classes, since it will have been clear to all that the agricultural thresholds corresponded to the economic levels of the contemporary liturgical, horse-owning, and leisure classes, respectively. Whatever a man's actual sources of wealth, he could be assessed or assess himself at one of these levels and register as a member of the corresponding property class.[23]

What our sources report, then, are property-class boundaries that were in use in the fourth century, though no longer of much significance, but had evidently been defined in the sixth century, before economic developments made their agricultural criteria obsolete.[24] A possible sign of change in the course of the sixth

---

[20] *Ath. Pol.* 7.4; Plut. *Sol.* 18.1–2; *Comp. Arist. Cat.* 1.2; Pollux 8.129–30 (= Hermias, *Scholia on Plato, Phaidros* 1.75; *Scholia vetera on Plato, Republic* 550c bis). The medieval *Lexica Segueriana* s.v. *zeugites* also gives the same number.

[21] Property classes were still actively used in a decree of 387/6 BCE, mentioning *pentakosiomedimnoi* in relation to settlers on Lemnos (*Agora* XIX, L3, l. 12).

[22] Candidates are asked 'to which property class do you belong?' (ποῖον τέλος τελεῖ); a *thes* will be allowed to lie: *Ath. Pol.* 7.4 (cf. 55.3: τὰ τέλη εἰ τελεῖ, surely 'if he belongs to the property classes', i.e. the highest three, rather than 'if he pays taxes', since the group of taxpayers at this time was far smaller than the three property classes eligible for office: see below). A man could serve in a post reserved by law for *pentakosiomedimnoi* 'even if he is extremely poor' (*Ath. Pol.* 8.1; 47.1): this is another case of *thetes* being allowed to lie (the alternative, that *pentakosiomedimnoi* could be genuinely poor is possible only if, as Cecchet posits in this volume, property-class status was hereditary, but, if so, the practice of partible inheritance would have made the property classes meaningless within a generation). Isaios 7.39: Pronapes holds office notionally reserved for *hippeis*, while submitting a low(er) property assessment for tax purposes.

[23] *Pace* Valdes Guia (2022), there is no need to posit a formal conversion to monetary qualifications. Note that Solon defined equivalencies between a *medimnos* of barley and a sheep, or a drachma of silver: fr. 80/2 L–R; de Ste. Croix (2004: 36–41, esp. 40).

[24] Valdes Guia and Gallego (2010) argue that these boundaries were first defined in 403, raising a supposedly much lower original Solonian threshold for *zeugites*-status, in order to restrict tax obligations to a narrower group. This seems unlikely: why would Solonian boundaries simply have been ignored at this time for political rights and military obligations (as the argument assumes), yet revised and applied to taxation, an area in which purely agricultural measures of wealth were certainly obsolete?

century is that the boundaries were defined in 'dry and liquid measures', although the name of the top class suggests a definition exclusively in dry measures, *medimnoi*. However, olive-oil production was an important enough part of the Athenian economy in Solon's time to be granted an exemption from his ban on agricultural exports (fr. 65 L–R), so surely Solon would already have taken 'liquid measures' into account when drawing his lines between the classes.

The only other possible hint at change comes in a law dealing with 'heiresses who belong to the class of *thetes*', which specified that the next of kin must either marry the heiress or else provide her with a dowry to marry someone else. If the next of kin was a *pentakosiomedimnos*, the dowry should be 500 drachmas, if a *hippeus* 300 drachmas, and if a *zeugites* 150 drachmas (frs 51/1–3 L–R). While this law is likely to have been enacted by Solon,[25] the amounts cited are too large for his time and were no doubt adapted when the laws were reinscribed in 410–399 BCE.[26] If the dowries were in proportion to the property–class thresholds, it would imply that at this time the dividing line between *thetes* and *zeugitai* was set at 150 measures of produce. It has been suggested that this was the original Solonian threshold,[27] but no satisfactory explanation has been offered for why our sources might have insisted on a higher level than the law implied. If the law represented the current threshold in the late fifth century, it would tend to confirm that the higher level attributed to Solon was plausible, although it would be unclear where our sources found this information, if not in the institutions of their own time. The simplest solution is to assume that the threshold at the time was 200 measures but that the law imposed a proportionally smaller obligation on *zeugitai* than on the other classes, just as the *zeugitai* paid proportionally smaller taxes.[28]

In short, there are no obstacles to accepting the property–class boundaries attributed to Solon as a coherent, meaningful set that matched social distinctions still existing in classical Athens but expressed these in terms of farming produce rather than monetary property values—exactly what one would expect property classes to look like in a pre-coinage agricultural society. I suspect that scholars would generally have drawn this conclusion if it had not been for the remarkable implication that there was no place for a 'middling' class of independent working farmers or other producers in Solon's scheme of things: everyone below the leisure-class threshold of the *zeugitai* was to him a *thes*, 'wage labourer'.

---

[25] The law is attributed to Solon by Diod. Sic. 12.18.3 (fr. 51/3) and Eustathios *ad Hom. Il.* 21.450 (fr. 51/2 L–R); Leão and Rhodes (2015: 87–91) make a strong case that it is genuinely Solonian, given both the role of the property classes and the fact that Solon legislated for heiresses in exhaustive detail, down to the number of times a month their husbands should have intercourse with them (fr. 52a L–R).

[26] Bravo (1992: 71–2) plausibly connects this law with another Solonian inheritance law (fr. 50ab L–R), which was reinscribed explicitly in 403/2 BCE.

[27] As proposed by Böckh (1886: 1.581).

[28] According to Pollux 8.129–30; see further van Wees (2013a: 91–7).

A class of middling farmers might in principle have covered more than half of the range between the leisure class and the destitute. A farm of only 6–8 ha under biennial fallow—about half of Solon's property threshold for *zeugitai*, producing only 85–115 *medimnoi* of barley annually—would have been large enough for a span of oxen to be economically viable. An even smaller farm of 4–6 ha was very probably enough for the owner to make an independent living and to serve as a hoplite in the citizen militia.[29] For men in this category, the label *thetes* rather than, say, *georgoi*, 'farmers', would have been deeply insulting. The position of a *thes* was regarded as even more humiliating than that of a *misthotos*, another term for wage labourer, as we shall see. If the terms *zeugitai* and *thetes* had been current as informal designations before Solon, meaning respectively those who owned a span of oxen or who actively engaged in wage labour, then anyone who owned a span but produced less than 200 measures would have suffered a serious loss of status in Solon's reform. Instead of being called 'yoke-owners', like their leisured superiors, they would have been demoted to 'wage labourers', like their social inferiors. Solon, as a self-proclaimed champion of the poor and of fairness for 'high and low alike' (fr. 36.18–20; cf. frs 4.23–6 and 6), would hardly have antagonized independent smallholders by giving them an insulting name.

The only reasonable conclusion we can draw is that around 600 BCE independent smallholders did *not* form a substantial group at Athens.[30] Most Athenians below the *zeugitai* threshold apparently did not have enough land to keep oxen, and really did need to earn at least part of their living by engaging in wage labour for their richer neighbours. Such a grim picture is entirely compatible with Solon's own portrayal of Athenian society as afflicted by the greed of the rich, by a widespread debt crisis, which he tried to resolve, and by radical demands for the redistribution of land, which he rejected.[31] Solon's property classes and poetry make sense only if he was dealing with an economically polarized society in which a leisured class monopolized most of the land, independent smallholders were few and far between, and most free persons owned very small plots of land, if any, so that they needed additional sources of income to survive.

---

[29] Minimum for span of oxen: Halstead (2014: 56) (3–4 ha without fallow); independent/hoplite status: Hanson (1995: e.g. 5, 22, 193, 478, n. 6); Halstead (2014: 61). Many of the hoplites in classical Athens would have had farms of this size, and would therefore not have been *zeugitai* but *thetes*: what that means for the relation between military service and property classes has been much debated (see van Wees 2006; Okada 2017; Pritchard 2018) but is not relevant to the present discussion.

[30] Valdes Guia (2019) attempts to find evidence that a 'middling' class of independent working farmers did exist c.600, but can cite only (*a*) Hesiod as a supposed representative in Boiotia, despite accepting (on p. 393) Halstead's verdict (2014: 61) that Hesiod's 'agricultural regime...reflects that of the richest landowners' (see also van Wees 2009: 445–50; 2013b: 226–9; Tandy 2018), not the working farmer; (*b*) Attic farmers falling into debt, although obviously dependent smallholders are if anything more likely to incur debts; (*c*) the importance of hoplites, although, in the absence of any indication of their numbers before 490 BCE, hoplite forces may have been drawn only from the propertied elite around 600 BCE.

[31] Cf. Edwards, Chapter 2, this volume.

## Size and Development of the Athenian Working Class

Just how large a proportion of free Athenians were 'wage labourers' in Solon's time, and how that proportion had changed by the fourth century, some further calculations can help us quantify. The Athenian leisure class is widely believed to have consisted in the fourth century of only 1,200 or at most 2,000 of a total 30,000 adult male citizens (4–7 per cent).[32] If the leisure class coincided with the three highest property classes, as we have argued, 93–6 per cent of citizens would therefore have fallen in the class of *thetes*. However, there are strong indications that the leisure class was much larger in classical Athens, and the proportion of *thetes* smaller.

In the mid-fifth century, when the property qualifications for office were still taken very seriously (as is clear from *Ath. Pol.* 26.2), Athens had thirty Treasurers annually selected among the *pentakosiomedimnoi*. On the assumption that one would usually hold this senior office only after the age of 40, and then only once, demographics imply that Athens must have had at least 1,500 adult men in that property class at the time.[33] Their numbers will have declined in the fourth century, in line with the overall population size, but surely not below 700–800.

Even more revealing is the size of the Athenian cavalry, recruited among those wealthy enough to keep horses, and so from the equivalent of Solon's *pentakosiomedimnoi* and *hippeis*.[34] In the mid-fourth century, Xenophon regarded as it as difficult but possible to recruit 'the full 1,000' horsemen (*Hipparch.* 9.3), and the strong association between cavalry and youth in all our Athenian sources suggests that most of the cavalrymen were aged 20–9. This age group would have formed about 30 per cent of all males aged 20–80, and 'the full 1,000' therefore implies that Athens even in the fourth century had more than 3,000 adult men (*c.*10 per cent of the citizen body) wealthy enough to belong to the two highest property classes.[35] If we add the *zeugitai*, presumably rather more numerous than either of the two higher classes, we end up with at least 5,000 members of the leisure class.

A similar number is suggested by the proposal of the oligarchic regime that briefly took power in 411 to abolish all pay for political office yet to share power

---

[32] As argued by Davies (1981: 28–9, 34–7); adopted by, e.g., Ober (1989: 128); Kron (2011: 129–30). This view is based on equating the leisure class with 'the 1,200', and potential 2,000, estates liable to both taxes and liturgies, 357–340 BCE (Dem. 14.16).

[33] Davies (1981: 36–7) made the point but did not pursue the implications, on the grounds that not all thirty positions were always filled. While this suggests that there were not quite enough *pentakosiomedimnoi*, there must still have been well over 1,000, with 3–4-talent properties. The cohort of 40 year olds would have amounted to 2% of all adult males (Hansen 1988: 21, table in n. 9).

[34] Davies (1981: 36) argues that cavalry numbers do not indicate the size of the leisure class, but, although it is true that cavalry did not coincide with the *hippeis* property class, cavalrymen were horse owners who belonged to the leisure class.

[35] Youth and wealth of cavalrymen: Spence (1993: 198–210, 272–86); Pritchard (2018: 58–63) (esp. 61: mid-fourth-century cavalry recruited from the wealthiest 9% of citizens). Demographic group: Hansen (1988: 21, table in n. 9); the maximum viable age range of 20–39 (55%) would still imply *c.*2,000 citizens in the top two classes.

with 'no more than 5,000' who could 'be of most use with their money and their bodies' (Thuc. 8.65.3; or 'no fewer than 5,000' according to [Ar.] *Ath. Pol.* 29.5). Their assumed ability to hold office without pay implies that these are men of leisure-class status. When the oligarchy was replaced by a body of Five Thousand, these were more broadly defined in principle as 'all who provided hoplite equipment' yet were in practice still limited to the leisure class because pay for office was not reinstated (Thuc. 8.97.1; *Ath. Pol.* 33.1). Moreover, the oligarchs' definition of the Five Thousand as able to serve the city 'with money' must refer to paying taxes, and, since only the *thetes* were exempt from taxation,[36] the Five Thousand must all have been in the top three classes. The leisure class thus included at least 5,000 men.[37] The reason for Thucydides' praise of this regime as Athens' best government, 'a measured blend of the few and the many' (Thuc. 8.97.2; cf. *Ath. Pol.* 33.2) may be that, unlike oligarchy, it included the whole leisure class, and, unlike democracy, it included nothing but the leisure class.[38]

What proportion of the citizen population 5,000 men would have constituted in 411 is hard to tell, but the best estimate of the total citizen body at this time is a minimum of 30,000,[39] so that the leisure class of 5,000 would have amounted to one-sixth (16 per cent). This may seem a high proportion, but we must remember that citizen families were only a part of the population, supported by many free non-citizen workers and a very large number of slaves. If non-citizens and non-free persons made up, say, half of the inhabitants of Attica, the leisure class would have constituted 8 per cent of the population.

The less-developed economy of Athens around 600 BCE would not have been able to sustain a leisure class of the same size, so it seems safe to infer that the three top property classes formed no more than 10–15 per cent of free Athenians under Solon. Let us assume for the sake of illustration that the adult male citizen population under Solon was 20,000 and that all available arable land was planted with barley, then a leisure class of 15 per cent (3,000 men) with properties of the size indicated by the property–class thresholds would have occupied *c*.81,000 ha or about 85 per cent of the highest estimate of available arable land in classical Attica (96,000 ha).[40] Since archaeology suggests that the cultivated area fell well

---

[36] Pollux 8.129–30 = Hermias, *Schol. On Plato, Phaidr.* 1.75; *Scholia vet. On Plato, Rep.* 550c bis. See van Wees (2013a: 91–7) for an explanation of this text.

[37] By implication, there was a major fiscal change in the fourth century, when most (or all) taxes and liturgies were restricted to 1,200 men (e.g. Isoc. 15.145), with a property threshold of 3–4 talents, as for the trierarchy (so, too, Gabrielsen 1994: 45–53, 176–82), rather than the 1–1.5 talents posited by the scholars cited in n. 32.

[38] See van Wees (2001: 56–9). These results lend some plausibility to Jones's view (1955: 147; 1957: 28–9) that there were 6,000 taxpayers, though his argument was not strong; he had no real basis for his assumed property threshold of only 2,500 dr.

[39] Hansen (1988: 27).

[40] Assuming 800 *pentakosiomedimnoi* with an average 40 ha (32,000 ha), 1,000 *hippeis* with av. 28 ha (28,000 ha), and 1,200 *zeugitai* with av. 17.5 ha (20,400 ha). Total arable land: see, e.g., Osborne (1987: 46).

short of the maximum extent in the archaic period,[41] this would leave no land at all for the 17,000 *thetes*. In practice, the elite would also have cultivated some crops that consumed less space (vines, olive trees intercropped with grain) and enjoyed non-agricultural income (above all from livestock), so that at least some land would have remained available to the lowest class. Even so, a smaller leisure class of 10 per cent (2,000 men), occupying 53,600 ha—56 per cent of the theoretically available arable and, say, 66 per cent of the land under cultivation in practice—seems more viable.[42] The 18,000 *thetes* would be left with 28,000 ha between them, an average of 1.5 ha (4 acres), half of what was needed to survive without engaging in wage labour.

Around 600 BCE, therefore, the property class of 'wage labourers' comprised about 90 per cent of the citizen body, and, in the absence of a substantial middling class, consisted very largely of persons who genuinely derived part or all of their livelihood from wage labour. A corollary is that only the 10 per cent of the citizen body that belonged to the leisure class had the resources to serve as hoplites or cavalry. Unless the wealthiest provided arms and armour for some of their dependants, which they may have done, early sixth-century Athenian hoplite and cavalry forces would have been very small. We are indeed told that the cavalry consisted of only 100 horsemen; no hoplite numbers are recorded.[43] The prominence in Athenian art of hoplites accompanied by a 'squire' and a pair of horses tends to confirm that hoplites came from a quite exclusive elite.[44]

By 490 BCE, however, Athens had a field army of 9,000 hoplites, implying a total body of hoplites aged 18–59 and cavalry of at least 12,500, perhaps just over 40 per cent of 30,000 adult male citizens.[45] By 431, the total number of hoplites and cavalry had climbed further to c.24,000, 40 per cent of an estimated 60,000 adult male citizens. In 322 BCE, inscribed records of 19- and 59-year-olds enable us to estimate a total number of 13,500 hoplites and cavalry, approximately 45 per cent of a total citizen population that had fallen back to about 30,000.[46] Assuming that the leisure class in the classical period had grown to 15 per cent of the citizen body, we now have an additional 25–30 per cent of adult citizen men capable of

---

[41] Uncultivated regions: Foxhall (1997: 122–9; 2013).

[42] Assuming 500 *pentakosiomedimnoi* with an average 40 ha (= 20,000), 700 *hippeis* with av. 28 ha (= 19,600), and 800 *zeugitai* with av. 17.5 ha (= 14,000). I assume here that 85% of potential arable (81,600 ha) was under cultivation c.600 BCE.

[43] Cavalry: Pollux 8.108; van Wees (2013a: 47–8, 74, 99). The only troop number mentioned is 500 volunteers for the capture of Salamis (Plut. *Sol.* 9.2), but these were also settlers and need not have been hoplites.

[44] Greenhalgh (1972); Brouwers (2007).

[45] 30,000 is the round number posited by Herodotos for 500 BCE (5.97.2); the total number of hoplites and cavalry is based on the assumption that the 9,000 in the field (Nepos. *Milt.* 5.1; Plut. *Mor.* 305b; Paus. 10.20.2) represented an emergency levy of all 20–49 year olds, who would form 72.7% of all males over 18 (Hansen 1988: 21, n. 9).

[46] 431: Thuc. 2.13.6–7; with van Wees (2004: 241–3; 322; see 2011: 99–100). Note also Lysias 20.13: in 411, 9,000 hoplites registered among the Five Thousand.

serving as hoplites who must have belonged to a new class of small but independent producers.

For 322, we can be slightly more precise about the composition of this new middling class. In this year, only 9,000 citizens had properties worth 2,000 drachmas or more. A sum of 2,000 drachmas would represent 40 *plethra* of land at the minimum price of 50 drachmas per *plethron*, i.e. 3.6 ha (9 acres), which very probably corresponds to the minimum amount needed to be an independent smallholder and serve as a hoplite. Since there were 13,500 hoplites in total at the time, this leaves 4,500 men whose properties did not meet the 2,000-drachma threshold but who evidently did have incomes large enough to serve as hoplites. Their incomes must have derived from crafts, trade, or services. In 322, therefore, the Athenian citizen body existed of approximately 15 per cent leisure class, 15 per cent independent working farmers, and 15 per cent independent craftsmen and other non-agricultural workers. Some of the remaining 55 per cent may still somehow have managed an independent living despite not being able to afford to serve as hoplites, but the great majority must surely have worked part-time or full-time as wage labourers.

The common scholarly view that wage labour played no significant role in the classical period is therefore untenable.[47] Instead, we must ask how 90 per cent of citizens found waged employment *c*.600 BCE, how a third of these achieved 'middling' independence and hoplite status by 490, and how most of the remainder continued to live off wage labour down to at least 322 BCE.

## The Condition of the Working Class in Archaic Athens

An obvious source of part-time employment would be seasonal labour at the time of the grain harvest and the vintage. The *Iliad* paints an idyllic picture in which a spirit of communal cooperation seems to animate such work, and the only reward is a lavish meal at the end of the day.[48] Reality may of course have been harsher. The term *thetes* is, however, applied not to these workers by Homer, but to labourers toiling under quite different conditions, typically on year-long basis. They receive food and clothing while they work, and an agreed 'wage' (*misthos*) at the end of the year.[49] Their lives are wretched (*Od.* 11.489–90) and their wages not only 'shameful' (*Il.* 12.433–5) but at risk of being withheld altogether by a menacing employer (*Il.* 21.444–57). Hesiod's advice to 'make a houseless man your *thes* and

---

[47] See de Ste. Croix (1981: 179–204); cf. Finley (1985: 65–9, 73–5); Cohen (2000: 142–3).
[48] *Il.* 18.550–560 (harvest by *erithoi*; an ox sacrificed to feed them), 561–72 ('maidens and youths' dance as they carry off baskets full of grapes).
[49] So rightly Bravo (1992: 83–5), citing *Il.* 21.441–52; *Od.* 18.357–61 (*pace* Cecchet, Chapter 4, this volume, who assumes that *thetes* are 'day or seasonal labourers' and that their wages consist merely of 'food and shelter for the duration of their activity').

seek an *erithos* without a child' (*Op.* 602–3)[50] points to the same conditions, since he hires these workers *after* the harvest, which makes sense only if they are contracted to work for a year, through to the end of the next agricultural cycle. The emphasis on hiring staff without families reveals an interest in getting the maximum amount of labour from these workers at minimal cost. Most relevantly, one of Solon's own poems singles out as a typical poor cultivator, not an independent small farmer, but one who 'serves for a year those who care about curved ploughshares' (fr. 13.47–8 West)—i.e. a labourer on an annual contract.[51]

Later sources, too, suggest that a *thes* is typically not a casual or seasonal labourer but someone contracted for a longer period. Several myths feature a year's service as *thes* as a form of compensation for a killing or injury.[52] Some legends speak of exiles who find long-term employment as *thetes* in a household abroad.[53] Odysseus employs 'foreigners' on a permanent basis (*Od.* 14.102), and his son, Telemachos, has *thetes* who, like his slaves, can be mobilized at short notice to man his ship (4.644). Plato regarded *thetes* as in some way different from other 'hirelings' (*misthotoi*, *Polit.* 1290a), and pictured a *thes* who was not merely a casual labourer but his employer's 'client' (*pelates*, *Euthy.* 4c). Dionysios of Halikarnassos thought that before Solon the relation between Athenian *thetes* and their employers was like that between clients and patrons in Rome, except that in Athens they were treated much worse (*Ant. Rom.* 2.9.2–3). Hellenistic scholars defined *thetes* as 'free men who serve as slaves for a wage': the latter is not just another way of saying 'hired man' but is suggestive of a long-term and humiliating position.[54] The notion that casual or seasonal wage labour is less 'slavish' than long-term wage labour in the exclusive service of a single employer is expressed clearly in Xenophon's much-cited story about Socrates' elderly friend Eutheros, who preferred performing manual labour for a wage, despite his age, to taking up a permanent position as a farm manager for a rich landowner, despite the financial security this would bring him in old age (*Mem.* 2.8).[55]

---

[50] Following the translation of Bravo (1992: 85–6) ('fare di un senza-casa un tuo *thes*'). West (1978: 309) suggests a different interpretation of the grammar but essentially the same meaning ('engage a man without a household').

[51] So de Ste. Croix (1981: 185; 2004: 126); Bravo (1992: 96); *contra* the translations by, e.g., Douglas Gerber in Loeb Classical Library and Martin West in Oxford World's Classics.

[52] In addition to *Il.* 21.441–52, cited above: Panyassis fr 3 West (Demeter, Hephaistos, Poseidon, Apollo, and Ares all serve mortal men for one year; cf. Pherekydes fr. 35 Fowler; Eur. *Alc.* 2, 6; Apollod. *Bibl.* 3.10.4 for Apollo serving Admetos; Isoc. 11.38; Dion. Hal. *Ant. Rom.* 2.19.2); Hellanikos *FGrH* 4 F 51; Apollod. *Bibl* 3.4.2 (Kadmos serves Ares for a year); Arist. *Eudemian Ethics* 1245b31 (Herakles serves as *thes*).

[53] Herod. 8.137 (Perdikkas and his brothers); Eur. *Electra* 205 (Orestes); Arist. fr. 485 Rose (Plut. *Thes.* 16.2: Athenian boys and girls 'grew old in Crete working as *thetes*').

[54] Aristophanes of Byzantium 279 Miller, and in Eustath. *ad Hom. Il.* 1246.10; Aristonikos on *Od.* 4.644; followed by Pollux 3.82; Ammonius 232; Herennius Philo s.v. *thes*; Suda θ3723–6; *Lex. Seg.* s.v. *theteia*; *Lex. Gud.* s.vv. *thes, thetes, thetikon*.

[55] See de Ste. Croix 1981: 181–2, and further below.

What kind of work did *thetes* do, if not seasonal or casual labour? Where their job is specified, they are usually herdsmen, especially in myth and legend but also in other contexts.[56] Herding is, of course, a year-round activity, so annual contracts make sense here. Moreover, although agriculture was the most widespread form of economic activity, the rich in archaic Greece evidently kept large herds as well. Not only do livestock, herders, and feasting on meat enjoy great prominence in Homeric epic, but countless graffiti from the hillsides around Vari attest to the presence of many shepherds and goatherds in sixth-century Attica. Solon's state-funded campaign to exterminate wolves is another indication that livestock-keeping was an important part of the archaic Athenian economy.[57] Many a *thes* will therefore have been hired to watch the flocks of the elite.

A simile in the *Iliad* shows that this sector of the economy also offered paid employment for women: 'an honest poor woman' weighs out wool to earn 'a wage [*misthos*] for her children' (12.433–5). The labour-intensive process of turning large amounts of wool into cloth could exceed the capacity of wives, daughters, and slave maids, and require additional work by *thetes*. Female labour might also be hired for other forms of domestic service. The goddess Demeter's year as a *thes* is spent as a nursemaid and housekeeper in Eleusis, where the local ruler engages her for 'a vast wage'.[58] A male *thes* working for 'a man without an allotment' (*Od.* 11.489–90), and hence not a farmer, is presumably employed by a craftsman. Both crafts and domestic service would demand year-round labour.

To account for as much as 90 per cent of the population being labelled *thetes*, however, we must assume that the majority worked in agriculture. The *Odyssey* speaks of a *thes* on a 'remote' farm 'gathering stones and planting tall trees' for a wage (18.357–9), which suggests terracing and olive cultivation. Given the role of olive-oil export under Solon (fr. 65 L–R), this will have been a major source of employment in Attica, too. Most important of all was the role of wage labour in arable farming, performed by the *hektemoroi*, 'sixth-parters', who 'worked the land of the rich' ([Ar.] *Ath. Pol.* 2.2).

Modern scholars have not usually regarded *hektemoroi* as wage labourers, because (Pseudo-)Aristotle said that *hektemoroi* gave the landowners one-sixth of the harvest as 'rent' (*misthosis*, *Ath. Pol.* 2.2), a notion also adopted by Plutarch (*Sol.* 13.2). This implies a form of sharecropping or tenancy on extremely generous terms, since a 50–50 split is common and widely regarded as fair.[59] Aristotle was forced to come up with a strained reason why this was nevertheless regarded as a kind of 'slavery' at the time—namely, that those who did not pay the rent 'and

---

[56] Hom. *Il.* 21.448; Hdt. 8.137; Soph. *OT* 1029; Eur. *Alc.* 6; *Cycl.* 77; Plato, *Rep.* 359d. Cf. Lys. 20.11: 'a poor man living in the countryside as a shepherd'.
[57] Graffiti: Langdon (2015); wolves: Solon fr. 81, 92 L–R.
[58] Panyassis fr. 3 West; *Hymn to Dem.* 101–4, 139–44, 166–73, 219–23.
[59] See, e.g., de Ste. Croix (2004: 116–17, 122) (who nevertheless accepts that *hektemoroi* paid this 'altogether exceptionally low rate').

even their children' could be sold as slaves. Why there would have been many defaulters when the rents were so low remains unclear.[60] As a result, modern scholars have felt obliged to imagine scenarios in which a one-sixth payment makes better sense—for example, if the cultivators needed an incentive to work marginal or previously uncultivated land,[61] or if they worked on their own land, not someone else's, and were repaying debts or paying 'protection money' or traditional tributes to powerful men.[62] Since none of these causes is even hinted at by our sources, other scholars have resorted to even more desperate measures and solved the problem by arguing that the *hektemoroi* were a fiction.[63]

However, several sources offer a quite different and more viable account of the *hektemoroi*. One would expect the term to mean 'those who *have* a sixth share', and there is a good deal of ancient support for the view that they did not pay one-sixth but received one-sixth of the harvest from the land they worked.[64] A law of Solon's spoke of *epimortos* land, which, Pollux's *Lexicon* (7.151) explained, is land 'cultivated for a share, and the *morte* is the share of the cultivators'.[65] Another lexicon, by Pollux's contemporary Pausanias the Atticist, speaking of 'clients' and *thetes*, said that 'the same persons are also known as *hektemoroi* because they cultivated the land for a sixth part of the crops' (s.v. *pelatai*; π15 Erbse). An anonymous third lexicon, probably also of the second century CE, was even more explicit: 'the *morte*... is the sixth part of the crops, which is given to the sixth-parters'.[66] Byzantine dictionaries followed suit and defined *hektemoroi* as receiving one-sixth of the harvest.[67] The unanimity of the Roman imperial lexica is striking, since they all went against the authority of Aristotle. Their unnamed source must be a Hellenistic or classical scholar of similarly high standing, such as the fourth-century historian Androtion, who gave an account of Solon's reform substantially different from Aristotle's (see below). Whoever the author was, unlike Aristotle he apparently cited evidence for his view: a Solonian law showing that the 'share' went to the cultivator, not the landowner.

---

[60] Stanley (1999: 184–5), rightly points out that 'in a sharecropping arrangement it would be impossible for the farmer not to pay his rent, unless he concealed it' (his own interpretation of the *hektemoroi* at 189–93 seems vastly overcomplicated).

[61] So, e.g., Cassola (1964: 49–51); Gallant (1982); Link (1991: 28–32); Rihll (1991); Sancisi-Weerdenburg (1993: 20–1).

[62] Debts: e.g. Starr (1977: 183); de Ste. Croix (2004: 123–5). Traditional tributes: e.g. Andrewes (1971: 115–17); Rhodes (1981: 94–5) ('feudal' dues); Harris (1997: 107–10) ('protection money').

[63] Ito (2004); Meier (2012).

[64] Cf. *isomoroi*, 'those who have an equal share', and *geomoroi*, 'those who have a share of land'. Cf., e.g., Link (1991: 25–32); van Wees (1999: 21–4); Faraguna (2012).

[65] Solon fr. 67 L-R. Leão-Rhodes adopt the text of Bethe's edition of Pollux which 'emends' two late MSS (F, S), garbled at this point; I translate instead the correct text of the older MSS (B, C: ἡ ἐπὶ μέρει γεωργουμένη καὶ μορτὴ τὸ μέρος τῶν γεωργῶν).

[66] Eustathios *ad Hom. Od.* 19.28 (1854.31). See Erbse (1950: 29–30, 222) on this anonymous lexicon (fr. 3); however, Erbse appears to have inadvertently altered the last word of Eustathios' text, then 'emended' the rest (noted by Meier 2012: 4, n. 11).

[67] Hesych. s.v. *hektemoroi* (ε1716); Phot. s.v. *pelatai* (π544), s.v. *hektemoroi* (ε504). The exception is Hesych. s.v. *epimortos* (ε4985), which follows *Ath. Pol.* and Plutarch.

A common objection to this view has been that it would have been impossible to survive on as little as a sixth of the produce of one's labour. This is easily countered by pointing out that one-sixth is the *largest* proportion of unthreshed grain that Cato the Elder thought a landowner should give to a sharecropper on the least fertile soil. On best-quality land, he recommended a share of as little as one-ninth (*De agricultura* 136). To survive on such small proportions would undoubtedly be hard, but evidently Cato believed it possible, probably assuming that the sharecropper would also have at least some land of his own to live off. On the estimates offered above of the number of *thetes* and the distribution of land around 600 BCE, if all the land owned by the leisured elite was cultivated by *thetes*, the average income from this work would have amounted to a single *choinix* of barley a day, a standard daily grain ration for an adult male,[68] but the average *thes* would also have had 1.5 ha (4 acres) of his own, perhaps cultivated intensively with vegetable and fruit crops to complement the wage in grain. Foraging and small-scale pasturing on common land will have helped make ends meet. Moreover, if the sixth share was a 'wage' on the Homeric model, *thetes* may have received daily rations as well as their share of the crop at the end of the year, and their livelihoods would begin to look sufficient to sustain a family.

Why, then, did Aristotle interpret the position of *hektemoroi* differently? The effect of presenting them as tenants on generous contracts, and calling them 'clients' (*pelatai, Ath. Pol.* 2.2), was to deny that the status of sixth-parter as such was exploitative, a problem that needed to be resolved. Isocrates similarly declared that in Solon's time 'the propertied classes' had been admirable in assisting the poor by 'letting them have farmlands for moderate rents' (7.32). For Aristotle, the only true problem facing Solon was the sale into slavery of those who had borrowed and defaulted on their loans. He attributed this, not to the greed of the lenders, but to the custom that 'all loans were on the security of the person before Solon', which in turn he implicitly explained by positing that 'all the land was in the hands of a few' (*Ath. Pol.* 2.2). Since the poor had no land, they could only pledge their bodies, and their creditors had no option but to sell them to recover their debts. Simply by cancelling all debt and banning future borrowing on the security of the person, Solon solved the problem (6.1; 9.1; 10.1; 11.2; 12.4) without needing to redistribute land (11.2; 12.3). While noting that Solon in his own poetry blamed the crisis on the rich (5.3), Aristotle thus largely exonerated them and implied that their monopolization of land was not in itself a problem, since they gave the poor access to low-rent tenancies.

---

[68] If 18,000 *thetes* cultivated 53,600 ha owned by 2,000 leisure-class men, they covered an average 3 ha each, minus fallow—i.e. 1.5 ha. They would each produce on average *c.*1,200 kg of barley, and receive as their share 200 kg—i.e. 7.3 *medimnoi* or 350 *choinikes*. Choinix as a standard ration: Foxhall and Forbes (1982: 51–65, 86–9).

The more plausible view that the cultivators received only a one-sixth share of the crop fits in with a different ancient theory about the situation before Solon. Androtion represented a minority view that Solon did not cancel debt but merely lowered interest rates and also reduced the value of the drachma to make repayment easier (*FGrH* 324 F 34). The same idea appeared in Diogenes Laertius' brief biography of Solon, which defined his reform as a 'redemption [*lutrōsis*] of persons and properties' (1.45), implying that Solon did not cancel debts but somehow enabled people to pay these off, and that debts were secured by mortgaging land as well as borrowing on the person.[69] Several Byzantine texts, alluding to the name 'shedding of burdens' given to Solon's reform, expanded on this: 'insofar as it was the custom at Athens for the debtors among the poor to labour in person for their creditors, it was as if they shed a burden when they paid back the loan.'[70] Although these texts are of very late date, Plutarch already hinted at the same ideas. He said that some defaulting debtors were made to work as 'slaves' in Attica—that is, as debt-bondsmen for their creditors—while others were sold abroad (*Sol.* 13.2), and he interpreted a poem of Solon's (fr. 36.4–5) to mean that many mortgaged their land (*Sol.* 15.5), rather than their persons.

All this adds up to a coherent view according to which the conditions posited by Aristotle to mitigate the actions of the elite did not exist: the poor did have some land and could mortgage it but were nevertheless forced to accept debt-bondage or sale into slavery, or 'to sell their own children or to go into exile from the city, on account of the harshness of the creditors', as Plutarch put it (*Sol.* 13.3). Solon's solution was simply to restrain the creditors by capping interest rates and prohibiting sale into slavery. Neither a cancellation of debt nor a redistribution of land was necessary on this view, which may well go back in its entirety to Androtion. *Hektemoroi* receiving only one-sixth of the crop fitted well in this context of an over-exploitative elite creating social problems. Both Plutarch and Diogenes called six-parters *thetes*, not 'clients', and attributed their willingness to accept this status to 'poverty', clearly separating them from debtors forced to work as bondsmen or slaves.[71]

Both Aristotle's interpretation and the view associated with Androtion have their implausible and anachronistic elements, and they were probably little more than scholarly hypotheses based on a few of Solon's poems and laws. This is not the place to discuss the cause and nature of Solon's reforms in full, but enough has been said to show that, as far as sixth-parters were concerned, Aristotle adopted a

---

[69] Identical wording in *Excerpta Vaticana* 26 Festa; a scholiast on Hermogenes *Peri Staseis* (7.146 Waltz) says that 'many...had mortgaged the land that they owned'. *Etym. Magnum* s.v. *seisachtheia* notes the theory that Solon merely reduced interest.

[70] Photius σ126; Suda σ286 (both s.v. *seisachtheia*); Apostolios 15.39.

[71] '*Either* they worked the land for the rich...*or* they incurred debts' (Plut. *Sol.* 13.2); in Diogenes, the construction *kai*...*kai* has the same effect: 'for they borrowed on the security of their bodies and, also, many worked as *thetes* on account of poverty' (*aporia*; 1.45; but Bravo (1992: 80) interprets *aporia* as 'inability [to pay back loans]').

view that suited his theory about the Solonian crisis but was far less plausible than the rival interpretation. Androtion was able to take the name *hektemoroi* at face value, could cite a Solonian law in evidence, and did not have to assume an unparalleled scenario in which *all* land was owned by the rich and *all* loans were on security of the person.[72] He merely had to posit that the archaic Athenian elite was greedy, as Solon himself said in his poems (frs 4.5–13; 4a–c; 6 West).

In agriculture as in animal husbandry, crafts, and domestic service, therefore, the propertied class employed free men and women as *thetes*, wage labourers on annual contracts. In arable farming, their typical wage was one-sixth of the harvest. This proportion was presumably arrived at because the main subdivision of the *medimnos* was the 'sixth' (*hekteus*, each in turn subdivided into 8 *choinikes*), and employers had been able to drive down wages to this low level. Since the propertied elite owned two-thirds or so of the arable land, while no doubt also occupying much common land with their livestock, and since they had the option of employing imported slaves and local debt-bondsmen,[73] they were able to impose exploitative terms on free labourers and force them to accept the bare minimum on which they could survive. Likewise, the workers who occupied this status did so, not because they were working off a debt or fulfilling traditional labour obligations or paying for protection, but because poverty forced them to accept a minimal reward. The 'standardization' of the status of *hektemoros* thus does not imply a rule imposed by central authority or a convention established by long tradition, but simply reflects economic forces converging on an established standard measure of volume as the typical wage.[74]

So long as *thetes* cultivated the great majority of land in Attica and had free access to common land, they would have been able to get by. However, as the propertied classes began to rely more on imported slave labour, enclosed some common land for their 'remote' farms (*eschatia*), and monopolized much of the common land that remained to pasture their expanding flocks and herds, *thetes* will increasingly have fallen below the subsistence margin and been forced to borrow food from their employers or wealthier neighbours. When they were unable to repay these loans, they could end up in debt-bondage and work under even worse conditions or be sold into slavery abroad by creditors who preferred money—perhaps to buy even more imported slaves—to cheap local labour.

---

[72] There is no evidence other than *Ath. Pol.* 2.2, 4.5 that land could not be mortgaged: Diod. 1.79.5 says only that weapons and agricultural tools could not be pawned.

[73] That imported slave labour was widely used in Attica and the Greek world before 600 BCE is now well established: see esp. Lewis (2018); van Wees (forthcoming). The presence of debt-bondsmen posited by Plutarch and the lexica (after Androtion?) is confirmed by Solon's claim to have set free people who 'trembled at the whim of their masters' in Attica (fr. 36.13–15).

[74] Similarly Bravo (1992: 95) (*hektemoroi* are free men working under contract for a wage); *pace* Edwards, Chapter 2, this volume (*hektemoroi* are like Helots, 'the Athenian elite's still incomplete project to secure their own population of epichoric slaves').

## The Condition of the Working Class in Classical Athens

Solon's cancellation of debts brought short-term relief and will have helped some *thetes* to establish themselves as independent farmers, but there is no evidence to suggest that he banned debt-bondage, which may even have increased when creditors lost the option to sell debtors into slavery abroad. Although the practice is rarely mentioned, debt-bondage was still current in Attica c.300 BCE.[75] Solon's law on *epimortos* land implies that wage labour for a 'share' remained a legitimate practice, and no source suggests that he forbade 'sixth-parter' contracts. The disappearance of *hektemoroi* by the classical period was simply the result of monetization: agricultural labourers were no longer paid in shares in kind at the end of the contract but in coin, in fixed sums or daily rates.

Solon's enigmatic claim to have 'freed the enslaved Earth' by 'pulling up boundary stones' (*horoi*, fr. 36.5–7 West) implies that some land changed hands. This may have involved restoring land seized by creditors—or simply seized illegally—to its original owners, or restoring enclosed land to communal use, and either way it will have helped some smallholders achieve independence. A ban on export of grain (fr. 65 L–R) will have been a disincentive to further exploitation of land and labour by the elite, while making it cheaper for the poor to borrow or buy grain. The cumulative effect of these and other measures[76] surely was to make it easier for smallholders to avoid falling into debt or having to accept wage labour on very unfavourable terms. However, Solon defied popular calls for a redistribution of land,[77] so the economic position of the *thetes* did not change structurally.

Material and legal help provided by Peisistratos in later decades (*Ath. Pol.* 16.2–9) no doubt made a significant difference, too, but the emergence of a substantial middling class and a larger leisure class must have been primarily because of broader economic developments. The expansion of both international commerce and local retail trade from c.550 onwards meant that smallholders could make themselves independent by using their plots for specialized high-value products—such as fine olive oil or honey—and craftsmen could sell to much wider markets. Increased mining of silver created a new stream of revenue for the leisure class as well as opportunities for the landless. In the fifth century, the resources of empire trickled down to still more Athenians. A combination of these trends enabled 15 per cent of citizens to establish themselves as leisure class, 15 per cent as independent working farmers, and at least 15 per cent as independent non-agricultural producers and providers of services.

---

[75] See esp. Harris (2002).    [76] See Humphreys (2019: 26–9).

[77] Edwards (Chapter 2, this volume) plausibly identifies *isomoirie* as the popular slogan. Solon fr. 149/1 L–R, a statement by Aristotle (*Pol.* 1266$^b$14–18) that Solon somehow legislated for a degree of equality of property, may refer only to whatever changes of ownership ensued from the 'pulling up of boundary stones'.

This still left up to 55 per cent of the citizen population in classical Athens in need of at least part-time wage labour.[78] For those who were not far below the threshold for economic independence, occasional pay for public service—on juries, at assemblies and festivals, in the fleet—may have been enough to avoid the need to work for a wage in private service. For those further down the economic scale, such limited revenues cannot have been enough, and wage labour must have been the only option. Our sources rarely touch upon wage labour, except in the context of formerly well-off families that have become impoverished (typically as a result of war), and now resort to wage labour, which is regarded as sad but 'necessary and appropriate'.[79] Similarly, the point of Xenophon's story about old Eutheros, who has lost his property and now works as a casual wage labourer, is not that this is an intolerable fate, but that it is hard to make a living from it in old age. Moreover, when Eutheros refuses to consider a permanent waged position because it will make him too dependent on a single employer, Socrates advises him to swallow his pride and take this kind of employment after all (*Mem.* 2.8.6).

If, despite their reluctance to engage in wage labour, even leisure-class families fallen on hard times could reconcile themselves to working as day or seasonal labourers, then those who had never been able to live in leisure or to work independently would surely have had no qualms about doing so. Aristotle argued that 'a free man does not live at the command of another' (*Rhet.* 1367$^a$27), but he assumed throughout *Politics* that a city needs a 'wage-labouring class' (*to thetikon*), which, he insists, will create the 'worst kind' of democracy and therefore should be denied citizen rights.[80] Since foreign residents and slaves were excluded from political rights by definition, this line of argument makes sense only if Aristotle imagined that many wage-labourers were free but poor citizens.[81]

Among the jobs poor free women might undertake for a wage were nursing, wool-work, and fruit- or grape-picking (Dem. 57.35; cf. 35, 42), in the classical period precisely as in Homer, Hesiod, and the *Homeric Hymn to Demeter*. For men, seasonal agricultural labour was a common option, as is clear from a military expedition in 372 BCE, when Iphikrates arranged for 'the majority' of the crews of his seventy ships—hoplites excepted—to sustain themselves by 'farming for the Corcyraeans' (Xen. *Hell.* 6.2.14, 37). The feasibility of putting as many as 13,000 men to work in this way shows both that there was a huge demand for seasonal hired labour, and that the poor citizens who formed a large part of these

---

[78] Contrast Ober (2015: 92, table 4.4): elite of 400 (1.3%), 'middling' group of 19,500–24,500 (65–81.7%), and a 'subsistence' group of 5,000–10,000 (16.7–33.3%).
[79] Dem. 57.42, cf. 35, 45; Isoc. 14.48. Cf. Xen. *Mem.* 2.8; Taylor (2017: 118–21, 135–47).
[80] Wage earners a vital part of society: Ar. *Pol.* 1258$^b$22–7; 1290b39–1$^a$8; 1321$^a$5–6; 1342$^b$19–20; must not have citizen political rights: 1278$^a$15–24; 1317$^a$25–9 (*thetikon* will create worst form of democracy); 1319$^a$26–8; 1329$^a$35–9 ('the whole *thetikon*' is needed but has no part in the army or decision-making); rejection of living at command of another: 1124$^b$29–5$^a$2; 1337$^b$18–22.
[81] On hired labour in classical Greece generally, see Hinsch (2021: 434–8, 502–5).

crews were able and willing to undertake such work.[82] They were no doubt used to it: hired free men are taken for granted as a key part of the agricultural workforce.[83]

In craft production, there is little direct evidence for wage labour by free men. Workshops mentioned in law-court speeches always seem to consist entirely of slaves, but this may be in part because the slaves are relevant as part of the properties being disputed in court, whereas wage labourers would not have been relevant in the same way. A major employer must have been the dockyards, where hundreds of warships were built and maintained, in part perhaps by hired labour.

In construction work, more metics than citizens are named in the building inscriptions of the Erechtheion and Eleusis, as has often been stressed,[84] but in the Eleusis accounts almost half of named individuals—many in lower-skilled work—are not identified either way, and there are anonymous work gangs, and payments to contractors whose workforces are not specified at all. Thus thirty unnamed wage labourers 'who eat at home' (*oikositoi*)—that is, do not receive rations—clear the debris of an 'old collapsed tower' (*IG* ii² 1672.44–6); the ground is prepared for rebuilding by a metic contractor whose workers are not mentioned (46–7); new blocks of stone are quarried by five men whose status is not specified (48–50), then transported by another four men of unspecified status (50–1), and put in position by a citizen contractor whose workforce is again not mentioned. All of these operations may have involved working-class citizens.[85]

Men looking for work gathered at the sanctuary of Eurysakes on the 'Hiring Hill' (*Kolonos Misthios*) near the agora at Athens, which gave rise to the expression 'You're late—off to the Hill you go!'[86] Presumably similar, smaller gathering places for available workers existed in most demes, providing the 'local hirelings' mentioned by Menander (*Dyskolos* 330–1). Few members of the Athenian working class may have been able to earn a full livelihood from a single form of waged employment, but many would have been able to scrape a living from a combination of a very small plot of land, occasional public service, and a variety of odd jobs on farms and building sites and in domestic service.

Recent work on Athenian society has offered upbeat assessments of the level of wages, especially in the late fourth century. Comparative study suggests that

---

[82] The same is true of a Peloponnesian fleet of c.100 ships on Khios in 406, who worked 'for a wage', until work dried up in winter: Xen. *Hell*. 2.1.1.

[83] Menander, *Dysk*. 330–1, implies that slaves, local hired men, and neighbours are normal sources of labour for a farmer: in this context, the hired men are evidently not slaves. Theophr. *Char*. 4.3–4 has the 'rustic man' tell 'the *misthotoi* who work for him all the news from the assembly', suggesting that they are citizens. Slaves might be hired for farmwork, too: Dem. 53.21. See Jameson (1977: 132). Dem. 18.51: harvester as typical hired labourer.

[84] The latest count: Feyel (2006: 320, 325); cf. Randall (1953).

[85] Dem. 49.51–2 assumes that heavy transport is a job for free hired men as well as for slaves; Aristoph. *Aves* 1152–4 assumes that walls are built by hired labour.

[86] Pollux 7.132–3; Harpokration and Suda s.v. *kolonetas*; Hesych. s.vv. *Kolonos* and *ops' elthes*; *Hypothesis II* to Soph. *Oedip. Colonus*; see Fuks (1985).

expressed in 'wheat equivalent' a bare subsistence income would be 1.2 litres per day for an individual and 4.7 litres of wheat for a family of four, while actual daily wages across historical periods tend to fall between 3.5 and 6.5 litres. By contrast, it is argued, the wage of 1.5 drachma per day for unskilled labour, attested in a building account from Eleusis of 329/8 BCE, amounted to 13–15.6 litres, so that even the cheapest Athenian worker received more than the best-paid labourer anywhere else from 1800 BCE to CE 1300.[87] The problem with this calculation is that it measures an exceptionally high wage against normal wheat prices, although the sources show that this wage was paid at a time when a food crisis caused wheat and other prices to rise steeply.

The building account that informs us of the 1.5-drachma wage does refer to wheat being sold at a normal price of 6 drachmas per *medimnos*, but this was a price fixed by a decree of the people (*IG* ii² 1672.287), not a market price. Other inscriptions show that at this juncture selling wheat at 5–9 drachmas per *medimnos* was deemed an act of generosity worthy of public honours,[88] and a contemporary speech reports a market price of 16 drachmas (Dem. 34.39). Barley and wine are said to have sold for three times their normal price (Dem. 42.20, 31). Other prices mentioned in the building account alongside the 1.5-drachma wage are much higher than they had been only four years earlier: caps and jackets for public slaves roughly doubled in price, while the cost of their shoes more than trebled.[89] Clearly the producers of these goods had raised their prices in line with the cost of food, and in the circumstances wages were raised too. Calculated against a market price of 16 drachmas, the 1.5-drachma wage amounts to only 4.9 litres of wheat, at the bottom of the family-subsistence range. Even the three carpenters who receive 2.5 drachmas per day each, the highest daily wage recorded in the inscription (*IG* ii² 1672.26–8), with a wheat equivalent of 8.1 litres, are only halfway between a bare subsistence and a 'respectable' income for a family of four (11.9 litres).[90]

The only other known wage that reached 1.5 drachmas was the payment for attendance at the 'principal assembly', which happened ten times a year; for the thirty ordinary assemblies pay was 1 drachma, and for jury service 0.5 drachma. If a citizen attended every assembly and served as a juror every day for the rest of the year—which was not in fact possible—he could thus earn a total of 207.5 drachmas p.a. At a normal price of 6 drachmas per *medimnos*, this would have bought him 4.9 litres of wheat a day, again a bare family subsistence. A citizen appointed to membership on the ruling Council would do better, with an annual

---

[87] Bare subsistence: Scheidel and Friesen (2009: 83 (with Ober 2015: 341, n. 50)). Actual range: Scheidel (2010: 441–2, 453); followed by Ober (2015: 91–8); Taylor (2017: 69–113).
[88] *IG* ii³ 1.339, 12–13; *IG* ii² 360, 9, 30, 56, 68.
[89] Detailed prices and references in Loomis (1998: 103, n. 17).
[90] Scheidel and Friesen (2009: 83) define 850 kg of wheat per capita per annum as 'respectable'— i.e. 3,400 kg/4,352 L p.a., or 11.9 per day, for four.

income of 310 drachmas and a daily wheat equivalent of 7.4.[91] Even the highest attested wage outside the Eleusis building account, 1 drachma a day for skilled craftsmen and public magistrates, amounted to no more than 8.7 litres of wheat, only halfway to 'respectability'.[92]

At the other end of the range, wages of 3 or 4 obols per day are often attested for military personnel. From 432 to 413 BCE, Athens paid soldiers and oarsmen a full drachma a day, but before and after this only the lower rates are attested. Even if Athens at the height of its imperial power was able to outbid everyone else with a high wage for sailors and rowers, the norm was clearly lower. Tellingly, by raising their wage offer from 3 to 4 obols in 408, the Spartans were able to hire oarsmen away from the Athenians and quickly man a fleet much larger than that of Athens.[93] A wage of 3 obols a day (4.3 litres of wheat) was enough for an individual but not for a family.

Moreover, to be competitive with slave labour, which was also available for hire, the wages of citizens could not be much higher than the pay of slaves. In the 350s, Xenophon proposed to hire out slaves at 1 obol per day, plus rations, for which he cited fifth-century precedents.[94] Rations may have cost as little as 1 obol: this is the food allocation to Councillors on all-day duty (*Ath. Pol.* 62.2), and Demosthenes reports an average of 0.83 obol a day on maintenance for his slaves.[95] In the Eleusis building account, the food allowance for seventeen public slaves and their supervisor is 3 obols a day per person,[96] but, since food prices were at three times the normal level, this is consistent with 1 obol as the norm. If one could hire a slave for the equivalent of 2 obols, then free men looking for occasional work as harvesters, building labourers, and the like could hardly demand much more: 2.9 litres wheat equivalent, only 62 per cent of a nuclear family's subsistence needs.

## Conclusion

We have arrived at a very different picture of Athenian society than has been suggested in recent studies. The elite was much wider than the 'liturgical' class

---

[91] Wages: *Ath. Pol.* 62.2 (Council: 5 ob p.d., but 1 dr p.d. during their 36-day prytany).

[92] The evidence is collected by Loomis (1998). Normal wheat price of 6 dr: Markle (1985: 279, 293–4). It is often said that unskilled labour also received 1 dr p.d. in the Erechtheion building accounts, but, as noted by Randall (1953: 202–3), these accounts cover only the final phases of construction, which involved a range of highly skilled craftsmen but few unskilled labourers: those who perform such work in the these accounts are therefore skilled masons and carpenters temporarily diverted from their main jobs and paid at their normal rates.

[93] Xen. *Hell.* 1.5.4–7; Plut. *Alc.* 35.4; *Lys.* 4.3–4. Military pay: Loomis (1998: 32–61); cf. Scheidel (2010: 455–6).

[94] *Poroi* 4.14–15, 23; see Powell (2021) for critical discussion of Xenophon's numbers.

[95] Dem. 27.35: 700 dr p.a. for fourteen slaves (see 27.6, 18–19).

[96] *IG* ii² 1672.4–5, 42–3, 117–18, 141–2, 233–4.

with which it has usually been identified. The liturgical class corresponded in practice to the property class of *pentakosiomedimnoi*, with an income of at least 7.5 times subsistence, even if they cultivated nothing but barley, the cheapest staple, and in practice no doubt a good deal more.[97] The elite, defined as those with enough property to be able to afford to live at leisure, also included the *hippeis* and *zeugitai* classes, the latter with incomes of at a minimum 3 to 4.5 times subsistence. In all, they amounted to about 15 per cent of the citizen population in the classical period and perhaps 10 per cent in Solon's time. The existence of such a broad elite helps explain the prevalence of egalitarian ideals from an early date in Greece: for most of the archaic period, the often-invoked *polis* or *demos* was in practice the leisure class, demanding equal treatment and political participation.

The 'middling' class, defined as independent working farmers and other producers, consisted in classical Athens of the next most well-off 30 per cent of the citizen population. In the fifth and fourth centuries, this entire class was able to afford military service as hoplites.[98] In terms of the property classes, they were all *thetes* and thus, according to some sources, not legally obliged to serve. If so, they must have fought as a matter of moral rather than legal obligation, until the property classes were abandoned as the basis for military mobilization.[99] About half of this class consisted of working farmers, while the other half consisted of self-employed craftsmen, traders, and service providers. Most importantly, we have found that this middling class was nearly non-existent around 600 BCE, and emerged only when economic growth made this possible in the latter half of the sixth century. The rise of these new middling classes, agricultural and non-agricultural, drove a development beyond elite egalitarianism towards broader participation and the creation of democracy from 508 BCE onwards.

The remaining citizens formed the 'working class', here defined as those who relied on employment by others for part or all of their livelihood. Under Solon, they made up as much as 90 per cent of the population and their work as *thetes*, 'wage labourers', gave a name to their formal property class. By the classical period, part-time and full-time wage labourers still amounted to 50 per cent of the citizen population. As the economy diversified and became monetized, their typical terms of employment changed from working on annual contracts for a sixth of the crops to seasonal and casual labour for daily pay, but optimistic

---

[97] Their 500 *medimnoi* of barley p.a. minus a quarter for seed grain would leave 375 *med.*, which could be sold at 4 dr each, raising 1,500 dr, which could buy 250 *med.* of wheat at 6 dr each—i.e. 13,000 litres p.a. or 35.6 litres p.d. This is precisely where Ober (2015: 93–4) sets his 'elite' level, derived from an estimate of the income of the *decuriones*—i.e. the narrow ruling elites of cities under the Roman Empire (Scheidel and Friesen 2009: 82–3). This suggests long-term continuity in the economic level of the ruling class within the socio-economic elite of Greek cities.

[98] I have elsewhere referred to this group as 'working-class hoplites' to distinguish them from the leisure-class hoplites of the three higher property classes, but in the present chapter I am using 'working class' only for wage labourers.

[99] See van Wees (2018) for full discussion.

modern assessments notwithstanding, the evidence suggests that they remained at subsistence level, with wages in the same range as those of labourers across most of history.

## Works Cited

Andrewes, A. (1971). *Greek Society*. London.

Bissa, E. (2009). *Governmental Intervention in Foreign Trade in Archaic and Classical Greece*, Mnemosyne Supplements 312. Leiden and Boston.

Blok, J., and A. Lardinois (2006) (eds). *Solon of Athens*. Leiden and Boston.

Böckh, A. (1886). *Die Staathaushaltung der Athener*. 3rd edn. Berlin.

Bravo, B. (1992). 'I thetes ateniesi e la storia della parola *thes*', *Annali della Facoltà di Lettere e Filosofia di Perugia. 1. Studi classici*, 15/16: 69–97.

Brouwers, J. J. (2007). 'From Horsemen to Hoplites: Some Remarks on Archaic Greek Warfare', *BaBesch*, 82: 305–19.

Cassola, F. (1964). 'Solone, la terra e gli ectemori', *La Parola del passato*, 19: 26–68.

Cohen, E. E. (2000). *The Athenian Nation*. Princeton.

Davies, J. K. (1971). *Athenian Propertied Families*. Oxford.

Davies, J. K. (1981). *Wealth and the Power of Wealth in Classical Athens*. Salem.

de Ste. Croix, G. E. M. (1981). *The Class Struggle in the Ancient Greek World from the Archaic Age to the Arab Conquest*. London.

de Ste. Croix, G. E. M. (2004). *Athenian Democratic Origins and Other Essays*, ed. D. Harvey and R. Parker. Oxford.

Duplouy, A. (2014). 'The So-Called Solonian Property Classes: Citizenship in Archaic Athens', *Annales: Histoire, sciences sociale* (English-language version), 69/3: 411–39 (also published as 'Les Prétendues classes censitaires soloniennes: À propos de la citoyenneté athénienne archaïque', *Annales: Histoire, sciences sociales*, 69: 629–58).

Erbse, H. (1950). *Untersuchungen zu den attizistischen Lexika: Abhandlungen der deutschen Akademie der Wissenschaften zu Berlin, Philosophisch-historische Klasse*. Berlin.

Faraguna, M. (2012). '*Hektemoroi, isomoirie, seisachtheia*: Ricerche recenti sulla riforme economiche di Solone', *Dike* 15: 171–93.

Feyel, C. (2006). *Les Artisans dans les sanctuaires grecs aux époques classique et hellénistique à travers la documentation financière en Grèce*. Paris.

Finley, M. I. (1985). *The Ancient Economy*. 2nd edn. London.

Foxhall, L. (1997). 'A View from the Top: Evaluating the Solonian Property Classes', in Mitchell and Rhodes (1997: 113–36).

Foxhall, L. (2003). 'Cultures, Landscapes, and Identities in the Mediterranean World', *Mediterranean Historical Review*, 18: 75–92.

Foxhall, L. (2013). 'Can we See the "Hoplite Revolution" on the Ground?', in Kagan and Viggiano (2013: 194–221).

Foxhall, L., and H. Forbes (1982). '*Sitometreia*: The Role of Grain as a Staple Food in Classical Antiquity', *Chiron*, 12: 41–90.

Fuks, A. (1985). '*Kolonos Misthios*. Labour Exchange in Classical Athens', in A. Fuks, *Social Conflict in Ancient Greece*, 303–5. Jerusalem.

Gabrielsen, V. (1994). *Financing the Athenian Fleet: Public Taxation and Social Relations*. Baltimore.

Gallant, T. (1982). 'Agricultural Systems, Land Tenure, and the Reforms of Solon', *Annual of the British School at Athens*, 77: 111–24.

Gallant, T. (1991). *Risk and Survival in Ancient Greece*. Stanford.

Greenhalgh, P. A. (1972). *Early Greek Warfare: Horsemen and Chariots in the Homeric and Archaic Ages*. Cambridge.

Halstead, P. (2014). *Two Oxen Ahead: Pre-Mechanised Farming in the Mediterranean*. Chichester.

Hansen, M. H. (1988). *Three Studies in Athenian Demography*. Copenhagen.

Hanson, V. D. (1995). *The Other Greeks*. New York.

Hanson, V. D. (2013). 'The Hoplite Narrative', in Kagan and Viggiano (2013: 256–76).

Harris, E. M. (1997). 'A New Solution to the Riddle of the *seisachtheia*', in Mitchell and Rhodes (1997: 103–12).

Harris, E. M. (2002). 'Did Solon Abolish Debt-Bondage?', *Classical Quarterly*, 52: 415–30.

Hinsch, M. (2021). *Ökonomik und Hauswirtschaft im klassischen Griechenland*. Historia Einzelschrift 265. Stuttgart.

Humphreys, S. C. (2019). *Kinship in Ancient Athens: An Anthropological Analysis*. Oxford.

Ito, T. (2004). 'Did the *hektemoroi* Exist?', *La parola del passato*, 337: 241–7.

Jameson, M. (1977). 'Agriculture and Slavery in Classical Athens', *Classical Journal*, 73: 122–45.

Jones, A. H. M. (1955). 'The Social Structure of Athens in the Fourth Century BC', *Economic History Review*, 8: 141–55.

Jones, A. H. M. (1957). *Athenian Democracy*. Oxford.

Kagan, D., and G. Viggiano (2013) (eds). *Men of Bronze: Hoplite Warfare in Ancient Greece*. Princeton.

Kron, G. (2011). 'The Distribution of Wealth in Athens in Comparative Perspective', *Zeitschrift für Papyrologie und Epigraphik*, 179: 129–38.

Lambert, S. D. (1997). *Rationes Centesimarum: Sales of Public Land in Lykourgan Athens*. Archaia Hellas 3. Amsterdam.

Langdon, M. K. (2015). 'Herders' Graffiti', in A. P. Matthaiou and N. Papazarkadas (eds), *Axon. Studies in Honor of Ronald S. Stroud*, 49–58. Athens.

Leão, D., and P. J. Rhodes (2015). *The Laws of Solon: A New Edition with Introduction, Translation and Commentary*. London.

Lewis, D. (2018). *Greek Slave Systems in their East Mediterranean Context, 800–146 BC*. Cambridge.

Link, S. (1991). *Landverteilung und sozialer Frieden im archaischen Griechenland*. Stuttgart.

Loomis, W. (1998). *Wages, Welfare Costs and Inflation in Classical Athens*. Ann Arbor.

Markle, M. M. (1985). 'Jury Pay and Assembly Pay at Athens', in P. A. Cartledge and F. D. Harvey (eds), *Crux: Essays Presented to G. E. M. de Ste. Croix on his 75th Birthday*, 265–97. Exeter.

Meier, M. (2012). 'Die athenischen Hektemoroi—eine Erfindung?', *Historische Zeitschrift*, 294: 1–29.

Mitchell, L., and P. J. Rhodes (1997) (eds). *The Development of the Polis in Archaic Greece*. London.

Moreno, A. (2007). *Feeding the Democracy: The Athenian Grain Supply in the Fifth and Fourth Centuries BC*. Oxford.

Ober, J. (1989). *Mass and Elite in Democratic Athens: Rhetoric, Ideology and the Power of the People*. Princeton.

Ober, J. (2015). *The Rise and Fall of Classical Greece*. Princeton.

Okada, T. (2017). 'Zeugitai and Hoplites: A Military Dimension of Solon's Property Classes Revisited', *Japan Studies in Classical Antiquity*, 3: 17–37.

Osborne, R. (1987). *Classical Landscape with Figures*. London.

Powell, J. (2021). '"An obol a day net": Problematising Numbers in Xenophon's *Poroi*', *Historia*, 70: 2–28.

Pritchard, D. (2018). 'The Horsemen of Classical Athens: Some Considerations on their Recruitment and Social Background', *Athenaeum*, 106: 439–53.

Raaflaub, K. A. (2006). 'Athenian and Spartan *eunomia*, or: What to Do with Solon's Timocracy?', in Blok and Lardinois (2006: 390–428).

Randall, R. H., Jr (1953). 'The Erechtheum Workmen', *American Journal of Archaeology*, 57: 199–210.

Rhodes, P. J. (1981). *A Commentary on the Aristotelian* Athenaion Politeia. 2nd edn (1993). Oxford.

Rhodes, P. J., and R. Osborne (2003). *Greek Historical Inscriptions 404–323 BC*. Oxford (= RO).

Rihll, T. E. (1991). '*EKTHMOPOI*: Partners in Crime?', *Journal of Hellenic Studies*, 111: 101–27.

Sallares, R. (1991). *The Ecology of the Ancient Greek World*. Ithaca, NY.

Sancisi-Weerdenburg, H. (1993). 'Solon's *hektemoroi*', in H. Sancisi-Weerdenburg, R. J. van der Spek, H. C. Teitler and H. T. Wallinga (eds), *De Agricultura. In Memoriam Pieter Willem de Neeve*, 13–30. Amsterdam.

Scheidel, W. (2010). 'Real Wages in Early Economies: Evidence for Living Standards from 1800 BCE to 1300 CE', *Journal of the Economic and Social History of the Orient*, 53: 425–62.

Scheidel, W., and S. Friesen (2009). 'The Size of the Economy and the Distribution of Income in the Roman Empire', *Journal of Roman Studies*, 99: 61–91.

Schmitz, W. (1995). 'Reiche und Gleiche: Timokratische Gliederung und demokratische Gleichheit der athenischen Bürger im 4. Jahrhundert v. Chr.', in W. Eder (ed.), *Die athenische Demokratie im 4. Jahrhundert v. Chr. Vollendung oder Verfall einer Verfassungsform?*, 573–97. Stuttgart.

Spence, I. (1993). *The Cavalry of Classical Greece: A Social and Military History with Particular Reference to Athens*. Oxford.

Stanley, P. V. (1999). *The Economic Reforms of Solon*. St. Katharinen.

Starr, C. (1977). *The Economic and Social Growth of Early Greece 800–500 BC*. New York.

Tandy, D. (2018). 'In Hesiod's World', in A. Loney and S. Scully (eds), *The Oxford Handbook of Hesiod*, 43–60. Oxford.

Taylor, C. (2017). *Poverty, Wealth and Well-Being. Experiencing* Penia *in Democratic Athens*. Oxford.

Valdes Guia, M. (2019). 'The Social and Cultural Background of Hoplite Development in Archaic Athens: Peasants, Debts, *zeugitai* and Hoplethes', *Historia*, 68: 388–412.

Valdes Guia, M. (2022). '*Zeugitai* in Fifth-Century Athens: Social and Economic Qualification from Cleisthenes to the End of the Peloponnesian War', *Pnyx: Journal of Classical Studies*, 1: 45–78.

Valdes Guia, M., and J. Gallego (2010). 'Athenian zeugitai and the Solonian Census Classes: New Reflections and Perspectives', *Historia*, 59: 257–81.

van Wees, H. (1999). 'The Mafia of Early Greece', in K. Hopwood (ed.), *Organized Crime in Antiquity*, 1–51. London.

van Wees, H. (2001). 'The Myth of the Middle-Class Army', in L. Hannestad and T. Bekker-Nielsen (eds), *War as a Cultural and Social Force*, 45–71. Copenhagen.

van Wees, H. (2004). *Greek Warfare: Myths and Realities*. London.

van Wees, H. (2006). 'Mass and Elite in Solon's Athens', in Blok and Lardinois (2006: 351–89).

van Wees, H. (2009). 'The Economy', in K. A. Raaflaub and H. van Wees (eds), *A Companion to Archaic Greece*, 444–67. Malden.

van Wees, H. (2011). 'Demetrius and Draco: Athens' Property Classes and Population in and before 317 BC', *Journal of Hellenic Studies*, 131: 95–114.

van Wees, H. (2013a). *Ships and Silver, Taxes and Tribute: A Fiscal History of Archaic Athens*. London.

van Wees, H. (2013b). 'Farmers and Hoplites: Models of Historical Development', in Kagan and Viggiano (2013: 222–55).

van Wees, H. (2018). 'Citizens and Soldiers in Archaic Athens', in A. Duplouy and R. Brock (eds), *Defining Citizenship in Archaic Greece*, 103–43. Oxford.

van Wees, H. (forthcoming). *Slave and Free Labour in Early Greece, 750–450 BC: Joseph C. Miller Memorial Lecture Series. Bonn Centre for Dependency and Slavery Studies.* Berlin.

West, M. L. (1978). *Hesiod:* Works and Days. Oxford.

# 6

# The Local Slave Systems of Ancient Greece

*David M. Lewis*

## Preface

A key objective of this volume is to explore the history of groups that are either underrepresented in our ancient literary sources and/or overlooked in modern scholarship. These may include, for instance, women, metics and immigrants, lower-class labourers, and slaves. Slavery is the subject of this chapter; but when we talk about slavery in ancient Greece, the tendency to date has been to talk about slavery in Athens, a choice that may seem odd in a world of a thousand or so far from uniform *poleis*. That choice has been justified in part because of the distribution of evidence: Athens simply represents the focal point of the vast majority of our literary sources, while slavery in the vast majority of other *poleis* goes completely unattested (though it is *prima facie* likely to have played a significant role in economy and society).

There is a second reason for the focus on Athens, however; and that is to do with taxonomy and scholarly tradition. For much of the twentieth century, labour systems described as systems of slavery in classical Greek sources have been categorized as something else by modern scholars. Most prominent among these labourers are the Helots of Lakonia and Messenia; analogous groups include the Penestai of Thessaly, the Klarotai of Crete, and the Mariandynoi of Herakleia Pontike. These have typically been counted not as slave populations but as 'serfs', 'dependent peasantry', or 'unfree labourers'.

The present chapter has two aims. The first is to show that the classification of such systems as something other than slavery is unwarranted: it depends on overlooking more reliable early sources (which classify these populations as slaves, privately owned and subject to sale) in favour of less reliable late sources written long after these systems of slavery had ceased to exist (which classify them as something other than slaves). A source-critical method enjoins us to take seriously these early sources and readmit such systems into our overall framework, seeing Greek slavery not just as Athenian slavery writ large, but as a patchwork of diverse epichoric slave systems whose distinctive features were adaptive responses to local historical developments. The second aim of this chapter is to illustrate the diversity of Greek slave systems, and thereby the experiences of those exploited in them, through a series of thumbnail sketches: Thessaly, Lokris, Herakleia Pontike, and Khios. Although such a survey is far from comprehensive, its range should indicate how the experience of work, supervision, and violence was extremely varied across the Greek world.

\* \* \* \* \*

## Introduction

Around the middle of the fourth century BCE, a man named Apollodoros insulted Phormion, an ex-slave of his father who had prospered in banking, in front of an Athenian law court:

> I should think that you all know that when this man was up for sale, if a cook or an artisan in some other trade had bought him, he would have learned the trade of his owner and been far removed from his present fortune. But since our father, a banker, bought him and taught him letters and educated him in his business and put him in charge of lots of money, he has become prosperous... ([Dem.] 45.71–2)

Apollodoros' remark, however vituperative, underscores an important truth. The experiences of subordinates in general, and slaves in particular, are profoundly shaped by the nature of their work. Most of a slave's waking life was spent at work: Aristotle (*Pol.* 1334$^a$20) repeats a proverb, 'no leisure for slaves!', and, while we might not expect every single day of a slave's year to have been spent at work, the slave's scope for leisure was more curtailed than that of individuals from any other status group. Accordingly, much of a slave's time will have been spent learning some skill and then applying it on a daily basis. Work shaped what a slave did and where, and to a significant degree with whom he or she interacted.

Phormion was sold in Athens, perhaps the most economically complex city in the Eastern Mediterranean at that time. When he was up for sale, the number of possible occupations he might have been forced into numbered close to two hundred.[1] But Athens was in many ways an unusual *polis*. The economy of Athens in which Phormion worked, and the laws that set the parameters of his exploitation, were not the same as those of other regions of the Greek world. What of the experiences of slaves beyond Attica? Put this way, a useful first step for investigating the theme of this volume might be to analyse patterns of labour and law more broadly. Such an enquiry does not, of course, represent the only way the question

---

[1] On the range of jobs in the Athenian economy, see now Lewis (2020).

of slave or subordinate experiences might be approached.[2] But it could prove a useful way of framing the issue prior to undertaking more focused analyses.

Several obstacles confront the historian who wishes to undertake this task. The most serious is the uneven distribution of evidence, in terms of both quantity and generic diversity, which places Athens in a privileged position.[3] But, although our evidence for other regions is comparatively meagre, this does not rule out analysis altogether: Alain Bresson's fine recent study of slavery in north-west Greece, drawing mainly on epigraphical sources, illustrates what can be done if sufficient attention is given to the local political and economic context, and shows the degree to which the working lives of slaves there were quite different from those of slaves in Attica.[4] But another obstacle lies in modern historiographical tradition. In several regions of classical Greece there existed systems of labour exploitation (most notably in Sparta, Thessaly, and Crete) that have traditionally been categorized as forms of serfdom or some equivalent (but at any rate non-slave) status. I have argued elsewhere, building on the work of several scholars (especially Jean Ducat, Stefan Link, and Nino Luraghi), that these systems were in fact systems of slavery, and therefore ought not to be viewed as something categorically different from the Attic model, but instead as local variations of a panhellenic practice.[5] Yet disagreement on this issue is still widespread. One key reason why scholars have resisted categorizing such populations as slaves lies in the importance accorded to a passage from Pollux's *Onomasticon* (3.83, second century AD):

> Between free men and slaves are the Helots of the Lakedaimonians, the Penestai of the Thessalians, the Klarotai and Mnoitai of the Cretans, the Dorophoroi of the Mariandynians, the Gymnetes of the Argives, and the Korynephoroi of the Sikyonians.[6]

The tendency to treat Pollux's claim as accurate has been pervasive, leading to various alternative classifications. The label 'serfdom' has proven influential in the Anglo-American sphere;[7] while various German scholars have preferred labelling such systems as forms of 'Unfreiheit', but not 'Sklaverei'.[8] In a recent synthesis,

---

[2] One might, for example, employ a comparative approach, as does Forsdyke (2012, 2021). The other chapters in this volume illustrate alternative approaches.
[3] Cf. Vlassopoulos (2016: 659–70).    [4] Bresson (2019).
[5] Lewis (2018: 125–65, esp. 143–6).
[6] Μεταξὺ δὲ ἐλευθέρων καὶ δούλων οἱ Λακεδαιμονίων Εἵλωτες καὶ Θετταλῶν Πενέσται καὶ Κρητῶν Κλαρῶται καὶ Μνῶιται καὶ Μαριανδυνῶν Δωροφόροι καὶ Ἀργείων Γυμνῆτες καὶ Σικυωνίων Κορυνηφόροι.
[7] See especially de Ste. Croix (1981: 147–51); Cartledge (1988); cf. most recently Hunt (2016; 2018: 77–85) and Forsdyke (2021: 41–7). Finley (1981: 142) criticized the use of the 'serf' category; his preference was to talk about 'unfree' statuses.
[8] The major German study is Lotze (1959), for whom these groups are subjected to a master class as a form of 'Kollektivsklaverei'. But see Schumacher (2001: 13) ('unfrei, doch keine Sklaven'); similarly, Hermann-Otto (2009) lists the Helots under 'Sonderformen der Unfreiheit' and defends Pollux 3.83. Welwei (2008) is more critical of Pollux, but also treats Helotage, etc., as forms of 'Unfreiheit' and avoids the language of slavery.

Jean Andreau and Raymond Descat exclude the Helots of Lakonia and Messenia, the dependent populations of Crete, the Mariandynoi of Herakleia Pontike and the Penestai of Thessaly from their purview. In discussing *Onomasticon* 3.83, they write:

> Such a text says both little and much. It shows a clear awareness of the following social fact: one cannot confuse non-slave dependants either with slaves, or with free persons. Is it correct to place them 'in the middle', 'between' free persons and slaves? For sure, it can be debated; but since these dependants are not entirely the private property of a master, as we shall see, it is not necessarily false to regard their status as intermediary between the two extreme categories. The essential point is there, in the difference between two statuses: slavery proper and serfdom.[9]

But do other sources align with Pollux's claim? What is surprising in recent historiography is the degree to which many scholars have ascribed special status to Pollux's remark, while according lesser status to earlier (contradictory) evidence. In some cases, Pollux 3.83 has been the first (and sometimes also the last) port of call for those interested in this question.[10] The tendency to exclude the Helots and analogous populations from the category of slavery has had wide-reaching effects, in two senses. First, Greek slavery has come to be conterminous with Attic slavery, meaning that the institution in general has taken on a strongly athenocentric complexion.[11] Secondly, apart from Helotage (which, given the high interest in Sparta, has always garnered much attention), the categorization of analogous groups as something other than slaves has shuffled them out of the investigative spotlight.[12]

This chapter continues the argument for a different paradigm. I take up the status question once more, but with a close analysis of Pollux 3.83 and its standing in recent historiography at its core. I aim to show that the trust placed in Pollux's remark is unwarranted, and that the classical sources that describe the aforementioned populations as privately owned slaves are a more reliable guide to

---

[9] Andreau and Descat (2006: 11–12): 'Un tel texte en dit à la fois peu et beaucoup. Il montre une conscience claire du fait social suivant: on ne peut confondre les dépendants non esclaves, ni avec les esclaves, ni avec les libres. Est-il juste de les placer «au milieu», «entre» les libres et les esclaves? On peut en discuter, certes; mais puisque ces dépendants ne sont pas entièrement propriété privée d'un maître, comme nous allons le voir, il n'est pas nécessairement faux de considérer leur statut comme intermédiaire entre les deux catégories extrêmes. Le point essentiel est bien là, dans la différence entre deux statuts: l'esclavage proprement dit et le servage.'

[10] e.g. Christiansen (2002: 25); Morgan (2003: 191); Hall (2007: 238); Migeotte (2009: 41).

[11] Despite their numerous virtues, the books of Schumacher (2001), Andreau and Descat (2006), Hermann-Otto (2009), Hunt (2018), and Forsdyke (2021) are similar in this respect.

[12] As Peter Hunt (2016: 71) has rightly noted, there is no discipline of 'serf studies' comparable to 'slavery studies'. Since slaves gain the lion's share of attention, the categorization of any of these groups as serfs means a corresponding drop in historical interest.

classical realities. This opens the door to a different view of Greek slavery: not an Attic-style Ideal Type, but a vast patchwork of local variants whose distinct features arose from the fact that they were embedded in their regional contexts and shaped by local socio-economic and historical developments. The bulk of this chapter analyses several of these systems, a series of soundings in epichoric history[13] that in part presents the key evidence and in part engages in analysis of specific historical problems, especially the reasons behind this or that slave system's distinctive attributes. Since I have recently discussed the slave systems of classical Sparta and Crete at some length, I will not touch on them in any detail here.[14] The first section will explore a northern-Greek region, Thessaly, and the second section a central-Greek region, Western Lokris; their slave populations have been compared to the Helots, the former in antiquity, the latter in modern times. The third section will look at a 'colonial' slave system—namely, the Mariandynoi of Herakleia Pontike. The fourth section turns to the Aegean islands and examines the system of slavery in Khios. In each case I shall demonstrate that we are dealing with slavery *sensu stricto* before analysing the distinctive local features of the slave system in question. This will, I hope, bring out more fully the striking regional differences between classical Greek slave systems, and thereby set the scene for a more granular analysis of local differences in slave experiences.

## Slavery or Something Else?

We begin with Pollux 3.83. The story of this passage's fate in twentieth-century scholarship on Greek slavery is a curious one, for it might easily have suffered the fate of other late lexical oddities such as the claim of the Medieval *Etymologicum Gudianum* (s.v. Εἴλωτες) that the Penestai and Helots were 'free men who work as slaves for a salary', a strange and justifiably ignored remark;[15] or that of Pausanias the Atticist, a contemporary of Pollux who categorized these populations as metics.[16] However, it was not ignored, and the story of its role in twentieth-century scholarship begins with a footnote in an otherwise almost forgotten article of 1905 by Heinrich Swoboda. In a brief discussion of the passage, Swoboda wrote that:

> This passage originates, as the comparison with the excerpts in E. Miller, *Mélanges de littérature grecque* 434 shows, from Aristophanes of Byzantium...who dealt

---

[13] A term coined by Figueira (1993: 1).   [14] Lewis (2018 125–65; forthcoming).
[15] οἱ <ἐπὶ> μισθῷ δουλεύοντες ἐλεύθεροι. Brief discussion in Ducat (1994: 31–2). As Ducat (1990: 38) points out, this entry looks like a garbled version of Theopompos BNJ 115 F122b, which is a scholion on Theokritos, *Idyll* 16.35. I agree with Ducat (1990: 48–9) that the 'fragment' is really a muddled gloss on Theopompos dating to the Roman era. For a useful recent illustration of the sorts of problems that can creep into late lexical sources, see Węcowski (2018).
[16] K33 s.v. Κλαρῶται Erbse. See Ducat (1990: 37).

extensively with these legal relations; this is also evident in the interest in which his student Kallistratos took in these things.[17]

And that was that; or at least until 1959, when Swoboda's connection of the passage with Aristophanes was once more reiterated in a work in German, Detlef Lotze's *Metaxu Eleutheron kai Doulon*. In the first page of this book, Lotze wrote that 'the passage presumably goes back to Aristophanes of Byzantium', citing Swoboda.[18] Yet the significance of the passage only truly took off with the publication of M. I. Finley's influential article 'Between Slavery and Freedom' in 1964. Here, Finley wrote regarding Pollux's *Onomasticon*:

> It is of no use pretending that this work is very penetrating or systematic; at least in the abridged form in which it has come down to us, but the foundation was laid in a much earlier work by a very learned scholar, Aristophanes of Byzantium, who flourished in the first half of the third century BCE.[19]

It is true that Pollux did draw extensively on Aristophanes' work in compiling his *Onomasticon*; but the crux lies in whether the *metaxu* formula derives from Aristophanes. Finley is more explicit a few pages later, writing of 'large numbers of men who could not be socially located as either slave or free, who were "between slavery and freedom", in the loose language of Aristophanes of Byzantium and Julius Pollux'.[20] Finley clearly did not share Lotze's more cautious stance, for there is no 'vermutlich' in his phrasing. This move catalysed the intellectual significance of Pollux's remark in two ways. First, it raised it from an offhand comment in a lexicographical work of the Second Sophistic to the learned opinion of one of the Hellenistic period's foremost scholars, who furthermore stood centuries closer in time to the heyday of these aforementioned servile systems. Secondly, the passage gained the imprimatur of M. I. Finley, the doyen of late-twentieth-century scholarship on Greek slavery. Subsequent scholarship has generally respected this attribution to Aristophanes.[21]

With each repetition of this view, the idea that the Helots and comparable populations were not slaves has worn an ever-deeper rut of intellectual path

---

[17] Swoboda (1905: 252, n. 1): 'Dieser Passus stammt, wie der Vergleich mit den Exzerpten bei E. Miller, *Mélanges de littérature grecque* 434 beweist, aus Aristophanes von Byzanz...der sich mit diesen Rechtsverhältnissen eingehend beschäftigt haben wird; dafür zeugt auch das Interesse, welches sein Schüler Kallistratos an diesen Dingen nahm.'

[18] Lotze (1959: 1): 'Vermutlich geht der Passus auf Aristophanes von Byzanz zurück.'

[19] Finley (1964: 233).

[20] Finley (1964: 237). The loose language, however, is Finley's, for Pollux does not write of slavery and freedom. As Ducat (1990: 51) notes regarding Finley's rendering: 'Le texte dit: «entre les hommes libres et les esclaves», ce qui n'est pas la même chose.'

[21] de Ste. Croix (1981: 139); Garlan (1988: 87); Fisher (1993: 22); Cartledge (2002 [1979]: 139); cf. Cartledge 2011: 79); Paradiso (2007: 29, n. 26); Hodkinson (2008: 287); Urbainczyk (2008: 91); Welwei (2008: 1); Luraghi (2009: 261); Zurbach (2013: 959).

dependence. Yet, if one checks the sources, it quickly becomes clear that the ascription of the slogan to Aristophanes is far from secure. We may consider, first, p. 434 of Emmanuel Miller's *Mélanges de littérature grecque* on which Swoboda relied, which presents a fourteenth-century manuscript from Athos that Miller attributed to Aristophanes. The text shows only a superficial resemblance to Pollux 3.83, a mere three groups (the Mnoitai, Penestai, and Helots) listed in a different order from Pollux's list, and, more importantly, without any mention of the *metaxu* slogan; instead, most remarkably of all, the passage equates them with freedmen, something Swoboda neglected to mention to his readers.[22]

The second prop of Swoboda's claim concerns Aristophanes' student Kallistratos, whom he rightly claimed was interested in the Helots and comparable groups. Yet the passage in question, Athen. *Deip.* 6.84.263d–e, far from supporting Swoboda's case, actually undermines it:

> Kallistratos the student of Aristophanes says that they called the Mariandynoi 'Gift Bearers' (*dorophoroi*) to take away the bitterness of the term 'slaves' (*oiketai*), just as the Spartans did regarding the Helots, the Thessalians regarding the Penestai, and the Cretans regarding the Klarotai.[23]

Kallistratos' point, then, is that these groups *were* slaves, but were given euphemistic names to take the sting out of their condition. If Aristophanes had thought these groups to be 'between free men and slaves', his student disagreed. Now, one ought not to assume that students always repeat unquestioned the views of their teachers; perhaps Aristophanes held a different stance. But Swoboda's citation of Kallistratos adds nothing to the likelihood of his claim about Aristophanes being correct, for his point that Kallistratos took an interest in the Helots and analogous groups could equally be made of Plato, Aristotle, or Theopompos.[24] In sum, the whole hypothesis of Aristophanes' authorship of the

---

[22] Miller (1868: 434): Ἀπελεύθερος τῷ δεσπότῃ, καὶ ἐξελεύθερος ὁ αὐτός· οὓς ἐν Κρήτῃ μινώτας, καὶ ἐν Θετταλίᾳ πενέστας, καὶ ἐν Λακεδαίμονι εἵλωτας ἐκάλουν. Slater (1986: 111) writes: 'These servile names could not have been identified with the preceding freedmen. Either there is a lacuna before οὕς or the epitomator has carelessly combined two sets of glosses.' This may well be so, and it is difficult to believe that Aristophanes made such a blunder; but, if we uncouple the relative clause from the preceding text, as Slater suggests, that only leaves us with the mention of three servile groups to attribute to Aristophanes, and thus removes any evidence that he thought these groups were not slaves.

[23] λέγει δὲ καὶ Καλλίστρατος ὁ Ἀριστοφάνειος ὅτι τοὺς Μαριανδυνοὺς ὠνόμαζον μὲν δωροφόρους ἀφαιροῦντες τὸ πικρὸν τῆς ἐπί τῶν οἰκετῶν προσηγορίας, καθάπερ Σπαρτιᾶται μὲν ἐποίησαν ἐπὶ τῶν εἱλώτων, Θετταλοὶ δ' ἐπὶ τῶν πενεστῶν, Κρῆτες δ' ἐπὶ τῶν κλαρωτῶν. On the term *oiketai*, see Lewis (2018: 295–305).

[24] Paradiso (2007: 30–1) cites a scholion on Ar. *Thesm.* 917 Nauck, noting Kallistratos' disagreements with Aristophanes. At pp. 31–2 she points out the problem of 'καὶ Μαριανδυνῶν Δωροφόροι' at Poll. *Onom.* 3.83: Asheri (1972: 18, n. 36) explains this as a partitive genitive, which works grammatically, but makes no sense in context, where the genitive is used for the master classes of the other servile groups; the Mariandynoi *were* Dorophoroi, and were not their masters. Pollux thus commits a factual error of a sort unlikely to have been made by Aristophanes, and which Kallistratos did not make (cf. Burstein 1976: 114). As Whitehead (1981 *passim*) demonstrates, Pollux also mistakenly uses

*metaxu* slogan rests squarely on one (possibly corrupt) source that says that the Helots were freedmen, and another that says they were slaves. Unless we are simply to split the difference between them, these sources do not support Swoboda's contention.

However, the most convincing reason to reject the *metaxu eleutheron kai doulon* idea—and to treat it as belonging to the same category as Pausanias the Atticist's contemporary claim that the Helots were metics—comes from a close examination of the early sources. Whereas Pollux groups the Helots and analogous populations together on the criterion of status (they are neither slaves nor free men, but something in between), writers at the very beginning of the tradition of comparing Sparta's Helots to other servile groups used a completely different criterion: the fact that the Helots and other groups were monoglot populations. This was seen as worrisome in the context of debates over slave management in the ideal states of Plato and Aristotle.[25] Plato in the *Laws* (776c–d) compares the Helots to the Penestai and Mariandynoi in discussing restive slave populations and proposes (*Leg.* 777c–d) that the ideal slave system should draw its slaves from many different races, implying that these restive slave populations were monoglot and ethnically uniform.[26] Aristotle extended the Helot comparison to Crete (*Pol.* 1271$^b$41–1272$^a$1). At *Politics* 1269$^a$34–$^b$12 he points out that the Penestai and Helots often revolted against their masters, but the same had not occurred in Crete. Later (*Pol.* 1330$^a$25–33) he comes to the same solution as Plato: those who cultivate the soil in the ideal state should preferably be slaves drawn from a multitude of races.

There is no sign in the first sources to compare the Helots to other servile groups that their authors thought them to have been anything other than slaves. As Jean Ducat has pointed out, the classical authors who discuss these groups do so using the standard vocabulary of slavery.[27] The remarks of early historians concur: Thucydides (8.40.2) claimed that the Khians had the most *oiketai* of any Greek *polis* except Sparta, while Theopompos of Khios (*BNJ* 115 F122) claimed that the Khians were the first Greeks to have paid a price (*time*) for their slaves; the Spartans and Thessalians had previously enslaved their Helots and Penestai, respectively, through conquest. In neither author is there any sign that they were comparing apples and oranges, and Theopompos' contrast is to do not with status but with methods of acquiring slaves. In another fragment (F 81), Theopompos refers to Agathokles, 'a slave (*doulos*) by birth, and of the Penestai in Thessaly'.

---

the term Κορυνηφόροι instead of the correct term Κατωνακοφόροι, probably through muddling them up with Peisistratos' club bearers (Hdt. 1.59). Cf. Hansen's remarks in Hansen and Hodkinson (2009: 474–5).

[25] Luraghi (2009: 265–6).

[26] Cf. Luraghi (2009: 266): 'The key element of the similarity between them was the ethnic homogeneity of the slaves.' Plato's analysis of the causes of slave revolt is rather monolithic; for a more sophisticated analysis, see Cartledge (1985), with the further observations of Luraghi (2009: 270).

[27] Ducat (1990: 46–7).

Kritias even claimed that the Helots were the most slavish of all slaves in Greece (88B 37 D-K), a remark that, as Nino Luraghi has noted, is almost the exact opposite of the *metaxu* slogan.[28]

Based on belief in Pollux's essential accuracy, some scholars have claimed that these early sources display a degree of juridical naivety, and that they were utilizing a fairly vague, broad conception of *douleia* that went beyond the traditional property definition employed by most ancient and modern scholars.[29] Yet a look at some other early sources confirms the picture painted by Plato, Aristotle, Kritias, Thucydides, and Theopompos. Ephoros (*BNJ* 70 F117) writes that the Helots were slaves held under special conditions—namely, that their masters were not allowed to manumit them nor 'to sell (them) beyond the boundaries', πωλεῖν ἔξω τῶν ὅρων. As Luraghi has observed, if Ephoros had meant an outright ban on sale, 'it would have been enough to conclude the sentence with πωλεῖν, without mentioning the borders'.[30] We find a similar detail in Arkhemakhos of Euboia's *Euboika* (*BNJ* 424 F1): the Thessalians were banned both from killing the Penestai and from taking them out of the country. Likewise, Poseidonios (*BNJ* 87 F8) remarks that the Mariandynoi could be sold only within the territory of Herakleia. In all three cases we find a restricted form of private ownership of slaves, one that had geographical limits placed on the range within which these slaves could be sold.[31]

Our most convincing evidence comes from Gortyn on Crete, another region where 'serfdom' is held to have prevailed. Gortyn's inscriptions contain two terms for slave, *dolos* and *woikeus*. Some have claimed that these terms refer to different statuses, and that *woikeis* were 'serfs' bound to the soil.[32] But, as Finley rightly pointed out, there are good reasons to question this view; and, even if one accepts it, we know from *IC* IV 41 IV 6–14 that *woikeis* could be sold by their private owners.[33] To sum up so far: all of our early sources depict the Helots and analogous groups as privately owned slaves potentially subject to sale (in several

---

[28] Luraghi (2009: 262).

[29] Cartledge (2002 [1979]: 139); Harvey (1988: 48); Forsdyke (2021: 45). On the property definition of slavery, see Lewis (2016; 2018: 25–55). Whether or not one chooses the traditional definition or Patterson's substitute definition, the Helots qualify as slaves: on the traditional definition applied to Helots, see Lewis (2018: 125–41); on Patterson's definition applied to Helots, see Luraghi (2002: 228–33).

[30] Luraghi (2002: 229). Forsdyke (2021: 43) claims that even the early sources on the Helots show confusion over status, and that Ephorus simultaneously believed the Helots to be private property and some manner of public slaves. But the comment about public slavery belongs not to Ephorus but to Strabo, because it is prefaced by the remark that Helotage lasted down to the Roman conquest (a remark excised by ellipsis in Forsdyke's quotation of the passage). See Hodkinson (2000: 117) for detailed discussion.

[31] Ducat (1990: 19–29; 1994: 72); Luraghi (2002: 229); Lewis (2018: 128–9.) On variations in restrictions on ownership across cultures, see Lewis (2018: 30–55).

[32] e.g. Gagarin (2010).

[33] *Dolos-woikeus* debate: Finley (1981: 135–7); Link (2001); Welwei (2008: 2–3); Lewis (2018: 155); Lewis (forthcoming). Bound to the soil: Gagarin (2010: 22) accepts that *woikeis* could be sold but argues that they were sold along with land plots to which they were bound, an idea with no evidentiary basis but that is supplied by his categorization of *woikeis* as 'serfs'.

cases within a restricted range). To believe the claim of Pollux that these groups were not slaves, then, is to suppose that these early sources were wrong, yet that this Roman-era compiler of words was correct. That seems rather improbable. The tradition of comparing the Helots to other servile groups must be recognized as fractured, contradictory, and composed of sources of highly unequal value, and it is largely through repetition of Finley's views that many scholars have given pride of place in their discussions to one of the least credible sources in that tradition.[34] Rigorous source criticism reveals that Pollux 3.83 tells us more about the reception of classical Greek slavery during the Second Sophistic than it does about fifth- and fourth-century realities.

The consequence of this alternative view, if it is accepted, is that Greek slavery ought not to be treated as roughly the same thing as slavery at Athens (with the occasional nod to Delphi, Corinth, Aegina, and so on). Attic slavery constitutes just one piece of a larger and more complex puzzle: Sparta, Crete, Thessaly, Herakleia, and so forth belong in the picture too; and, given Athens' long-held centrality to the subject, further progress requires reorientation towards the full range of evidence, especially epigraphy. That is not to say that the potential for work on Attic slavery has been exhausted—far from it—but that, for a better appreciation of Greek slavery *as a whole*, much work remains to be done on other regions, and old habits of thought subjected to critical scrutiny. In terms of the focus of this volume, such a gearshift can only encourage the study of the experiences of slaves beyond Athens. How might we think of the working life of a slave shepherd in the backcountry of Ozolian Lokris? Or of a slave girl working for one of the grand families of Thessaly? Or of a Mariandynian slave belonging to a Herakleote oligarch, engaged in collecting the summer nut harvest? Or of a Phrygian trafficked to Khios and set to work in a vineyard far from the city? We can begin by considering the basic local parameters of the slave systems in which these individuals worked, as the following four case studies will illustrate.

## Thessaly: A Northern-Greek Slave System

According to Jean Ducat, the Thessalian Penestai system most closely resembles the kind of slavery depicted in the Homeric poems: opulent aristocratic houses, with extensive landholdings cultivated by large numbers of slaves involved in a mixture of arable and pastoral farming.[35] Theokritos, in his sixteenth *Idyll*

---

[34] By comparison with the widely held view that Pollux 3.83 contains reliable information and ought to be mentioned prominently when discussing Helot status, early evidence that contradicts the orthodoxy (e.g. Ephoros) tends to be treated with much more scepticism: cf. Hunt (2016: 65) (who, to his credit, comes to grips with Ephoros, unlike most scholars of a traditional leaning). As one can see from general works touching on the issue (see n. 10), Pollux 3.83 remains the 'go to' reference on Helot status.

[35] Ducat (2015: 194, building on Ducat 1994, 1997). For Homeric slavery, see Harris (2012); Lewis (2018: 107–24); van Wees (2021). On Thessalian decadence, see Pownall (2009).

(16.34–47), harks back to several (now lost) poems by the late-archaic poet Simonides praising the wealth and athletic achievements of several grand Thessalian aristocratic families:

> Many were the Penestai that drew their rations month by month in the halls of Antiochos and king Aleuas; many the calves that with the horned cattle were driven bellowing to the byres of the Skopadai; countless the choice sheep that for the honourable Kreondai the shepherds pastured afield over the plain of Krannon. Yet of these no joy they had when once they had discharged their dear spirits into the capacious raft of the ferryman old and grim. And leaving that rich store, unremembered would they have lain long ages among the hapless dead had not a bard inspired, the man of Keos, tuned his varied lays to the lyre of many strings and made them famous among the men of later days; and even the swift steeds lacked not their meed of glory that brought them from the holy games the crown of victory. (trans. A.S.F. Gow, adapted)[36]

There are a number of archaic echoes here. Theokritos enlists the same rare term used for rations by Hesiod (*Op.* 560, 767), ἁρμαλιή; and the enumeration of the flocks and herds of the Skopadai of Krannon and of the Kreondai of Pharsalos resonates with Eumaios' enumeration of the livestock of Odysseus (Hom. *Od.* 14.99–104).[37] Just as Odysseus arms his slaves to meet his enemies (Hom. *Od.* 24. 496–501), so too do we learn from Demosthenes (23.199) that the Thessalian aristocrat Menon of Pharsalos had assisted the Athenians in their campaign at Eion in 476/5 with three hundred of his own mounted Penestai. Various classical Greek states armed their slaves on occasion, from Sparta's use of Helot infantrymen to Athens' use of slaves as rowers in the fleet at Arginousai in 406.[38] Menon's personal troop obviously shows an adaption of this traditional practice, playing to Thessaly's local strength in cavalry.[39]

The ethnic and linguistic homogeneity of the Penestai—which later gave rise to charter myths of their origins in mass conquests in the distant past—makes sense in terms of the geographical position of Thessaly, its aristocratic culture, and the broader economy of the region.[40] Thessaly is extremely fertile, allowing not only

---

[36] On Thessalian aristocrats and their patronage of the arts, see Stamatopoulou (2006).
[37] Of course, Theokritos is engaging in archaism for generic reasons; but Thessalian aristocratic culture lent itself well to this; some aristocratic Thessalians even started to build *tholos* tombs like those of early Greece during the classical period, cultivating links with the heroic past: Stamatopoulou (2016).
[38] Welwei (1974); Hunt (1998).
[39] See Aston and Kerr (2018). On Thessalian warfare more generally, see Sprawski (2014).
[40] Charter myths and folk etymologies: sources in Ducat (1994: 13–63); cf. Welwei (2008: 7), who rightly writes: 'Die angedeuten Herkunftslegenden haben keinen eigenständigen Quellenwert.' The approach of Luraghi (2003) could equally be applied to an 'Imaginary Conquest of the Penestai', which is not to rule out a role for warfare in the origins of the system, only the plausibility of a mythical conquest by an invading population; cf. Welwei (2008: 10).

for major stockbreeding but for grain yields well in excess of local requirements, which could be exported abroad.[41] Thessaly was therefore not dependent on food imports, and did not integrate as fully into Aegean trading networks as regions such as Attica, the Corinthiad, or islands such as Aegina, whose growing populations had already outstripped the carrying capacity of their *khorai* in the archaic period and whose economies were heavily dependent on overseas trade for their food supply.[42] Besides, despite the great size of the region, the only area accessible to seaborne merchants was the gulf of Pagasai.[43] Thessaly's aristocrats took an even more conservative stance regarding trade than the Spartans; for, although the latter eschewed *khrematistike*, they did engage in buying and selling in the *agora* (Thuc. 5.34; Xen. *Hell.* 3.3.5). The Thessalians, however, went so far as to construct separate *agorai* in their cities: there was a commercial *agora* of the usual sort; but Aristotle (*Pol.* 1331ª30–5) refers also to 'an *agora* of the kind customary in Thessaly, which they call a free agora, that is, one which has to be kept clear of all merchandise and into which no artisan or farmer or any other such person may intrude unless summoned by the magistrates' (trans. Rackham).

The ban on external sale of Penestai (Arkhemakhos *BNJ* 424 F1) may have emerged from the need to plug any potential leaks to the slave population and guarantee an adequate supply of slaves for an aristocratic class whose *habitus* involved a conscious abstention from direct involvement in trade.[44] Luraghi has also pointed out that the elites that owned slaves in such regions cleaved to a militaristic ideology: it served their purposes to own slaves who could be presented as the descendants of people captured by their forefathers, a conceit that would be hard to maintain had they routinely acquired new slaves by purchase. The ban on external sale may thus have served to stabilize the system of slave reproduction and perpetuate the ideology of original conquest.[45] Perhaps the issue of stability also played a role, for these sale bans are all attested for oligarchic regimes, which often impose restrictions of various kinds on the acquisition and exchange of positional goods in order to reduce the political instability caused by status competition among elites.[46] Whatever the origins of the system, and whenever this ban on external sale was introduced, the latter can only have led to greater dependence on reproduction through slave families, and, as a result, increasing linguistic and cultural homogeneity as time went by.[47]

---

[41] Xen. *Hell.* 6.1.11; [Herodes] *Peri Politeias* §14; Antiphanes fr. 36 K–A; Alexis fr. 196 K–A; cf. Theophr. *HP.* 8.7.4.

[42] See Bresson (2016: 402–38).

[43] Hermippos fr. 63 K–A mentions slaves exported from Pagasai to Athens, as well as tattooed men (one of the latter turns up, of all places, in the Epidaurian *iamata*: *IG* iv² 121, ll. 48–68); while Aristophanes (*Plut.* 519–21) notes the Thessalian reputation for *andrapodistai*, kidnappers who sell their victims into slavery. Such references hint at aspects of slavery in Thessaly occurring beyond and alongside the aristocracy's Penestai system.

[44] Cf. Ducat (1990: 23); Luraghi (2002: 229, 234); van Wees (2003: 70).

[45] Luraghi (2009: 267–8). In a similar vein, see Link (2004).

[46] Bernhardt (2003); Simonton (2017: 89–93). [47] Cf. Luraghi (2002: 239).

There are further differences between the Penestai and the Helots; for, whereas the Spartans sought for ideological reasons to humiliate their Helots through an ongoing *Kulturkampf*, marking out the distinction between slave and citizen through, for example, forms of dress, the same does not appear to have occurred in Thessaly, or at least not consistently: two of our sources note the existence of powerful Penestai who achieved wealth and status.[48] Yet there were similarities in practices with other regions: Baton of Sinope (*BNJ* 268 F5), for instance, refers to a Thessalian role-reversal festival of the sort that can be paralleled in various Greek communities.[49] The Thessalian Penestai-system survived into the Hellenistic period; but its demise is as shrouded in mystery as its origins.[50]

## Lokris: A Central-Greek Slave System

Most Lokrians lived in central Greece, their settlements lying either side of Phokis. To the west of Phokis lived the Western (or Ozolian) Lokrians; to the east lived the Eastern (Opountian, Hypoknemidian, and Epiknemidian) Lokrians. Despite this territorial separation, they remained a single *ethnos* joined by kinship, dialect, and a shared identity.[51] A colonial population, the Epizephyrian Lokrians, had dwelt in southern Italy since the colony's establishment in the seventh century. The mainland Lokrians are of interest here because they have been drawn into the debate over 'helotic' slavery and Greek 'serfdom', despite the fact that no ancient author ever drew the connection—not even the lexicographers whose lists of Helot comparanda include various groups not mentioned by writers of the classical period.[52] The view is based on two texts. *SIG*³ 47 (= Tod no. 24) dates to the early fifth century and relates to the Eastern Lokrian colony at Naupaktos in Western Lokris. Among the regulations is a stipulation concerning magistrates, who are required to grant trials to prospective litigants (ll. 43–5): 'If he does not grant the accuser a trial, he is to be disenfranchised and his property confiscated, his land portion along with his *woikiatai*.'[53] According to van Wees, these *woikiatai* were serfs bound to the land portion (*meros*).[54] But this

---

[48] Theopompos *BNJ* 115 F81; Arkhemakhos *BNJ* 424 F1. Agathokles, the powerful Penestes mentioned by Theopompos, may have been a freedman. For referring to manumitted slaves as if they were still slaves, see Lewis (2018: 299–300). For manumission in Thessaly see Ducat (1994: 72–3). For Spartan humiliation of the Helots, see Ducat (1974).
[49] For parallels in other Greek societies, see Zelnick-Abramovitz (2012).
[50] Ducat (1994: 105–13).  [51] See Nielsen (2004); Rousset (2004).
[52] Ducat (1990: 31–44). Note that Aristotle, whose students collected information on the Lokrians, never raises the comparandum of Lokris when discussing the Helots in the *Politics*. The idea of Lokrian 'serfdom' (or a status *metaxu eleutheron kai doulon*) is raised in Lotze (1959: 56); Vidal-Naquet (1986: 212) ('the Locrian *woikiatas*...is effectively a helot'); Garlan (1988: 101); van Wees (2003: 62); Dominguez (2007: 411–12).
[53] αἴ κα μὴ διδῶι τῶι ἐνκαλειμένωι τὰν δίκαν, ἄτιμον εἶμεν καὶ χρήματα παματοφαγεῖσται, τὸ μέρος μετὰ ϝοικιατᾶν.
[54] Van Wees (2003: 62); see also Welwei (2008: 20).

presupposes rather than demonstrates a system of serfdom: all that the text says is that the errant magistrate's land and *woikiatai* are to be confiscated, not that the latter are in any way bound to the former.[55] Could the term ϝοικιάτας indicate a serf rather than a slave? The word is the equivalent in the Lokrian dialect of north-west Greek to οἰκιήτης in Ionic and οἰκέτης in Attic; the Attic term applies exclusively to slaves in texts of the classical period.[56] *Woikiatas* is used in a fifth-century inscription from Mantinea (*IG* V, 2 262 = *IPArk* 8), which states that, if someone is found guilty by divine judgement, he must forfeit his property (*tōn khrēmatōn*), including his *woikiatai*, to the goddess Athena Alea; but there is nothing about a plot of land here, and Veneciano translates the term *woikiatai* simply as 'slaves'.[57] It also appears in a fifth-century inscription from Epidauros, listing an Argive suppliant named Kallipos along with his *woikiatai*; again there is no mention of land.[58] The term οἰκιάται also appears in several early honorific inscriptions from Thessaly, which grant the honorand *asylia*, the coverage of which extends over his *oikiatai*.[59] These too say nothing about land, but are guarantees that the honorand and his property, slaves included, will be immune from seizure, which is an occasional feature of such grants.[60] The corpus of Boiotian dedication inscriptions sometimes use the term ϝυκέτας for slaves dedicated to a deity (e.g. *IG* VII 3082; 3198; 3199; 3200; 3201). Finally, the several mentions of *woiketai/oikiatai* in the Dodona *lamellae* fit the same pattern and make no mention of land.[61]

The linguistic parallels, therefore, point to slavery, not serfdom, and the epigraphic parallels align perfectly well with this translation. Rather than serfdom, it is more probable that the Lokrians practised an old-fashioned form of slavery not vastly different from what we find in the works of Homer and Hesiod (namely, a focus on agriculture and animal husbandry; slaves largely acquired from war, raids, and reproduction rather than commerce); for Thucydides (1.5–6) compares the customs of the Ozolian Lokrians, that is, those living near Naupaktos, to those of the heroic age: they go about armed and live in an old-fashioned society devoted to warfare and slave-raiding, just like the Greeks of early times.[62]

---

[55] Besides, the Athenian Hermokopids had both land and slaves confiscated, and nobody has seen this as evidence for the latter being 'bound' to the former. The parallel with Gortynian 'serfdom' (more specifically, *IC* IV 72 IV 33–6) adduced by Vidal Naquet (1986: 212) and Dominguez (2007: 411) misses the mark, for this passage does not show slave ownership of land or cattle: see Lewis (2013: 406–8); and esp. Probert (2015: 374–7).

[56] Lewis (2018: 295–305).  [57] Veneciano (2014: 153).

[58] *SEG* xxvi 449: Κάλλιπος: ηικέτας/Εὔκλος hυιὸς/τὸν Ἐπιδαύριον/παρ' Ἀπόλλονος/Πυθίο Ἀργεῖος/ἀρχὸς καὶ ϝοικιάται: 'Kallipos, son of Eukles, an Argive leader [or: magistrate] and his *woikiatai*, a suppliant of the Epidaurians from Apollo Pythios.'

[59] *IG* ix. 2 257 (5th c. BCE); *SEG* 23:422 = *BCH* 88 (1964): 407, 8 (4th c. BCE); *MDAI*(A) 59 (1934) 56, 14 (4th c. BCE).

[60] Will Mack points out to me parallels in *I.Olbia* 5 and *IosPE* I² 20. See further the remarks of Osborne (2009: 337–9).

[61] Meyer (2018: 152).

[62] Cf. Welwei (2008: 20). The Ozolian Lokrian way of war was positively Homeric: compare Thuc. 3.94–5 and Xen. *Hell.* 4.2.17 with van Wees (1994). For the extreme conservatism of the Epizephyrian

Our second text, Timaios *BNJ* 556 F11a, has been interpreted to the effect that slavery did not exist at all among the Lokrians and Phokians until the mid-fourth century BCE.[63] (The alleged absence of slavery *sensu stricto* thus leaves a void that modern scholars have filled with a conjectural 'serf' population.)

> Timaios of Tauromenion says in the ninth book of his *Histories* that 'It was not customary among the Greeks of early times to be served by bought slaves,' writing as follows: 'they completely admonish Aristotle for mistaking the customs of the Lokrians: for it was not a custom among the Lokrians, nor equally among the Phokians, to buy either female or male slaves, apart from in recent times. But the first to be followed by two female slaves was the wife of Philomelos the captor of Delphi. And similarly Mnason, the companion of Aristotle, having acquired a thousand slaves, was brought into disrepute among the Phokians, since so many of the citizens had their necessary livelihood taken away from them. For in their houses it was a custom for the young men to serve the older men.'

Both Finley and de Ste. Croix believed that there was something fishy about this passage, but neither made any arguments to justify their unease.[64] But arguments there are. For one thing, we might be suspicious of the claim that the Phokians had no slaves down to the 350s, when Hesiod, writing of Askra two and a half centuries earlier but only thirty or so miles from Phokis, offered plenty of advice to his brother about how to buy and manage slaves.[65] Above all, Timaios' claims in F11a ought not to be read as an isolated statement, but as bound up with his famous assault on Aristotle, and Polybios' bilious reaction to it. Aristotle (or at least the peripatetic author of the lost *Constitution of the Lokrians*—Aristotle as far as Timaios was concerned) claimed that the inhabitants of Epizephyrian Lokris were the descendants of slaves and free Lokrian women from the mainland ([Arist.] *apud* Polyb. 12.5–11 = fr. 547 Rose). Timaios, who was notoriously hostile to Aristotle (Polyb. 12.8.1–6), viewed this as a slander on the Lokrians and an opportunity to tarnish Aristotle's reputation. To counter Aristotle, he first claims that the early Greeks had no slaves; this was a known trope,[66] and, since Aristotle's claims are about the foundation of Epizephyrian Lokris long ago, he can weaponize this trope as belonging (vaguely) to the same timeframe. Having set up this slave-free backdrop, he then cites a fourth-century change in Phokian

---

Lokrians regarding legal innovation, see Dem. 24.139–43; cf. Polyb. 12.16.13. Given the terrain, one would expect these slaves to have been more heavily involved in animal husbandry, especially sheep-herding, than arable farming, as Bresson (2019) points out. On herders, see Roy (2012).

[63] How and Wells (1912: 123); Schmidt (1995: 95); van Wees (2003: 62); Schmitz (2004: 37–8).
[64] Finley (1980: 168, n. 63); de Ste. Croix (1981: 202).
[65] Hes. *Op.* 37–41; 405–6; 441–7; 469–71; 502–3; 571–3; 597–9; 765–8.
[66] Hdt. 6.137; Palaeph. 6; Cratin. fr. 176 K–A; Crates Com. fr. 16 K–A; Pherecr. fr. 10 K–A.

society to the effect that the role of domestic servants—a role previously filled by young free males—had been monopolized by an influx of purchased slaves; Timaios' clear implication is the sudden introduction of slavery to a region where it had previously not existed.

The idea of a traditional Greek society using free servants at least in certain contexts has a parallel in Homer, where young free men called *therapontes* perform various tasks in the household alongside slaves (although slaves are the main workforce on elite landholdings).[67] The practice is attested in archaic Lesbos (Sappho fr. 203 Voigt), and variants persisted in some traditional, conservative regions of the Greek world such as Crete, where Ephoros (*BNJ* 70 F149 §20) and Pyrgion (*BNJ* 467 F1) write that young citizen men would serve their elders in the messes, and also in certain contexts on Rhodes (Dieuchidas *BNJ* 485 F7). Royal 'pages' in Macedon may represent a version of this custom.[68] It would appear that the Phokians had the same practice until the fourth century, when they began to ape the fashions of their southern neighbours, who had long used slaves in domestic service (to the point where the term *therapon* in classical Attic had come to be used exclusively for slaves). But the evidence that Timaios cites regarding Philomelos and Mnason attests to a restricted change, nothing more than a new fashion, just as black African slaves came to be popular manservants in grand English houses of the eighteenth century.[69] Most significantly, the only concrete historical examples that Timaios can cite relate to two Phokian generals, not Lokrians. Timaios makes two specious leaps here: first, lacking any evidence for Lokris, Timaios extrapolates the social changes reported for Phokis concerning domestic service to neighbouring Lokris based on no evidence at all. Secondly, he moves quickly to the conclusion that slavery must not have existed in Lokris or Phokis *in general*, despite the fact that his evidence concerns only the narrow labour role of personal service. We ought to be wary here: Timaios' claim is not a neutral, antiquarian report made in passing, but part of a bitter polemic in which he builds a case more sweeping than the facts warrant to disparage Aristotle.

Besides, the Phokian capture of Delphi in 356 under Philomelos became a moralizing example of the corrupting effect of wealth, somewhat like the supposedly novel introduction of precious metals to Sparta after the Peloponnesian War.[70] One might note too Ephoros' claim (*BNJ* 70 F96) that the wives of the Phokian generals made off with famous items of jewellery from the shrine, which J. K. Davies has called a 'gossip-column account'.[71] Ephoros' and Timaios' reports

---

[67] *Therapontes*: Greenhalgh (1982); slave labour: Harris (2012); Lewis (2018: 107–24); van Wees (2021).
[68] See Hammond (1990) and Węcowski (2013) for further discussion.
[69] Various examples in Dresser and Hann (2013).
[70] Athen. *Deip.* 6.231c; 232e; cf. 233b–d; Diod. Sic. 16.37.4; Theopompos *BNJ* 115 F248. On the Spartan case, see Hodkinson (2000: 26–30).
[71] Davies (2007: 82).

about the behaviour of the Phokians after the Delphic *hierosylia* represent the exact opposite of traditional Lokrian mores, exemplified by the statutes of the austere lawgiver Zaleukos; for, according to Diodoros (12.21.1), Zaleukos banned free women from going around with more than one slave attendant and from wearing jewellery. (Ephoros is probably Diodoros' source on Zaleukos: cf. *BNJ* 70 F139.)

Fragment 11a of Timaios, then, forms part of a much larger polemic; the 'facts' reported in this fragment are the distillate of a highly tendentious diatribe. Finley and de Ste. Croix were right to think Timaios' claims were fishy; in particular, it should be emphasized that Timaios had to base his account of changes in Lokrian customs wholly on Phokian examples. The likelihood is that in Phokis until the fourth century, as in other Greek societies in which certain archaic practices persisted, some limited service roles were performed by citizen boys; that is the sum total of what can be taken as factual from Timaios' account. His 'evidence' for Lokris, on the other hand, looks to be contrived.

Skipping forward in time, the West Lokrian manumission inscriptions show that this conservative Greek society had, by the Hellenistic period, opened up somewhat to the broader market for slaves, though reproduction probably remained more important than trade; although a slight majority of the individuals of known origin were homeborn, we also hear of slaves from Asia Minor (Galatia, Tibarania, Phrygia), Thrace, Sarmatia, and the Near East (Cyprus, Arabia, Antioch, Phoenicia, Media, Syria).[72]

## Herakleia Pontike: A Colonial Slave System

Plato (*Leg.* 776c–d) compared the slave population of Herakleia Pontike to the Helots and Penestai. These slaves were called Mariandynoi after a local non-Greek people, part of which was enslaved by the Herakleotes.[73] That we are dealing with slaves rather than serfs is clear, not only from Plato[74] but also from Poseidonios (*BNJ* 87 F8), who, as we noted above, mentions explicitly that the Mariandynoi

---

[72] References to *IG* IX 1² 3: 624 (Galatia); 638,13 (Tibarania); 640 (Phrygia); 624–5, 638,5 and 639,2 (Thrace); 638,3 and 679 (Sarmatia); 622 (Cyrpus); 624 (Arabia, Antioch); 629 (Phoenicia); 638,2 (Media); 630, 638,6, 638,8, 639,10, 785, *SEG* lvi 576; *SEG* xxv 640 (Syria). See, in general, Blavatskaja (1972: 7–62).

[73] Burstein (1976: 28–30); Bittner (1998: 10–2); Baralis (2015: 198–209).

[74] *Leg.* 776d uses the terms *douleia*, *oiketai*, and *douloi*. Plato was in a good position to know about the Mariandynoi: see Burstein (1976: 41–2); Baralis (2015: 200). There is an obscure reference to Mariandynoi at Pherecr. fr. 74 K–A, suggesting that some knowledge of them circulated in Athens in the late fifth century. I do not agree with Baralis (2015: 215) that Plato is using *douleia* vaguely; Baralis' categorization of the Mariandynoi *metaxu eleutheron kai doulon* depends on a flawed analogy with Cretan servile 'rights': see Lewis (2013; forthcoming), and n. 55 above. Burstein's suggestion (1976: 29–30) that Aristotle (*Pol.* 1327ᵇ11–12) wrote of two Mariandynian slave populations seems to me to be an overly mechanical interpretation of a casual pleonasm.

could be sold by their owners, but not outside the territory of Herakleia. During the Hellenistic period, antiquarian interest grew concerning the origins of this system of slavery (which had disintegrated in the 360s following a popular revolution against the oligarchic elite: Justin 16.5.1-4). Poseidonios considered their subjection to have originated in a voluntary submission to the mastery of the Herakleotes: the Mariandynoi, on this view, recognized their natural inferiority and proposed an exchange of services in return for protection.[75] A different tradition is found in Strabo (12.3.4): the Mariandynoi were subjected by conquest, following which the ban on external sale was imposed.[76] These stories look very much like later attempts to reverse-engineer information on the origins of the system from two facts—namely, that in the classical period, (i) there existed a ban on external sale, and (ii) the slave population was ethnically and linguistically homogeneous, drawn from the local non-Greek population. Other nearby locals lying beyond the borders of the Herakleian *khora* (such as Paphlagonians) were not protected from external sale and appear occasionally as slaves in the core regions of the Greek world.[77]

The functioning of the Herakleote slave system is poorly understood, but some clues might be gleaned by looking at the broader economy of the colony. Herakleia was no economic backwater, lying as it did on a key trade route along the southern Black Sea littoral; it could boast an impressive navy ([Arist.] *Oec.* 1347$^b$3: forty warships); and Aristotle (*Pol.* 1327$^b$11-14) pointed out that the Mariandynians who tilled the Herakleote *khora* were enlisted as rowers in their triremes. Just as Menon of Pharsalos adapted the old practice of arming slaves to play to the Thessalian strength in cavalry, so too did the Herakleotes use slaves in the branch of the military in which they excelled. Like the Penestai, it is likely that the Mariandynoi worked mainly for a landed elite; for it was this class that was overthrown in Herakleia's fourth-century revolution.[78] Klearkhos, the revolution's leader, declared the slaves free; they sided with the *demos*, much like the alliance between the *demos* at Syracuse and the Killyrioi in their revolt against the elite Gamoroi ('land-portion holders') over a century earlier (Hdt. 7.155).

At any rate, perhaps it is overly simplistic to think of the Mariandynoi only as cereal farmers; for the colony exported not just grain but nuts (Athen. *Deip.* 2.53b-54c; cf. Hermipp. fr. 63 K-A), a major product of the region to this day, as well as wine and other commodities. Burstein's characterization nicely captures the economic realities of the late fifth century:

---

[75] Discussion in Garnsey (1996: 146-50).
[76] Detailed discussion of both traditions in Paradiso (2007) and Baralis (2015).
[77] Paphlagonian slaves in Attica: Theophr. *Char.* 9.3; *IG* i$^3$ 1032.131, 255; *IG* ii$^2$ 10051.1; 2940.6; 2940.8; 11679/80; Delphi: *SGDI* II 1696; Khios: see n. 90; Rhodes: Maiuri, *NSER* 136.
[78] Asheri (1972: 23, n. 61); Luraghi (2009: 268).

With the labor provided by the Mariandynoi, Heracleote landowners were raising vines and barley and running herds of cattle and flocks of sheep on their estates in addition to the nuts, wheat, and olives that are indicated by other sources. The result was that, while benefiting from the general growth in the Pontic trade during the fifth century, Heraclea developed her own foreign trade. By the end of the century it had not only attained a moderate volume but its geographical extent was notable. Heracleote merchants or Heracleote wine could then be found almost everywhere in the Pontus, in the cities of the north and south coasts, the villages of Bithynia, and probably also those of Paphlagonia.[79]

It should be noted that the city's *khora* expanded westwards over time, pushing beyond the Hypios River by 424 BCE until, by *c*.400, it possibly bordered Bithynia at the Sangarios River.[80] This gave its oligarchs access to the rich Hypios River valley, whose location over 50 km from Herakleia must have led to absenteeism and had consequences for the organization and supervision of the Mariandynoi; perhaps this is why, in his discussion of restive slave populations, Plato (*Leg.* 776c) says that the system was almost as controversial as helotage.

Once more, it appears that the slave system of Herakleia was tailored to local needs, drawing its manpower from the nearby non-Greek population and exploiting the potential of the local environment and its products; its military functions were, again, attuned to the *polis*'s specific strengths and position as a maritime power. When we consider the landscape across which these slaves were deployed, as well as take into account the fractious class relations in the *polis* of Herakleia, it is not hard to see why its slave system was noted for its instability.[81]

## Khios: An Island Slave System

The Greek world contained many island slave systems.[82] The most famous was Khios, which, according to Thucydides (8.40.2), possessed the largest number of slaves of any single Greek *polis* except Sparta. As Finley shrewdly suggested, this

---

[79] Burstein (1976: 36). Cf. Bittner (1998: 117–50); Kac (2003).

[80] Burstein (1976: 28); Baralis (2015: 209–13); but cf. Bosworth and Wheatley (1998: 158, n. 36), who argue that the border did not extend quite as far as the Sangarios.

[81] Class relations: Burstein (1976 *passim*); factors causing instability: Cartledge (1985); for economic exploitation, cf. Hodkinson (2008).

[82] Naxos, according to Herodotus (5.31.1), had a large slave population in the early fifth century BCE. The slave population of Corcyra was sufficiently large at the time of the Peloponnesian War to sway the course of the island's civil war (Thuc. 3.73–4). The figure for the slave population in Aigina cited from Aristotle by Athenaios (6.272ᶜ) is unbelievable; but the notion that the Aiginetans had many slaves is not. See Figueira (1981: 35–7, 51), with Hansen (2006: 5–18). Rhodes: some preliminary remarks in Lewis (2017); see also Bresson (1997) and especially Maillot (forthcoming). On Delos, see Bruneau (1989); on Crete, Link (1994: 30–48); Lewis (2018: 147–65; forthcoming).

claim is probably based not on a census of absolute numbers, but on the perceived density of the slave population relative to the free population.[83] In the subsequent century, Theopompos of Khios (*BNJ* 115 F122) repeated what was perhaps a local tradition that the Khians were the first of the Greeks to buy slaves from non-Greeks. We may doubt the verity of this tradition; for, when we recall that Theopompos also made the dubious claim that viticulture was invented at Khios, having been taught to the Khians by the god Dionysos' son Oinopion (*BNJ* 115 F276, a claim he elsewhere contradicted by writing that viticulture originated at Olympia: F277), we can see that his story about the Khians pioneering slave-trading ought to be taken with a grain of salt, and seen as part of the wider Greek tendency to attribute this or that practice or invention to a *protos heuretes*.[84] That said, the connection between mass slavery and export-oriented viticulture at Khios has been noted several times;[85] and the Khians may have been exploiting slaves for the production of wine for export on a significant scale as early as the eighth century BCE, if the recent discovery of Khian transport amphorae at Methone and Abdera are anything to go by.[86] Even though Theopompos was simply repeating a piece of 'intentional history', it is still possible that the Khians were involved in commercially orientated slavery from quite an early date.

The findspots of these early amphoras in northern Greece tempt one to suppose that the Khians acquired at least some of their slaves from that vast northern reservoir of enslaveable persons, Thrace.[87] Yet Khios was even closer to the other main reservoir of slave labour exploited by the Aegean Greeks: Anatolia. Khian wine amphoras have been discovered in significant numbers in centres of elite activity in Phrygia such as Daskyleion and Gordion; and it is probable that elite Anatolian intermediaries organized the enslavement and export of their fellow countrymen in return for wine and fine wares from the Greek world.[88] Inscriptions from the late fifth century BCE (*PEP Chios* 61 and 62) are of particular interest regarding the ethnic origins of Khios' slave population, for they group numerous individuals with ethnic and foreign names in squads of ten; Louis Robert remarked that 'La δεκάς est essentiellement une unité militaire' and suggested that we are looking at groups of ex-slaves enfranchised in return for military

---

[83] Finley (1981: 102). On slavery in Khios, see Luraghi (2009: 268–70).

[84] Kleingünther (1933); cf. Fisher (1993: 20).

[85] e.g. Davies (1981: 46); Cartledge (1985: 35–6); Luraghi (2009: 269); Bresson (2016: 126).

[86] Methone: Tzifopoulos (2012: 184–219); Abdera in the seventh century BCE: Dupont and Skarlatidou (2012). I owe this point to Alain Bresson. Finds of stamped Khian amphoras from the classical period have mainly been found in the Crimea: Panagou (2015: 218); this continued into the Hellenistic period, but for that era we find a wider range of findspots: Panagou (2015: 220–1).

[87] On Thrace as a slave source, see Velkov (1964); Lewis (2018: 284–5). Selene Psoma points out to me in this respect the fortuitous location of the Khian colony of Maroneia, established c.650 on the Thracian coast. Other Greek port towns perched on the Thracian littoral are known as slave export points: Abdera (*SEG* xlvii 1026); Perinthos (Xen. *Anab.* 7.4.2).

[88] See Lewis (2015: esp. 319–21) on the slave trader Manes mentioned in *SIG*[3] 4, an honorific decree from Kyzikos dating to the late sixth century BCE; cf. Lewis (2018: 285–6). Daskyleion: Yaldır (2011).

service.[89] The predominance of Anatolian ethnic and foreign names is striking.[90] Like Herakleia, Khios possessed a considerable fleet,[91] and we know from Thucydides (8.15) that the Khians drafted their slaves to serve in it. As at Sparta, Thessaly, and Herakleia, Khios' slave population was famously restive (Thuc. 8.40; Nymphodoros *BNJ* 572 F4), which can be explained through a combination of large slaveholding units, an unfavourable slave–free ratio, absenteeism, rugged terrain capable of sheltering maroon communities, and fractious class relations among the citizenry.[92]

The overall picture that emerges is of a well-connected island economy catalysed by the growth of commerce in the archaic period, establishing a grisly feedback loop where the export of slave-produced wine to slave-supply zones (and elsewhere) perpetuated the system of exploitation, acquiring new slaves in exchange for the products of slave labour, all the while enriching the Khian elite. As in Thessaly and Herakleia, military use of slaves was attuned to local military traditions. The large number of slaves on Khios and their high-intensity exploitation, however, made for an unstable system prone to disruption and revolt.

\* \* \* \* \*

The preceding thumbnail sketches serve to illustrate two basic points. First, Greek slavery was diverse. Such a brief and selective survey cannot fully capture the range of diversity; but I trust it can provide suggestive impressions of alternatives to the Attic model. Secondly, this diversity emerged for a range of reasons. The apparently distinctive slaving practices pursued in this or that region were not random, but can be explained as often as not by investigating their particular local contexts. When we do so, we find that local slaving strategies were generally attuned to the prevailing socio-economic, cultural, and political trends of the region in question; each system was the product of its own, local process of historical development.[93]

---

[89] Robert (1938: 124).
[90] See Robert (1938: 118–26). The foreign and ethnic names include: Παφλαγων[ί]δης, three individuals named Τίβειος, individuals named Μάνιππος, Φρύξ, Μίδας, and Κιλίκας, two individuals named Ἀρτύμης, and two individuals named Σῦρος. It is interesting in this regard to note Herodotus' story of Panionios (8.105), a Khian who bought slave boys, castrated them, and sold them at Ephesos and Sardis, whence they entered the eastern market for eunuchs. For Khios and Ephesos as slave markets, see Aristophanes fr. 556 K–A. On eunuchs in the Persian Empire, see Lenfant (2012).
[91] Hdt. 6.15; Thuc. 1.116; 2.56; 4.13; 5.84; 6.43; 7.20.
[92] See Cartledge (1985: 38–9). Large slaveholding units and disparity in slave–free ratio: Thuc. 8.40.2; rugged terrain: Nymphodoros *BNJ* 572 F4; factional strife among the citizenry: Hdt. 8.132; Thuc. 8.9; 14.2; Xen. *Hell.* 3.2.11; Arist. *Pol.* 1303ᵃ34–5; Diod. 13.65.3–4. On absenteeism, note that Khios is the only *polis* counted for the island by Rubinstein (2004), though she notes (pp. 1064–5) several second-order settlements. Most elite Khians with an interest in politics will have been *polis*-dwelling absentee landlords.
[93] Lewis (2022) treats the processes of convergence and divergence that, over the *longue durée* of c.750–400 BCE, produced such a variety of local formations.

## Conclusions

Once we recognize the error of placing our faith in late lexical sources such as Pollux and recognize that our classical-era sources show most of the systems he mentions to have been systems of private slavery, we can progress towards a more nuanced and textured picture of Greek slavery as a mosaic of epichoric slave systems. Capturing regional diversity, ultimately, was one of M. I. Finley's aims; for he drew an illuminating parallel between differing forms of dependent labour in the Greek world and regional variations in, for example, coinage and weight standards.[94] Finley's approach went astray, however, by viewing these systems of dependent labour in terms of a spectrum of 'unfree' statuses between slavery and freedom, a perspective that is fraught with methodological and empirical problems.[95] Finley erred in seeing diversity mainly in terms of statuses *beyond* slavery, whereas the evidence shows diversity in terms of many different local forms *within* the larger category of slavery. By bracketing off 'slavery' as a term applicable only to systems that imported barbarian outsiders, and by overlooking contradictions between the early and late sources, Finley's approach produced an unintended consequence—namely, the marginalization of forms of slavery that did not fit the Athenian Ideal Type. Classical Greek slavery was not, then, Attic slavery replicated in so many carbon copies; but neither is it necessary to recategorize everything that does not fit that model as something other than slavery. The classical Greeks certainly did not see things this way, and this was due not to juridical ineptitude, but to a picture of contemporary forms of slavery that was unobscured by viewing them through foggy, Second-Sophistic goggles clouded by three or four centuries of charter myths, folk etymologies, and scholarly armchair speculation.

Such a shift in conceptualization of Greek slavery, if it is accepted, has the potential to reframe the study of slave experiences, because it locates the differences in the regional forms of slavery in terms of local cultural, political, and economic factors. These all had an important bearing on the lives of slaves, for they shaped the occupations in which slaves were exploited (which were often sharply gendered), the proximity of their owners, the frequency of slave families, the prospects of manumission, and the intersection of slavery with war and violence. Such a shift allows us to move away from generalizations about 'the slave experience,' to specific circumstances, calibrated in terms of regional specificities.

## Acknowledgements

This chapter builds on Lewis (2018), which contains a lengthy discussion of Sparta and Crete and a critique of Finley's discussion of status; I have, furthermore, written this

---

[94] Finley (1981: 140).   [95] Lewis (2018: 72–6) for detailed discussion.

chapter as a companion piece to Lewis (2022), which explores the diachronic processes that produced such variety in the classical-era slave systems. As well as the welcome comments of the audience at Oxford and remarks of the editors and readers for OUP, Edward Harris, Mirko Canevaro, Kostas Vlassopoulos, Jason Porter, Stephen Hodkinson, Ulrike Roth, Moritz Hinsch, Tony Edwards, and Sara Forsdyke kindly read and commented on this chapter. This essay has benefited greatly from their remarks; none of them should be held complicit in my argument. This essay is dedicated to the Starkeys of Coniamstown, ἐπιχώριοι καλοί.

## Works Cited

Andreau, J., and R. Descat (2006). *Esclave en Grèce et à Rome*. Paris.

Archer, L. (1988) (ed.). *Slavery and Other Forms of Unfree Labour*. London.

Asheri, D. (1972). 'Über die Frühgeschichte von Herakleia Pontike', in *Forschungen an der Nordküste Kleinasiens*, 9–34. Vienna.

Aston, E., and J. Kerr (2018). 'Battlefield and Racetrack: The Role of Horses in Thessalian Society', *Historia*, 67: 2–35.

Baralis, A. (2015). 'Le Statut de la main-d'oeuvre à Héraclée du Pont et en Mer Noire', in Zurbach (2015: 197–234).

Bernhardt, R. (2003). *Luxuskritik und Aufwandsbeschränkungen in der griechischen Welt*. Stuttgart.

Bittner, A. (1998). *Gesellschaft und Wirtschaft in Herakleia Pontike: Eine Polis zwischen Tyrannis und Sebstverwaltung*. Bonn.

Blavatskaja, T. V. (1972). 'Zur Geschichte der Sklavenhaltung in den nordwestlichen Gebieten Griechenlands', in T. V. Blavatskaja, E. S. Golubcova, and A. I. Pavlovskaja (eds), *Die Sklaverei in Hellenistischen Staaten im 3.–1. Jh. V. Chr.*, 3–105. Wiesbaden.

Bodel, J., and W. Scheidel (2016) (eds). *On Human Bondage: After Slavery and Social Death*. Malden, MA.

Bosworth, B., and P. Wheatley (1998). 'The Origins of the Pontic House', *Journal of Hellenic Studies*, 118: 155–64.

Bresson, A. (1997). 'Remarques préliminaires sur l'onomastique des esclaves dans la Rhodes antique', in M. Moggi and G. Cordiano (eds), *Schiavi e dipendenti nell' ambito dell' oikos e della famiglia*, 117–26. Pisa.

Bresson, A. (2016). *The Making of the Ancient Greek Economy: Institutions, Markets, and Growth in the City-States*. Princeton.

Bresson, A. (2019). 'Slaves, Fairs and Fears: Western Greek Sanctuaries as Hubs of Social Interaction', in K. Freitag and M. Haake (eds), *Griechische Heiligtümer als Handlungsorte*, 251–77. Stuttgart.

Bruneau, P. (1989). 'L'Esclavage à Délos', in *Mélanges Pierre Lévêque III: Anthropologie et société*, 41–52. Besançon.

Burstein, S. M. (1976). *Outpost of Hellenism: The Emergence of Heraclea on the Black Sea*. Berkeley and Los Angeles.

Cartledge, P. A. (1985). 'Rebels and Sambos in Classical Greece: A Comparative View', in P. Cartledge and F. D. Harvey (eds), *Crux: Essays in Greek History Presented to G. E. M. de Ste. Croix on his 75th Birthday*, 16–46. London.

Cartledge, P. A. (1988). 'Serfdom in Classical Greece', in Archer (1988: 33–41).

Cartledge, P. A. (2002 [1979]). *Sparta and Lakonia: A Regional History, 1300–362 BC*. London.

Cartledge, P. A. (2011). 'The Helots – a Contemporary Review', in K. Bradley and P. A. Cartledge (eds), *The Cambridge World History of Slavery*, i. *The Ancient Mediterranean World*, 74–90. Cambridge.

Christiansen, E. (2002). 'The Moses Finley Approach to Slavery and Slave Society', in K. Ascani, V. Gabrielsen, K. Kvist, and A. H. Rasmussen (eds), *Ancient History Matters: Studies Presented to Jens Erik Skydsgaard on his Seventieth Birthday*, 23–8. Rome.

Davies, J. K. (1981). *Wealth and the Power of Wealth in Classical Athens*. New York (repr. Salem, NH, 1984).

Davies, J. K. (2007). 'The Phokian *hierosylia* at Delphi: Quantities and Consequences', in N. Sekunda (ed.), *Corolla Cosmo Rodewald*, 75–96. Gdansk.

de Ste. Croix, G. E. M. de (1981). *The Class Struggle in the Ancient Greek World*. London.

Dominguez, A. J. (2007). 'Fear of Enslavement and Sacred Slavery as Mechanisms of Social Control among the Ancient Locrians', in Serghidou (2007: 405–22).

Dresser, M., and A. Hann (2013). *Slavery and the British Country House*. Swindon.

Ducat, J. (1974). 'Le Mépris des Hilotes', *Annales: Économies, Sociétés, Civilisations*, 29: 1451–64.

Ducat, J. (1990). *Les Hilotes*. Bulletin de correspondance hellenique supplément 20. Athens.

Ducat, J. (1994). *Les Pénestes de Thessalie*. Besançon.

Ducat, J. (1997). 'Bruno Helly et les Pénestes', *Topoi*, 7: 183–9.

Ducat, J. (2015). 'Les Hilotes à l'époque archaïque', in Zurbach (2015: 165–95).

Dupont, P., and E. Skarlatidou (2012). 'Archaic Transport: Amphoras from the First Necropolis of Clazomenian Abdera', in M. Tiverios, V. Misailidou-Despotidou, E. Manakidou, and A. Arvanitaki (eds), *Η ΚΕΡΑΜΙΚΗ ΤΗΣ ΑΡΧΑΪΚΗΣ ΕΠΟΧΗΣ ΣΤΟ ΒΟΡΕΙΟ ΑΙΓΑΙΟ ΚΑΙ ΤΗΝ ΠΕΡΙΦΕΡΕΙΑ ΤΟΥ (700–480 π.Χ)*, 253–64. Thessaloniki.

Figueira, T. J. (1981). *Aegina: Society and Politics*. Salem, NH.

Figueira, T. J. (1993). *Excursions in Epichoric History*. Lanham, MD.

Finley, M. I. (1964). 'Between Slavery and Freedom', *Comparative Studies in Society and History*, 6: 233–49.

Finley, M. I. (1980). *Ancient Slavery and Modern Ideology*. London.

Finley, M. I. (1981). *Economy and Society in Ancient Greece*, ed. B. Shaw and R. Saller. London.

Fisher, N. R. E. (1993). *Slavery in Classical Greece*. London.

Forsdyke, S. (2012). *Slaves Tell Tales: And Other Episodes in the Politics of Popular Culture in Ancient Greece*. Princeton.

Forsdyke, S. (2021). *Slaves and Slavery in Ancient Greece*. Cambridge.

Gagarin, M. (2010). 'Serfs and Slaves at Gortyn', *Zeitschrift der Savigny-Stiftung für Rechtsgeschichte, Romanistische Abteilung*, 127: 14–31.

Garlan, Y. (1988). *Slavery in Ancient Greece*, trans. J. Lloyd. Ithaca, NY.

Garnsey, P. (1996). *Ideas of Slavery from Aristotle to Augustine*. Cambridge.

Greenhalgh, P. A. L. (1982). 'The Homeric *therapon* and *opaon* and their Historical Implications', *Bulletin of the Institute of Classical Studies*, 29: 81–90.

Hall, J. (2007). *A History of the Archaic Greek World, ca. 1200–479 BCE*. Oxford.

Hammond, N. G. L. (1990). 'Royal Pages, Personal Pages, and Boys Trained in the Macedonian Manner during the Period of the Temenid Monarchy', *Historia*, 39: 261–90.

Hansen, M. H. (2006). *Studies in the Population of Aigina, Athens and Eretria*. Copenhagen.

Hansen, M. H., and S. Hodkinson (2009). 'Spartan Exceptionalism? Continuing the Debate', in S. Hodkinson (ed.), *Sparta: Comparative Approaches*, 473–98. Swansea.

Hansen, M. H., and T. H. Nielsen (2004) (eds). *An Inventory of Archaic and Classical Poleis*. Oxford.

Harris, E. M. (2012). 'Homer, Hesiod, and the "Origins" of Greek Slavery', *Revue des études anciennes*, 114: 345–66.

Harris, E. M., D. M. Lewis, and M. Woolmer (2015) (eds). *The Ancient Greek Economy: Markets, Households and City-States*. Cambridge.

Harvey, F. D. (1988). 'Herodotus and the Man-Footed Creature', in Archer (1988: 42–52).

Hermann-Otto, E. (2009). *Sklaverei und Freilassung in der griechisch-römischen Welt*. Hildesheim.

Hodkinson, S. (2000). *Property and Wealth in Classical Sparta*. Swansea.

Hodkinson, S. (2008). 'Spartiates, Helots and the Direction of the Agrarian Economy: Toward an Understanding of Helotage In Comparative Perspective', in E. Dal Lago and C. Katsari (eds), *Slave Systems, Ancient and Modern*, 285–320. Cambridge.

How, W. W., and J. Wells (1912). *A Commentary on Herodotus*, ii. Oxford.

Hunt, P. (1998). *Slaves, Warfare and Ideology in the Greek Historians*. Cambridge.

Hunt, P. (2016). 'Slaves or Serfs? Patterson on the Thetes and Helots of Ancient Greece', in Bodel and Scheidel (2016: 55–80).

Hunt, P. (2018). *Ancient Greek and Roman Slavery*. Malden, MA.

Kac, V. I. (2003). 'A New Chronology for the Ceramic Stamps of Herakleia Pontike', in P. Guldager Bilde, J. Munk Højte, and V. F. Stoba (eds), *The Cauldron of Ariantas: Studies Presented to A. N. Sceglov on the Occasion of his 70th Birthday*, 261–78. Aarhus.

Kleingünther, A. (1933). Πρῶτος εὑρετής: *Untersuchungen zur Geschichte einer Fragestellung*. Leipzig.

Lenfant, D. (2012). 'Ctesias and his Eunuchs: A Challenge for Modern Historians', *Histos*, 6: 257–97.

Lewis, D. M. (2013). 'Slave Marriages in the Laws of Gortyn: A Matter of Rights?', *Historia*, 62: 390–416.

Lewis, D. M. (2015). 'The Market for Slaves in the Fifth- and Fourth-Century Aegean: Achaemenid Anatolia as a Case Study', in Harris et al. (2015: 316–36).

Lewis, D. M. (2016). 'Orlando Patterson, Property and Ancient Slavery: The Definitional Problem Revisited', in Bodel and Scheidel (2016: 31–54).

Lewis, D. M. (2017). 'Notes on Slave Names, Ethnicity, and Identity in Classical and Hellenistic Greece', *Studia Źródłoznawcze. U Schyłku Starożytności*, 16: 169–99.

Lewis, D. M. (2018). *Greek Slave Systems in their Eastern Mediterranean Context, c.800–146 BC*. Oxford.

Lewis, D. M. (2020). 'Labour Specialization in the Athenian Economy: Occupational Hazards', in E. Stewart, E. M. Harris, and D. M. Lewis (eds), *Skilled Labour and Professionalism in Ancient Greece and Rome*, 129–74. Cambridge.

Lewis, D. M. (2022). 'The Homeric Roots of Helotage', in J. Burnhardt and M. Canevaro (eds), *From Homer to Solon: Continuity and Change in Archaic Greece*, 64–92. Leiden.

Lewis, D. M. (forthcoming). 'Did Serfdom Exist in Classical and Hellenistic Crete?', in P. Schreibelreiter (ed), *Symposion 2022: Akten der Gesellschaft für griechische und hellenistische Rechtsgeschichte*. Vienna.

Link, S. (1994). *Das griechische Kreta*. Stuttgart.

Link, S. (2001). 'Dolos und Woikeus im Recht von Gortyn', *Dike*, 4: 87–112.

Link, S. (2004.) 'Snatching and Keeping: The Motif of Taking in Spartan Culture', in T. Figueira (ed.), *Spartan Society*, 1–24. Swansea.

Lotze, D. (1959). *ΜΕΤΑΞΥ ΕΛΕΥΘΕΡΩΝ ΚΑΙ ΔΟΥΛΩΝ: Studien zur Rechtsstellung unfreier Landbevölkerungen in Griechenland bis zum 4. Jahrhundert v.Chr.* Berlin.

Luraghi, N. (2002). 'Helotic Slavery Reconsidered', in A. Powell and S. Hodkinson (eds), *Sparta: Beyond the Mirage*, 229–50. London.

Luraghi, N. (2003). 'The Imaginary Conquest of the Helots', in N. Luraghi and S. Alcock (eds), *Helots and their Masters in Laconia and Messenia: Histories, Ideologies, Structures*, 109–141. Cambridge, MA.

Luraghi, N. (2009). 'The Helots: Comparative Approaches, Ancient and Modern', in S. Hodkinson (ed.), *Sparta: Comparative Approaches*, 261–304. Swansea.

Maillot, S. (forthcoming). 'Esclaves de naissance à Rhodes', in R. Bouchon, L. Lamoine, and S. Maillot (eds), *Familles d'esclaves: Esclaves dans la famille, monde grec et romain II$^{ème}$a.C.–II$^{ème}$p.C.* Clermont-Ferrand.

Meyer, E. (2018). 'Slavery and paramonē in the Dodona *lamellae*', in L. Soueref (ed.), *Dodona: The Omen's Questions: New Approaches in the Oracular Tablets*, 151–7. Ioannina.

Migeotte, L. (2009). *The Economy of the Greek Cities*, trans. J. Lloyd. Berkeley and Los Angeles.

Miller, M. E. (1868). *Mélanges de littérature grecque*. Paris.

Morgan, C. (2003). *Early Greek States beyond the Polis*. London.

Nielsen, T. H. (2004). 'East Lokris', in Hansen and Nielsen (2004: 664–73).

Osborne, R. (2009). 'Reciprocal Strategies: Imperialism, Barbarism and Trade in Archaic and Classical Olbia', in P. G. Bilde and J. H. Petersen (eds), *Meetings of Cultures between Conflicts and Coexistence*, 333–46. Aarhus.

Panagou, T. (2015). 'Patterns of Amphora Stamp Distribution: Tracking down Export Tendencies', in Harris et al. (2015: 207–29).

Paradiso, A. (2007). 'Sur la servitude volontaire des Mariandyniens d'Héraclée du Pont', in Serghidou (2007: 23–33).

Pownall, F. (2009). 'The Decadence of the Thessalians: A Topos in the Greek Intellectual Tradition from Critias to the Time of Alexander', in P. Wheatley and R. Hannah (eds), *Alexander and his Successors: Essays from the Antipodes*, 237–60. Claremont, CA.

Probert, P. (2015). *Early Greek Relative Clauses*. Oxford.

Robert, L. (1938). *Études épigraphiques et philologiques*. Paris.

Rousset, D. (2004). 'West Lokris', in Hansen and Nielsen (2004: 391–8).

Roy, J. (2012). 'Le Bérger, un personnage en marge de la société grecque classique', in F. Rduzzi Merola (ed.), *Dipendenza ed emarginazione nel mondo antico e moderno*, 219–25. Rome.

Rubinstein, L. (2004). 'Ionia', in Hansen and Nielsen (2004: 1053–1107).

Schmidt, R. V. (1995). 'Rapports et servage en Thessalie avant la période hellénistique: Question des "structures" de la Grèce esclavagiste', in *Esclavage et dépendance dans l'historiographie soviétique récente*, 93–102. Besançon.

Schmitz, W. (2004). *Nachbarschaft und Dorfgemeinschaft im archaischen und klassischen Griechenland*. Berlin.

Schumacher, L. (2001). *Sklaverei in der Antike: Alltag und Schicksal der Unfreien*. Munich.

Serghidou, A. (2007) (ed.). *Fear of Slaves—Fear of Enslavement in the Ancient Mediterranean. Actes du XXIX Colloque du GIREA, Rethymnon 4–7 Novembre 2004*. Besançon.

Simonton, M. (2017). *Classical Greek Oligarchy*. Princeton.

Slater, W. (1986). *Aristophaniis Byzantii Fragmenta*. Berlin.

Sprawski, S. (2014). 'Peltasts in Thessaly', in N. V. Sekunda and B. Burliga (eds), *Iphicrates, Peltasts and Lechaion*, 95–112. Gdansk.

Stamatopoulou, M. (2006). 'Thessalian Aristocracy in the Age of Epinikian', in S. Hornblower and C. Morgan (eds), *Pindar's Poetry, Patrons, and Festivals*, 309–41. Oxford.

Stamatopoulou, M. (2016). 'Forging a Link with the Past: The Evidence from Thessalian Cemeteries in the Archaic and Classical Periods', in O. Henry and U. Kelp (eds), *Tumulus as Sema: Space, Politics, Culture and Religion in the First Millennium BC*, 181–204. Berlin.

Swoboda, H. (1905). 'Beiträge zur griechischen Rechtsgeschichte 2. Über die altgriechische Schuldknechtschaft', *Zeitschrift der Savigny-Stiftung für Rechtsgeschichte, Romanistische Abteilung*, 26: 190–280.

Tzifopoulos, Y. Z. (2012) (ed.). *Μεθώνη I: Επιγραφές, χαράγματα και εμπορικά σύμβολα στην υστερογεωμετρική και αρχαϊκή κεραμική από το 'Υπόγειο'*. Thessaloniki.

Urbainczyk, T. (2008). *Slave Revolts in Antiquity*. Berkeley and Los Angeles.

van Wees, H. (1994). 'The Homeric Way of War: The *Iliad* and the Hoplite Phalanx', *Greece and Rome*, 41: 1–18.

van Wees, H. (2003). 'Conquerors and Serfs: Wars of Conquest and Forced Labour in Archaic Greece', in N. Luraghi and S. Alcock (eds), *Helots and their Masters in Laconia and Messenia: Histories, Ideologies, Structures*, 33–80. Cambridge, MA.

van Wees, H. (2021). 'Slaving Practices in the Early Greek World', in S. Hodkinson, K. Vlassopoulos, and M. Kleiwegt (eds), *The Oxford Handbook of Greek and Roman Slaveries* (online version.) Oxford.

Velkov, V. (1964). 'Zur Frage der Sklaverei auf der Balkanhalbinsel während der Antike', *Études balkaniques*, 1: 125–38.

Veneciano, G. (2014). 'The Structure of the Legal Norm in Archaic Greece: A Case Study ("*Ivo*" 7)', *Zeitschrift für Papyrologie und Epigraphik*, 192: 143–55.

Vidal-Naquet, P. (1986). *The Black Hunter: Forms of Thought and Forms of Society in the Greek World*, trans. A. Szegedy-Maszak. Baltimore.

Vlassopoulos, K. (2016). 'Qui savons-nous vraiment de la société athénienne?', *Annales: Histoire, sciences sociales*, 71: 659–82.

Węcowski, M. (2013). 'Slaves or Aristocrats? Naked Boys in the Archaic *Symposion*', *Przegląd Humanistyczny*, 2: 37–43.

Węcowski, M. (2018). 'The So-Called "Bouleutic Ostracism" and Other Late Byzantine Nonsenses on the Athenian Ostracism', *Scripta Classica Israelica*, 37: 7–23.

Welwei, K.-W. (1974). *Unfreie im antiken Kriegsdienst*, i. *Athen und Sparta*. Wiesbaden.

Welwei, K.-W. (2008). 'Ursprung, Verbreitung und Formen der Unfreiheit abhängiger Landbewohner im antiken Griechenland', in E. Herrmann-Otto (ed.), *Unfreie und abhängige Landbevölkerung*, 1–52. Hildesheim.

Whitehead, D. (1981). 'The Serfs of Sicyon', *Liverpool Classical Monthly*, 6: 37–41.

Yaldır, A. K. (2011). 'Imported Trade Amphoras in Daskyleion from the Seventh and Sixth Centuries BC and the Hellespontine–Phrygia Route', *World Archaeology*, 43: 364–79.

Zelnick-Abramovitz, R. (2012). 'Slaves and Role Reversal in Ancient Greek Cults', in S. Hodkinson and R. Geary (eds), *Slaves and Religions in Graeco-Roman Antiquity and Modern Brazil*, 96–132. Newcastle upon Tyne.

Zurbach, J. (2013). 'La Formation des cités grecques: Statuts, classes et systèmes fonciers', *Annales: Histoire, sciences sociales*, 68: 957–98.

Zurbach, J. (2015) (ed.). *La Main-d'oeuvre agricole en Méditerranée archaïque: Statuts et dynamiques économiques*. Paris.

# 7

# How to Find a New Master

## The Agency of Enslaved Persons in Ancient Greece[1]

*Sara Forsdyke*

### Preface

Full-scale rebellions by enslaved individuals against their enslavers are rare in history.[2] Nevertheless, historians of the modern world have demonstrated the many indirect ways that enslaved individuals and other subaltern groups have resisted authority in order to improve their conditions.[3] It remains true, however, that the existence of widespread resistance to slavery in the ancient world is doubted, and some have suggested that it is a modern fantasy.[4] Against this scholarly background, this chapter attempts to broaden the appreciation of the ways that enslaved individuals did in fact attempt to resist their enslavers and improve their conditions either within slavery or outside of it. Moreover, this chapter focuses on some sophisticated strategies of resistance that suggest that enslaved individuals developed considerable knowledge of Greek legal culture and formed networks of support both among themselves and within the free population. While the chapter does not claim that all enslaved individuals were in a position to resist their enslavers in these ways, it suggests that they were constantly on the lookout for ways to improve their conditions and sometimes used clever strategies—including the manipulation of law and religious customs—to avoid the potential risks and maximize the gains of their actions.

---

[1] This chapter is one part of a two-part investigation of the agency of enslaved individuals in ancient Greece. The companion paper is published separately (Forsdyke 2019). For a broader account of resistance by enslaved groups and individuals in ancient Greece, see Forsdyke (2021).

[2] Genovese (1979) analyses slave revolts in the modern world and explains their relative frequency in the Caribbean compared to the American South. Cartledge (1985) draws on Genovese to explain the general absence of slave revolts in ancient Greece and their relative frequency at Sparta. Earlier scholarship explained the absence of slave revolts in Greece by the heterogeneous nature of the slave population which – they claim – lacked a common language or culture: see e.g., de Ste. Croix (1981: 146).

[3] See, for example, Genovese (1974), Scott (1985, 1990); Johnson (1999).

[4] McKeown (2007).

## Introduction

In the second-century comic biography of Aesop, the following dialogue takes place between the enslaved Aesop and a potential buyer, the philosopher Xanthus:

XANTHUS: I wish to buy you, but you won't try to run away, will you?
AESOP: If I wish to do this, I will not make you my advisor in this enterprise, as you take me for your advisor. But who determines whether I run away? You or me?
XANTHUS: Clearly, you do.
AESOP: No, you do.
XANTHUS: Why do I?
AESOP: If you are a good master, no one, fleeing the good, goes to the bad, giving himself over to wandering and the expectation of hunger and fear. But if you are a bad master, I will not stay one hour with you, not even half an hour, not even a second. (Vita G, 26)

While this fictive episode clearly comically exaggerates or even reverses real-life relations between the enslaved and their enslavers, I suggest that it nevertheless captures something of the truth about the perspectives and experiences of enslaved individuals in ancient Greece.[5] In particular, the passage reflects enslaved individuals' careful calculations of the costs and benefits of remaining with or fleeing from their enslavers.[6] Indeed, many enslaved individuals—perhaps most—found the risks of flight overwhelming and remained with their enslavers. On the other hand, many other enslaved individuals did in fact flee their enslavers, judging the costs of staying greater than the uncertainties of flight.[7] In this chapter, I examine the evidence for some intermediate strategies between remaining and fleeing that, I suggest, enlarge our understanding of the scope of resistance by enslaved individuals in ancient Greece. In particular, I show that some enslaved individuals maneuvered to get transferred to new more lenient enslavers rather than either remain with their current owners or risk the unknowns of flight. The strategies by which the enslaved sought new owners are interesting, moreover, because they show not only that enslaved persons obtained sufficient understanding of

---

[5] For a similar argument about the utility of the comic biography of Aesop for understanding the dynamics of slavery in the ancient world, see Hopkins (1993, repr. in Hopkins 2018).
[6] The same idea is expressed by Xenophon in the *Oeconomicus*. For example, he observes that in some households slaves are all chained yet run away frequently; whereas elsewhere they are unchained and wish to work and to remain (3.4); later at 5.15–16, he suggests that a vital part of household management is the ability to make 'the workers eager and willing to obey', further clarifying that slaves need positive incentives just like free men, indeed even more so, 'so that they may wish to stay'.
[7] For the evidence of flight, see Forsdyke (2021: 211–16).

Greek law and religious custom to be able to exploit them to their own advantage, but also that they were often able to recruit allies among the free population to aid them in their quest for transfer to a new enslaver.

In making this argument, I do not intend to minimize the brutality and oppression experienced by enslaved individuals in ancient Greece. In fact, it was precisely the extreme cruelty of masters towards those whom they held in slavery that often drove the enslaved to seek a middle way between remaining with their enslavers and fleeing into an uncertain future. The modes of resistance examined in this chapter, therefore, do not prove that ancient slavery was milder than modern forms of slavery. Rather they illustrate the often ingenious ways that the enslaved responded to a system that frequently subjected them to intolerable conditions.

## The Problem of Agency

Before launching into the evidence and arguments, it is important to acknowledge some recent challenges to the idea that enslaved individuals resisted their domination.[8] One challenge came in the form of an article by Walter Johnson, a historian of slavery in the American South, in an article titled 'On Agency' that was published in the *Journal of Social History* in 2003. Johnson was responding to the trend in scholarship on slavery in the American South (including his own prize-winning book) that emphasized the ways that enslaved individuals resisted their enslavement.[9] These works argued that, while full-scale rebellion was often too risky, enslaved individuals engaged in other everyday actions of resistance, including working slowly, breaking tools, and playing sick.[10]

In his article of 2003, Johnson criticized the tendency of this scholarship to humanize enslaved individuals primarily by acknowledging their agency in the cause of their own autonomy and freedom. For Johnson, the conceptualization of enslaved individuals as human beings with 'independent will and volition' is too strongly shaped by nineteenth-century liberal thought and was not applicable to enslaved individuals whose historical condition was one of 'objectification and choicelessness'. For Johnson, the enslaved individual's humanity should be equated not with 'agency' or 'free will', but rather with their conditions of suffering, and even sometimes flourishing, in slavery. Johnson stressed the enslaved individual's ordinary human emotional states—for example, their capacity for feeling hungry, cold, tired, as well as feeling love and amusement. Indeed, Johnson

---

[8] See Ben-Ur (2018), who provides a survey of this development. [9] Johnson (1999).
[10] On resistance, see the classic work of Genovese (1974, 1979) as well as the work of Scott (1985, 1990). For a more recent discussion, see Johnson (1999). For recent discussions of resistance in ancient Greece, see McKeown (2011) and Hunt (2018).

points out that enslavers not only exhibited fundamentally human behaviours in their use of torture, rape, and exploitation but also made use of aspects of the enslaved individual's humanity—their ability to feel hatred, fear, desire—in order to keep them enslaved. His point was that the enslaved individual's humanity cannot be conflated with 'resistance', and indeed that some aspects of their humanity were precisely what enabled their continued enslavement.

A second challenge came from Niall McKeown, in a book of 2007 with the provocative title *The Invention of Ancient Slavery?* McKeown raised the question of whether our view of ancient slavery is an invention of the modern era—that it is thoroughly conditioned by our own beliefs and concerns so that we reconstruct it in the way that we want to see it ('slaves as heroic freedom fighters and abolitionists') rather than as it was ('slaves passively accepting slavery or at best strategizing to improve their individual situations whether by acquiescence to the system or through its manipulation').

Any attempt to discuss slave resistance must acknowledge these critiques and recognize the ways that enslaved individuals' humanity both enabled enslavement and also provided the means of resisting it. It is important not to glamorize enslaved individuals as heroic freedom fighters, when their historical conditions all but precluded this self-conceptualization or possibility.

What I am doing in this chapter, however, is attempting to recover some middle ground of resistance—between everyday acts and flight or full-scale rebellion—that actually enlarges our view of the myriad of ways that an enslaved individual could act to change his or her conditions. Indeed, the modes of resistance examined in this chapter involve being transferred to a new owner and therefore not escaping slavery at all, let alone resisting the system of slavery itself. In highlighting these examples, therefore, I am demonstrating some of the ways that enslaved individuals engaged in self-directed action to improve their conditions *in slavery*.[11]

Even more importantly, I hope to demonstrate that enslaved individuals in the ancient world thought rationally about the possibilities for improvement of their circumstances within the system of slavery and sometimes made use of the law to do so. I will further suggest that the examples that I will discuss are indicative of the striking sophistication of the tactics of some enslaved persons, implying their familiarity with Greek law and their capacity for collaboration with free persons to meet common objectives. As we shall see, such collaborations required effective communication and negotiation to ensure that the interests of both parties were met. As such, these examples provide strong evidence of the agency of this central subaltern group in classical Athens.

---

[11] In Forsdyke (2019, 2021) I examine the ways that enslaved persons used the law to escape slavery altogether and even, sometimes, to become citizens.

## The Agency of the Enslaved in Ancient Greece

My first examples of the agency of the enslaved are found in two laws, both of which appear in Plato's treatise, the *Laws*. The legislation in Plato's *Laws* is, of course, not a direct record of historical legislation, but rather a creative reworking of contemporary legislation in service of Plato's vision of a well-ordered society.[12] We must be cautious, therefore, in assuming that any Platonic law reflects historical legislation. In the case of Plato's laws on slavery, however, Glenn Morrow has convincingly demonstrated that they have many similarities with existing historical legislation.[13] As we shall see, moreover, the two laws discussed below have verbal and substantive parallels with Athenian laws, suggesting a close relation.

The two laws in question concern procedures for dealing with damage or wounding caused by slaves. I quote the laws in full before discussing their significance for capturing slave agency in ancient Greece.

Law on Damage (Plato *Laws* 936c–e)

δοῦλος δ' ἂν ἢ δούλη βλάψῃ τῶν ἀλλοτρίων καὶ ὁτιοῦν, μὴ συναιτίου τοῦ βλαβέντος αὐτοῦ γενομένου κατ' ἀπειρίαν ἤ τιν' ἑτέραν χρείαν μὴ σώφρονα, ὁ τοῦ βλάψαντος δεσπότης ἢ τὴν βλάβην ἐξιάσθω μὴ ἐνδεῶς, ἢ τὸν βλάψαντ' αὐτὸν παραδότω· ἐὰν δ' ἐπαιτιώμενος ὁ δεσπότης κοινῇ τοῦ βλάψαντος τέχνῃ καὶ τοῦ βλαβέντος ἐπ' ἀποστερήσει φῇ τοῦ δούλου γεγονέναι τὴν αἰτίαν, διαδικαζέσθω μὲν κακοτεχνιῶν τῷ φάσκοντι βλαβῆναι, καὶ ἐὰν ἕλῃ, διπλασίαν τῆς ἀξίας τοῦ δούλου κομιζέσθω ἧς ἂν τιμήσῃ τὸ δικαστήριον, ἐὰν δὲ ἡττηθῇ, τήν τε βλάβην ἐξιάσθω καὶ τὸν δοῦλον παραδότω.

If a male or female slave does damage to someone else's property [and] if the person who was harmed is not himself also to blame owing to lack of experience or some other use that is not prudent, let the master of the slave who did the damage make full amends for the damage or let him hand over the slave who did the damages. But if the master who is accused asserts that the slave is to blame through a common intrigue of the slave doing the damage and the one who was harmed for the purpose of depriving him of his slave, let him make a suit for evil scheming against the one who says that he was harmed. If he wins, let him receive twice the value of the slave that the court assesses. If he loses, let him repair the damage and let him hand over the slave.

Law on Wounding (Plato *Laws* 879a–b)

δοῦλος δ' ἐάν τις ἐλεύθερον ὀργῇ τρώσῃ, παραδότω τὸν δοῦλον ὁ κεκτημένος τῷ τρωθέντι χρῆσθαι ὅτι ἂν ἐθέλῃ· ἐὰν δὲ μὴ παραδιδῷ, αὐτὸς τὴν βλάβην ἐξιάσθω.

---

[12] Schofield (2016: 3) writes that 'Plato's…legal code is much of it a reworking of contemporary Athenian law'.
[13] Morrow (1939). Cf. Morrow (1960).

ἐὰν δὲ ἐκ συνθήκης αἰτιᾶται τοῦ δούλου καὶ τοῦ τρωθέντος μηχανὴν εἶναί τις τὸ γεγονός, ἀμφισβητησάτω· ἐὰν δὲ μὴ ἕλῃ, τριπλασίαν ἐκτεισάτω τὴν βλάβην, ἑλὼν δέ, ἀνδραποδισμοῦ ὑπόδικον ἐχέτω τὸν τεχνάζοντα μετὰ τοῦ δούλου.

If a slave wounds a free man in anger, let the owner hand over the slave to the wounded man to treat as he sees fit. If the owner does not hand the slave over, let the owner himself make full amends for the damage. If anyone contends that the affair is a scheme resulting from an agreement between the slave and the wounded party, let him bring a suit. And, if he does not win the case, let him pay three times the damages. And, if he wins the case, let him prosecute on a charge of kidnapping the one who colluded with the slave.

These laws raise many questions, but, before we address them, it is important to observe that there are two parts to these laws. The first part of each law lays out remedies for damages or wounding caused by the slave of a free person to the property or person of another free person. The second part of each law addresses situations in which an enslaved person colludes with a free person to exploit the provisions of the first part of the law in order to get transferred to a new owner. Let us examine the two parts of the law in turn.

Regarding the first part of each law, it is provided that the master of the slave who perpetrated the offence is responsible for making amends or he must hand over his slave to the victim. In this part of the laws, then, provision is made for compensating a free person for damages caused by the slave of another free person, either through direct transfer of money or by handing over the slave as the equivalent of a certain monetary value. The law on wounding, moreover, suggests that the slave—besides serving as monetary compensation—might also be physically punished by the victim of the crime ('the victim may treat the slave as he sees fit'). In this portion of the text, then, the law makes provision for compensating a victim of a crime committed by a slave, as well as for punishing the slave.

This provision corresponds with an actual Athenian law, reported in a speech by Hyperides from a legal case at Athens. The Athenian law similarly states that masters are responsible for compensating victims of crimes committed by slaves who work for them.

Σόλων...ἔθηκε νόμον δίκαι[ον, ὡς] παρὰ πάντων ὁμολογεῖται, τὰς ζη[μίας ἅς ἂν] ἐργάσωνται οἱ οἰκέται καὶ τὰ ἀ[δικήμ]ατα διαλύειν τὸν δεσπότην παρ᾽ ᾧ [ἂν ἐργάσ]ωνται οἱ οἰκέται.

Solon...passed a law, which everyone admits is just, stating that any offences or crimes committed by slaves shall be the responsibility of whichever master they work for.[14]

---

[14] Hyp. Ath. 22.

The liability of masters for crimes committed by their slaves is confirmed in other law-court speeches in which masters are said to have paid compensation for wrongs done by their slaves. For example, the speaker in another Athenian case reports that one Arethousios 'took compensation and gave it, whenever [Kerdon, his slave] committed some offence, since he was his master'.[15] In this case, the offences appear to be fairly minor, since a simple transfer of a sum of cash was sufficient to compensate the victim.[16] When a transfer of cash was insufficient to remedy the damage, however, the law provided for more substantial compensation in the form of the enslaved person himself. If the master was unable or unwilling to hand over monetary compensation, he was obligated to hand over the offending slave himself/herself, both as financial compensation and often also for punishment in his/her own person.

As Glenn Morrow notes in his book, *Plato's Law of Slavery*, this provision is 'the familiar *noxae datio* of Roman law, i.e., the gift of the *noxa*, or offending object, to the injured party. With the delivery of the offending slave, the master is quit of all further liability, but the slave becomes the property of the person who has been injured.'[17] Morrow further notes that this provision 'seems to be the general procedure of Greek law, as far as we can determine', since it is attested in several laws of the Hellenistic period.[18] In regard to Athenian law specifically, Morrow notes that, although there is no 'conclusive evidence that the *noxae datio* was permitted ... for the offences of slaves', some evidence suggests it.[19] Most significantly, Xenophon

---

[15] Demosthenes 53.20.

[16] One might note that an enslaved person could knowingly use this part of the law to cause financial losses to his enslaver. He or she would, of course, risk punishment from his or her enslaver for such behaviour, so this would be a risky proposition.

[17] Morrow (1939: 60).

[18] Morrow (1939: 60). P. Lille I.29, ll. 29–31. Although fragmentary, the papyrus seems to allow an owner to resolve a suit by handing over his slave. The text dates to the third century BCE and contains a legal code from Egypt. Nevertheless, the code has striking parallels with Athenian law, and its editors have concluded that it has Greek and particularly Athenian origins. A law from Andania in Messenia is more complete. It concerns regulations for a mystery cult and dates to 92 BCE. It runs as follows: 'Concerning crimes: if someone is found to have committed theft or some other crime during the festival and the celebration of the Mysteries, let him be brought before the priests. Let a free person pay double if he is condemned; let a slave be whipped and let him pay back double the amount of the stolen goods; and, for the other crimes, [let him pay back] a penalty of twenty drachmae. And if he does not pay the penalty right away, let his master hand over the slave to the victim for the purpose of working off his debt, and if not, let the master be liable for double the amount' (ἀδικημάτων· ἂν δέ τις ἐν ταῖς ἁμέραις, ἐν αἷς αἵ τε θυσίαι καὶ τὰ μυστήρια γίνονται, ἁλῶι εἴτε κεκλεθὼς εἴτε ἄλλο τι ἀδίκημα πεποιηκώς, ἀγέσθω ἐπὶ τοὺς ἱερούς, καὶ ὁ μὲν ἐλεύθερος ἂν κατακριθᾶ ἀποτινέτω διπλοῦν, ὁ δὲ δοῦλος μαστιγούσθω καὶ ἀποτεισάτω διπλοῦν τὸ κλέμμα, τῶν δὲ ἄλλων ἀδικημάτων ἐπιτίμιον δραχμὰς εἴκοσι· ἂν δὲ μὴ ἐκτίνει παραχρῆμα, παραδότω ὁ κύριος τὸν οἰκέταν τῶι ἀδικηθέντι εἰς ἀπεργασίαν, εἰ δὲ μή, ὑπόδικος ἔστω ποτὶ διπλοῦν (LSCG 65, ll. 75–80). Finally, among the lexica in Bekker's *Anecdota Graeca* (i. 187) is found the entry 'to give surety: whenever someone who is convicted hands over a slave instead of himself for punishment' (ἐγγυῆσαι· ὅταν τις κρινόμενος παράσχῃ δοῦλον ἀνθ' ἑαυτοῦ τιμωρηθῆναι). While these examples demonstrate the principle of surrender of the slave to the victim, it should be noted that the law from Andania requires that the slave be handed over until he works off his debt, rather than true noxal surrender, whereby the slave becomes the permanent property of the victim. I thank David Lewis for drawing my attention to this distinction.

[19] Morrow (1939: 60).

seems to draw on the idea of *noxae datio* in a speech that he gives to Thrasybulus, the leader of the Athenian democratic counter-revolution in 403 BCE. In the speech, Thrasybulus suggests that the Spartans had handed over the 'men of the city' to the People of Athens who had been wronged, just as an offending dog is handed over to the victim for punishment.[20] On the basis of such evidence, Morrow notes that scholars have plausibly argued that, 'since *noxae datio* is known to have been permitted in the case of offending animals, it must likewise have been permitted when the injury was caused by slaves'.[21]

It is this provision for handing over an enslaved person to an injured party that gives rise to the second part of the law. For it appears that enslaved persons themselves and free persons who coveted enslaved persons belonging to others contrived together to take advantage of the provisions in the first part of the law in order to remove the enslaved person from the ownership of his enslaver. Indeed, one might hypothesize that the second part of the law was an addition to the original law, and that it aimed to prevent the unforeseen strategic exploitation of first part of the law by imposing a new legal procedure and stiff penalties to deter and/or deal with such cases of collusion.

Notably, the second part of the law on damage caused by an enslaved person provides for a new 'suit for evil-scheming' (δίκη κακοτεχνιῶν) against the alleged victim, and grants the master twice the value of the enslaved person if he is able to win the case. In the law on wounding, the reward for a successful prosecution in a new suit for 'kidnapping' (ἀνδραποδισμός) is not specified, but we can imagine it to be comparable. Interestingly, the law on wounding *does* specify a penalty for the master if he loses his suit for kidnapping. In this case, the victim wins three times the damages.[22]

It is important to stress that a 'private suit for evil-scheming' (δίκη κακοτεχνιῶν) and probably a 'public suit for kidnapping' (γραφὴ ἀνδραποδισμοῦ) existed in Athenian law.[23] The suit for evil-scheming seems to have been directed against those who provided false testimony in court and therefore is similar to the 'private suit for false witnessing' (δίκη ψευδομαρτυριῶν). While the latter suit targeted the witness himself, the former suit was aimed at the person who had arranged for the false testimony.[24] As Harrison notes, we have no direct evidence for a public

---

[20] Xen. *Hell.* 2.4.41.
[21] Morrow (1939: 60), citing Beauchet (1897: 456). See also Meier (1824: 653, nn. 472–3).
[22] It is interesting to speculate why the law is so concerned with punishing a master for a false claim for collusion between an enslaved person and the victim. In such a case, it would seem that a master was trying to scapegoat a slave for an attack against a free person that he himself had orchestrated. The law, it seems, was concerned to punish and deter such use of one's slaves.
[23] Morrow (1939: 62) notes that 'kidnapping was a grave crime in Athens, punished in some periods at least (perhaps in all) by death'. He cites Lycurgus fr.62 Blass and Xen. *Apol.* 25. In Athenian law, a kidnapper (*andrapodistes*) was an evildoer (*kakourgos*) who was subject to summary arrest if caught in the act (Harrison 1968: 165–6).
[24] Morrow (1939: 61.) Cf. Scafuro 1994.

suit for kidnapping, but the existence of such a suit is implied in the sources. The term 'kidnapper' covered both those who stole slaves and those who abducted free men.[25] Kidnappers who were caught in the act were subject to summary arrest. It is likely that a public suit was available for prosecuting cases in which the wrongful seizure was in the past. In sum, we may conclude that these parallels confirm the close ties between Plato's legislation and historical Greek, and specifically Athenian, law.

There are several possible scenarios that might have given rise to the second part of these laws. One scenario is that a free person schemed to deprive another free person of his slave by colluding with the enslaved person to make a claim for damages or wounding. In such cases, the would-be owner of the enslaved person would hope that the actual owner would rather settle the case by handing over his slave than by paying for damages, so that the former would gain ownership of the enslaved person. In such cases, the would-be owner presumably would have had to make a claim for damages worth at least the value of the enslaved person, if he expected to have a chance of gaining possession of them.

A second possible scenario is that it was the enslaved persons themselves who arranged with a third-party free person to make a claim for damages in the hope that they would be 'handed over' to a new owner, whom they expected to be more lenient, or even willing to grant them their freedom. Again, the claim would have to be fairly high if the enslaved person expected his enslaver to be willing to hand him over to a new master in compensation.

Several details of the laws suggest that the enslaved person was an active collaborator, and possibly the prime mover, in these schemes. The law on damage, for example, specifies that the slave and the third-party free person engage in a 'common ruse' (κοινῇ τέχνῃ). In the law on wounding, moreover, the ruse is described as a 'scheme' (μηχανή) resulting from 'a compact between the slave and the wounded party' (ἐκ συνθήκης...τοῦ δούλου καὶ τοῦ τρωθέντος). Even more striking is the fact that the law on damages appears to envision that the enslaved person was to blame for the collusion when it states: 'If the master who is accused says that the slave is to blame...' (τοῦ δούλου γεγονέναι τὴν αἰτίαν...).

Even if the third-party free person was contriving to gain a new slave, it would seem that he would have to offer the enslaved person something in order to gain his or her cooperation. Conversely, if the enslaved person were initiating the ruse, he or she too would have to offer the prospective master something in return—loyal service or continued good service after emancipation. The important point is that, either way, the enslaved person would expect to improve his or her situation and thus must be recognized as an active player in this legal game.

---

[25] Harrison (1968: 166, n. 1).

The implications of this conclusion are important for understanding the behaviour of enslaved persons. For it would seem that the enslaved were willing collaborators in a legal ruse that improved their conditions. It is unknowable and ultimately irrelevant whether enslaved persons had first-hand knowledge of the law on damages and devised the ruse themselves or were informed and persuaded by third-party free persons to collude for mutual benefit. What is important is that enslaved persons were active partners in the manipulation of the law for mutual benefit.

That said, it is crucial to remember that enslaved persons did not have legal rights and therefore could not initiate a legal claim themselves.[26] Rather, enslaved persons wishing to exploit the law on damages needed to conscript a free person to make the legal claim. Without the cooperation of a free person, an enslaved person could not initiate this ruse. This fact implies that enslaved individuals developed close relationships with free persons who were not their masters and negotiated skilfully with them to entice them to act in their interests, or at least for their own mutual benefit.

One plausible situation in which such a sort of collaboration might occur is in the case of a romantic and/or sexual relation between the third-party free person and an enslaved person. In such cases, it is possible that the enslaved person granted sexual favours in order to gain the cooperation of the free person in the legal ruse. In this regard, it is noteworthy that the law on damages envisions either male or female slaves (δοῦλος ἢ δούλη) as participants in this legal dodge. This fact strengthens the likelihood that romantic or sexual relations could be a motivating factor for the perpetration of such ruses.

I have suggested that enslaved persons might have learned from self-interested free persons about the laws on damages and wounding. Regardless of where the information originated, however, it is likely that such legal knowledge spread quickly through the enslaved population, and we may well wonder how many enslaved individuals took advantage of this legal loophole. The fact that the laws on damages and on wounding both had to be supplemented with an extra provision to deal with cases of collusion suggests that exploitation of this loophole happened frequently enough to necessitate further legislation. At the end of the chapter, I will return to the question of what these examples imply about the frequency of exploitation of such opportunities by enslaved persons.

## A Modern Comparandum

An example of how knowledge of a legal loophole could spread among a slave population can be found in a remarkable episode in American history.

---

[26] Kamen (2013: 12–14); see also Kamen, Chapter 9, this volume.

One morning in 1861, three enslaved youths rowed across the James River in Virginia and asked for asylum in a citadel, Fort Monroe, belonging to the Union. These young men had been leased out to the Confederate Army to construct defences at a strategic point across the river from Fort Monroe. Although Virginia had seceded from the Union earlier that year, the Union had retained control of Fort Monroe. The commander at Fort Monroe was one Benjamin Butler, a lawyer by training and an opponent of slavery. Butler declared the fugitives 'contraband of war', shrewdly arguing that, if Virginia considered itself to be a foreign power by seceding from the Union, then he was under no obligation to return the fugitives, as would otherwise be required by the Fugitive Slave Act of 1850.

Almost immediately after this decision, a massive flood of enslaved individuals began streaming towards Fort Monroe. According to one account of this incident, 'within weeks...slaves were reported flocking to the Union lines just about anywhere there *were* Union lines'.[27] A soldier who was present at Fort Monroe wrote to his family in wonderment at what he called the 'mysterious spiritual telegraph which runs through the slave population'. The soldier wrote that it was enough to 'proclaim an edict of emancipation in the hearing of a single slave on the Potomac, and in a few days it will be known by his brethren on the gulf'.[28]

That such a 'mysterious spiritual telegraph' existed among enslaved persons in ancient Greece (and I think the barriers of language and ethnicity have been vastly exaggerated—but that is another topic) is suggested by evidence of similar unified responses to opportunities for freedom that we hear of in our sources.[29] For example, Thucydides reports that more than twenty thousand enslaved persons in Attica fled to Deceleia after it was occupied by the Spartans in 413 BCE. On Corcyra in 427 BCE, moreover, he records that enslaved persons in the countryside fled to the side of the democrats when a civil war erupted there. Finally, on Khios in 411 BCE, Thucydides writes that enslaved persons fled *en masse* to the Athenian fortification when the Athenians invaded the island after it had revolted from the Athenian empire.[30] While these examples concern situations of external or civil war rather than everyday life, nevertheless they illustrate the effectiveness of communication among enslaved populations, including those dispersed in the rural hinterlands of ancient Greek city states.

Before we turn to another striking example of enslaved persons exploiting Greek law in order to get transferred to a new master, it is worth mentioning in

---

[27] Goodheart (2011: 59).

[28] For a similar example of an enslaved person making use of the law to gain freedom, see Miles (2017: 152–8), who demonstrates how enslaved persons in the Detroit area used the Northwest Ordinance of 1787 to manoeuvre for freedom, among other legal strategies. In one case, a newly freed couple managed to get the cooperation of a white lawyer and appealed to the principle of habeas corpus in an (ultimately unsuccessful) bid to gain freedom for their children (Miles 2017: 177–8).

[29] For refutation of the idea that the enslaved were too culturally diverse to communicate and organize resistance, see Forsdyke (2021: 168–81).

[30] Thuc. 7.27.5; 3.73; 8.40.2.

passing several other legal dodges that closely parallel the use of *noxae datio* discussed above. For example, it is possible that enslaved individuals made use of the Athenian democratic institution of property exchange (*antidosis*) to arrange transfer to a new master. The speaker in Lysias 4, for example, states quite boldly that his opponent offered to exchange property only because he wanted to obtain possession of a girl who was enslaved to the speaker. It is possible that the enslaved girl was a helpless pawn in the legal battles of these Athenian citizens, but it is also possible the enslaved girl took an active role in instigating this legal manoeuvre. The same speech, moreover, provides evidence that masters might even free their slaves in order to prevent them from testifying under torture and thereby revealing incriminating information.[31] As in the case of *noxae datio*, such legal manoeuvres had to be initiated by a free person, but there is no reason to doubt that enslaved persons could have actively prompted the free person to initiate these legal actions. After all, enslaved persons were often major beneficiaries of these legal strategies.

The potential benefits for enslaved individuals are particularly clear about a third legal strategy—namely, the practice of offering information on one's enslaver's alleged seditious activities to public authorities in exchange for a grant of freedom. This scenario is most famously attested in the case of the profanation of the mysteries in 415 BCE, when enslaved individuals came forward with information against their enslavers in exchange for freedom. While the circumstances of 415 were clearly exceptional, it is possible that enslaved individuals could resort to this strategy whenever they perceived that their enslavers had done anything against the public interest.[32]

\* \* \*

## Finding a New Master at a Temple

In the second half of this chapter, I turn to a further example of enslaved individuals exploiting Greek law in order to be transferred to more lenient masters. This example involves the Greek law of asylum at temples.

It was a long-established Greek custom that suppliants at temples could be granted asylum and thereby be protected from any reprisals that might threaten them.[33] In many cases, the right of asylum would have been invoked by free persons. For example, Thucydides relates the story of Cylon, the would-be

---

[31] Lys. 4.2, 14.
[32] Thuc. 6.53–61; And. 1; Lys. 7.16. See Hunter (1994) on the power that the exchange of information for freedom gave slaves to 'police' their masters.
[33] For discussion of this phenomenon, see Sinn (1990, 1993) and Chaniotis (1996). For supplication in the ancient world, including temple supplication, see Naiden (2006).

Athenian tyrant, whose partisans fled to the sanctuary of the Semnai Theai when their coup failed c.630 BCE.[34] Similarly, Thucydides relates the story of the Spartan regent Pausanias, who sought refuge in the 'Brazen House', a temple of Athena, when he was detected in seditious activity in Sparta c.470.[35] In both these cases, infamously, the right of asylum was violated, and the suppliants were dragged from the temples and killed.[36] Indeed, our sources usually report incidents only when the right of asylum was violated.[37]

Enslaved persons were also protected by this right of asylum, and particular temples were known to give refuge to the enslaved. The temple of Poseidon at Tainaron in Laconia and the temple of Theseus in Athens are two well-known examples.[38] Thucydides mentions that, in the 460s BCE, the Spartans expelled a group of helots who were presenting themselves as suppliants at a temple of Poseidon at Tainaron. The Spartans then executed the helots, and Thucydides reports that 'even the Spartans believe that the great earthquake [of 464 BCE] was a result of this impiety.'[39] Aristophanes alludes to the function of the sanctuary of Theseus as a place of refuge in his play *Knights* of 424 BCE, and an ancient commentator on the play explains that enslaved persons who fled to the sanctuary of Theseus gained asylum (ἀσυλίαν εἶχον).[40] In the fourth century, Aeschines mentions the sanctuary of Theseus as the place where magistracies were allotted, and an ancient commentator adds a reference to a law regarding slaves who fled to the temple: 'There was a law that those who fled to the precinct of Theseus should be inviolate.'[41] A long lexicographic tradition echoes and confirms this function of the sanctuary of Theseus in classical Athens.[42]

On the basis of the surviving literary and epigraphic evidence, Ulrich Sinn summarizes the process of requesting asylum as follows:

> If someone...wished to avail himself of the protection of a sanctuary, he had to appear openly and set forth the reasons for his coming. After such a presentation, the sanctuary was in turn obliged to work towards a solution of the problem, as a rule by undertaking the role of a go-between.[43]

---

[34] Thuc. 1.126.   [35] Thuc. 1.134.
[36] The violation of the right of asylum by slave-owners is also dramatized in several plays, including Menander's *Girl from Perinthos* and Plautus' *Rudens*. I thank Peter Hunt for these references.
[37] Sinn (1993: 93).
[38] See Christensen (1984) for a complete list with sources. See also Kudlien (1988: 243–5) and Gottesman (2014). The Athenians apparently made some efforts to keep runaways from the sanctuaries on the acropolis, as attested in an inscription concerning a wall to keep them out (*IG* i³ 45; Chaniotis 1996: 72).
[39] Thuc. 1.128.   [40] Ar. *Eq.* 1311–2 with scholion to l. 1312.
[41] Aeschin. 3.13 with scholion: νόμος δ' ἦν τοὺς ἀποφυγόντας τῶν ἱκετῶν εἰς τὸ τοῦ Θησέως τέμενος ἀτιμωρήτους εἶναι.
[42] Hsch., Phot., Suda, Ed.Gud., Et.Mag., s.v. Θησεῖον.   [43] Sinn (1993: 91).

While Sinn's description of the process concerns all types of suppliants, including criminals seeking to escape punishment and high-status citizens fleeing violence at the hands of their political opponents, it also holds for enslaved suppliants.

But what reasons might an enslaved person set forth for fleeing his master? On the basis of the scant surviving evidence, it seems that an enslaved person needed to accuse his or her enslaver of unjust treatment. For example, in Achilles Tatius' novel *Leukippe and Kleitophon* (second century CE), we learn that an enslaved woman who fled to the temple of Artemis at Ephesus made formal accusations of wrongdoing against her enslaver (ἐγκαλοῦσα τῷ δεσπότῃ).[44] A fragment of Eupolis's play *Cities*, moreover, features an enslaved woman who prefaces her reasons for fleeing to the Theseion by saying that she is suffering the evil things of the sort that she will now enumerate (κακὰ τοιάδε πάσχουσα).[45] Unfortunately the fragment breaks off before the specific offences are listed.

Scholars have pointed to the fact that, at Athens, enslaved persons were covered by the law on hubris, which forbade outrageous treatment of one human being by another.[46] Acts of hubris, therefore, were possibly cited by slaves to justify a claim to asylum at the sanctuary of Theseus.[47] While it is difficult to discern what exactly constituted hubris towards enslaved persons at Athens, it is likely, however, that intolerable physical abuse by enslavers—beating or starving an enslaved person to the point of death—was the basis of an enslaved person's request for asylum.[48] Plutarch's *Life of Theseus* comments on the general humanity exhibited at the sanctuary of Theseus towards the vulnerable, including enslaved persons. The sanctuary, Plutarch writes, was 'a place of refuge for slaves [οἰκέταις] and all the weak [πᾶσι τοῖς ταπεινοτέροις] who fear the stronger, since Theseus himself was an advocate and helper and he received humanely [φιλανθρώπως] the appeals of the weak [τῶν ταπεινοτέρων].'[49]

Cases of asylum were decided by the priests of the sanctuary themselves, or by other magistrates in the polis.[50] An inscription from Andania dating to 92 BCE, for example, indicates that the sanctuary is to serve as a refuge for slaves (φύγιμον

---

[44] 7.13, with Chaniotis (1996: 81).     [45] Kassel-Austin fr. 229, quoted below.

[46] See Kamen, Chapter 9, this volume, who argues persuasively, however, that it was difficult, practically speaking, for enslaved persons to gain redress for mistreatment under this law (see next two notes for some of the reasons). If Kamen is right that legal redress was very difficult for enslaved persons, then flight to a sanctuary was all the more likely a response to severe abuse.

[47] Christensen (1984), with earlier scholarship cited therein. It is important to emphasize that slaves, who had no legal rights at Athens, depended on their master or another citizen to prosecute a case of hubris. If the master himself were the perpetrator, then the slave would have had no legal recourse except flight to the Theseion, where even slaves could be heard (see below). On the law of hybris in relation to slaves, see Fisher (1995), Canevaro (2018), and Kamen, Chapter 9, this volume.

[48] There were laws concerning cases in which a master killed his own slave, and they are referenced in several Athenian sources. For example, see Antiphon 6.4, where it is noted that a slave who is killed by his own master goes unavenged, although the master still purifies himself and avoids polluting shrines. Lycurgus, at *Leoc.* 65, suggests that, in the old days, the penalty for killing a slave and free man is the same (death), implying that it was different in the fourth century.

[49] Plut. *Thes.* 36.4.     [50] Chaniotis (1996: 79).

εἶμεν τοῖς δούλοις) and specifies that priests (ἱεροί) are to adjudicate such cases.[51] On Samos in the third century BCE, temple officials (νεωποίαι) preside over the court responsible for interrogating the slave and his or her master.[52] In Achilles Tatius' novel, 'magistrates' (ἄρχοντες) arbitrate between an enslaved woman and her enslaver.[53]

There were three possible outcomes of the process. If the enslaver won the case, then the suppliant was to be handed back to him. If the enslaved person won, then either the enslaved person was dedicated to the god and became an enslaved worker at the sanctuary or he or she was sold to a new master.[54] Herodotus reports that, even up to his own time, any enslaved person who fled to the temple of Heracles at the mouth of the Nile became inviolate if he permitted himself to be branded with sacred marks and gave himself over to the god.[55] Herodotus seems to suggest that the enslaved person served at the temple, and this seems plausible, given that both branding and enslaved workers at temples are well attested in ancient Egypt.[56]

A similar outcome may have resulted for helots who fled to the temple of Poseidon at Tainaron. A remarkable set of six inscriptions dating to the fourth century records the dedication of individuals to the god.[57] While there is some question whether these individuals were Spartan helots or enslaved persons belonging to the free non-citizen inhabitants of Laconia (the *perioikoi*), it is nevertheless clear that these inscriptions involve dedications of enslaved individuals. A further question, however, is whether, by entrusting themselves to the god, helots became enslaved workers at the temple or free persons? This question arises because, in later periods, consecration at a temple became a standard mode of liberating an enslaved person.[58]

In regard to the temple at Tainaron, Jean Ducat has argued that there is no need to consider dedication and manumission as exclusive options. By dedicating the enslaved individual to the god, the enslaved person gained the god as his new owner, and the god protected him from being seized by his former

---

[51] *LSCG* 65, ll. 80–4, cited in Chaniotis (1996: 80, n. 56). [52] Habicht (1972: 226–31, n. 59).
[53] Ach. Tat. 7.13.
[54] Chaniotis (1996: 83), who states that 'supplication did not change their legal condition but only their owner. There is no evidence that they were manumitted.' Cf. Kudlien (1988: 243–5).
[55] Hdt. 2.113.2.
[56] Asheri et al. (2007: 323) with references. For temple-slavery in ancient Greece, see Eur. *Ion* 309–10. There, slaves are said to be either dedicated or sold to the temple (ἀνάθημα πόλεως, ἤ τινος πραθεὶς ὕπο).
[57] *IG* v¹ 1228–1233; Ducat (1990). That said, the fact that only six survive is a puzzle. What happened to the many more helots/slaves who must have fled there over the centuries? Why are there only six dedications, if this is the regular procedure? What makes these special? The loss of much of the epigraphical record cannot be the only answer.
[58] Sokolowski (1954) proposed that sacral manumission originated in the right of asylum at temples, following Latte (1920: 105–8). Contra: Bömer (1960: 14).

(human) enslaver. The formerly enslaved person was, therefore, free with regard to his former enslaver, but was bound to perform certain services for the god. As Ducat observes, this paradoxical condition is exemplified in an inscription from Cos (third century BCE) in which an enslaved man, Libys, and his descendants are dedicated to a sanctuary of Heracles and declared free (ἐόντω δὲ ἐλευθέρο[ι]), if they perform certain services (ποιοῦντες τὰ συντεταγμένα).[59] In several other inscriptions, moreover, specific services, such as assistance with sacrifices, are enumerated.[60] For our purposes, what is clear is that this sort of partially free status was an amelioration of the enslaved person's former condition.[61]

Such an improvement of one's condition was also probably the effect of the third possible outcome of a slave's flight to a temple—namely. sale to a new owner. This outcome seems to have been the expectation of enslaved individuals who fled to the temple of Theseus at Athens. As Kerry Christensen observes in her careful reconstruction of the evidence, the second-century CE lexicographer Pollux cites two fragments from lost comedies that attest to the fact that enslaved fugitives at this sanctuary were given the opportunity to seek a new master. They did this by formally 'requesting a sale'.[62]

> What people now say is that enslaved persons 'request' a sale, but in Aristophanes' *Horai*, they 'find' a sale:
> 'For me it is best to flee to the sanctuary of Theseus
> and there to remain, until I find a sale.'
> Conversely, in Eupolis' *Cities*,
> 'Such evils I suffer
> and so should I not request a sale?'

The clear impression that this comic evidence gives is that enslaved suppliants sought a sale to a new master in order to improve their conditions. Yet, in a recent article, Peter Hunt exhibits considerable scepticism about whether this institution provided any relief for slaves. Hunt wonders: 'who would buy a slave who had caused his master trouble by alleging ill-treatment and seeking sanctuary?' He then suggests: 'Only slaveholders whose operations were based on brute violence

---

[59] *LSCG* 177, ll. 5–6.   [60] Ducat (1990: 192–3).
[61] For other examples of such partially free status, see Zelnick-Abramowitz (2005). Zanovello (2018), however, disputes that enslaved persons consecrated to a god were partially free as a matter of law, even if they were de facto free. See also Sosin (2015).
[62] Christensen (1984: 24), citing Pollux 7.13, who cites in turn lines from Aristophanes' lost play *Horai* and Eupolis' *Poleis* (translated here): ὃ δ' οἱ νῦν φασὶ τοὺς οἰκέτας πρᾶσιν αἰτεῖν, ἔστιν εὑρεῖν ἐν Ἀριστοφάνους Ὥραις· ἐμοὶ κράτιστον ἐς τὸ Θησεῖον δραμεῖν, / ἐκεῖ δ', ἕως ἂν πρᾶσιν εὕρωμαι, μένειν (= 577 Kassel-Austin), ἄντικρυς δ' ἐν ταῖς Εὐπόλιδος Πόλεσι· κακὰ τοιάδε πάσχουσα / μηδὲ πρᾶσιν αἰτῶ (= 229 Kassel-Austin). Cf. Plut. *Mor.*166D.

and physical constraint, such as mill or mine operators,' would be willing to buy such slaves.[63]

While I greatly admire Peter Hunt's work on slavery, on this small detail I wonder if this explanation of the institution can be correct? I would pose the contrary question: what enslaved person would flee to a temple, if he were bound to be sold to a master 'whose operations were based on brute violence and physical constraint', including the two most brutal and dangerous occupations such as milling and mining? In other words, what was in it for the enslaved, if their conditions were bound to be bad and probably worse than what they had escaped? We might further observe, slightly modifying the passage from the comic biography of Aesop cited at the beginning of this chapter, that 'no one, fleeing the better, goes to the worse'.

The answer to this puzzle, it seems to me, is to acknowledge the capacity of the enslaved to negotiate with a potential new owner in such a way as to ensure that *both* parties' interests were met. In fact, we have comparative evidence for negotiations between prospective owners and enslaved individuals in the process of sale. In his study of slave markets in the antebellum American South, Walter Johnson demonstrates how enslaved individuals—despite their weaker position— were able to influence the outcome of sales in significant ways. Indeed, Johnson writes that 'many slave sales had to be negotiated twice through— once with the buyer and once with the merchandise'.[64] One example from Johnson's book will help illustrate how this worked and sheds light on the sort of negotiations that might have taken place between an enslaved individual who had taken refuge in a sanctuary and a potential new owner in ancient Greece.

Johnson relates the story of an enslaved man named Edward Hicks, who 'used flight to renegotiate the terms of his own sale'. When Hicks learned that he had been sold to a slave trader, he ran away. Hiding out in the woods, Hicks remained in contact with his 'friends and brothers' in town, 'who told him that he had been advertised as a runaway' and 'advised him to go to an old house where the cotton was kept and there to stay until the advertisement was over'. Hicks followed these instructions and hid out in the house until 'the slave trader gave up and set off for New Orleans without him'. When the slave trader returned for another season of buying the next spring, somehow there was a white man in the town who wanted to buy Hicks. The trader then sold to this white man 'the chance of Hicks's capture in the woods'—a common practice at the time. The price for Hicks was set at 800 dollars. and, once the deal was made, the white man sent

---

[63] Hunt (2016: 153–4). Hunt (personal correspondence) notes that, according to Watson (1987: 121), in Roman law, it was 'standard practice in buying a slave to demand a guarantee that he had not fled to the statue [of the emperor and thus afforded protection]'.

[64] Johnson (1999: 30).

out some of his boys to tell Hicks, and a few days later Hicks presented himself to his new owner.[65]

By hiding out and yet remaining in contact with the community of the enslaved—and apparently also potential buyers—Hicks avoided being sold away from his community and even exerted some control over the terms of his purchase. As Johnson writes:

> The connection between Hicks and the man who eventually bought the chance of his capture is obscure…What is clear is that he had plenty of help from neighboring slaves in escaping, hiding and deciding when to come out. With the help of the very community from which he was to be separated by the trade, Hicks stayed away until he was satisfied with the terms of his own sale.[66]

For Hicks, the key condition for allowing himself to be captured would probably have been a prohibition on future sale. In return, Hicks would have promised his new master loyal service.[67]

*Mutatis mutandis*, this scenario sheds light on how enslaved individuals in ancient Greece might have negotiated their sale to a new master by seeking refuge in a sanctuary. It is noteworthy, moreover, that one might reasonably ask in the modern example, as Hunt does of the ancient example, 'who would buy a runaway?' The modern example emphatically shows that there were buyers even for runaways, and, more importantly, that such sales were a product of negotiations between potential buyers and the enslaved themselves.[68]

A fifth-century law from Gortyn may have implications for this reconstruction of negotiations between enslaved suppliants and potential buyers. The law forbids the sale of enslaved suppliants (or serfs) for a year after they have fled to the sanctuary.[69] Some scholars think that this delay was intended to allow time for extensive negotiation between the enslaved and the enslaver before a sale was allowed.[70] Gagarin and Perlman write, for example, that '[t]he time interval, up to a year,

---

[65] Johnson (1999: 32–3).  [66] Johnson (1999: 33).
[67] Another modern example can be found in the ways that enslaved runaways managed to negotiate down the terms of their enslavement after the passage of the Northwest Ordinance in 1787. After the passage of the law, enslaved individuals in the Detroit area 'ran away more frequently and refused to return unless they could negotiate better circumstances' (Miles 2017: 152). One tactic was to agree to return only as an indentured person (voluntary slavery was not prohibited by the Northwest Ordinance), thereby establishing a time limit on servitude. Miles recounts the story of an enslaved man named John Reed, whose tactic of flight and negotiation with a bounty hunter has striking parallels with Hicks's actions. Like Hicks, Reed negotiated favourable terms for his return: time-limited indenture rather than slavery.
[68] Johnson (1999: 45–6) reproduces a list of twenty-two slave sales recorded by a slave trader. One entry concerns a slave who is noted to be a runaway, and, although he is sold at a loss (bought at $750 and sold at $540), he is nevertheless sold.
[69] Gagarin and Perlman (2016: G41.4; cf. G72.1.39–49).   [70] Chaniotis (1996: 82).

would be intended to allow the serf's master time to persuade the serf to return to his service; if he could not, then the serf would be sold'.[71] But it is equally true that such an extensive waiting period allowed an enslaved suppliant plenty of time to identify a potential new buyer and conduct the necessary negotiations regarding future treatment. Aristophanes' coinage of a term for one who hangs out in the sanctuary of Theseus, a 'Theseion-loiterer' ($\theta\eta\sigma\epsilon\iota\acute{o}\tau\rho\iota\psi$), similarly suggests a long period of waiting and hence ample time for such negotiations.[72]

Summing up, one might conclude from this discussion that enslaved individuals in ancient Greece exploited Greek beliefs about the sanctity of temples and the right of divine protection in order to improve their conditions of enslavement. Contrary to what Peter Hunt argues, I suggest that the enslaved would not have fled to sanctuaries if their conditions were only bound to get worse. Knowledge of the outcomes for enslaved individuals who fled to sanctuaries would have spread quickly among the community of the enslaved, and the practice would have ended if it regularly resulted in worse outcomes for the enslaved than their previous conditions. That the practice did not end, and indeed was a common feature of life in fifth-century Athens, is again suggested by Aristophanes' coinage mentioned above, the 'Theseion-loiterer'. The most likely outcome of such situations, I would argue, is that enslaved individuals would have been sold to new owners who entered into a bargain with the enslaved individual to swap humane treatment for loyalty.

Once again, we see in this example how enslaved individuals may have exploited Greek laws—this time religious laws—to improve their conditions in slavery. The example illustrates the knowledge of Greek law and customs possessed by enslaved individuals, as well as their ability to negotiate successfully with potential new owners.

## Conclusion

A big question that remains is how frequently enslaved individuals actively manipulated the law in order to improve their conditions. If the examples discussed in this chapter are simply rare cases, then there is reason to conclude that, in most cases, enslaved individuals were unable to exercise control over their fate in this way. Here we may recall Johnson's critique of scholarship on modern slavery, including his own book on the slave market from which the example of the runaway Hicks was drawn. Johnson argues that he and other scholars may have overemphasized the extent to which enslaved individuals were able to manipulate

---

[71] Gagarin and Perlman (2016: 298).
[72] Et.Mag. s.v. $\theta\eta\sigma\epsilon\iota\acute{o}\tau\rho\iota\psi$ with Gottesman (2014: 178).

their owners to gain their own objectives. In regard to ancient slavery, moreover, we must also take to heart the warnings of McKeown about the insufficiency and ambiguity of the evidence, as well as modern scholars' (including my own) desire to view the enslaved as active agents in the cause of their own autonomy.

In response to these critiques, it should be acknowledged that the enslaved in classical Athens were variously situated and not all of them will have had the opportunity to exploit the tactics discussed in this chapter. A person chained in the mines or imprisoned in a mill is unlikely to have had the opportunity to flee to a sanctuary, let alone engage in the type of legal ruse mentioned in the laws on damages and wounding.[73] On the other hand, many enslaved individuals were embedded in the everyday life of the *polis* and would have had ample opportunity not only to gain knowledge of the laws and customs of their owners but also to develop social ties (networks) with citizens as well as other enslaved individuals.[74] Some enslaved persons, of course, were fellow Greeks (if not Athenian specifically), in which case they would have been familiar with Greek customs concerning asylum and might even have come from states that had similar laws to Athenian legislation on damages and wounding.[75]

Furthermore, a key part of the argument of this chapter is that the evidence we do have suggests that these actions by the enslaved were not rare. The formulation of laws responding to the problem of collusion between enslaved individuals and third parties in suits for damages and wounding indicate that the problem was thought, at least by Plato, to be common enough to require legislation. The ubiquity of sanctuaries—some specially designated for the enslaved—in the Greek world, moreover, and the plentiful evidence for their importance at Athens and Sparta, suggest that the enslaved resorted to this option with some frequency. In short, while I would not argue that all or even most enslaved persons engaged in these tactics, there is enough evidence to show that such manoeuvres were a significant element of their efforts to improve their conditions in slavery.

---

[73] As Adriaan Lanni has pointed out to me, the legal ruse outlined in the laws on damages and wounding is more sophisticated than flight to a temple and may have been a tactic employed only by rather privileged slaves. On the other hand, if my reconstruction of the evidence for slave suppliants is correct, slaves would have needed considerable networks and negotiation skills, not to mention speaking ability, to obtain the optimum outcome.

[74] There is a growing body of scholarship on the ways that citizens and slaves interacted in daily life, despite rigid legal categories: Jones (1999); Cohen (2000); Vlassopoulos (2007, 2009); Taylor and Vlassopoulos (2015). If the total enslaved population of Athens was 80,000–100,000, then somewhere between 10% and 20% of the enslaved population may have been in the mines or mills. Demographic estimates are based of course on perilously little evidence, but these numbers are generally accepted.

[75] See, e.g., the laws concerning the liability of enslaved persons at Gortyn, as discussed by Lewis (2020).

## Acknowledgements

I would like to thank audiences at Oxford University, the Ohio State University, the University of Texas at Austin, the University of Michigan, and Harvard Law School for helpful comments on this chapter.

## Works Cited

Asheri, D., et al. (2007). *A Commentary on Herodotus Book I–IV*. Oxford.

Beauchet, L. (1897). *L'Histoire du droit privé de la république athénienne*. Paris.

Ben-Ur, A. (2018). 'Bound Together? Reassessing the Slave Community and Resistance Paradigms', *Journal of Global Slavery*, 3: 195–210.

Bömer, F. (1960). *Untersuchungen über die Religion der Sklaven in Griechenland und Rom*. Wiesbaden.

Canevaro, M. (2018). 'The *graphe hybreos* against Slaves: The *time* of the Victim and that of the *hybristes*', *Journal of Hellenic Studies*, 138: 100–26.

Cartledge, P. A. (1985). 'Rebels and Sambos in Classical Greece: A Comparative View', in P. A. Cartledge and F. Harvey (eds), *Crux: Essays in Greek History Presented to G. E. M. de Ste. Croix*, 16–46. London (repr. in P. A. Cartledge, *Spartan Reflections*. Berkeley and Los Angeles, 2001, 127–52).

Chaniotis, A. (1996). 'Conflicting Authorities: Asylia between Secular and Divine Law in the Classical and Hellenistic Poleis', *Kernos*, 9: 65–86.

Christensen, K. (1984). 'The Theseion: A Slave Refuge at Athens', *American Journal of Ancient History*, 9: 23–32.

Cohen, E. E. (2000). *The Athenian Nation*. Princeton.

de Ste. Croix, G. E. M. (1981). *The Class Struggle in the Ancient Greek World*. London.

Ducat, J. (1990). 'Esclaves au Ténare', in *Mélanges Pierre Léveque*, iv. *Religion: Annales littéraires de l'Université de Besançon*, 173–93. Besançon.

Fisher, N. R. E. (1995). 'Hybris, Status and Slavery', in A. Powell (ed.), *The Greek World*, 44–84. London.

Forsdyke, S. (2019). 'Slave Agency and Citizenship in Classical Athens', in G. Thür, Uri Yiftaḥ-Firanko, and Rachel Zelnick-Abramovitz (eds), *Symposion: Gesellschaft für griechische und hellenistische Rechtsgeschichte*, 346–66. Vienna.

Forsdyke, S. (2021). *Slaves and Slavery in Ancient Greece*. Cambridge.

Gagarin, Michael, and Paula J. Perlman (2016). *The Laws of Ancient Crete: c.650–400 BCE*. Oxford.

Genovese, E. (1974). *Roll Jordan Roll: The World the Slaves Made*. New York.

Genovese, E. (1979). *From Rebellion to Revolution: Afro-American Slave Revolts in the Making of the Modern World*. Baton Rouge.

Goodheart, A. (2011). 'The Shrug that Made History', *New York Times Magazine*, 3 April: 59.

Gottesman, A. (2014). *Politics and the Street in Democratic Athens*. Cambridge.

Habicht, C. (1972). 'Hellenistische Inschriften aus dem Heraion von Samos', *Mitteilungen des Deutschen Archäologischen Instituts, Athenische Abteilung*, 87: 191–228.

Harrison, A. R. W. (1968). *The Law of Athens. Volume 1. The Family and Property*. Oxford.

Hopkins, K. (1993). 'Novel Evidence for Roman Slavery', *Past and Present*, 138: 3–28 (repr. in K. Hopkins, *Sociological Studies in Roman History*, ed. C. Kelly (Cambridge, 2018), 398–424).

Hunt, P. (2016). 'Violence against Slaves in Classical Greece', in W. Reiss and G. Fagan (eds), *The Topography of Violence in the Greco-Roman World*, 136–61. Ann Arbor.

Hunt, P. (2018). *Ancient Greek and Roman Slavery*. Malden, MA.

Hunter, V. (1994). *Policing Athens. Social Control in the Attic Lawsuits, 420–320 BC*. Princeton.

Johnson, W. (1999). *Soul by Soul: Life Inside the Antebellum Slave Market*. Cambridge, MA.

Johnson W. (2003). 'On Agency', *Journal of Social History*, 37: 113–24.

Jones, N. F. (1999). *The Associations of Classical Athens: The Response to Democracy*. Oxford.

Kamen, D. (2013). *Status in Classical Athens*. Princeton.

Kudlien, F. (1988). 'Zur sozialen Situation des flüchtigen Sklaven in der Antike', *Hermes*, 116: 232–52.

Latte, K. (1920). *Heiliges Recht: Untersuchungen zur Geschichte der sakralen Rechtsformen in Griechenland*. Tübingen.

Lewis, D. (2020). 'Legal Knowledge in Gortyn: Debt Bondage and the Liability of Slaves in Gortynian Law', in C. Ando and W. P. Sullivan (eds), *The Discovery of the Fact*, 72–90. Ann Arbor.

McKeown, N. (2007). *The Invention of Ancient Slavery?* London.

McKeown, N. (2011). 'Resistance among Chattel Slaves in the Classical Greek World', in K. Bradley and P. Cartledge (eds), *The Cambridge World History of Slavery*, i. *The Ancient Mediterranean World*, 153–75. Cambridge.

Meier, M. (1824). *Der Attische Process*. Berlin.

Miles, T. (2017). *The Dawn of Detroit: A Chronicle of Slavery and Freedom in the City of the Straits*. New York.

Morrow, G. (1939). *Plato's Law of Slavery in its Relation to Greek Law*. Urbana, IL.

Naiden, F. (2006). *Ancient Supplication*. Oxford.

Scafuro, A. (1994). 'Witnessing and False Witnessing: Proving Citizenship and Kin Identity in Fourth-Century Athens', in A. Boegehold and A. Scafuro (eds), *Athenian Identity and Civic Ideology*, 156–98. Baltimore.

Schofield, M. (2016). (ed.). *Plato Laws*. Translated by Tom Griffith. Cambridge.

Scott, J. (1985). *Weapons of the Weak: Everyday Forms of Peasant Resistance*. New Haven.

Scott, J. (1990). *Domination and the Arts of Resistance: Hidden Transcripts*. New Haven.

Sinn, U. (1990). 'Eine sakrale Schutzzone in der korinthischen Peraia', *Mitteilungen des deutschen archäologischen Instituts, Athenische Abteilung*, 105: 53–116.

Sinn, U. (1993). 'Greek Sanctuaries as Places of Refuge', in R. Hägg and N. Marinatos (eds), *Greek Sanctuaries: New Approaches*, 88–109. London.

Sokolowski, F. (1954). 'The Real Meaning of Sacral Manumission', *Harvard Theological Review*, 47: 173–81.

Sokolowski, F. (1969). *Lois sacrées des cités grecques*. Paris (= *LSCG*).

Sosin, J. (2015). 'Manumission with Paramone: Conditional Freedom?', *Transactions of the American Philological Association*, 145: 325–81.

Taylor, C., and K. Vlassopoulos (2015) (eds). *Communities and Networks in the Ancient Greek World*. Oxford.

Vlassopoulos, K. (2007). 'Free Spaces: Identity, Experience and Democracy in Classical Athens', *Classical Quarterly*, 57: 33–52.

Vlassopoulos, K. (2009). 'Slavery, Freedom and Citizenship in Classical Athens: Beyond a Legalistic Approach', *European Review of History/Revue européenne d'histoire*, 16: 347–63.

Watson, A. (1987). *Roman Slave Law*. Baltimore.

Zanovello, S. (2018). 'Some Remarks on Manumission and Consecration in Hellenistic Chaeronea', *Journal of Global Slavery*, 3: 129–51.

Zelnick-Abramowitz, R. (2005) *Not Wholly Free: The Concept of Manumission and the Status of Manumitted Slaves in the Ancient Greek World*. Leiden.

Sara Forsdyke, *How to Find a New Master: The Agency of Enslaved Persons in Ancient Greece* In: *Voiceless, Invisible, and Countless in Ancient Greece: The Experience of Subordinates, 700–300 BCE*. Edited by: Samuel D. Gartland and David W. Tandy, Oxford University Press. © Sara Forsdyke 2024. DOI: 10.1093/9780191995514.003.0008

# 8
# Spoken from the Grave
## The Construction of Social Identities on the Funerary Monuments of Metics in Classical Athens

*Sara Wijma*

### Preface

My interest in the position of metics in classical Athens does not originate from a personal or academic interest in the position of subordinated groups in general. Rather, it was in the context of a large project on Athenian citizenship at the University of Utrecht, in the Netherlands, that my first steps into the research of Athenian *metoikia* were made. Publications associated with this project and earlier publications that inspired it have facilitated a paradigm shift in our understanding of Athenian citizenship. They suggest that we should no longer define Athenian citizenship as a juridical status that encompassed certain strictly demarcated political and juridical rights, privileges, and duties. Instead, we should focus on 'being a citizen', on belonging to the Athenian *polis* by descent, which was embodied by the active and acknowledged participation of the Athenians in the public affairs of their *polis*, including sharing in the community's obligations towards the gods (see especially Manville (1994) and Blok (2017)). My own work on the implications of this new paradigm for our understanding of Athenian *metoikia*—in what ways did the details of the participation of metics in Athenian *polis* religion inform their status in society at large? (Wijma (2014))—not only ties in with these recent studies of Athenian citizenship, but also with works more broadly concerned with the multifaceted and sometimes fuzzy demarcations of status in Athens in general, like Cohen (2000) and Vlassopoulos (2007).

These latter works and more recent ones, like Osborne (2011), with its emphasis on the invisibility of status in visual arts, and Kamen (2013), which argues for a spectrum of statuses, have made it abundantly clear that belonging to one of the three main status groups in classical Athens did not fully define and dictate the lives and experiences of the people living in the *polis*. Investigating these polis inhabitants as either citizens, metics, or slaves only offers a partial understanding of their position in Athens. If we zoom in on metics, it should furthermore be observed that formal metic status was solely articulated by the Athenians. In addition, we have to acknowledge that almost all testimonies explicitly relating to *metoikia* come from Athenian sources. This means that scholars working on *metoikia*, including myself, will by necessity have to adhere to a subordinator's perspective. Of course, the lives and experiences of the people living in classical Athens as metics were greatly informed (and limited) by their official status, as they were accordingly excluded from political and juridical offices, could not own land, were to pay a specific metic tax, had to serve in the Athenian army, could not marry an Athenian, had to participate in several *polis* festivals in a specific way, and so on, but it cannot automatically be assumed that this imposed metic status completely defined them.

The generous invitation of the editors to fill a 'metic-shaped hole' in the current volume allowed me to pursue my growing discomfort with the heuristic use of the concept of *metoikia* to approach the position of free foreigners in Athenian society. In search of the voices of people who could be labelled metics, it quickly became clear that by far the majority of these voices come from a funerary context. Inspired by the numerous studies on the representation of subordinated groups on funerary monuments in the Roman Empire (such as Joshel (1992), Hope (1998) and (2000), and Mouritsen (2005)), I have compiled a corpus of 125 (fragments of) funerary monuments and around 500 funerary inscriptions from the fifth and fourth centuries BCE[1] that may, cautiously, be associated with metics, in order to investigate the ways in which these people represented themselves in the public context of Attica's cemeteries.

## Introduction

πάντων ἀνθρώπων νόμος ἐστὶ κοινὸς τὸ ἀποθανεῖν

'A law common to all mankind, is that one must die'
(beginning of the grave epigram for Theoites,
a Tegean (*IG* ii² 10435.1–2)

As one of the main status groups that made up Athenian society, metics and their metic status (*metoikia*) have always received much scholarly attention, both as a subject on its own and as an ideological challenge to the concept of Athenian citizenship. As such, many studies have been devoted both to the size and to the (economic) activities of Athens' metic population and to the historical origins, development, and ideology of Athenian *metoikia*.[2] A serious shortcoming in most

---

[1] All dates are BCE, unless stated otherwise.
[2] Clerc (1893) is the first comprehensive account on the topic of metics. Most important still is Whitehead (1977). Most recent on the size and activities of Athens's metic population is Akrigg (2019: 120–38). Most recent on the ideological force of the 'perpetual immigrant' in Athenian political thought is Kasimis (2018).

of these studies, including my own,³ is that they all, by necessity, largely adhere to an intrinsically Athenian perspective. For, with the single exception of a famous passage in Lysias' speech against one of the assailants of his family during the rule of the Thirty (12.20), metics never explicitly referred to their metic status nor to themselves as metics. Besides this short passage in Lysias, himself a metic, it is only in Athenian sources that we find explicit references to metics and *metoikia*.⁴ When modern scholars talk about these topics, they are therefore bound to echo the master narrative of the Athenian *demos* about the metics living in their midst, which included all visitors from abroad who stayed in Athens for longer than thirty days, all more or less permanent immigrants and freedmen, and all their descendants.⁵ This Athenian bias is perhaps most clearly present in the notion that metics constituted a clearly definable and coherent status group, a neatly defined 'metic community', while the great variation in economic, social, and ethnic backgrounds among the thousands of people who could be considered metics simply defied such an all-encompassing categorization.⁶ To use terms like 'metics' and 'metic status' might even be considered a form of othering, whereby subordinators, among many other things, consistently present the people they wish to control as a homogeneous collective, as an unruly mass that has been stripped of any individual characteristics.⁷

Since the late twentieth century, scholars have been challenging the social simplification that is inferred by terms such as 'metic status', 'metic community', or 'slave population', as they began to question the validity of the traditional division of Athenian society into three neatly demarcated status groups of citizens, metics, and slaves. In 1994, for instance, Robert Connor challenged the tidiness of official Athenian civic ideology by presenting several examples from classical Athens where boundaries between status groups were not so clearly marked and seemed rather fuzzy instead.⁸ In 2000, Edward Cohen placed a small explosive underneath the tripartite division of Athenian society, when he, perhaps a bit too vehemently, emphasized the openness and fluidity of status boundaries in ancient Athens.⁹ Kostas Vlassopoulos, moreover, introduced a valuable concept into the debate, by analysing the Athenian Agora as a 'free space of identity'—that is, as a location or

---

³ Wijma (2014).
⁴ See also Lucia Cecchet (Chapter 4, this volume), who works from a similar lack of self-identification of working-class citizens as thetes, and as such reveals the limits of the traditional (elitist) categories often employed to study the ancient world.
⁵ Sosin (2016) convincingly argues (against Kamen 2013: 43–54) that the legal category of 'metics' included *all* free non-Athenians who stayed at Athens for longer than thirty days, including freedmen and their descendants. After this period of thirty days had transpired, they all had to register as a metic and pay a specific annual metic tax.
⁶ Garland (2001: 61) estimates 28,000–30,000 metics, male and female, living in Attica around 431.
⁷ See, most famously, Said (2003 [1978]) on the specific othering of 'The East' by western colonial powers. On othering in ancient Athens/Greece, see Hall (1989) and Cartledge (2002).
⁸ Connor (1994).    ⁹ Cohen (2000).

institution where the formal status of citizen, metic, or even slave did not seem to play such a decisive role.[10]

The 2010s witnessed a further disqualification of the once so beloved tripartite division of Athenian society, which seems to have paved the way for a critical re-evaluation of the usefulness of the concept of 'metic status' to approach Athenian society. In 2011, for instance, Robin Osborne made a strong case for the near invisibility of the differences between citizen and metic status in Athenian art.[11] Deborah Kamen, following an old lead by Moses Finley, has furthermore argued for a spectrum of statuses, showing us the many nuances and subcategories that were applied to designate different groups of *polis* inhabitants, including several groups of (privileged) metics.[12] By the same token, Rebecca Futo Kennedy has studied the largely ignored topic of metic women and the particular social realities they were living in and the particular challenges they were facing, thereby further tearing down the coherence implied by the term 'metic status'.[13]

What should we do then with concepts like 'metics' and 'metic status'? As things stand now, *metoikia* appears to have mattered most of all to the Athenians and particularly in the context of their official civic ideology. Motivated by administrative, fiscal, policing, and ideological reasons, the Athenian *demos* was the sole architect in the ongoing articulation of a formal metic status in the fifth and fourth centuries. However, the fact that the people who were labelled 'metics' were not actively participating in this master narrative on their status in Athenian society does not mean that they were completely silent or silenced on this matter. It is at this point, I think, we could learn a great deal from scholars who have been working on the funerary monuments and epitaphs of subordinated groups in the Roman Empire.[14]

Introducing her outstanding study of occupational inscriptions at Rome, Sandra Joshel proposes 'new strategies of listening' to get away from the dominant narrative of Roman authors on freedmen and to get closer to how people who referred to their occupations in their epitaphs saw and presented *themselves*. She proposes to do so, first, by focusing on inscriptions as evidence and, secondly, by incorporating 'a rigorous sense of partiality' in studying what these inscriptions tell us about the social relations these men and women deemed significant enough to be mentioned on their tombstones.[15] In a similar way, I wish to argue that

---

[10] Vlassopoulos (2007). Cf. Sawtell (2018) on the cemetery as a 'free space of identity' in classical Athens.
[11] Osborne (2011: esp. 105-23).
[12] Kamen (2013, with 43-54 on metics and 55-61 on privileged metics).
[13] Kennedy (2014).
[14] Taylor (1961) and Zanker (1975) have been pivotal for the study of tombstones of freedmen. More recent on this topic: Mouritsen (2005). See also Hope (1998; 2000).
[15] Joshel (1992: 3-24). See also Sarah Murray, Chapter 3, this volume, in which she examines a methodology to uncover the lives and experiences of the urban workers in Greek history by focusing on archaeological and epigraphic sources, in order to counterbalance the negative attitudes and open hostility towards work and the working classes in elitist Athenian texts.

memorials and funerary inscriptions with references to the ethnic background of the deceased, by means of so-called *ethnika*, offer us a valid and valuable opportunity to listen in on the personal narratives of individual metics about their position and status in Athenian society as they *themselves* saw and presented it. By investigating how they represented their loved ones in the public context of Attica's cemeteries, I hope to arrive at a greater appreciation of the multifaceted and varied social identities of these free foreigners living in classical Athens, while also tracing some of the more broadly shared social relations and moral values they promoted on their grave monuments.[16]

In what follows, we will see that by far the majority of the memorials for metics conformed to Athenian norms and practices, partly because of the standardized repertoire available in the workshops of Athens, at which sculptors seem to have worked from pattern books and also offered stones in stock, and partly because of the choice of the buyers of these stones, as the deceased's family could always choose/pay to have various (personal) details added, to have completely unique designs created, or even to have complete memorials imported from outside Athens.[17] The conformity displayed in and on the memorials therefore seems to suggest that these metic families were actively presenting themselves as willing participants in this Athenian arena for the display of status. But in what particular ways did they conform to the norms of their subordinators? In what ways were they expressing divergent voices? What were some of the distinctive aspects of the social identities they wished to commemorate in public? In short, what do these mixed voices of conformity and nonconformity tell us about the position and experiences of metics in Athenian society from their own, subordinated, point of view? In addressing these questions with a 'rigorous sense of partiality', this chapter is aimed to counterbalance somewhat the Athenian bias in our understanding of the people living as metics in Athens as it sets out to listen to what the free foreign residents *themselves* had to say about their status.

---

[16] It is generally unclear who were responsible for the burial of dead metics or in what ways metics could obtain a burial plot for their loved ones. In a few epigrams, allusions are made to who had been responsible for the memorial, but the relationship of this person to the deceased usually remains obscured. For instance, the monument for the daughter of the *isoteles* Apollodoros, from Plataia, appears to be set up by (the Athenian?) Hippostrate (or her family?), of whom the unnamed deceased was a nurse (*IG* ii² 7873). In the epitaph for the copper-smelter Sosinous, from Gortyn, we find a rare explicit mention—namely, to his children, who had erected 'a monument to his sense of justice, his prudence, and his excellence' (*IG* ii² 8464.2–3). We should most likely envisage family members, perhaps in concord with an Athenian *prostates*, taking care of the burial of a metic.

[17] See Kurtz and Boardman (1971: 137) on the probable use of pattern books and clients having to choose from stock. However, discussing the funerary reliefs found in the Athenian Agora, Janet Burnett Grossman (2013: 3) notes 'the virtual infinite variety and creative use of a set of figure types and motifs by the ancient sculptors.' On p. 72 she furthermore discusses the East Mediterranean origins of some of the funerary stones and iconography from the late classical and early Hellenistic period. The many deviations from standard Athenian iconography discussed in this chapter are a further reminder of the freedom people could experience/buy in their choice of funerary markers.

## Redefining the Athenian Master Narrative on Funerary Monuments

A funerary monument—including its general layout, inscription, iconography, location, and positioning[18]—functions first and foremost as a testimony to a family's and/or community's grief and loss. At the same time, it offers the next of kin a unique opportunity to present to a larger public an idealized and socially acceptable image of the deceased, who can be presented both as an individual, with an emphasis on his or her defining and obviously highly esteemed attributes, and as belonging to various communities, the membership of which, so it is emphasized, had informed that person's social persona up to an important degree. In that sense, funerary monuments can be highly informative as to what moral values and social relationships were deemed worthy of public praise in a certain place at a certain time for a certain group of people.

If we turn to classical Athens, we can clearly see this general principle at work. For instance, from the mid-fifth century onwards, there was a radically new interest in depicting domestic scenes on funerary monuments, with many placing women centre stage. Robin Osborne has associated this iconographic trend with the new importance attached to the legitimate, Athenian birth of one's mother to qualify as a citizen after Pericles' Citizenship Law of 451/0.[19] Similarly, from the late fifth century onwards, epitaphs of Athenian male citizens increasingly included demotics, which could indicate a growing need among these men publicly to express their affiliation with an ancestral deme, thereby promoting their citizenship's legitimacy, as Elisabeth Meyer has argued.[20] Karen Stears likewise observed that, when occupations are portrayed on funerary monuments for women, these exclusively centre on a few domestic activities, most importantly child-raising and wool-working. Most epigrams for women, in addition, typically praise the *sophrosyne* of the deceased. These activities and values were all highly respected by Athenian ideology as the ideal concerns and proper demeanour of women.[21] Athenian families could thus publicly advertise a highly idealized and socially desirable image of the deceased by means of a funerary monument, emphasizing both the individual qualities and the social affiliations that represented, or even renegotiated, the deceased's social identity in Athenian society at large.

---

[18] Morris (1992) has been crucial in emphasizing the interconnectedness of these different aspects of funerary monuments. Material pertaining to ancient Athenian memorials is, unfortunately, published in strict isolation: inscriptions are accessible through the *Inscriptiones Graecae (IG)*, which can be accessed online through the PHI website <inscriptions.packhum.org (accessed January 2023), with new founds published annually in the *Supplementum Epigraphicum Graecum (SEG)* (cf. Oliver 2000a); epigrams are accessible through the Latin editions of Hansen's *Carmina Epigraphica Graeca (CEG)* (1983; 1989), with many significant ones translated and commented on in Clairmont (1970); most memorials can be found in Clairmont (1993) (*CAT*); archaeological information can be very difficult to come by, as these data are published dispersed over several journals.

[19] Osborne (1997; repr. 2010).   [20] Meyer (1993).   [21] Stears (1995).

Significantly, although the highly idealized representations on funerary monuments—and the artists producing these—were clearly influenced and bounded by the dominant Athenian narratives on, for instance, citizenship or gender, these essentially private memorials also offered the Athenians one of only few opportunities publicly to construe and to display, and thereby publicly to (re)define the markers and affiliations they themselves thought pivotal to one's social persona. So, while public memorials for the Athenian war dead listed those who had died in combat under the *phyle* they had belonged to, 'normal' Athenian dead were never associated with their *phyle*, but were named with their *demotika* instead. Also, while Athenian ideology praised the invisibility of Athenian women, many funerary monuments depicted virtuous, Athenian-born women, publicly advertising their most defining assets. In that sense, funerary monuments may be understood as bottom-up reinterpretations of what was narrated top-down about what to be and how to behave as part of the larger Athenian polis community.[22]

## Funerary Monuments and the Self-Representation of Metics

With these observations in mind, the funerary monuments of metics would appear to offer us a unique opportunity to investigate both the self-representation of these people in public and the ways in which they reinterpreted what was narrated top-down about what qualities to embody and how to behave as part of the Athenian community, both in general and as a metic. In order to do so, I have assembled 125 (fragments of) funerary monuments and around 500 funerary inscriptions from the fifth and fourth centuries that can to some degree be associated with metics.[23] Despite recent scholarly attention for several remarkable individual memorials[24] and for the tombstones of specific groups of metics, such as female and non-Greek metics,[25] this material is (almost[26]) never used as a whole

---

[22] Meyer (1993: 109–10).
[23] I have collected the monuments from Osborne and Byrne (1996) and Bergemann (1997: 138–48, with Anhang 2.1), with the corresponding entries in Clairmont (1993). The epigraphical material comes from Osborne and Byrne (1996) and the relevant entries in *IG* i³, *IG* ii², and *Agora* XVII. The *SEG* has been scanned for any new material. I have used Sawtell (2018) to check and complement my own corpus.
[24] Hagemajer Allen (2003) (on the funerary monument of Nikeratos and Polyxenos from Histria = Bergemann (1997: L2) = Garland (1982: L2)) and Stager (2005) (on the funerary monument of the Phoenician Antipatros = *CAT* 3.410).
[25] Bäbler (1998) (on the tombstones of barbarians); Garland (2001: 62–71) (on the tombstones of metics in Piraeus); Kennedy (2014: 55–8) (on the tombstones of immigrant women).
[26] Urdahl (1959) is greatly outdated and too descriptive in nature, in addition to being nearly impossible to locate in libraries worldwide. There is a group of scholars working from the Copenhagen database of Attic tombstones (http://www.dyabola.de/en/indexfrm.htm?page=http://www.dyabola.de/), who pay specific attention to the funerary monuments of metics. However, they do so to investigate to what degree metics emulated the civic values that are so zealously displayed on the tombs of Athenian citizens—e.g. Salta (1991: 161–239); Scholl (1996: 171–83); Bergemann (1997: 131–50); cf. Bäbler (1998: 199–203). Any publication deriving from Sawtell (2018) on the iconography of non-citizen commemoration in classical Attica will make a most welcome contribution to this topic.

to investigate the self-representation of these subordinated *polis* inhabitants. Admittedly, there are some troublesome issues, but none of them is alarming enough to refrain from using this material all together.

First of all, and most importantly, we are faced with the fact that the deceased are never explicitly referred to as metics in their epitaphs. The only cases where we can be certain that we are dealing with a metic is when the deceased is referred to as an *isoteles*, which is the official term for a metic who had received the honour of paying taxes on the same footing as Athenian citizens.[27] What we do have, are epitaphs with an *ethnikon*, which refers to the (non-Athenian) ethnic background of the deceased. Most pressingly, this makes it impossible to distinguish with absolute certainty between more or less permanent resident *metoikoi*, on the one hand, and merely visiting *xenoi*, on the other.[28] However, we cannot deny that a vast majority of these tombstones will have belonged to metics. As David Whitehead put it drily, 'is it really likely that many foreign visitors happened to die in Athens?'[29] As such, they do indeed seem to offer us an exceptional chance to arrive at a greater appreciation of the varied social realities of those living in Athens as metics, but only if we do not put too much emphasis on individual memorials, as a rare case might belong to a mere visitor.

Another reason why this material has received so little attention as a whole is because, at first sight, almost all metics seem to have completely conformed to Athenian funerary practices, probably partly because of what was in stock at the workshops and partly by choice. This, so it is often implied, would then only reveal something about the pressures on metics to conform to Athenian norms and, by extension, their willingness to yield to Athenian subordination.[30] However, conformity in itself indicates more than compliant acceptance of a state of subordination. Even more significant is the fact that, within the context of the highly formulaic Athenian funerary language, we do actually find metics articulating the social identities of their loved ones in their own, divergent ways. Actually, on all tombs with *ethnika* there is a remarkable degree of hybridity, consisting of both typically Athenian funerary forms and norms and several elements differentiating

---

[27] There are fourteen epitaphs (*IG* ii² 7863–5; 7868–9; 7873; 7875; 7877; 7879; 7881; *SEG* 18.112–13; 21.940; 57.228) and five funerary monuments (*CAT* 1.969; 2.360d; 2.461; 2.885; NM 3518) that belong to *isoteleis* and date to the classical period. On *isoteleia*, see Whitehead (1977: 11–13).

[28] Slaves, in addition, are largely absent from this group of epitaphs with *ethnika*. They will generally not have been in a position to obtain grave plots for themselves and will, by and large, have been dependent on their owners for this. Those slaves so valued were most often commemorated with a single name, typically inscribed on a simple slab and placed inside the *peribolos* of the family to whom the slave belonged; cf. Nielsen et al. (1989). To be on the safe side, I have excluded those epitaphs with *ethnika* in which the deceased is commemorated as *chrestos* (useful), which is commonly thought to have been exclusively used for slaves—even though it associated with a metic at least once: in *CEG* II 571 (= *IG* ii² 7873) the daughter of the *isoteles* Apollodoros is referred to as χρηστὴν τίτθην (5); cf. Kennedy (2014: 134–6).

[29] Whitehead (1977: 111, further 33–4). Also see Scholl (1996: 174–5); Vestergaard (2000: 83–4).

[30] E.g. Schmaltz (1979); Stears (1995: 128); Bergemann (1997: 147); Osborne (1997: 29, n. 53).

non-Athenians from Athenians. This betrays a definite sense of agency and self-awareness on the part of metics, who do not at all appear to have been slavish followers or powerless victims of overbearing Athenian customs and ideology. How, then, were metics represented on their tombstones?

## The Funerary Monuments with *ethnika*

### The Dead

As previously said, there are 125 (fragments of) funerary monuments and around 500 funerary inscriptions from the classical period that will by and large have belonged to metics. The main criteria for inclusion here are a secure Attic provenance, a date in the fifth or fourth century, and the occurrence of an *ethnikon*, which establishes the foreign background of the deceased beyond doubt.[31] Before we begin our investigation of how metics represented their loved ones on these memorials, it is important to acknowledge the fact that funerary material is never representative for any demographic or social group in any straightforward manner.[32] In our case this means that our corpus cannot be understood as a perfect, representative cross-section of all metics living and dying in Athens, as social, economic, cultural, and archaeological factors will have resulted in several distortions of the representativeness of our material.

First of all, an important consequence of our focus on memorials with *ethnika* in search for metic voices is that metics with a strong ethnic identity or awareness are probably over-represented, while metics with a reduced sense of an ethnic identity, like some manumitted slaves or people descending from former slaves, are possibly under-represented, as they might have been less inclined to commemorate a loved one with an *ethnikon*. This means that the material in our corpus might have a tendency to over-represent immigrants and their descendants, at the expense of manumitted slaves and their descendants. Metics who were not commemorated with an *ethnikon* were probably referred to only by name, but it is impossible to identify them in our material.[33]

---

[31] This means that a few reliefs without *ethnika* for which it has been (convincingly) argued that they belonged to metics are here excluded on principle, most importantly *CAT Suppl.* 5.470 (the so-called Charon relief, with Scholl (1993)) and *CAT* 1.630 (for Xanthippos, who is represented as a cobbler).
[32] Hopkins (1966–7; 1987) has been ground-breaking in exposing the problems of using Roman funerary material as demographic data. Cf. Damsgaard-Madsen (1988) on the problems of using Greek material for demographic purposes.
[33] These metics commemorated without an *ethnikon* can be included among a very large group of persons whose background is uncertain. To give an impression: in *IG* ii², which covers all extant Attic inscriptions from the archonship of Euklides in 403/2 until the Roman period, epitaphs with demotics run from number 5228 to 7861 and those with *ethnika* from 7882 to 10530, while those of uncertain origin (*tituli sepulcrales hominum originis incertae*) run from 10531 to

Next, we have to admit that chance survival and differing cultural habits among the free foreigners living in Athens must have resulted in several distorted representations in our corpus. A telling example is presented by the Kitians living in Attica. In 334, the Athenian *demos* granted a group of Kitian merchants the right to purchase land, on which to build a sanctuary for Aphrodite (*IG* ii² 337 = RO no. 91). This seems to imply that this particular group of Phoenicians was enough of a recognized presence in Athens to request and receive this strictly guarded right of *enktesis*. Yet, we have only seven epitaphs and no monumental tombstones from the classical period that definitely belong to Kitians.[34] A case of significant over-representation, on the other hand, seems to be exemplified by the very large number of Milesians among the funerary inscriptions from Attica, although historical circumstances can partly explain this anomaly.[35]

Finally, we should consider who were most likely to be commemorated with a grave monument, or, more correctly, with a non-perishable memorial that could stand a chance against time. Concerning the economic background of the Athenian dead buried in an archaeologically visible way there now seems to be a general consensus that most of the preserved memorials from Attica must, in fact, commemorate Athenians of ordinary means. The well-to-do, often equated with the Athenian leiturgical class, do not seem to constitute a disproportional presence, while the poorest Athenians will have to remain mostly invisible to us, as they were most likely to receive simple, perishable grave markers that will not have survived the passage of time.[36] The dead commemorated with an *ethnikon* appear to present a similar pattern. Rich metics were buried in ostentatious family grave precincts—ten so-called *periboloi* have been associated with metic families,[37] while metics of more modest means received more modest, painted or sculpted reliefs, so-called *Bildfeldstelen*, or simple slabs that were inscribed with only a name and an *ethnikon*. The poorest metics will, similar to the Athenian poor, have to remain mostly invisible to us. We may, therefore, conclude that with the memorials and epitaphs including an *ethnikon* we have the best chance to get closer to the self-presentations of rich metics and of metics of more modest means, with a probable under-representation of poor metics and (descendants of) former slaves.

---

13085. The latter mostly come from very simple slabs and usually give only a proper name. There is no consensus as to exactly what kind of people these are referring to. That said, many of these epitaphs carry typical slave names or refer to the deceased as χρηστός, an epithet most commonly used for (ex-)slaves. Others probably belonged to children or other subordinated members of the *oikos* buried in a family's *peribolos*, in which case a central *stele* would fully identify the key members of the *oikos*, on which see Nielsen et al. (1989); Meyer (1993: 99–101); Fraser (1995: 66–8); Stears (1995: 114–15). These persons of *originis incertae* undoubtedly included some metics, most certainly some former slaves, but it is impossible to tell them apart.

[34] *Ag.* xvii 521; *IG* ii² 9031+*SEG* 25.276; *IG* ii² 9032–6.   [35] Vestergaard (2000).
[36] Bergemann (1997: 131–6), generally reaffirming Nielsen et al. (1989).
[37] Bergemann (1997: 138–9, with n. 71 and Anhang 2.1), largely following Garland (1982).

## Organization

The majority of funerary memorials and inscriptions with *ethnika* were excavated in the cemeteries of Athens, Piraeus, and the area between the two, called the Elaion. In addition, there are several isolated cases from rural demes.[38] Within these areas, metics were not buried together as a group. That is to say, there are no indications what so ever for the existence of separate 'metic cemeteries' or specific areas within Athenian cemeteries that were specially marked off for metics. Although on some occasions the Athenians wished to approach the free foreigners living in their midst as a coherent group of metics, these same metics were apparently relatively free to choose their own burial locations.[39] As such, certain social ties and attachments could be emphasized by means of the choices the deceased's family made about where and with whom they wished their loved ones to be buried.

A common affiliation found among the burials of metics is, similar to that found among most Athenian citizens, the (extended) family unit, with husbands and wives, parents and children, and sometimes grandparents and grandchildren being buried together. For example, Kydrokles, son of Kaikylos, from Kos, was commemorated together with Stephanos, who is identified as Kydrokles' son (*IG* ii² 9143). Peithias, son of Leon, from Salamis, was commemorated together with his son Leon, but also with Plangon, who is identified as the wife of a certain Charios, with Thraitta, who was probably a slave in Peithias' *oikos*, and with another Peithias, who was probably the grandson of the first Peithias and the son of Leon (*IG* ii² 10208).

Another form of organization commonly found in the ways metics were buried is the interment of individual metics. In a discussion of metic tombstones from Piraeus, Robert Garland remarks that, of a total of 182 funerary inscriptions with *ethnika*, of which 110 date to the fourth century, only twenty commemorate two or more metics.[40] The entries of epitaphs with an *ethnikon* in the *IG* ii² and the *SEG* reveal a similar picture, with a large majority commemorating a single metic, such as Alexandros from Samos (*SEG* 22.188) or Timagora, the daughter of Demokritos, from Delphi (*IG* ii² 8478). From this we might conclude that most metics were also actually buried on their own. Significantly, compared to the number of tombstones commemorating Athenians on their own, there are, relatively speaking,

---

[38] Salta (1991: 171); Bäbler (1998: 53–7); Meyer (1993: 102, figs 4, 5). Cf. Clairmont, *Introductory vol.* (1993: 47–65), on the provenance of classical Attic tombstones in general. The distribution of epitaphs with an *ethnikon* shows a clear overlap with the important observation made by Whitehead (1986: 80–5), that of the 366 metics whose deme of residence were known to him, most lived either in (sub)urban Athens (223) or in Piraeus (69), while an entirely metic-less deme was probably a rarity. Meyer (1993: fig. 4) lists 262 'foreign' epitaphs for the fourth century in urban and suburban areas, against 28 scattered across rural Attica. Most funerary monuments and epitaphs of barbarians, i.e., non-Greek foreigners, derive from Piraeus: Bäbler (1998: 53–7).

[39] See also n. 16.   [40] Garland (2001: 64–6).

far more tombstones commemorating individual metics. Admittedly, the funerary reliefs for individual metics often show the deceased with his or her family. Timagora from Delphi, for instance, is most likely depicted with her parents, who bid her farewell (*CAT* 3.463) and on the relief on the grave monument for the Samian Alexandros, the deceased is leaning on a *loutrophoros*, while what are probably his parents approach him from the right (*CAT* 3.455). The inscribing of *patronymika* also subscribes to the notion that the deceased was commemorated as a member of an *oikos*. However, although emphatically commemorated as a beloved member of an *oikos*, the proportion of metic tombstones with a single name inscribed is striking enough to assume that many of these metics did not have the same extended kinship structures as Athenian citizens had, which should not surprise us very much.[41]

A further affiliation that should be considered is the grouped burial of people with the same ethnic background. The strongest evidence for this is found in the Kerameikos, where, along the South Path and at the feet of the South Hill, we find the so-called 'precinct of the Messenians'.[42] Inside this impressive *peribolos* of $c.145$ m$^2$, there are several elaborate funerary monuments, all dating to the middle of the fourth century and all belonging to the family of a certain Philoxenos from Messenia. It is what is underneath the surface that is of particular interest here: in addition to the burnt remains of those who are named on the monuments, there were found over fifty simple interments, also dating to the middle of the fourth century. A strong case has been made that these remains may well belong to fellow countrymen of the wealthy family whose *peribolos* it was, perhaps Messenian metics whose families were not in a position to acquire their own funerary plots and monuments. Ursula Knigge has even suggested that Philoxenos was a *proxenos*, who was (or felt?) responsible for the burial of Messenians who had died in Athens. That Philoxenos was a *proxenos* is perhaps also reflected in the location of his *peribolos* near the fifth-century honorary graves for a *proxenos* from Selymbria (*IG* i³ 1034), for two *proxenoi* from Kerkyra (*IG* ii² 5224), and for an envoy from Rhegion (*IG* ii² 5220).[43]

Another case of ethnic clustering is perhaps represented by two small *stelai* (*IG* ii² 8534, 8542) and a small, low pillar, a so-called *cippus* (*IG* ii² 8545), which were found in the vicinity of the Acharnian Gate. They commemorate Stephanos, Dexandros, son of Glauketos, and Praullis. The deceased are all from Epirus, but they are not further related in any observable way. Maria Salta has therefore suggested that the monuments derive from a communal grave district for people from

---

[41] Cf. Patterson (2000), on the isolated position metics held in court owing to their limited kin connections.
[42] Knigge (1988: 117–21, no. 21); Kovacsovics et al. (1990: 87–130); Bergemann (1997: A13) = Garland (1982: A13).
[43] Knigge (1988: 120). Cf. Kovacsovics et al. (1990: 96).

Epirus.[44] She has tried to build a similar case concerning a group of inscriptions from a grave district near the Sacred Road, which include a Boiotian *ethnikon* (*IG* ii² 10092 (Erylos of Plataia)), particular Theban names (*IG* i³ 1363a (Xenon) and *IG* i³ 1236bis (Timollo)) and names in Boiotian dialect or script (*IG* i³ 1363 a–g).[45] Salta argues that most metics from Boiotia probably lived in the western part of the city, near the main roads leading to Thebes. She suggests that those buried here were part of a closed, exclusively Boiotian group.[46] Based on the findspot of two epitaphs for Phoenicians that appear to be engraved by the same hand, Balbina Bäbler has similarly suggested 'ein spezieller Friedhof für die Phönizer' in the northern part of Piraeus, where, as she adds, several Phoenician cults and perhaps a Phoenician community were located.[47] Although none of these cases is entirely conclusive, that metics with the same ethnic background were buried together should remain a real possibility.[48] The scattered finds of tombstones with different *ethnika* all over Attica will, in turn, have to act as a reminder that there were never any strict and centralized rules that dictated that metics were to bury their fellow countrymen at specially designated burial plots.

Finally, we need to consider the location of the tombstones of metics in relation to other tombstones. However, only in the case of a few thoroughly excavated *periboloi* in the Kerameikos we can say anything about the positioning of particular graves and monuments. We have already come across the possibly meaningful position of the *peribolos* of Philoxenos from Messenia in the vicinity of the honorary graves for several *proxenoi* and envoys at the feet of the South Hill. Perhaps it is no coincidence that several more epitaphs were found in this same area that belonged to non-Athenians, of which six refer by means of their *ethnika* to several of Athens's allies in the Delian League, thereby perhaps intentionally expressing an association with the League by the location of their tombs.[49]

Another telling example of the meaningful positioning of a grave monument is provided by the *peribolos* of the brothers Agathon and Sosikrates from Herakleia, which is located on the Street of the Tombs at the Kerameikos and dated between 346/5 and 338.[50] With its impressive layout and monuments, which will be discussed later, it was constructed in-between what are perhaps the most familiar monuments of the excavated Kerameikos in modern times: Dexileos' famous grave *stele* that pictures the deceased on horseback and the equally famous statue of a charging bull that was placed on a large pillar to mark the *peribolos* of Dionysios of Kollytos (Figure 8.1).

---

[44] Salta (1991: 207, n. 2120).
[45] Cf. Ginestí Rosell (2012) on non-Athenian dialects and scripts on funerary monuments for non-Athenians, which was unfortunately unavailable to me.
[46] Salta (1991: 174–6). On Boiotian exiles in Athens, see also Gartland (2016).
[47] Bäbler (1998: 146), referring to her no. 61 (*IG* ii² 10271) and no. 67 (*CAT* 1.333).
[48] Shea (2018) argues for the predominance of ethnic clustering in the major Athenian cemeteries.
[49] Salta (1991: 172–3).
[50] On this *peribolos*, see Knigge (1988: no. 22); Bergemann (1997: A2) = Garland (1982: A2).

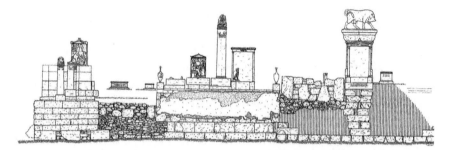

Figure 8.1 Reconstruction of the excavated remains of the *periboloi* of Dexileos (left), Agathon and Sosikrates (middle), and Dionysios (right) along The Street of the Tombs in the Kerameikos. Drawing by A. Brueckner and A. Struck 1909.

There is no question as to the affiliations this family wished to promote by the location of their graves: they were non-Athenians who hailed from Herakleia, as was clearly stated on their monuments (*IG* ii$^2$ 8550, 8551), who by the sheer ostentatiousness of their *peribolos* and its positioning in between two of the most remarkable memorials of the Kerameikos openly promoted their wealth *and* their participation in Athens's elite contest of conspicuous consumption, in which they wished to be considered the equals of Dexileos and Dionysios of Kollytos.

## Monumental Form

When it came to the choice of a particular type of monument, nearly all non-Athenians adopted local, Athenian funerary forms to commemorate their dead. Among the funerary monuments with *ethnika* there are several tall *Bildfeldstelen* and several so-called *naiskoi*, which took the form of a small temple, complete with columns and a pediment, inside which the deceased was often shown in a domestic setting—Johannes Bergemann catalogues fifty *Bildfeldstelen* and thirty *naiskoi* as 'für Metöken gesichert'.[51] These types are very familiar from the excavations in the Kerameikos and other Attic cemeteries, but are also widely attested outside Attica.[52] As such, they do not tell us much about any trend towards conformity among the metics living in Athens. Perhaps more remarkable, in that sense, is the adoption of the stone *loutrophoros* and the stone *lekythos* to mark the graves of non-Athenians.[53] These types of funerary monuments are attested only in Athens, where they were usually marking the grave of a young person. Several include an *ethnikon*: there are five *loutrophoroi* and thirteen *lekythoi* attested for non-Athenians, like the *loutrophoros* for Parthenios from Messenia (*CAT* 2.421b),

---

[51] Bergemann (1997: 229).   [52] Kurtz and Boardman (1971: 218–35).
[53] For the most important studies and collections of these funerary vase types, see Schmaltz (1970) and Kokula von Leitner (1984).

which was placed inside the district of the Messenians, or the pair of *lekythoi* for Hippias, son of Timotheos, from Lokris, which was decorated with an image of a seated, elderly bearded man (Timotheos?), shaking the hand of a younger unbearded man (Hippias?) (*CAT* 2.369 + 2.369d).[54] Non-Greek foreigners also used these funerary vases: a pair of *lekythoi* for Ada and Mikon from Sigeion (*IG* ii² 10575a; Peek no. 240), dating to 380–370, has been found near Laureion (*CAT* 2.349).

Of course, the Athenian workshops at which these grave monuments were bought were accustomed to these funerary forms and must have had many of these typically Athenian memorials in stock. However, throughout this chapter it will become clear that variations and deviations, also concerning the choice of a particular funerary monument, were always an option, especially for those who could afford it. The striking similarity between the monuments and their placement inside the *periboloi* of what must have been very wealthy metics and the monuments and their placement inside the *periboloi* of what must have been very wealthy Athenians therefore probably reflects a conscious choice. So, it was not only in the positioning of the *peribolos* of Agathokles and Sosikrates from Herakleia, in-between the *periboloi* of Dexileos and Dionysios of Kollytos, that we can see their claim to be affiliated with Athens's elite. They also completely adhered to Athenian practices in the highly conventional funerary forms they used and in the placement of these monuments inside their *peribolos* (Figure 8.2), which itself was already a typically Athenian way to bury the wealthy. As at most Athenian *periboloi*, we find at the centre of their grave district an impressive, tall *anthemion stele* that is inscribed with the full names of the main members of the family, who, in this case, are Agathon, son of Agathokles, from Herakleia, and Sosikrates, son of Agathokles, from Herakleia (*IG* ii² 8551). The *peribolos* of Agathon and Sosikrates further contained two marble *lekythoi* that were placed at the corners of the precinct's facade, which is remarkably similar to the placement of two *lekythoi* at the extremely costly *peribolos* of the Athenian Hierokles in Rhamnous.[55] In addition, there is a base for a small *naiskos* or statue (of a child?), another *naiskos* base, a large painted *naiskos* for Agathon of which only Agathon's full name (*IG* ii² 8550) and part of a man's legs are preserved, and the impressive *naiskos* for Korallion (*CAT* 4.415 (see Figure 8.4)), the wife of Agathon. None of these monuments and architectural remains refers in appearance to the non-Athenian background of Sosikrates

---

[54] Bergemann (1997: 144, nos 120–1), to which can be added *CAT* 280 (the body of a *lekythos* for Kritias and his daughter Archo, from Hephaistia) and *CAT* 1.303 (a *stele* with a *loutrophoros* in relief, for Nikomachos from Lemnos). The recent find of a *stele* for Xenokles from Samos, decorated with a relief of a *loutrophoros*, is reported in *SEG* 59.305.

[55] Bergemann (1997: 138; N5; Taf. 1.1) = Garland (1982: N5). One of the *lekythoi* that had been part of the *peribolos* of Agathon and Sosikrates has been found and possibly depicts the two brothers in a farewell scene (*CAT* 2.893).

**Figure 8.2** Reconstruction of the *peribolos* of Sosikrates and Agathon from Herakleia. Drawing by A. Brueckner and A. Struck 1909, https://commons.wikimedia.org/wiki/File:Kerameikos_Grabbezirk_des_Agathon_und_Sosikrates_Frontansicht_%28Der_Friedhof_am_Eridanos,_Abb._43%29.jpg.

and Agathokles; only the *ethnika* on the epitaphs betray their metic status. Equally remarkable is the fact that, in contrast to their neighbours, the family of Agathon and Sosikrates apparently did not wish to attract too much attention with ostentatious monuments that were openly challenging more conventional forms of commemoration, like Dionysios' unique charging bull or Dexileos' equally unique relief that showed him on horseback. Instead these Herakleians constructed a highly conventional, typically Athenian, and very elite narrative, which clearly expressed their wish to be counted among the elite of Athens, but not in an over-conspicuous way.

Indeed, most of the attested *periboloi* for rich metics appear consciously to mimic the most conventional monumental forms and layout of their rich Athenian counterparts. There is, however, one significant exception to this general rule of eager conventionalism and conformity. It highlights the degree of freedom rich metics could experience, and buy, and the active choice they had in the design of their final resting places and, therefore, in the social identities they wished to articulate. From Kallithea, located between Piraeus and Athens, comes a rather hybrid *peribolos*, dated to the second half of the fourth century, which belongs to a family from Histria, on the Black Sea coast (Figure 8.3).[56] The monument consists of a retaining wall that is topped by three marble steps. Two steps are decorated with sculpted friezes, one consisting of an Amazonomachy and one consisting of animal pairs. The third step contains an inscription naming the two deceased: Nikeratos, son of Polyidos, from Histria, and Polyxenos, son of Nikeratos (*SEG* 24.258). The steps lead up to a large *naiskos* that has the appearance of a small Greek temple. Inside the *naiskos*, framed by two Ionic columns,

**Figure 8.3** The grave monument for Nikeratos and his son Polyxenos, excavated at Kallithea. Piraeus Museum—photo by George E. Koronaios, https://commons.wikimedia.org/w/index.php?curid=70942232.

[56] Bergemann (1997: L2) = Garland (1982: L2).

there are three freestanding statues. We see a tall draped male figure, who is identified as Nikeratos, a smaller nude youth, probably Polyxenos, and a scarcely draped smaller figure, who is probably to be identified as a slave.

The monuments, the inscription, the focus on height, the monumentality, and the marked frontality of the tomb all communicate that we are dealing with a typically Athenian *peribolos*. However, both the layout of the wall, seemingly constructed to form a unified whole with the steps leading to a large single *naiskos*, and the peculiar decoration of these steps are unequalled among Attic tombs. By exhibiting these clearly non-Athenian aspects to this unprecedented degree, even evoking typically eastern mausoleums like the famous one from Halicarnassus, 'the tomb makes a noticeable statement about the non-Athenian identity of its owners', as Wendy Closterman convincingly argues.[57] Nikeratos and his son Polyxenos are, in sum, commemorated in an architectural setting that overtly pays tribute to their non-Athenian background, while the monument as a whole still lays claim to a place among Athens's finest.

## Iconography

As a key witness 'für die Assimilationsbereitschaft zumindest eines Teils der Metöken', Bergemann presents the *naiskos* of Korallion (Figure 8.4). Korallion was the wife of Agathokles from Herakleia, whom we have already met. Her *naiskos* was centrally placed in Agathokles' and his brother Sosikrates' *peribolos* (see Figure 8.2). Both the details of the *naiskos* and the composition as a whole are very familiar among the funerary monuments of classical Athens. Browsing through Clairmont's entries for 'tombstones with four to seven adults with child/children, dated to 350–300' (= *CAT* 4.400–4.499), it is not very difficult to find several *naiskoi* for Athenian citizens that look astonishingly similar to Korallion's.[58]

It indeed seems that also concerning the iconography on their funerary monuments, wealthy metics wished to associate themselves first and foremost with their equally wealthy Athenian peers through a conscious mimicry of their Athenian funerary language, and not with their more ordinary fellow countrymen, or with metics in general. In that sense it is perhaps more notable that the iconography on most of the more modest memorials with *ethnika*, which must have belonged to metics of more modest means, also looks very similar to that on their Athenian counterparts—we come across several seated non-Athenian women who have drawn their himations over the back of their heads,

---

[57] Closterman (2006: 63, with bibliographical references). Hagemajer Allen (2003) has convincingly demonstrated that the uniqueness of the Kallithea monument has generally been overstated. It was not simply an exceptional, one-time imitation of non-Greek tombs, but rather a convergence of various traditions that were already present in Athens.

[58] Cf. Bergemann (1997: 146, with n. 157).

Figure 8.4 The *naiskos* of Korallion. Athens, Kerameikos Museum P 688—photo by Tilemahos Efthimiadis, https://commons.wikimedia.org/wiki/File:Kerameikos,_Ancient_Graveyard,_Athens,_Greece_(4454536779).jpg.

non-Athenian loved ones shaking their hands in a gesture of consolation (the famous *dexiosis*), non-Athenian children depicted with birds or toys, servant maids holding jewellery boxes for their non-Athenian matrons, and bearded elderly non-Athenian men supporting themselves with sticks.

Most scholars have explained this conformity by reference to the overpowering dominance of Athenian democratic ideology in the cemeteries of Attica, with the notion of 'equality' not only dictating a highly formalized, uniform, and anonymous iconography but also resulting in a high degree of homogeneity in size, form, and even general quality among the Athenian funerary monuments. Karen Stears, for instance, suggested that 'these ideologies appear to have been so pervasive in social discourse that even those who stood no chance of entry into this fictional equality, metics (resident aliens), employed the same iconography'.[59] In the past, Robin Osborne similarly explained the general trend of conformity among the memorials of metics by referring to the 'pressures on the metic community to conform to local practice', in addition to the sculptural practices in the workshops

---

[59] Stears (1995: 128), referring to Schmaltz (1979), who was one of the first to argue this.

producing these monuments on citizens' demands.[60] In that way, we would have to envision highly passive metics, who were unable and/or unwilling to defend themselves against the democratic ideology of their Athenian hosts.

However, if we adhere to 'a rigorous sense of partiality', a slightly, though essentially, different image emerges. Recently, Rebecca Futo Kennedy has emphasized the specific gender roles praised in Athenian funerary iconography. She argues that funerary monuments for metic women created an opportunity for their families to show that these non-Athenian women had conformed to the gender expectations of their Athenian hosts—for instance, by marrying the 'right' (i.e. metic) partner, bearing only his (i.e. metic) children, and adhering to a general demeanour of *sophrosyne*.[61] In that sense, the conformity displayed on the funerary monuments of these female metics may be understood as an active statement of integration and acculturation. This is often emphasized in the case of several subordinated groups in the Roman Empire, such as gladiators or auxiliaries, who promoted typical Roman iconography on their funerary monuments, so it is argued, to show their familiarity with and integration into Roman culture.[62] The funerary monuments that show metic youths with objects that refer to the world of the gymnasium, such as the relief for Stephanos, son of Eucharides, from Phokis, who is depicted as a naked youth, scraping himself with a strigil (*CAT* 1.944), could be interpreted in a similar manner—that is, not as meaningless mimicry dictated by ideology and the practices in the workshops, but as showing young metic men adhering to Athenian gender expectations and to generally accepted rules for the expression of masculinity.[63]

The funerary monuments with *ethnika* that depict a non-Athenian deceased as a soldier or a warrior, like the relief for Menes, son of Kallias, from Argos, who is depicted on horseback, carrying a lance (*CAT* 1.429), or the memorial for Lisas from Tegea, which shows him charging to the left, holding a shield in his left arm (*CAT* 1.194), may be re-evaluated in the same light.[64] One could say these images are only empty echoes of Athenian civic ideology, which so highly praised the military defence of the *polis* as a pivotal aspect of Athenian citizenship. However, from the metic's point of view, they could also be read as a display of loyalty to his Athenian hosts. Metics were expected to contribute to the well-being of the Athenian *polis* in specific ways, and one of the things male metics were expected to do was to serve in the Athenian army.[65] The Athenians, though, seem to have approached the loyalty of metics with great suspicion and fear, for what actually

---

[60] Osborne (1997: 29, n. 53). Osborne (2011: 105–23, esp. 108, n.127) is far more elaborate and nuanced on this point.
[61] Kennedy (2014: 55–8).   [62] Hope (1998; 2000: 176, 179–80).
[63] See also *CAT* 1.221; 1.436; 1.713; 1.855; 2.461; 3.455. *CAT* 2.868 shows the deceased as a hunter, which, although more aristocratic in flavour, could be interpreted similarly.
[64] See also *CAT* 1.461; 2.392e; 2.746; 3.355b; 2.878a; Scholl (1996: no. 69).
[65] Whitehead (1977: 82–6).

tied these immigrants to their *polis* and what exactly could prevent them from leaving?[66] Wishing to express his loyalty to Athens as a metic, Lysias, among other things, explicitly refers to his dutiful payment of special war taxes (so-called *eisphora*) and the ransoming of many Athenian prisoners of war (12.20). The military scenes on memorials for metics may perhaps be interpreted similarly—that is, as an expression of military commitment and loyalty to the Athenian *polis*.

That metics were not simply passive duplicators is also borne out by the unmistakable foreign influences on classical Athenian funerary iconography in general. It is commonly believed that, when most of the great new public structures on the Akropolis were completed around 440–430, many of the foreign sculptors who had worked on these buildings probably found a living in Athens's sculptural workshops, where they were to work on monuments of a more private nature, such as dedications and grave monuments.[67] It was in these workshops that these metics, with their own local (i.e. Boiotian, Thessalian, Cycladic, and so on) commemorative traditions in mind, became largely responsible for the famous Athenian funerary iconography of the classical period, including the predominance of scenes depicting women in a domestic setting.[68] Stears has even suggested that these foreigners were possibly behind the reappearance of grave monuments in the decades between 470 and 450 to begin with, as their 'ignorance of, possibly exemption from, even their disdain for' Athenian funerary legislation may have expedited the end to the restraint shown in the Athenian cemeteries in the first half of the fifth century.[69] In that sense, these particular metics are to be understood as early adopters or even important innovators in the context of Athenian funerary iconography.

It is, however, in the deviations from the highly standardized Athenian funerary iconography that a certain agency on the part of metics becomes most clear. Let us first talk numbers: of the 125 memorials associated with metics, a large majority of 71 can be labelled 'conformist', while another 33 are too fragmentary to say anything about their composition with certainty.[70] The remaining 21 either have atypical features or are atypical as a whole. Some peculiar features should

---

[66] Cf. Bakewell (1999).
[67] Kurtz and Boardman (1971: 122); Robertson and Frantz (1975: 365); Stears (2000: 37–42).
[68] Stears (2000: 49–50). Cf. Hagemajer Allen (2003: 213), who extensively discusses the Kallithea monument of Nikeratos (see Figure 8.3) as 'an example of a convergence of traditions that would not have been possible without prior interaction and exchange'—that is, between the Greek world and 'the lands north, east, and south of the Aegean'.
[69] Stears (2000: 31–50). Cf. Garland (2001: 70–1). That metics did not feel compelled to abide by Athenian funerary legislation is perhaps also reflected in the fact that several of their memorials cannot be strictly dated to before 317, when Demetrios of Phaleron introduced his sumptuary laws banning all lavish display in Athenian cemeteries; cf. Bäbler (1998: 205–6); Grossman (2013: 14–16, 72).
[70] Too fragmentary: *CAT* 111; 153; 233; 0.874a; 0.878; 1.262; 1.303; 1.350; 1.399; 1.461; 1.758; 2.313b; 2.316; 2.321; 2.356a; 2.360d; 2.366e; 2.392; 2.399b; 2.424b; 2.458; 3.394a; PE 44–8; NM 2760; Ag. xvii. 408, 649; Schmaltz (1970: B30); Scholl (1996: no. 181); Kaltsas (2002: no. 401).

not be made too much of, like the intertwined fingers of Ktesileos from Erythrai (*CAT* 2.206), the hand of Erato from Plataia fully embracing the hand of her father, instead of merely shaking it (*CAT* 3.427a), the addition of a fourth figure with only part of the body showing on the relief of Symmachia and Theophile from Mende (*CAT* 4.950), or the unique combination of a box, a siren, and a sphinx on the pediment of the relief for Silenis from Boiotia (*CAT* 1.862). These details may easily be understood as experimentations on the sculptor's part.

Other atypical features could be considered the result of a misunderstanding of Athenian funerary language that might be associated with the deceased's or sculptor's non-Athenian background. For instance, on the *stele* for an unknown man from Olynthos (*CAT* 1.436), the deceased is depicted as an athlete: he holds an *aryballos*, and his naked upper body has an overtly robust appearance. However, he also wears a mantle, drawn over his left shoulder and draped around his waist, which makes him seriously overdressed for an athlete. Clairmont has suggested this has to do with the non-Athenian origin of the deceased.[71] Then there are two reliefs belonging to non-Athenians that depict a youth leaning against a *loutrophoros* (*CAT* 1.456, 3.455). Although leaning youths are a common sight on Athenian funerary monuments, they never do so against a *loutrophoros*. That the deceased persons in these reliefs do so is perhaps, again, to be associated with their non-Athenian background.[72]

Then there are monuments with a clear indication of the non-Athenian background of the people buried underneath them, with an individuality and expressiveness not found on tombs for Athenians. For instance, on the relief for Leon from Sinope (*CAT* 1), the deceased is suitably commemorated with the image of a lion. Such a direct allusion to the deceased's name is not found on memorials for Athenians. Next, there is the relief for Tokkes, son of Phyrron, from Aphytis, who is depicted as a bearded man, seated on a rock, holding an object in his hand, which could be a cup or a flask (*CAT* 1.388). Against the rock stands a wine amphora, which may be an unusual reference to Tokkes' place of origin, as this locality in Macedonia was famous for its vine culture.[73] However, it could equally well be a visual reference to the occupation of the deceased (in viticulture?), something we find on at least three and possibly seven other reliefs associated with non-Athenians.[74] On the *naiskos* for Sosinous from Gortyn, who is referred

---

[71] Clairmont (1993) on *CAT* 1.436. Another curious mixture of Athenian funerary iconography is the depiction of a youth who holds a stick in front of his chest (*CAT* 1.274). The relief was later inscribed to belong to [Askl]epiades, son of Lykophron, from Miletos. For the reuse of memorials in general, see Kurtz and Boardman (1971: 136–7).

[72] Clairmont (1993) on *CAT* 3.455.

[73] See also the sketch of a fragmentary *stele* for Abd-eshun ben Schalom, which is said to have once contained a painted image of a palm, which possibly referred to the Phoenician background of the deceased (*CAT* 1.333).

[74] The occupation of Philostrate (who possibly came from Melitaia or Miletos; cf. Kennedy 2014: 141–2) as a midwife and doctor (*IG* ii² 6873—μαῖα καὶ ἰατρὸς) of Antiphile is possibly alluded to in the depiction of Antiphile and her children, who are gathered around a seated Philostrate (*CAT* 2.890).

to as a copper-smelter in his epitaph (*IG* ii² 8486.1—χαλκόπτης), the deceased is depicted as seated, holding large circular, slightly hollow objects, while horizontal mouldings on the floor are probably best interpreted as forge bellows (*CAT* 1.202 (Figure 8.5)). Then there is the *stele* of Potamon, son of Olympichos, from Thebes, on which Potamon and his father Olympichos are both depicted as holding double flutes (*CAT* 2.235). In the accompanying epigram they are both praised for their flute playing (*IG* ii² 8883 = *CEG* II 509). A final example of an occupational allusion is found on the *stele* for Spokes (Seukes in *CAT* 1.380), on which the deceased is shown as holding a narrow, rectangular object. Clairmont has identified the object as a knife case, which perhaps refers to Spokes's occupation as a butcher.

**Figure 8.5** Funerary relief for Sosinous from Gortyn, depicted as a copper-smelter. Louvre Museum—photo by Tangopaso, https://commons.wikimedia.org/wiki/File:St%C3%A8le_fun%C3%A9raire_de_Sosinos_%28Louvre,_Ma_769%29.jpg.

On the *stele* for Antipatros from Sidon (*CAT* 3.410) references are possibly made to maritime trade by means of a boat's prow. Scholl (1993) believes the enigmatic scene on the so-called Charon relief (*CAT* 5.470) depicts metics who had been engaged in trade in the area of the Black Sea, their place of origin. A clear case in which we find a visual reference to an occupation is the relief for Xanthippos, on which the deceased is depicted as a cobbler, holding a boot tree (*CAT* 1.630). Xanthippos is commonly regarded as a metic, but, as an *ethnikon* is missing, he is excluded here.

Significantly, all these depictions show the deceased in highly conventional, Athenian schemata. It is only by means of the addition of one or two objects that a reference is made to the deceased's occupation. Still it suggests a deliberate choice, and thus the freedom to make such a choice, to include a visual reference to an occupation as an important aspect of the deceased's social persona and as an important feature of his life in Athens.[75]

An interesting comparison may be drawn with the occupational allusions so often found on Roman funerary monuments. Similar to the Athenians, Roman citizens appear to have generally avoided any allusion to any occupation on their memorials, with the exception of the honorary offices of the *cursus honorum*, which were always proudly presented in the epitaphs of the elite. However, funerary monuments for freedmen—to be easily identified as such because the deceased is explicitly referred to as 'the freedman/freedwoman of X'—commonly refer both in iconography and in inscriptions to the occupation the deceased held after they had been manumitted. In his work on *Invisible Romans*, Robert Knapp even suggests that 'perhaps half of all inscriptions of freedmen mention a craft or profession'.[76] These occupational allusions are most commonly interpreted as showcasing social mobility, as displaying the social and economic successes these freedmen had experienced after they had been manumitted. Significantly, these references to occupations, together with references to (gaining) freedom and (having started a) family, were marking out exactly those feats that set freedmen apart from slaves, thus clearly and carefully distinguishing ex-slaves from slaves.[77]

By contrast, we never come across such explicit references to the status of former slave, whether or not explicitly distinguished from the status of slave, among Athenian funerary monuments. In the context of Athenian cemeteries, freedmen seem to have been commonly and invisibly subsumed under the general category of non-Athenians, who were commemorated either with an *ethnikon* or with only a name. Still, the extraordinary visual (and epigraphic, as we will see) references to occupations on several memorials for metics could probably be interpreted similarly to those on the memorials for Roman freedmen, though not in the sense of emphasizing social mobility, away from the status of slave towards a higher status, but as showcasing the social and economic success of these non-Athenians in general.

Finally, there are several reliefs on tombstones containing an *ethnikon* with scenes that are altogether out of the ordinary. On the *stele* for Plangon, daughter of Tolmides, from Plataia, for instance, we see the deceased reclining on a couch in the process of giving birth. Plangon's father, Tolmides, stands by in dismay, as her mother and a female servant are trying to help her in vain (*CAT* 4.470 (Figure 8.6)). Memorials for Athenians also sometimes referred to death in childbirth,

---

[75] Cf. Bergemann (1997: 148); Bäbler (1998: 203–4).   [76] Knapp (2013: 190).
[77] Knapp (2013: 190–2). Cf. Joshel (1992) and Mouritsen (2005).

**Figure 8.6** Funerary relief for Plangon, daughter of Tolmides, from Plataia. National Archaeological Museum, Athens 749.

but mainly by means of a swaddled baby.[78] Plangon's family clearly felt a need to express the reason for their sorrows in a far more explicit, direct, and thereby individualistic manner than was commonly accepted. While Plangon is shown struggling for her life in her final hours, Athenian deceased are generally depicted in a non-dynamic way and as they were in life.

The same holds true for the enigmatic *stele* for Antipatros from Sidon, on which we see a lion standing on his hind legs attacking a naked (dead?) man, who is stretched out on a *kline*, while another man, with the prow of a boat behind him, is bending over him (*CAT* 3.410). Although the exact meaning of this relief will probably always remain an enigma, what is clear is that it shows an exceptional (and perhaps explicit) rendering of the deceased's way of passing, also alluded to in the accompanying epigram (*IG* ii² 8388 = *CEG* II 596).[79]

Of a completely different unique nature are the funerary reliefs with banquet scenes, so-called *Totenmahl* reliefs. These typically show a person (or persons)

---

[78] Bergemann (1997: 64, n. 318). Bergemann further notes that these scenes relating to an Athenian's death in childbirth are the only Athenian reliefs that clearly allude to a cause of death, though not explicitly showing it.

[79] On the various interpretations of this relief, see Stager (2005); Osborne (2011: 124–8).

reclining, who is commonly identified as the deceased, while another person, often female, is seated at their feet, with a table with food in front of them. Out of a total of nineteen known *Totenmahl* reliefs, ten preserve an epitaph. Of these, four can be associated with non-Athenians: three contain an *ethnikon*, while a fourth belonged to the *isoteles* Sparton.[80] Their iconography seems to be borrowed from Athenian votives with similar scenes that were commonly dedicated in the context of hero cults, showing the hero reclining at a heroic *symposion*. As such, the *Totenmahl* reliefs are often understood as an odd adaptation by ignorant non-Athenians, who would feel less uncomfortable showing the deceased in a heroic or sympotic and therefore elite context.[81] However, there are at least two certain cases of Athenians being commemorated by a *Totenmahl* relief (NM 990 and Piraeus 261). Wendy Closterman has furthermore made a convincing case against a heroic or sympotic reading of these scenes, in favour of reading them as domestic family gatherings, which would generally fit the corpus of Athenian funerary monuments much better.[82] Still, whatever their interpretation, these *Totenmahl* scenes remain puzzling deviations from the standard Athenian funerary iconography.

## Inscriptions

The final section of this chapter is concerned with the inscriptions on memorials with *ethnika*. There are around 500 attested in total, ranging from simple name inscriptions to elaborate elegiac epigrams. Perhaps the most remarkable aspect of these epitaphs is the fact that they never refer explicitly to the deceased as a metic (or a *xenos*, or a slave, or a freedman for that matter).[83] The only exception is a late sixth-century epigram in which the Naxian Anaxilas is honoured by the Athenians as a μετάοικον (SEG 22.79), a label that was never picked up by the free foreigners living in Athens to present themselves to a wider audience.[84] Nor did metics refer to themselves by mentioning their deme of residence in the form of 'living in deme X' (ἐν X οἰκῶν/οἰκοῦσα), a formula that was occasionally used to designate metics in official *polis* documents from the late fifth century onwards.[85] The only instances where it is made explicit that a particular tombstone actually

---

[80] NM 3785; Pir.Mus. 16 (= Scholl 1996: nos 200, 267); NM 1025; NM 3518 (= Closterman 2014: figs 1.4, 1.2).

[81] For this reason Clairmont (1993) has excluded these scenes from his catalogue.

[82] Closterman (2014). She presents an excellent bibliographic overview on this topic.

[83] Metics are referred to as such on tombstones at other *poleis*—e.g. at Rhodes, for which see Fraser (1995: 71–3).

[84] Cf. Baba (1984).

[85] Cf. Whitehead (1977: 31–2). A possible exception to this is perhaps found in the epitaph for Nikomachos from Lemnos, who is associated with Περαιεύς (IG ii² 7180), where he had presumably been living as a metic.

belongs to a metic are when the deceased is referred to as an *isoteles*, of which fourteen cases are attested.[86] As such, the epitaphs do not generally show any concern with the ideological tripartite division of Athenian society into citizens, metics, and slaves. Instead there was, in addition to a large group of Athenian citizens who referred to their ancestral deme by way of a *demotikon*, a large group of people who referred to their foreign background by way of an *ethnikon* and an even larger group of people who were commemorated with only a single name. Significantly, these labels, or, more accurately, lack thereof, represent the perspective of the deceased and their non-Athenian families rather than the top-down perspective of Athenian ideology.

Most commonly an *ethnikon* was engraved to designate the ethnic background of the non-Athenian deceased. The earliest epitaphs attested in Attica, dating to the late sixth and early fifth century already contain *ethnika*.[87] That the *ethnikon* was considered an important element of the social identities constructed on these monuments is also evident from the fact that its engraving was often larger than that of the proper name and, if present, of the *patronymikon* of the deceased. This is similar to the *demotikon*, which was also frequently in a larger engraving than the other elements of an Athenian's epitaph.[88] It is generally assumed that by means of these *ethnika* metics were referring to the highest formal status they possessed—that is, of being a citizen in the *polis* from which they originated. In this way, so it is argued, they were purposely passing over their more inferior status of being a metic in Athens.[89] However, this tight connection of *ethnika* with citizenship elsewhere does not quite correspond with current ideas of what Greek citizenship entailed in general. Many scholars now agree that ancient citizenship was not a strictly juridical or movable commodity that one could collect at the age of 18 and take with you to another *polis*. Citizenship, or 'being a citizen', was rather conceptualized as (the community's expectation of) one's active participation in the public affairs of one's *polis* of origin.[90] Nor does this connection between *ethnika* and citizenship agree with the fact that many foreign women are referred to with their own, feminine *ethnika*, while *demotika*, as an unambiguous indication of one's citizenship, are (almost[91]) completely lacking in their feminine forms for Athenian women. It therefore seems wise to understand the *ethnikon* as referring to a

---

[86] See n. 27.
[87] The earliest attested epitaphs are collected in *IG* i³ 1194–1281 (Athenians) and *IG* i³ 1340–79 (foreigners).
[88] Cf. Meyer (1993: 100). Patronyms were less frequently used in epitaphs with *ethnika* than in those with *demotika*, which can perhaps be explained by reference to the absence of patronyms on tombs outside Athens, on which see Salta (1991: 169–70).
[89] See, for instance, Whitehead (1977: 33–4); Stears (2000: 115).
[90] On this conceptualization of Athenian citizenship, see now most importantly Blok (2017).
[91] *IG* ii² 10483 (late fifth century) and *IG* ii² 6285 (before the middle of the fourth century) possibly include a female *demotikon*.

different, probably broader horizon of reference, one that was shared by non-Athenian men and women alike.[92]

Everything discussed so far has demonstrated that a primary function of Athenian funerary monuments is that they indicated belonging, for instance to a particular family, to Athens's elite, or to the Athenian community in general. Along these lines, the *ethnika* found on tombstones could be interpreted as signalling that the deceased belonged to a group of people with the same ethnic background—that is, as originally deriving from the same locality and usually sharing a common (mythological) ancestor.[93] This group would not have been restricted to the active citizens, the *politai*, of a particular *polis*, but would embrace a larger community of people who would find each other in shared traditions, myths, rites, customs, histories, and memories, which, being away from one's place of origin, would most probably gain in weight over active participation in the public affairs of a faraway *polis*. In that way, Philonikos, son of Bithys, from Thrace (Θρᾶιξ) (*IG* ii² 8927), or [K]teso from Thrace ([Θ]ρᾶιττ[α]) (*Ag.* xvii 508), were by means of their Thracian *ethnikon* referring not only to their *ethnos* up north, to which they and their families originally belonged by descent, but probably also, or especially so, to the vibrant and widely attested community of Thracians who lived in Athens in the classical period.[94] In the 420s, this community was granted the exceptional right to own land (so-called *enktesis*) to build a sanctuary for Bendis. Bendis was a Thracian goddess who, from the late fifth century onwards, was honoured with a *polis* cult and an impressive annual *polis* festival, the Bendideia, in both of which her Thracian worshippers played a key role.[95]

In a similar manner, Tolmides from Plataia (Πλαταεύς) and his daughter Plangon from Plataia (Πλαταική) (*IG* ii² 10096) were probably to be associated not only with their *polis* in Boiotia, but also with the Plataians who lived in Athens and who assembled at the fresh-cheese market on the same day of each month, as Lysias tells us (23.6–7). Perhaps they would commemorate the mass grant of Athenian citizenship a group of Plataian refugees had received in 427, after their city had been sacked by Sparta and Thebes. These Plataian refugees, and their descendants, would be formally registered not as metics but as citizens, yet their experiences as non-Athenians would to a certain extend mirror that of 'true' metics. The fact that many Plataians had their *ethnikon* engraved on their tombstones also points towards something of an in-between position, between naturalized Athenian citizens, on the one hand, and non-Athenians who proudly held on to their ethnic background, on the other.[96] The occurrence of feminine *ethnika*, like [Θ]ρᾶιττ[α] or Πλαταική, could furthermore indicate that women were considered to belong to these ethnic groups more or less on their

---

[92] Cf. Hansen (1996). [93] On this topic Hall (1997) has been pivotal.
[94] Wijma (2014: 127–33). [95] Wijma (2014: 126–55, 2022).
[96] Cf. Gartland (2016: 148–55).

own account, while Athenian women belonged to an Attic deme only by proxy of their Athenian husbands or fathers.[97]

In contrast to the *ethnikon*, by which these foreigners were actively setting themselves apart from Athenian citizens, there is also one aspect of the inscriptions that demonstrates a clear case of conformity to Athenian norms: all epitaphs, even those of non-Greek people, were written in the Greek script and language, most commonly in the Attic dialect.[98] This can, of course, largely and easily be ascribed to the local engravers who were responsible for these epitaphs. Significantly, there is one group of highly informative deviations from this common use of Attic/Greek in Athenian cemeteries. It concerns a group of nine bilingual epitaphs (out of a total of eighteen) epitaphs attested for Phoenicians. The nine inscriptions are written in both Greek and Phoenician and all date to the fourth century.[99] They belong to Phoenicians from Kition, Sidon, Naukratis, and Byzantion, while a ninth bilingual epitaph possibly includes a more general reference to 'Phoenicia'.[100] The Greek epitaphs all give a transcribed or translated version of the Phoenician name of the deceased. Their Semitic and often theophoric names are usually equated with Greek deities. So, Abdanitos, son of Abdšemešos, from Sidon has become Artemidoros, son of Heliodoros (*IG* ii² 10270), while Asepte, daughter of (E)symelem, from Sidon is the same as Asepta, daughter of Ešmun-šillem, whose tombstone, as only the Phoenician epitaph adds, was erected by (her brother?) Yatan-bel, son of Ešmun-šillem, high priest of Nergal (*IG* ii² 10271).

One epitaph, that of Sem (Antipatros), son of Abdestartes (Aphrodisios), from Askalon, even includes an epigram that is rendered in both Greek and Phoenician (*IG* ii² 8388 = *CEG* II 596). Both epigrams offer a curious retelling of the events that also inspired the enigmatic grave relief of a lion attacking a naked man on a *kline*, which we came across earlier (*CAT* 3.410). Significantly, the two version are not identical. As such 'the imagery and the epigram...reveal different amounts of information to different viewers', as Jennifer Stager states in her stimulating discussion of the bilingual aspects of this strange monument. She concludes that 'the monument constitutes a kind of unequal bilingual, weighted not toward the Greek reader, despite the greater abundance of Greek text, but toward the Phoenician reader, to whom the full message of the imagery was directed'.[101]

---

[97] On which, see Bäbler (1998: 66–9). This may also be reflected in the fact that we find several *metronymika* on metic tombstones, while Athenians largely refrained from explicitly referring to their mothers on their tombstones.

[98] There are some epitaphs with names or *ethnika* that are engraved in dialects from outside Attica: e.g. for Sko[-]eas from Messenia (*IG* i³ 1355—written Μεσάνιος instead of Μεσσήνιος), or Nikaso from Aigina (*IG* ii² 7963—Αἰγιναία instead of Αἰγινῆτις). Despite this, these epitaphs must have remained completely legible for the people visiting these cemeteries. Cf. Ginestì Rosell (2012).

[99] *IG* ii² 8388 (Bäbler no. 51); 8440 (52); 9031 (53); 9033 (55); 9034 (56); 9035 (57); 10270 (60); 10271 (61); *CAT* 1.333 (67), with Xagorari-Gleissner (2009). There is also one archaic Carian/Greek epitaph: *IG* i³ 1344.

[100] On *CAT* 1.333 only a Ξ can be read, which is sometimes restored as [ΦΟΙΝΙ]Ξ.

[101] Stager (2005: 446).

Not all memorials containing a Phoenician *ethnikon* are as radically unconventional as the monument for Sem (Antipatros) from Askalon. A very conformist grave relief was, for instance, set up for the Phoenician Erene (*sic*) from Byzantion (*CAT* 2.849). She is shown seated, with her himation drawn over the back of her head, while a young woman, probably a servant maid or a female relative, is holding a swaddled baby—apparently Erene had died in childbirth, which is rendered in a very conventional, Athenian way. But even on such a conformist grave relief, we find Erene's name engraved in both Greek and Phoenician (*IG* ii² 8440).[102] In all these cases, the Phoenician epitaph emphatically pays homage to the Phoenician background of the deceased by means of a Phoenician *ethnikon* and the use of the Phoenician language and script, while the rendering of epitaphs and epigrams in both Phoenician and Greek seems to convey the aspiration to participate, or at least be able to communicate, within this Athenian arena of ideological self-representation.[103]

Finally, we need to consider those epitaphs that consist not only of a name and an *ethnikon*, and sometimes a *patronymikon*, but also of an epigram. Twenty epigrams dating to the classical period can be associated with non-Athenians.[104] In them we find the same hybridity as in the other aspects of the funerary monuments for foreigners. By having an epigram engraved on the tomb of a loved one, the family could, first of all, display a familiarity with Greek funerary traditions, something especially non-Greek metics might wish to display.[105] A familiarity with Greek, or even specifically Athenian culture, is furthermore communicated by means of references to Greek deities or to Homeric or even exclusively Athenian heroes. On the tomb for the daughter of the *isoteles* Apollodoros, for instance, we find an epigram with a reference to Persephone and Ploutos (*IG* ii² 7873.10). The epigram for Atotas from Paphlagonia contains a reference to Achilles (*IG* ii² 10051.5), while the epigram for Symmachos from Khios mentions the Athenian mythological king Kekrops (*IG* ii² 10510). Several epigrams for non-Athenians also emphasize the same fundamental virtues we see so often praised on the tombstones of Athenians, such as σωφροσύνη (on the tomb for Aristokrateia from Korinth—*IG* ii² 9057.2), δικαιοσύνη and ἀρετή (for Sosinos from Gortyn—*IG* ii² 8464.2), or being worthy of praise and eulogy in general (*IG* ii² 8593.6-7 (ὧν εὐλογίας καὶ ἐπαίνων ἄξιός εἰμι); *IG* ii² 8883.3-4 (αὔξετ' ἔπαινος)).

Besides these Greek and even specifically Athenian features, there are also elements that are clearly associated with the deceased's non-Athenian background. For instance, there are several epigrams that contain a reference to the deceased's

---

[102] Cf. Kennedy (2014: 107, with fig. 4.2).
[103] Bäbler (1998: 122–4), suggests that the Phoenician community in Athens could have had its own masons and engravers, which is perhaps reflected in the peculiar Greek used in the epigram of Antipatros and the peculiar relief decorating his tomb (*CAT* 3.410).
[104] *IG* i³ 1361 (*CEG* I 87); *IG* ii² 7873 (*CEG* II 571); 7965 (532); 8388 (596); 8464 (*CEG* I 96); 8523 (*CEG* II 485); 8593 (533); 8708 (544); 8870 (545); 8883 (509); 9057 (486); 9112 (534); 10051 (572); 10108; 10113 (605); 10435 (487); 10510 (606); *SEG* 18.120 (586); 12.193 (587); 59.305.
[105] Bäbler (1998: 203).

land of origin, in addition to the *ethnikon* in the epitaph. It is often made explicit that the deceased was born somewhere else, even though he or she is now buried in Athens. So, in the epigram for Symmachos, son of Simon, we find a reference to Khios, his fatherland, while it is also stated that he was buried in the plains of Kekrops (*IG* ii$^2$ 10510.4–5). Similarly, in the epigram for Theogeiton, son of Thymochos, it is specified that he was born in Thebes, while he will now forever rest in glorious Athens (*IG* ii$^2$ 8870.5–8). In these epigrams, one's fatherland is marked as just as important for someone's social persona as one's final resting place.

Most remarkable in these epigrams, however, and corresponding to some of the most unconventional iconography found on the tombstones of several non-Athenians, is the emphasis on the personal life of the deceased, often in the form of a reference to an occupation or an activity as a key aspect of one's life. In the epigram for Mannes from Phrygia, for instance, it is stated that he was a wood-cutter (ὑλοτόμον), who had fallen in war (*IG* i$^3$ 1361.5–6), which probably refers to his participation as a metic in the Athenian army during the Peloponnesian War, as his memorial is dated to c.431–421. The tomb for the daughter of the *isoteles* Apollodoros contains an epigram that repeatedly emphasizes that she was, is, and will be honoured for having been such a worthy nurse (τίτθην) for the children of Hippostrate (*IG* ii$^2$ 7873). Similarly, Malicha from Kytheria is honoured as 'the most trustworthy nurse (τίτθην) from the Peloponnesos for the children of Diogeiton' (*IG* ii$^2$ 9112).[106] The epigram for Atotas from Paphlagonia states that he was a miner (μεταλλεύς—*IG* ii$^2$ 10051.1–2). Sosinos from Gortyn is referred to as a copper-smelter (χαλκόπτης), whose tomb with the relief of what appears to be a copper-smelter (*CAT* 1.202 (Figure 8.6)) is 'a memorial to his justice, good sense and his virtue, set up by his children' (*IG* ii$^2$ 8464). Then there is Potamon, son of Olympichos, from Thebes, whom we also met earlier (*CAT* 2.235), and who, according to his epigram, had been assigned first prize in the flute-player's art by Hellas (*IG* ii$^2$ 8883).[107] So, also concerning their inscriptions these memorials with *ethnika* openly emphasize the non-Athenian background of the deceased, sometimes revealing interesting details about their lives, which is generally absent from the memorials for Athenians, while many other aspects, by contrast, powerfully adhere to their specifically Athenian context.

## Conclusions

In the social realities of classical Athens, metic status seems to have mattered most of all to the Athenians. It was in their interest, and in their interest alone,

---

[106] Both the relief for the daughter of Apollodoros and the one for Malicha are discussed by Kennedy (2014: 133–6) as indications for metic women working in the context of domestic childcare.

[107] See also the mention of an occupation in *IG* ii$^2$ 9979 (Ἡρα[κ]λείδ[α]ς Μυσὸς κατ[α]παλταφέτας); *IG* ii$^2$ 7967 (<'Ε>ρμαῖος ⋮ Αἰγύπτιος ⋮ ἐχ Θηβῶν [γ]ναφαλλουφάντης) and *IG* ii$^2$ 8755 (Ὄλυμπος Τιμοθέου Ἡρακλειώτης κυβερνήτης). In addition, Polykleos, from Akanthos (*SEG* 56.75), and Diogeiton (*IG* ii$^2$ 9304) are both commemorated as *proxenos*.

that immigrants and all other free foreigners living in their midst were to be organized and differentiated from other *polis* inhabitants. In the course of that process, metics were excluded from political decision-making, could not own land, had to register in a deme, were to participate in several *polis* festivals in a certain way, had to pay a specific metic tax, were liable for certain additional financial obligations, had to serve in the Athenian army, had to bring their legal cases before the polemarch, were liable under Athenian laws, which included some specific cases and penalties concerning metics, and, after Pericles' Citizenship Law of 451/0, became disqualified, in fits and starts, as legitimate partners for Athenian citizens. All these measures underscored the notion of a clearly demarcated status, known as *metoikia*.

Most significantly, this narrative of *metoikia* was an exclusively Athenian narrative. Except for a short passage in Lysias, there are no voices of metics themselves expressing ideas about their status *qua* metics. I have argued that the funerary monuments from classical Athens that include an *ethnikon* offer a unique opportunity to listen in on how the free foreigners living in Athens themselves conceptualized their own position in Athenian society. My aim has been twofold. First, by focusing on the narratives of individual non-Athenians, I hope to have brought about a greater appreciation of the multifaceted and diverse aspects of the social identities and experiences of the free foreigners living in classical Athens, thereby somewhat counterbalancing the Athenian master narrative with its frequently implied notion of a coherent and homogenous metic community.

My second aim has been to arrive at a better understanding of the social ties and the values that the free foreigners in Athens deemed worthy of commemorating in public and therefore pivotal to their social identities. First, it cannot be emphasized enough that metic status was not an organizing principle in the context of Athenian cemeteries, nor was it explicitly displayed by the people who could be labelled as such. Still, despite the absence of a coherent metic community in death, there can be found some commonalities among the social markers and affiliations that were displayed on the tombs with *ethnika*. Most importantly, these tombs all share a hybridity in organization, form, iconography, and epigraphy that seems to be typical of immigrant (and, on a completely different note, (post)colonial) identity in general. The specific hybridity displayed on these memorials for non-Athenians consists first of all of an extensive and cogent conformity to the practices of their Athenian hosts and a conscious and powerful display of familiarity with Greek and Athenian culture and values in general. But nonconformity was also clearly present, most generally through the emphasis on the ethnic affiliations of the deceased and more specifically through references to personal narratives, most importantly to the occupation of the deceased or to the way in which he or she died. Significantly, this specific hybridity was present in tombs of both very wealthy and more ordinary metics, who apparently all felt the need to promote both their integration into Athenian society and their non-Athenian background at the same time.

## Acknowledgements

I would very much like to thank Samuel Gartland and David Tandy for their constructive comments and for inviting me to join their project in the first place. Thanks must also go to Rebecca Futo Kennedy and to the three anonymous readers for the Oxford University Press, who have commented on earlier drafts of this chapter. All errors remain, of course, my own.

## Works Cited

Akrigg, B. (2019). *Population and Economy in Classical Athens*. New York and Cambridge.

Baba, K. (1984). 'On Kerameikos Inv. I 388 (*SEG* XXII, 79): A Note on the Formation of the Athenian Metic-Status', *Annual of the British School at Athens*, 79: 1–5.

Bäbler, B. (1998). *Fleissige Thrakerinnen und wehrhafte Skythen: Nichtgriechen im klassischen Athen und ihre archäologische Hinterlassenschaft*. Stuttgart.

Bakewell, G. (1999). 'Lysias 12 and Lysias 31: Metics and Athenian Citizenship in the Aftermath of the Thirty', *Greek, Roman, and Byzantine Studies*, 40: 5–22.

Bergemann, J. (1997). *Demos und Thanatos: Untersuchungen zum Wertsystem der Polis im Spiegel der attischen Grabreliefs des 4. Jahrhunderts v. Chr. und zur Funktion der gleichzeitigen Grabbauten*. Munich.

Blok, J. H. (2017). *Citizenship in Classical Athens*. Cambridge.

Boegehold, A. L., and A. C. Scafuro (1994) (eds). *Athenian Identity and Civic Ideology*. Baltimore.

Cartledge, P. (2002). *The Greeks: A Portrait of Self and Others*. 2nd edn. Oxford.

Clairmont, C. W. (1970). *Gravestone and Epigram: Greek Memorials from the Archaic and Classical Period*. Mainz.

Clairmont, C. W. (1993). *Classical Attic Tombstones*. 8 vols. Kilchberg (= *CAT*).

Clerc, M. (1893). *Les métèques Athéniens: Étude sur la condition légale, la situation morale et le rôle social et économique des étrangers domiciliés à Athènes*. Paris.

Closterman, W. E. (2006). 'Family Members and Citizens: Athenian Identity and the *Peribolos* Tomb Setting', in C. B. Patterson (ed.), *Antigone's Answer: Essays on Death and Burial, Family and State in Classical Athens*. Helios Supplement 33, 49–78. Lubbock.

Closterman, W. E. (2014). 'Family Meals: Banquet Imagery on Classical Athenian Funerary Reliefs', in K. F. Daly and L. A. Riccardi (eds), *Cities Called Athens: Studies Honoring John McK. Camp II*, 1–22. Lewisburg, PA.

Cohen, E. E. (2000). *The Athenian Nation*. Princeton.

Connor, W. R. (1994). 'The Problem of Athenian Civic Identity', in Boegehold and Scafuro (1994: 34–44).

Damsgaard-Madsen, A. (1988). 'Attic Funeral Inscriptions: Their Use as Historical Sources and Some Preliminary Results', in A. Damsgaard-Madsen, E. Christiansen, and E. Hallager (eds), *Studies in Ancient History and Numismatics Presented to Rudi Thomsen*, 55–68. Aarhus.

Fraser, P. M. (1995). 'Citizens, Demesmen and Metics in Athens and Elsewhere', in M. H. Hansen (ed.), *Sources for the Ancient Greek City-State*, 64–90. Copenhagen.

Garland, R. (1982). 'A First Catalogue of Attic *Peribolos* Tombs', *Annual of the British School at Athens*, 77: 125–76.

Garland, R. (2001). *The Piraeus: From the Fifth to the First Century BC*. 2nd edn. London.

Gartland, S. D. (2016). 'A New Boiotia? Exiles, Landscapes, and Kings', in S. D. Gartland (ed.), *Boiotia in the Fourth Century BC*, 147–64. Philadelphia.

Ginestí Rosell, A. G. (2012). *Epigrafia funerària d'estrangers a Atenes (segles VI–IV aC)*. Tarragona.

Grossman, J. B. (2013). *Funerary Sculpture*. The Athenian Agora XXXV. Princeton.

Hagemajer Allen, K. (2003). 'Becoming the "Other": Attitudes and Practices at Attic Cemeteries', in C. Dougherty and L. Kurke (eds), *The Cultures within Greek Culture: Contact, Conflict, Collaboration*, 207–36. Cambridge.

Hall, E. (1989). *Inventing the Barbarian: Greek Self-Definition through Tragedy*. Oxford.

Hall, J. M. (1997). *Ethnic Identity in Greek Antiquity*. Cambridge and New York.

Hansen, M. H. (1996). 'City-Ethnics as Evidence for Polis Identity', in M. H. Hansen and K. Raaflaub (eds), *More Studies in the Ancient Greek Polis*, 169–96. Stuttgart.

Hansen, P. A. (1983). *Carmina Epigraphica Graeca saeculorum VIII-V a. Chr. n.* Berlin (= *CEG* I).

Hansen, P. A. (1989). *Carmina Epigraphica Graeca: saeculi IV a. Chr. n.* Berlin (= *CEG* II).

Hope V. M. (1998). 'Negotiating Identity and Status: The Gladiators of Roman Nîmes', in R. Laurence and J. Berry (eds), *Cultural Identity in the Roman Empire*, 179–95. London and New York.

Hope, V. M. (2000). 'Inscription and Sculpture: The Construction of Identity in the Military Tombstones of Roman Mainz', in Oliver (2000b: 155–85).

Hopkins, K. (1966). 'On the Probable Age Structure of the Roman Population', *Population Studies*, 20: 245–64 (repr. in K. Hopkins (2018) 93–104).

Hopkins, K. (1987). 'Graveyards for Historians', in F. Hinard (ed.), *La mort, les morts et l'au-delà dans le monde romain*, 113–26. Caen (repr. in K. Hopkins (2018) 105–34).

Hopkins, K. (2018). *Sociological Studies in Roman History*, ed. C. Kelly. Cambridge.

Joshel, S. R. (1992). *Work, Identity, and Legal Status at Rome: A Study of the Occupational Inscriptions*. Norman, OK.

Kaltsas, N. (2002). *Sculpture in the National Archaeological Museum, Athens*, trans. D. Hardy. Los Angeles.

Kamen, D. (2013). *Status in Classical Athens*. Princeton.

Kasimis, D. (2018). *The Perpetual Immigrant and the Limits of Athenian Democracy*. Cambridge.

Kennedy, R. F. (2014). *Immigrant Women in Athens: Gender, Ethnicity, and Citizenship in the Classical City*. New York.

Knapp, R. C. (2011). *Invisible Romans: Prostitutes, Outlaws, Slaves, Gladiators, Ordinary Men and Women... the Romans that History Forgot*. London.

Knigge, U. (1988). *Der Kerameikos von Athen: Führung durch Ausgrabungen und Geschichte*. Athens.

Kokula von Leitner, G. (1984). *Marmorlutrophoren*. Mitteilungen des Deutschen Archäologischen Instituts, Athenische Abteilung 10. Berlin.

Kovacsovics, W. K., S.C. Bisel, C. Dehl, and F. Willemsen (1990). *Die Eckterrasse an der Gräberstrasse des Kerameikos*. Kerameikos 14. Berlin.

Kurtz, D. C., and J. Boardman (1971). *Greek Burial Customs*. London.

Manville, P. B. (1994). 'Toward a New Paradigm of Athenian Citizenship', in Boegehold and Scafuro (1994: 21–33).

Meyer, E. A. (1993). 'Epitaphs and Citizenship in Classical Athens', *Journal of Hellenic Studies*, 113: 99–121.

Morris, I. (1992). *Death-Ritual and Social Structure in Classical Antiquity*. Cambridge.

Mouritsen, H. (2005). 'Freedmen and Decurions: Epitaphs and Social History in Imperial Italy', *Journal of Roman Studies*, 95: 38–63.

Nielsen, T. H., L. Bjertrup, M. H. Hansen, L. Rubinstein, and T. Vestergaard (1989). 'Athenian Grave Monuments and Social Class', *Greek, Roman, and Byzantine Studies*, 30: 411–20.

Oliver, G. (2000a). 'An Introduction to the Epigraphy of Death: Funerary Inscriptions as Evidence', in (Oliver 2000b: 1–23).

Oliver, G. (2000b). (ed.). *The Epigraphy of Death: Studies in the History and Society of Greece and Rome*. Liverpool.

Osborne, M. J., and S. G. Byrne (1996). *The Foreign Residents of Athens: An Annex to the Lexicon of Greek Personal Names: Attica*. Studia Hellenistica, 33. Leuven.

Osborne, R. (1997). 'Law, the Democratic Citizen and the Representation of Women in Classical Athens', *Past and Present*, 155: 3–33 (repr. in R. Osborne, *Athens and Athenian Democracy*, Cambridge, 2010, 244–66).

Osborne, R. (2011). *The History Written on the Classical Greek Body*. Cambridge.

Patterson, C. W. (2000). 'The Hospitality of Athenian Justice: The Metic in Court', in V. J. Hunter and J. Edmondson (eds), *Law and Social Status in Classical Athens*, 93–112. Oxford.

Rhodes, P. J., and R. Osborne (2003). *Greek Historical Inscriptions 404–323 BC*. Oxford (= RO).

Robertson, C. M., and A. Frantz (1975). *The Parthenon Frieze*. London.

Said, E. W. (2003 [1978]). *Orientalism*. London.

Salta, M. (1991). 'Attische Grabstelen mit Inschriften: Beiträge zur Topographie und Prosopographie der Nekropolen von Athen, Attika und Salamis vom Peloponnesischen Krieg bis zur Mitte des 4. Jhs. v. Chr.'. Ph.D. dissertation. Tübingen.

Sawtell, C. (2018). 'Non-Citizen Commemoration in Fifth and Fourth Century BC Attica'. Ph.D. dissertation. Sheffield.

Schmaltz, B. (1970). *Untersuchungen zu den attischen Marmorlekythen*. Berlin.

Schmaltz, B. (1979). 'Verwendung und Funktion attischer Grabmäler', *Marburger Winckelmann-Programm*, 1979: 13–37.

Scholl, A. (1993). 'Das "Charonrelief" im Kerameikos', *Jahrbuch des Deutschen Archäologischen Instituts*, 108: 353–73.

Scholl, A. (1996). *Die attischen Bildfeldstelen des 4. Jhs v. Chr.: Untersuchungen zu den kleinformatigen Grabreliefs im spätklassischen Athen*. Mitteilungen des Deutschen Archäologischen Instituts, Athenische Abteilung 17. Berlin.

Shea, T. D. (2018). 'Mapping Immigrant Communities through their Tombstones in Archaic and Classical Athens'. Ph.D. dissertation. Duke University.

Sosin, J. D. (2016). 'A Metic was a Metic', *Historia*, 65/1: 2–13.

Stager, J. M. S. (2005). '"Let No One Wonder at this Image": A Phoenician Funerary Stele in Athens', *Hesperia*, 74/3: 427–49.

Stears, K. (1995). 'Dead Women's Society: Constructing Female Gender in Classical Athenian Funerary Sculpture', in N. Spencer (ed.), *Time, Tradition and Society in Greek Archaeology*, 109–31. London.

Stears, K. (2000). 'The Times they are a-Changing: Developments in Fifth-Century Funerary Sculpture', in (Oliver 2000b: 25–58).

Taylor, L. R. (1961). 'Freedmen and Freeborn in the Epitaphs of Imperial Rome', *American Journal of Philology*, 82/2: 113–32.

Urdahl, L. B. (1959). 'Foreigners in Athens: A Study of the Grave Monuments'. Ph.D. dissertation. Chicago.

Vestergaard, T. (2000). 'Milesian Immigrants in Late Hellenistic and Roman Athens', in Oliver (2000b: 81–109).

Vlassopoulos, K. (2007). 'Free Spaces: Identity, Experience and Democracy in Classical Athens', *Classical Quarterly*, 57: 33–52.

Whitehead, D. (1977). *The Ideology of the Athenian Metic*. Cambridge.

Whitehead, D. (1986). *The Demes of Attica, 508/7-ca. 250 BC: A Political and Social Study*. Princeton.

Wijma, S. M. (2014). *Embracing the Immigrant: The Participation of Metics in Athenian Polis Religion (5th-4th century BC)*. Stuttgart.

Wijma, S. M. (2022). 'Between Private and Public: *Orgeones* in Classical and Hellenistic Athens', in A. Cazemier and S. Skaltsa (eds), *Associations and Religion in Context: The Hellenistic and Roman Eastern Mediterranean*. Kernos Supplement 39, 21–43. Liège.

Xagorari-Gleißner, M. (2009). 'Attische bilingue Grabreliefs des 4. Jhs. v. Chr.', *Archäologischer Anzeiger*, 2009/2: 113–27.

Zanker, P. (1975). 'Grabreliefs römischer Freigelassener', *Jahrbuch des Deutschen Archäologischen Instituts*, 90: 267–315.

# 9
# Varying Statuses, Varying Rights
## A Case Study of the *graphē hubreōs*

*Deborah Kamen*

## Preface

This chapter addresses the extent to which various status groups in classical Athens were able to make use of a right (notionally) offered them by law: namely, protection from *hubris*. In this way, it builds on recent work on status in classical Athens, which has compared the relative statuses of enslaved people, metics, and citizens (e.g. Fisher 2006; Kapparis 2019: ch. 2), explored the mechanics of mobility between status groups (e.g. Deene 2014; Taylor 2015; Davies 2017), and laid out the full range of statuses in Athens, including those existing between enslaved, metic, and citizen (Kamen 2013).

By exploring the discrepancy between the ideology of equal protection from *hubris* and the reality of variable access to this protection, this chapter also contributes to scholarship on the various gaps between ideology and practice in Athens (Kamen 2013), such as that between the ideology of autochthony and the reality of Athenians of mixed ancestry (e.g. Lape 2010), between the ideology of fixed status groups and the reality of status fluidity (e.g. Vlassopoulos 2009), and between the ideology of equality and the reality of differing access to rights for citizens of different socio-economic groups (e.g. Cecchet, Chapter 4, this volume).

## Introduction

Access to legal rights and protections in classical Athens varied considerably according to one's status: that is, whether one was enslaved, metic (resident foreigner), citizen, or somewhere in-between, and whether one was a man, woman, or child.[1] Nonetheless, despite this variation, there was one important right that was, at least notionally, available by law to everyone, regardless of their status: namely, protection from *hubris*, an offence conventionally defined, following

---

[1] On the spectrum of statuses in classical Athens, see Kamen (2013).

Nick Fisher, as a deliberate insult to another's honour.[2] Fisher bases his definition of *hubris* on Aristotle's discussion in the *Rhetoric*, which reads in part: 'He who commits *hubris* against another also slights him; for *hubris* consists in causing damages or annoyance whereby the sufferer is disgraced, not to obtain any other advantage for oneself besides the performance of the act, but for one's own pleasure' (Arist. *Rhet.* 2.2.6, 1378$^b$23–5). While Douglas MacDowell, Douglas Cairns, and most recently Mirko Canevaro all agree with Fisher that dishonour was for Aristotle an important component in *hubris*, they argue that disposition—namely, the disposition of exuberant arrogance—plays an equally large or greater role.[3]

However, when it comes to the *technical* or *legal* sense of *hubris*—that is, as a crime that could be prosecuted, my concern in this chapter—the intention to insult another person appears to be key.[4] After all, there needs to be a victim in order for an Athenian lawsuit to be brought.[5] This interpretation of the legal meaning of *hubris* allows for the importance of disposition while also acknowledging that, in the specific context of the *graphē hubreōs* (γραφὴ ὕβρεως), it was disposition *manifested in the form of an insult* that was most salient. As I have demonstrated elsewhere, insults were an enormous concern for the Athenians, given the importance of honour in their society.[6] Indeed, even though they passionately defended freedom of speech, they simultaneously prohibited any insult that was thought especially damaging to its target's social or legal standing.[7]

---

[2] *Hubris* is 'a deliberate and willful attempt to inflict serious humiliation and dishonour' (Fisher 1976: 181); 'the serious assault on the honour of another, which is likely to cause shame, and lead to anger and attempts at revenge' (Fisher 1992: 1); 'the deliberate infliction of serious insult on another human being' (Fisher 1995: 45); 'seriously insulting behaviour which threatens the honour and personal integrity of the citizen' (Fisher 2005: 69).

[3] MacDowell (1990); Cairns (1996); Canavero (2018 = 2019) (with which Vlassopoulos 2021: 132–3 agrees). Cf. D. Cohen (1995: 144–51), who stresses, more than Fisher does, the pleasure gained by hubristic action.

[4] See Kamen (2020: ch. 5 on *hubris*, esp. 118–19) on the importance of intentionality. For example, in *Against Medias* (discussed further below), Demosthenes says that not only in the case of damage and homicide, but in all cases, 'the laws may be seen to be severe against those who are willfully hubristic [τοῖς ἐκ προαιρέσεως ὑβρισταῖς]' (21.44), where *ek prohaireseōs* has a meaning roughly similar to *hekōn*, 'voluntary', and *ek pronoias*, 'with forethought', used of intentional damage and murder, respectively, in the previous paragraph (21.43). This meaning also seems to apply when Demosthenes says that 'on every occasion [Meidias] has shown a deliberate intention to insult me [προῃρημένος μ' ὑβρίζειν]' (21.38).

[5] Even Canevaro (2018: 107 = 2019: 55), who stresses the primacy of disposition in conceptualizing *hubris*, concedes that 'Athenian charges originated from specific acts and therefore necessitated a victim—"victimless" *hubris* would have hardly been liable to a *graphē hubreōs*'. To my mind, however, this does not necessarily mean that the victim had *in fact* been dishonoured, rather that the action being prosecuted with a *graphē hubreōs* was perceived as one *intended* to dishonour that person. We might compare the suit for 'wounding with attempt to kill' (τραῦμα ἐκ προνοίας), where what is prosecuted is the *intent* to murder the victim.

[6] See Kamen (2020). On the importance of honour in Greek society, see, e.g., Cairns (1993). On the relationship between insults and honour in Athens, see also McHardy (2008: 85–102).

[7] Kamen (2020: chs 4, 5).

My focus in this chapter is on the degree to which individuals of different statuses could, in practice, make use of their right to be protected from insults they perceived as *hubris*. More specifically, I will argue that subordinate members of Athenian society—that is, all who were not fully enfranchised male citizens— were, to varying degrees, less able to obtain redress after suffering *hubris* than the law purported to offer.[8] I suggest further that this inability to access their (notional) right would have reminded them, in turn, of their precarious status. In this way, the seemingly generous law on *hubris* paradoxically reinforced the subordination of most members of Athenian society.

## Access to Legal Rights and Protections

Before turning to a discussion of *hubris*, it will be useful to survey what access, in general, various status groups in Athens had to the legal system. At the lowest end of the status spectrum were chattel slaves, who were classified legally as property[9] and who had virtually no access to any rights or protections.[10] They could not bring lawsuits, either private suits (*dikai*) or public ones (*graphai*), nor could they defend themselves or their loved ones in court (Pl. *Gorg.* 483b). Technically, lawsuits could be brought on behalf of an enslaved person, but it would have to be by someone—most likely his or her owner—with a vested interest in the slave's well-being or value as property. Starting in the mid-fourth century BCE, enslaved people were allowed to engage in mercantile lawsuits (*dikai emporikai*), which were open to individuals of any status.[11] In practice, however, the only enslaved people who had access to this right were the 'privileged' slaves who worked semi-independently in commerce.[12]

Metics, who could be either freeborn or formerly enslaved individuals, had greater access than enslaved people to the Athenian legal system, though they were at least somewhat dependent on their patrons (*prostatai*) in doing so.[13] (For freeborn metics, their *prostatēs* was a citizen of their choosing; for formerly enslaved metics, it was usually their former owner.) The precise level of

---

[8] This argument stands in contrast to, e.g., the work of Edward Cohen (e.g. E. E. Cohen 2000: 159–67; 2015: 124–30), who argues that all members of Athenian society were in fact protected by the law on *hubris*.
[9] See Vlassopoulos (2011) on the debate about whether Greek slavery was defined as a relationship primarily of property or of domination (he argues for the latter); but cf. Lewis (2018), who returns to the property definition.
[10] On the status of chattel slaves in classical Athens, see, e.g., Kamen (2013: ch. 1); Kapparis (2019: 96–101).
[11] On these *dikai*, see E. E. Cohen (1973); Lanni (2006: 149–74).
[12] On the status of 'privileged' slaves, see Kamen (2013: ch. 2).
[13] On the status of metics, see Whitehead (1977); Kamen (2013: chs 4, 5); Kapparis (2019: 88–96). On female metics, see Kennedy (2014).

involvement of the *prostatēs* in the metic's legal affairs is unclear,[14] but rather than speaking on behalf of the metic in court (as the owner did with his slave), he most likely simply gave the latter legal advice.[15] Perhaps in consultation with their *prostatai*, then, metics could sue and be sued in any kind of *dikē*. However, unlike in *dikai* involving two citizens (which came before whichever magistrate held jurisdiction over that type of suit, before being handed over to a court), these suits were always heard first by the polemarch, the magistrate in charge of all private suits involving metics ([Arist.] *Ath. Pol.* 58.2). (This was, in a sense, a 'separate but equal' way of handling metics' legal affairs.) In most instances, the polemarch then assigned these *dikai* by lot to judges in each of the ten tribes ([Arist.] *Ath. Pol.* 58.2), but there were some cases that the polemarch presided over himself, including the *dikē apostasiou* (for formerly enslaved people 'standing apart' from their former owner and seeking a new *prostatēs*) and cases having to do with metics' inheritance ([Arist.] *Ath. Pol.* 58.3). In the fifth century, the polemarch also dealt with *graphai* involving metics, but in the fourth century these suits seem to have been handled in the same way as *graphai* involving citizens.[16] There were some exceptions, however: for example, even in the fourth century the *graphē aprostasiou* (for metics failing either to register a *prostatēs* or to pay the metic tax) was under the jurisdiction of the polemarch ([Arist.] *Ath. Pol.* 58.3).[17]

For the most part, then, metics (or at least male metics[18]) had fairly robust rights vis-à-vis the courts, but, as Cynthia Patterson has convincingly demonstrated, this supposedly 'equal access' did not match the access granted to citizens.[19] First of all, metics often lacked a strong support network of friends and family[20] and were denied membership in the main groupings of Athenian society (for example, phratry, deme, tribe); both were relied upon by litigants in fashioning their cases. In addition to the prejudices that metics faced simply by virtue of

---

[14] Arist. *Pol.* 3.1.3, 1275ᵃ11–13 says that in many places (πολλαχοῦ) a metic needs a *prostatēs* in order to bring suits or defend himself, but he does not specify exactly what the role of the *prostatēs* would be.

[15] See Whitehead (1977: 90–1); Kamen (2013: 47–8).

[16] MacDowell (1978: 223); Rhodes (1981: 652).

[17] On the *graphē aprostasiou*, see, e.g., Meyer (2010: 43–7 and *passim*).

[18] On the more precarious position of female metics, see Kennedy (2014: ch. 4).

[19] Patterson (2000: 94): 'Within a system that may indeed have given some degree of "equal" or "symmetrical" treatment to the resident alien, the metic was nonetheless isolated as an independent legal persona, without connection to the Athenian land or to Athenian household and kinship structures so important to Athenian litigation.'

[20] Recent work, however, has illuminated the degree to which metics were engaged in, and benefited from, social networks that cut across status lines: see, e.g., Steinhauer (2014: 48–9); Taylor (2015). Moreover, some formerly enslaved metics may have been able to rely on the built-in network of their former owner's family. See Akrigg (2015), who argues that many of the metics in Athens were in fact freed slaves, rather than (as is usually thought) economic migrants (he does not, however, fully account for refugees, who at times must have constituted a portion of the metic population: see Rubinstein 2018).

being foreigners,[21] these factors presented real obstacles for metics trying to win over a jury of Athenian citizens. Secondly, even if metics could seek justice in the Athenian courts, it was sometimes lesser justice than that attainable by citizens. For instance, the killing of a metic (just like that of an enslaved person), even if it was premeditated, was held in the same court where cases involving the *unintentional* killing of citizens were heard ([Arist.] *Ath. Pol.* 57.3), and the penalty in these instances was (only) exile (Dem. 23.71–3), whereas the premediated killing of a citizen could be punished with death (Dem. 21.43).[22]

Citizens, unlike enslaved people and metics, had complete access to the courts, at least notionally. Even so, variation in social and even legal status among citizens also entailed variation in the ability to access one's legal rights. An extreme case is the disenfranchised citizen (*atimos*): depending on the degree to which a citizen was disenfranchised—disenfranchisement (*atimia*) could be partial or complete—he might not have the right to bring *dikai* or *graphai* at all.[23] A naturalized citizen, like a natural-born citizen, technically had full access to the judicial system, but, like the metic, he faced the social stigma of being foreign born, which was a potential impediment, if not an insurmountable one, to acquiring the jury's favour.[24] A male citizen under the age of 18, not yet in possession of full civic rights,[25] would in general have had his interests represented by a parent or another adult, and a female citizen could not speak in court but had to be represented by her guardian (*kurios*), whether it was her husband (if she was married) or father (if she was not) or another guardian.[26] And finally, male citizens—that is, those who were neither disenfranchised, nor naturalized, nor underage—technically had full and equal access to the courts,[27] but even here we find some variation. Poor citizens were less likely than rich ones to come to court,[28] both because of the costs involved in doing so (not only hiring a speechwriter but also missing a day's wages[29]), and because juries tended to be better disposed towards the wealthy, or at least towards the wealthy who had made benefactions to the

---

[21] See Cooper (2003) on hostility to foreigners in the Athenian courts. See also Bakewell (1999) on Lysias' strategy of tarring his citizen opponents as 'metaphorical metics', and Kennedy (2014) on the particular prejudices faced by metic women.

[22] On these penalties, see also Todd (1993: 274).

[23] On the status of *atimoi*, see Kamen (2013: ch. 7).

[24] On the status of naturalized citizens, see Kamen (2013: ch. 8).

[25] According to Aristotle, children are 'citizens in a sense [$\pi\omega\varsigma$ $\pi o\lambda\acute{\iota}\tau\alpha\varsigma$], yet not quite absolutely, with the qualification "incomplete" [$\mathring{\alpha}\tau\epsilon\lambda\epsilon\hat{\iota}\varsigma$]' (*Pol.* 3.1.4, 1275$^a$16–17; see also *Pol.* 3.3.2, 1278$^a$5–6).

[26] On the status of female citizens, see Kamen (2013: ch. 9.) On 'female citizenship' in Athens, see, e.g., Patterson (1986); Blok (2017). On the obstacles faced by citizen women in court, see Kennedy, Chapter 10, this volume.

[27] On the status of male citizens, see Kamen (2013: ch. 10). On Athenian citizenship more broadly, see Blok (2017).

[28] On poverty in Athens, see Cecchet (2015); Taylor (2017). On the limitations faced by poor citizens, see also Cecchet, Chapter 4, this volume.

[29] See, e.g., [Dem.] 44.4 for a portrait of a poor man, a public crier in the Piraeus, who (apart from this lawsuit) has never come to court because he needs to spend all day in the agora.

city.[30] Thus, while citizens in general had greatest access to the courts, not all citizens were equally capable of exercising this right.

## The *graphē hubreōs*

Let us turn now to the experience of individuals seeking legal recourse specifically in the case of *hubris*. Theoretically, this was available to everyone. The law against *hubris*, as cited in Demosthenes' *Against Meidias*,[31] states whom the law protects and the procedure to be followed in an indictment for *hubris* (i.e. the *graphē hubreōs*):

> If anyone treats with *hubris* any person, either child or woman or man, free or slave, or does anything unlawful against any of these, let anyone who wishes, of those Athenians who are entitled, submit a *graphē* to the *thesmothetai* [judicial officers]. Let the *thesmothetai* bring the case to the people's court within thirty days of the submission of the *graphē*, if no public business prevents it, or otherwise as soon as possible. Whoever the people's court finds guilty, let it immediately assess whatever penalty it thinks right for him to suffer or pay. Of those who indict [i.e. submit a *graphē*] according to the law, if anyone does not proceed [to trial], or when proceeding does not get one-fifth of the votes, let him pay one thousand drachmas to the public treasury. If he [i.e. the convicted assailant] is assessed to pay money for his *hubris*, let him be imprisoned, if the *hubris* is against a free person, until he pays it. (Dem. 21.47)

One of the most surprising features of this law—apparently surprising even to the Athenians—is that it protects *everyone*, including enslaved people, from *hubris*.[32] (The distinct treatment of those convicted of committing *hubris* against a *free* person, and unable to pay the fine, should, however, be noted.) Demosthenes explains that 'the lawmaker' included slaves in the law because the very act of *hubris*, regardless of the identity of its victim, was deemed intolerable (Dem. 21.46). Aeschines adds that the lawmaker's concern was not so much for the slaves themselves as it was to prevent undemocratic behaviour on the part of the citizens of Athens (Aesch. 1.17). Some scholars have followed the lead of Demosthenes and Aeschines, arguing that the reason for protecting (even) enslaved people was to demonstrate how unacceptable any and all *hubris* was,[33] with the aim of preventing behaviour that was thought damaging to the *polis* as a

---

[30] On juries' complex attitudes towards wealthy litigants, see, e.g., Ober (1989: 192–247).
[31] Many scholars think this law is genuine, but cf. Harris (1992: 77; 2013: 224–31); Leão and Rhodes (2015: 163); Canevaro and Harris (2019).
[32] See also Aesch. 1.15; Lyc. fr. 10–11.12; Hyp. fr. 120 Jensen.
[33] See, e.g., Fisher (2001: 141–2 (ad loc. Aesch. 1.17)).

VARYING STATUSES, VARYING RIGHTS   249

whole.[34] Others have suggested, alternatively or in addition, that the law protected enslaved people from *hubris qua* vehicles of their owner's honour,[35] *qua* part of the owner's household,[36] or *qua* human beings who possessed some (albeit small) share of honour that warranted protection.[37] Most likely, the reasons behind this provision are manifold, reflecting some combination of these explanations.[38]

Regardless of its motivations, I think we can, and should, explore the degree to which this protection was actually afforded to enslaved people and other subordinate members of Athenian society. Unfortunately, we have no preserved speeches from *graphai hubreōs* and very few references to *hubris* suits that came to trial, making it difficult to know how often such cases were brought, both in general and specifically on behalf of members of particular status groups.[39] For this reason, what I will try to do is determine how *likely* it would have been for a person of any given status to receive justice after suffering *hubris*. To do so, I will consider the incentives and obstacles in bringing a *graphē hubreōs* that might have existed either for the victim of *hubris* or for someone acting on his or her behalf. The incentives are perhaps obvious—bringing this kind of suit was a way to preserve one's own honour or that of someone one wanted to protect—but, as we shall see, the potential obstacles were manifold. In what follows, I will proceed 'upward' in status, moving from the most subordinated enslaved people to the most elite citizens.

As mentioned above, enslaved people could not bring lawsuits themselves (apart from commercial suits in the mid-fourth century); they would have needed to rely on another person to bring a *graphē hubreōs* for them. However, if their owner were the one treating them with *hubris*, it is very unlikely that a *graphē* would be brought:[40] an owner obviously would not bring a suit against himself, and one would think that others would generally be reluctant to bring a suit, explicitly on behalf of an enslaved person, against the latter's owner—in part because they probably had their own slaves at home whom they treated however they wished, in part because doing so might stir up enmity from the defendant, who would be likely to retaliate with another suit or by some other means.[41] Most

---

[34] See, e.g., Lanni (2016: 88–93) (the law's concern was with prohibiting behaviour that posed a threat to the democracy); Ober (2012: 840–3) (*hubris* threatened the collective civic dignity of the *dēmos*); Canevaro (2018 = 2019) (*hubris* against anyone, including slaves, entailed overestimating one's claims to *timē*, thereby violating community standards); Kapparis (2019: 97) (the law's purpose was 'to safeguard the rules of civilized society').

[35] See, e.g., Mactoux (1988: 336–8); Murray (1990: 145).    [36] Dmitriev (2016).
[37] Fisher (1995: 48–62).    [38] Todd (1993: 189–90).
[39] See also Kapparis (2018: 158–61, 238–41; 2019: 223–5) on the slim evidence for *graphai hubreōs*; he argues that it is unlikely these suits came to court at all.
[40] Instead, an enslaved person treated with *hubris* by his or her owner might seek refuge in a sanctuary in the hope of acquiring a new owner: see Forsdyke (2021: 229; Chapter 7, this volume).
[41] Enslaved people did, however, find other ways to collude with third parties who might rescue them from their owners: see Forsdyke (2018; 2021: 223–35; Chapter 7, this volume).

realistically, then, a *graphē hubreōs* would have been brought only against an individual who had committed *hubris* against someone *else*'s slave.[42] But what incentive would an owner have had to bring a *graphē hubreōs* on his slave's behalf rather than another kind of suit? Given the financial risk inherent in bringing any kind of *graphē* (namely, the penalty for not getting enough votes), and the difficulty in proving that someone acted with the intent to insult (especially with the intent to insult a slave!), the owner would have stood a much better chance of winning a private suit for property damage (a *dikē blabēs*). Moreover, with the latter, and unlike with a *graphē hubreōs*, he would have seen a financial payout if he won.

How do we explain, then, Demosthenes' claim in *Against Meidias* that the Athenians 'have punished with death many men [πολλούς]' who have, contrary to the law, treated enslaved people with *hubris* (Dem. 21.49)? To unpack this statement, we have to keep in mind its context: it is part of a hypothetical scenario posited by Demosthenes, in which he says that, if an Athenian were to bring the *hubris* law to the very *barbaroi* (foreigners) from whom the Greeks get their slaves, these foreigners would surely be so impressed by the Athenians' civility that they would want to appoint the Athenians as their *proxenoi* (ambassadors) (Dem. 21.48-50). This is, of course, a ludicrous situation, in a number of respects: first, it is very unlikely that an Athenian spokesman would travel to 'barbarian' lands to read aloud Athenian laws to them, and it is technically impossible for these peoples to select *all* Athenians as their *proxenoi*.[43] It is, then, within this improbable scenario that Demosthenes speculates about what the spokesman might say to these *barbaroi*: namely, that the Athenians are so benevolent and civilized that, even in the face of hostility from foreign peoples, they nonetheless refuse to treat the slaves purchased from these lands with *hubris*, and have even made a law against it. In fact, the spokesman would claim, they had already put to death 'many men who have transgressed the law' (Dem. 21.49). Everything about this episode is over the top, and I am inclined to think this statement is an exaggeration as well.[44] This is not to say that violence against enslaved people could not be considered hubristic—it certainly could[45]—just that we should not accept

---

[42] Harrison (1968: 172); Todd (1993: 189–90); Harris (2013: 225); Lanni (2016: 93–8).

[43] It is true that Mausolos, satrap of Caria, along with his wife/sister Artemisia, awarded proxeny to the entire polis of Knossos (RO no. 55), but such a grant to a state is highly unusual; as Rhodes and Osborne (2003: 264) write, Mausolos and Artemisia acted either 'from ignorance or by a deliberate stretching of the concept'. I thank Samuel Gartland for bringing this inscription to my attention.

[44] See also MacDowell (1990: 269 (ad loc. Dem. 21.49)): 'it is surprising if many free men were really put to death for treating slaves with *hybris*. No instance is known to us.'

[45] For example, in his speech *Against Konon*, Ariston says that Konon's sons were abusive to Ariston's slaves (ἀκολούθους), 'omitting no brutality or *hubris*', and then turned this violence against his (Ariston's) men (Dem. 54.4). It should be noted, however, that, while Ariston is bringing an assault charge against Konon, he is not charging Konon's sons with *hubris*.

at face value this claim that many people were actually brought to court and convicted of *hubris* against slaves.

But, even if 'many men' were not tried for *hubris* against slaves, might it at least have happened sometimes? Edward Cohen has argued that it did, citing *hubris* suits that he says were brought on behalf of enslaved people, as well as the Athenian ideal of coming to the defence of others.[46] He points, for example, to a passage of Deinarchos' speech *Against Demosthenes*, where Deinarchos says to the jury: 'You punished with death Themistios of Aphidna, because he assaulted [ὕβρισεν] the Rhodian lyre-player at the Eleusinian festival, and Euthymachos, because he put the Olynthian girl in a brothel' (Dein. 1.23).[47] We do not have any reason to assume, however, that either the Rhodian lyre-player or the Olynthian girl was necessarily enslaved.[48]

Cohen also points to an episode alluded to by both Demosthenes and Aeschines in their paired speeches about Aeschines' actions on the embassy to King Philip II of Macedon.[49] According to Demosthenes, the drunken guests at a symposium attended by Aeschines tried to make an Olynthian captive girl sing for them, as if she were a *hetaira* ('courtesan'[50]) or professional entertainer. But because she did not know how to sing, she became distressed (ἀδημονούσης) and refused to perform. Aeschines and another man, thinking she was acting too high and mighty for an Olynthian captive, ordered a slave to be brought in to whip her. She tried to utter something (εἰπούσης τι)—perhaps a plea for them to spare her—and began crying (δακρυσάσης), but to no avail: the slave tore off her dress and repeatedly whipped her bare back (Dem. 19.196–7). Beside herself (ἔξω...αὑτῆς) at this degrading treatment (τοῦ κακοῦ καὶ τοῦ πράγματος),[51] she sought the only justice she could: she fell, in desperation, to the knees of one of the guests, a man named Iatrokles, who Demosthenes says saved her from death (Dem. 19.198).

Aeschines, in turn, relates that Demosthenes accused (κατηγόρει) him of committing drunken violence (ὕβριν) on the girl (Aesch. 2.4, 154), and says that the people kicked (ἐξεβάλλετε) Demosthenes off the speakers' platform as he was making the accusation (αἰτίαν) (Aesch. 2.4). Aeschines also asserts that Demosthenes tried (unsuccessfully) to bribe an Olynthian man to testify falsely

---

[46] E. E. Cohen (2000: 160–6; 2014: 185–90; 2015: 126–9). That it probably happened at least 'on certain occasions', see Vlassopoulos (2021: 132–3).

[47] E. E. Cohen (2015: 126–7). On this episode, see also Glazebrook (2021).

[48] Moreover, despite the use of the verb ὑβρίζειν, it is not entirely clear that a *graphē hubreōs per se* was brought against either Themistios or Euthymachos.

[49] E. E. Cohen (2015: 127).

[50] Cf. Kennedy (2014: 68–74, 85–7; 2015), who objects to this translation of *hetaira*. She argues that the word originally referred to elite women who participated in sympotic culture and in time came to designate women, often metics, who acted independently of a *kurios*.

[51] Westgate (2015: 82) notes the girl's degradation of status in this episode from freeborn captive to *hetaira* to lowly slave; see similarly Hobden (2009: 75).

that Aeschines had committed this violence (2.154–5). It seems unlikely, then, that Demosthenes succeeded in bringing to trial a *graphē hubreōs* against Aeschines or the other symposiasts, though it is certainly possible he tried to do so. However, it should also be noted that this Olynthian girl is not a run-of-the-mill chattel slave: she is referred to as 'free' (ἐλευθέραν) by both men (Dem. 19.196; Aesch. 2.4), presumably referring to the fact that, although she is now a captive, she was born free, and Demosthenes even bestows the lofty adjectives 'attractive' (εὐπρεπῆ) and 'prudent' (σώφρονα) on her (Dem. 19.196). The girl's freeborn status—as well as the fact that she came from Olynthos (an ally of Athens), that the symposium took place in Macedon (with which Athens was in conflict), and, most importantly, that Demosthenes apparently did not actually bring a *graphē* to trial—means that this episode should not be taken as evidence for the likelihood of a *graphē hubreōs* being brought for an average slave.

Another potential *graphē hubreōs* on behalf of an enslaved person is mentioned in Aeschines' *Against Timarchos*, in which we hear about a suit for *hubris* involving an individual named Pittalakos, who at the time of the incident was either a (relatively privileged) public slave or perhaps already freed.[52] Aeschines tells the jury that the defendant, Timarchos, had been hired as a prostitute by the wealthy Pittalakos (1.54) until Timarchos was lured away by another man named Hegesandros (1.57). In his jealousy, Pittalakos began stalking Hegesandros' house (Aesch. 1.58), and Hegesandros and Timarchos responded by breaking into Pittalakos' home, destroying his property, tying Pittalakos to a pillar, and giving him a terrible whipping. The next day, Pittalakos sought refuge at the altar of the Mother of the Gods and was approached by Hegesandros and Timarchos, who persuaded him to get up, promising they would give him some sort of justice (Aesch. 1.59–62). But they never delivered on their promise, and so, according to Aeschines, Pittalakos 'brought a suit [δίκην...λαγχάνει] for *hubris* [ὕβριν]' against his abusers (1.62). However, when the case was about to come to trial, Hegesandros alleged that Pittalakos was actually his slave, which led to lawsuits between Hegesandros and a man named Glaukon, who defended Pittalakos' freedom. Eventually, Aeschines tells us, Pittalakos lost confidence in himself (καταμεμψάμενος ἑαυτόν), asking himself who he was (ἐκλογισάμενος ὅστις ὤν) to try to fight against such men, and decided not to pursue his case (1.62–4).

Unfortunately, we do not know exactly what kind of lawsuit Pittalakos attempted to bring against his attackers, or how he did so. Although Aeschines uses the word *hubris* in §62, suggesting that the suit may have been a *graphē hubreōs*, he also uses the word *dikē* (rather than *graphē*), which implies that it

---

[52] Enslaved: E. E. Cohen (2000: 131); Hunter (2006: 2–8); Ismard (2017: 69–70). Formerly enslaved: Jacob (1928: 158–62); Fisher (2004: 66–7; 2008); Vlassopoulos (2009: 352); Forsdyke (2018: 359). For further discussion, see Kamen (2013: 25–6).

might instead have been a private suit for damages (*blabēs*) or assault (*biaiōn*).[53] If Pittalakos was still enslaved at the time of the incident, he presumably could not have brought *any* kind of suit himself and would have needed to rely on someone else to do so for him.[54] (Who would that have been? As a public slave, his owner was the *polis*, so maybe it was Glaukon, who was clearly willing to act as his vindicator?[55]) If, on the other hand, Pittalakos had been manumitted by this point, he could have brought a *graphē hubreōs* or another kind of suit on his own behalf before the polemarch. Either way, the fact that Pittalakos was intimidated into dropping his suit reveals that, even if a privileged slave (or formerly enslaved person) had the *ability* to initiate a suit with the assistance of a citizen, he might have lacked the confidence to bring the case to court, let alone win it.[56] As Claire Taylor has pointed out, although the networks that Pittalakos formed were in many ways useful to him—earning him social capital and helpful friends like Glaukon—they were ultimately insufficient in the face of attacks from prominent citizens.[57] The possibility of being able to make use of the *graphē hubreōs*, then, provided Pittalakos with false hope, since it seemed to open a door that was in effect still closed. Indeed, this glimpse of an ultimately inaccessible right may have made him feel worse than if it had not been offered in the first place.

On the basis of these two stories—those of the Olynthian captive and Pittalakos—I think we can assert that it is at least *possible* that a *graphē hubreōs* might be brought on behalf of an enslaved person. At the same time, I do not think it is a coincidence that the only two circumstances we hear of where a *graphē hubreōs* may have been attempted—and, it should be noted, not even ultimately brought to court—involve a beautiful freeborn captive and a privileged public slave (or possibly someone who had already been manumitted).[58] That is, to the extent that a citizen might have been motivated to defend an enslaved person from *hubris*, there would have been greater incentive for him to do so for one of higher status.

Freed slaves, in turn, should have been in a better position than privileged slaves to take advantage of the *graphē hubreōs*, since as metics they could bring cases before the polemarch. That said, we have no definitive evidence for this happening. We have already discussed Pittalakos, who may have been a freed slave,

---

[53] Fisher (2001: 199–200 (ad loc. Aesch. 1.62)). See also E. E. Cohen (2015: 103, n.77), who states that Pittalakos brings a *dikē*; and Taylor (2015: 49–50), who suggests that it is a *dikē aikeias*.
[54] Cf. Hunter (2006: 6), who asserts that Pittalakos must have had the right to bring the suit himself *qua* public slave.
[55] See also Hunter (2006: 7), who suggests that Glaukon may have served as Pittalakos' 'protector' (if such a role, otherwise unattested, existed for public slaves).
[56] See similarly Fisher (1995: 70), who says that Pittalakos' dropped suit 'does not suggest that it would be easy for such privileged slaves, or for freed persons, to succeed in the courts, let alone for ordinary slaves'.
[57] Taylor (2015: 49–51). On the usefulness of Pittalakos' citizen connections, see also Forsdyke (2018: 358–60).
[58] Fisher (1995: 65) also makes this point.

and who appears to have at least attempted to bring a *graphē hubreōs* (or perhaps another kind of suit). The only other possible example we hear of is the formerly enslaved prostitute Neaira, who, according to Apollodoros (the main speaker in [Dem.] 59), confided in her client Stephanos about the abuse (ὕβριν) she had faced at the hands of her previous client Phrynion.[59] Afraid (φοβουμένη) of Phrynion and his wrath, she 'placed herself under the protection' (προΐσταται) of Stephanos, which may have involved making him her *prostatēs* ([Dem.] 59.37).[60] Stephanos reassured her that he would take care of her and boasted that Phrynion would regret it if he laid a hand on her again ([Dem.] 59.38). And indeed, shortly thereafter, when Phrynion tried to carry off Neaira as his slave, Stephanos protected her by asserting that she was in fact free ([Dem.] 59.40), similarly to what we saw in Glaukon's defence of Pittalakos. Once again, however, these actions entailed not a *graphē hubreōs* but another procedure, a 'taking-away into freedom' (ἀφαίρεσις εἰς ἐλευθερίαν), designed to rescue someone who had been wrongly claimed as a slave.[61] Thus, while Neaira succeeded in securing protection for herself, she did not see justice specifically for the earlier *hubris* committed against her. We might imagine, then, that this was a bittersweet victory for her, especially if she was aware that, technically at least, she should have been protected by the law on *hubris*.

It is possible that *freeborn* foreigners (especially male ones) stood a better chance than formerly enslaved metics of seeking redress for *hubris* they suffered. In fact, we have two examples of what might be *graphai hubreōs* involving (most likely freeborn) foreigners, although it is also possible they represent a different kind of public suit, that for an 'offence concerning a festival' (ἀδικεῖν περὶ τὴν ἑορτήν), which I will call for the sake of convenience a 'festival suit'.[62] I mentioned above that Themistios of Aphidna was put to death because he committed *hubris* (ὕβρισεν) against a Rhodian lyre-player—who was certainly a foreigner, less certainly enslaved—at the Eleusinian festival (Dein. 1.23). Given the venue of this assault, a festival suit may indeed have been most appropriate in this context. In the second instance, a Thespian man named Euandros, when he was in Attica for the Eleusinian Mysteries, lay hold of (ἐπελάβετο) a Carian man named Menippos, who owed him two talents after being defeated in an earlier mercantile case (Dem. 21.176). Menippos then brought a preliminary accusation (*probolē*) against him in the Assembly (Dem. 21.175), where the people voted against Euandros, and the matter proceeded to court. Apparently, the jury was ready to impose the death penalty, but they ultimately ruled instead that Euandros should forfeit the monetary award from the earlier case and pay damages in addition

---

[59] On the abuse faced by Neaira and her limited options for legal recourse, see Kennedy (2014: 103–6).
[60] For this interpretation of *proïstatai*, see Patteson (1978: ad loc.); Carey (1992: ad loc.).
[61] On the *aphairesis eis eleutherian*, see, e.g., Kamen (2013: 35–6); Gottesman (2014: 163–9).
[62] On this type of suit, see MacDowell (1990: 14–16).

(Dem. 21.176). Again, the suit Menippos brought *may* have been a *graphē hubreōs*, but it may just as well have been a festival suit or something else entirely.[63] Nonetheless, we might extrapolate from Menippos' successful navigation of the Athenian legal system that, even if the suit he brought was not a *graphē hubreōs*, it technically would have been feasible for him to bring one. If, however, he chose to bring a different kind of suit, it may have been because he thought that, as a foreigner, he had a slightly better chance of winning a festival suit: after all, no Athenian juror would want to take lightly a crime that took place at one of their festivals. It might also have been a hard case for Menippos to make that his honour had been deliberately slighted, especially because, as a metic, he was less likely to have a network of friends and family to attest to his standing.

Citizens, unsurprisingly, would have stood a much greater chance than enslaved people or metics of making use of the *graphē hubreōs*, but, even within the category of those who were citizens, the likelihood of its use may have depended on what type of citizen one was (for example, naturalized versus natural-born, child versus adult, woman versus man, poor versus rich). Interestingly, one of the few definite *graphai hubreōs* we hear about was brought by the aforementioned Apollodoros, the son of a formerly enslaved man named Pasion who was granted citizenship. Apollodoros appears to have been a bit touchy about his origins,[64] and it may be for this reason that he found it so insulting when his father's freed slave Phormion, who continued to run Pasion's bank and shield factory after Pasion had died, married Apollodoros' mother Archippe (Dem. 45.3). This arrangement, even though it had apparently been mandated by Pasion's will,[65] not only deprived Apollodoros of his inheritance but also, at least from Apollodoros' perspective, implicitly suggested that Apollodoros and his family were on the same footing as Phormion.[66] This made Apollodoros very angry (πόλλ' ἀγανακτήσας), and he could not bear it (χαλεπῶς ἐνεγκών) (Dem. 45.3). His response to this slight was to indict Phormion for *hubris* (γραφὴν... ὕβρεως γράφομαι), but the suit never actually came to trial. Apollodoros cites as the reason the postponement of the trial and the fact that his mother and Phormion had children in the meantime (Dem. 45.4), but we might speculate that he also thought he did not have a good chance of winning his case, either because of the jurors' bias against him as the son of a naturalized citizen[67] or because a *hubris*

---

[63] Harris (1992: 73–4) thinks that it is a *dikē blabēs*.
[64] Trevett (1992: 160) refers to Apollodoros' 'sensitivity about his own servile origins'.
[65] It was, moreover, not an unusual type of arrangement: see Dem. 36.28–30.
[66] Fisher (1992: 42) says the reason was the 'gross insult done to him by the deprivation of his estates and by the marriage, imposed by an allegedly forged will, of his mother to an ex-slave'.
[67] In another speech, Apollodoros says that he insisted on a fine rather than the death penalty in the case of a citizen who had wronged him, saying that he did not want it said that the son of a naturalized citizen was responsible for the death of an Athenian ([Dem.] 53.18).

accusation would have been especially hard to prove in this instance.[68] At any rate, it is possible that Apollodoros' (already present) feelings of status insecurity may have been stoked by his realization that he did not have as much protection against *hubris* as a natural-born citizen did.

Another category of citizen mentioned in the context of *hubris* legislation is (citizen) children: 'If anyone treats with *hubris* any person, either child or woman or man, free or slave...' (Dem. 21.47; cf. Aesch. 1.15). In fact, Aeschines specifically emphasizes the law's protection of children: 'If any Athenian shall commit *hubris* [ὑβρίσῃ] against a free-born child, the parent or guardian of the child shall prosecute him before the *thesmothetai*, and shall demand a specific penalty' (Aesch. 1.16). This part of the *hubris* law is considered not to be genuine, in part because it differs from the (probably authentic) law preserved in Dem. 21.47, in part because the documents in this speech are generally thought to be spurious.[69] I would add that it is unlikely that the *graphē hubreōs* would have been limited to the child's parent or guardian, as this law (or 'law') implies. Rather, it would have been open to anyone entitled to bring a *graphē*, even if the parent or guardian would have been the individual most invested in bringing it. We do hear once about individuals other than parents planning to bring a *graphē hubreōs* for *hubris* committed against a citizen child. In his speech *Against Nikostratos*, Apollodoros says that his enemy Nikostratos and his cronies sent an Athenian boy to pick flowers from Apollodoros' rose bed so that Apollodoros would put the boy in bonds or strike him, thinking he was a slave. The idea is that they would then have been able to indict Apollodoros for *hubris* (γραφήν με γράψαιντο ὕβρεως ([Dem.] 53.16). But Apodolloros did not fall for their scheme, and so they were not able to bring the suit. Interestingly, the logic of Nikostratos' plan seems to imply that a suit for *hubris* would in practice be brought only if the victim was a *freeborn* child, despite what the law on *hubris* states ('child... free or slave').[70]

The law on *hubris* also specifically mentions the protection of (citizen) women. While we never hear of *graphai hubreōs* being brought on behalf of female citizens, there is occasional mention of citizen women, often alongside one of their male family members, being treated with *hubris*. It should be noted, however, that in none of these instances is the action described as *hubris* the main charge of the suit. So, for example, in the speech *Against Simon*, the speaker says that, when his opponent Simon learned that his beloved Plataian boy was staying at his (the speaker's) house, Simon broke down the doors of the speaker's house and even

---

[68] Apollodoros probably made the right decision. In a different lawsuit, a speaker on behalf of Phormion asserts (in passing) that Apollodoros was the one who had committed *hubris* (Dem. 36.47), and one could imagine a similar argument being made by Phormion if Apollodoros had brought his *graphē hubreōs* to trial.

[69] MacDowell (1990: 263 (ad loc. Dem. 21.47)); Fisher (2001: 139 (ad loc. Aesch. 1.15–16)); van Wees (2011: 119).

[70] Both Todd (1993: 190) and Bers (2003: 62, n. 30) take this passage to mean that striking the boy would not have counted as *hubris* if he were enslaved.

dared to enter the women's chambers—all of which, including the implied insult to the women of the house, are described as *hubris* (Lys. 3.6). Similarly, in *Against Meidias*, Demosthenes describes the actions of Meidias and Thrasylochos—who burst into Demosthenes' house and used bad language in front of him, his sister, and his mother—as 'acts of *hubris*' (ὑβρίσματα) (Dem. 21.80). And, in the speech *On the Murder of Eratosthenes*, the speaker Euphiletos repeatedly says that Eratosthenes' adulterous liaisons with his (Euphiletos') wife constituted *hubris* (Lys. 1.2) against both himself and his wife (Lys. 1.4, 16, 25). But again, despite the use of *hubris* language, a *graphē hubreōs* was apparently not brought in any of these instances of women being insulted. Presumably a *hubris* suit could have been brought, especially in the case of a grievous offence like rape, but such cases either never came to court or simply have not been preserved.[71] In general, citizen women seem to have been plaintiffs or defendants in trials only infrequently, and, as mentioned above, they could not speak on their own behalf in court. It is perhaps in part for these reasons that we do not find citizen women featured as key players in *graphai hubreōs*. Additionally, we have to keep in mind that, for a male citizen, any desire to preserve the honour of his insulted female relative would have had to be weighed against the shame of calling further attention to the fact that she had been dishonoured. In most cases, regardless of how aggrieved a woman might have felt—and how aware she might have been that she was owed protection from *hubris*—it would probably have seemed more favourable for her reputation to limit her exposure to the publicity afforded by a trial.

Perhaps unsurprisingly, given both the importance of honour to male citizen identity and the fact that the vast majority of our preserved lawsuits concern male citizens, the bulk of our evidence for *graphai hubreōs* pertains to male citizens. Indeed, the only attested *graphē hubreōs* that we know made it to court involves *hubris* against a male citizen. In a lawsuit *On the Estate of Kiron* (Is. 8), the speaker (a grandson of Kiron) alleges that a certain Diokles not only illegally claimed Kiron's property but also imprisoned and disenfranchised (ἠτίμωσε) one of his own brothers-in-law (Is. 8.41). For the actions against his brother-in-law, Diokles was apparently indicted for *hubris* (γραφὴν ὕβρεως γραφείς), though he had not yet been punished (Is. 8.41). The speaker then says that the jury 'will learn' more about Diokles when 'we enter into [εἰσίωμεν] a suit [δίκην] against him' (Is. 8.44). If '*dikē*' here alludes loosely to the *graphē hubreōs* mentioned in §41,[72] we have to assume that the *hubris* suit against Diokles was still pending at the time of Is. 8. We do know that it eventually came to court, since the title (and a couple of lines) of a lawcourt speech by Lysias entitled 'Against Diokles, for *Hubris* [ὕβρεως]'

---

[71] See also Omitowoju (2002), who argues that, while technically a *graphē hubreōs* could be brought on behalf of a woman who had been raped (pp. 39–49), there are various reasons why a *kurios* would be reluctant to bring one (pp. 122–8). On *hubris* and sex, see also D. Cohen (1991; 1995: 143–62); Fisher (1992: 104–11).

[72] Wyse (1904: ad loc.); Forster (1927: 318–19); Edwards (2007: 145, n. 36).

survives. Assuming that it was the speaker of Is. 8 who brought this *hubris* suit, we can imagine he must have had a strong incentive to do so: not only defending the status of a fellow citizen (who, having been disenfranchised by Diokles, could not bring the *graphē* himself), but perhaps more importantly (and more self-interestedly) ensuring his own place in the circle of inheritance by getting Diokles out of the picture.

In a number of other instances, a lawsuit is brought for an action described as *hubris* without it being clear if the suit is, strictly speaking, a *graphē hubreōs*. The most prominent such example is Demosthenes' speech *Against Meidias*, in which Demosthenes accuses Meidias of slapping him at the theatre during the City Dionysia. The majority of scholars think this speech was delivered (if it was delivered at all), not in a *graphē hubreōs*, but in a festival suit,[73] though Edward Harris has argued in favour of identifying the suit as a *graphē hubreōs*, on the grounds that Demosthenes is clearly trying to show that Meidias committed *hubris*.[74] It is true that Demosthenes repeatedly describes Meidias' behaviour as *hubris*, but he also says that Meidias will argue that he (Demosthenes) *should have* brought a *graphē hubreōs* (Dem. 21.25), a statement that makes sense only if the current suit is *not* a *graphē hubreōs*. Similarly, in the speech *Against Konon*, the speaker Ariston says that his friends and relatives told him he *could* bring an *apagōgē* ('summary arrest') or a *graphē hubreōs* against his opponent, but they advised him not to take on a suit he was not equipped to handle at his young age, suggesting that he bring a *dikē aikeias* (a private suit for assault) instead (Dem. 54.1). Ariston follows their advice, but he never lets the jury forget that he could have brought a *graphē hubreōs*.[75] Thus, I think that, even if Dem. 21 is not a *graphē hubreōs*, it is clear that Demosthenes (like Ariston) could have brought this kind of suit for Meidias' actions. Perhaps he chose the indictment he did because he thought it would be easier to win.

A number of other incidents of *hubris* against citizens are alluded to where it is even less clear whether a *graphē hubreōs* was brought. For example, we hear of a man, the father of an archon and assessor (*paredros*) for his son, who was accused of a festival offence after he grabbed hold of (ἥψατο) a spectator at the City Dionysia and kicked him out of the theatre (Dem. 21.178). The victim brought a *probolē*, arguing that neither the man nor his son had the authority to treat him in this way. The Assembly voted against the assailant, but, because he died before the case came to trial, it is not entirely clear what kind of suit this would have been: either a *hubris* or a festival suit would have been possible. In another instance, we

---

[73] See, e.g., MacDowell (1990). That both the accusation before the Assembly and the subsequent trial were called *probolai*, see MacDowell (1990: 16).
[74] Harris (1992: 73–4; 2013: 210, 211; 2019). See also Canevaro (2018: 108 = 2019: 56).
[75] Ariston says, e.g., 'I think it has become clear in many ways that the blows I suffered were not ordinary or insignificant, but that I was in extreme danger because of the *hubris* [ὕβριν] and brutality [ἀσέλγειαν] of these men, and I have instituted a suit far less severe than appropriate' (Dem. 54.13).

are told that, after a man named Ktesikles drunkenly whipped another man—presumably a fellow citizen—during a procession, he was found guilty of having acted 'with *hubris*' and was sentenced to death (Dem. 21.180). The use of *hubris* language here might indicate that he was prosecuted with a *graphē hubreōs*, but again a festival suit would also have been appropriate. In a third instance, a fragmentary suit of Lysias that Dionysios of Halicarnassus calls a 'narrative of a type of *hubris*' (διήγησίν τινα...ὑβριστικήν), the speaker says that he and his friend Archippos went to a certain Teisis' house, where Teisis' cronies seized Archippos and fastened him onto a pillar. Teisis then struck Archippos with a whip and locked him in a room, and later ordered his slaves to tie Archippos to a pillar a second time and whip him again (Lys. fr. 279 Carey). The speech narrating this episode might be a *graphē hubreōs* (based on Dionysios' description), but it might also be something like a *dikē aikeias*.[76] At any rate, the treatment of Archippos—that is to say, his being treated like a slave—is certainly in keeping with what would have been considered hubristic behaviour.

Lastly, we sometimes hear about instances where it is evident that *hubris* was committed against a citizen, but it is unclear whether any kind of lawsuit was brought. For example, in *Against Meidias*, Demosthenes says that Meidias intends to mention previous victims of *hubris*, including a *prohedros* (chairman of the Assembly) who was hit by a certain Polyzelos at an Assembly meeting, and a *thesmothetēs* who was hit while rescuing a female piper from a drunk man (Dem. 21.36). However, we do not know whether lawsuits were actually brought in either of these instances, and, if they were, whether they were *graphai hubreōs*. Given that there was a recognition of *hubris* being inflicted, the most we can say is that these victims, or others on their behalf, *could have* brought suits for *hubris*. And it is possible, though not certain, that, as office-holders—a *prohedros* and a *thesmothetēs*—these individuals stood a better chance of making the case that an assault against them was especially dishonouring. Or, to put it another way, individuals acting in an official capacity on behalf of the *polis* probably faced the fewest obstacles to securing the rights promised them by the law on *hubris*.

## Conclusions

In sum, although subordinates in classical Athens were, as a general rule, deprived of the full range of legal protections granted to their superiors, they were, exceptionally, protected from *hubris*—even if it was less for their own sake than a side effect of a policy that was meant to benefit the *polis* as a whole. The reality, however, seems to have been that not everyone was in fact equally protected from

---

[76] Todd (2000: 347) suggests that it was a *dikē aikeias* because the word *dikē* is used, and on analogy with Dem. 54.1, where the speaker says he is bringing a *dikē aikeias* despite being treated with *hubris*.

*hubris*, in part because of the impediments faced in actually bringing a *graphē hubreōs* to trial. As we have seen, some individuals (for example, enslaved people) simply were not allowed to bring these suits and had to rely on someone else to do it for them (an unlikely scenario in the case of most enslaved people). Others could do so only with difficulty, either because of their lesser access to the courts, or because of a social stigma they bore, or both (for example, formerly enslaved people, freeborn metics, and possibly naturalized citizens). Even some citizens—whether because of their gender, their inexperience, or a lack of funds—may have felt it was safer to bring a different kind of suit, or no suit at all. There were, moreover, certain obstacles to bringing a *graphē hubreōs* that were faced by everyone. For example, as with all *graphai*, not securing one-fifth of the jury's votes would have incurred a hefty penalty, a measure that disincentivized everyone but the super-wealthy (and perhaps sometimes even them). In addition, bringing any kind of lawsuit not only was expensive but also ran the risk of stirring up animosity on the part of the defendant or his friends and family—and possibly also on the part of the jurors, who disdained those who were overly litigious. Finally, the specific charge of *hubris* may have been especially difficult to substantiate (it is very hard to prove intent, particularly intent to dishonour) and therefore less appealing than one of a number of charges that were easier to prove (for example, the *dikē aikeias*). For all of these reasons, even though everyone in Athens was theoretically protected by the law on *hubris*—and therefore had a way of preserving their honour, regardless of their legal status—this would probably not have been the case in practice. In fact, the variable access to a right that was notionally granted to all may have had the effect, intended or not, of upholding the status hierarchy.

## Works Cited

Akrigg, B. (2015). 'Metics in Athens', in Taylor and Vlassopoulos (2015: 155–73).

Bakewell, G. (1999). 'Lysias 12 and Lysias 31: Metics and Athenian Citizenship in the Aftermath of the Thirty', *Greek, Roman, and Byzantine Studies*, 40: 5–22.

Bers, V. (2003). *Demosthenes, Speeches 50–59*. Austin.

Blok, J. (2017). *Citizenship in Classical Athens*. Cambridge.

Cairns, D. L. (1993). *Aidōs: The Psychology and Ethics of Honour and Shame in Ancient Greek Literature*. Oxford.

Cairns, D. L. (1996). '*Hybris*, Dishonour and Thinking Big', *Journal of Hellenic Studies*, 116: 1–32.

Canevaro, M. (2018). 'The Public Charge for *Hybris* against Slaves: The Honour of the Victim and the Honour of the *Hybristēs*', *Journal of Hellenic Studies*, 138: 100–26.

Canevaro, M. (2019). 'L'accusa pubblica di *hybris* contro gli schiavi: L'onore della vittima e l'onore dell'*hybristes*', *Rivista di diritto ellenico*, 9: 43–90.

Canevaro, M., and E. M. Harris (2019). 'The Authenticity of the Document at Demosth., *In Mid.* XXI.47', *Rivista di Diritto Ellenico*, 9: 91–108.

Carey, C. (1992). *Apollodoros Against Neaira [Demosthenes] 59*. Warminster.

Cecchet, L. (2015). *Poverty in Athenian Public Discourse: From the Rise of the Peloponnesian War to the Rise of Macedonia*. Stuttgart.

Cohen, D. (1991). 'Sexuality, Violence and the Athenian Law of *Hubris*', *Greece and Rome*, 38: 171–88.

Cohen, D. (1995). *Law, Violence, and Community in Classical Athens*. Cambridge.

Cohen, E. E. (1973). *Ancient Athenian Maritime Courts*. Princeton.

Cohen, E. E. (2000). *The Athenian Nation*. Princeton.

Cohen, E. E. (2014). 'Sexual Abuse and Sexual Rights: Slaves' Erotic Experience at Athens and Rome', in T. Hubbard (ed), *A Companion to Greek and Roman Sexualities*, 184–98. Malden, MA.

Cohen, E. E. (2015). *Athenian Prostitution: The Business of Sex*. Oxford.

Cooper, C. (2003). '"Worst of all he's an Egyptian"', *Syllecta Classica*, 14: 59–81.

Davies, P. A. (2017). 'Articulating Status in Ancient Greece: Status (In)consistency as a New Approach', *Cambridge Classical Journal*, 63: 29–52.

Deene, M. (2014). 'Let's Work Together! Economic Cooperation, Social Capital, and Chances of Social Mobility in Classical Athens', *Greece and Rome*, 61: 152–73.

Dmitriev, S. (2016). 'The Protection of Slaves in the Athenian Law against *Hubris*', *Phoenix*, 70: 64–76.

Edwards, M. (2007). *Isaeus*. Austin.

Fisher, N. (1976). '*Hybris* and Dishonour: I', *Greece and Rome*, 23: 177–93.

Fisher, N. (1992). *Hybris: A Study in the Values of Honour and Shame in Ancient Greece*. Warminster.

Fisher, N. (1995). '*Hybris*, Status and Slavery', in A. Powell (ed), *The Greek World*, 44–84. London.

Fisher, N. (2001). *Aeschines, Against Timarchos*. Oxford.

Fisher, N. (2004). 'The Perils of Pittalakos: Settings of Cock Fighting and Dicing in Classical Athens', in S. Bell and G. Davies (eds), *Games and Festivals in Classical Antiquity*, 65–78. Oxford.

Fisher, N. (2005). 'Body-Abuse: The Rhetoric of *Hybris* in Aeschines' *Against Timarchos*', in J.-M. Bertrand (ed), *La violence dans les mondes grec et romain*, 67–89. Paris.

Fisher, N. (2006). 'Citizens, Foreigners, Slaves', in K. Kinzl (ed), *A Companion to the Classical Greek World*, 327–49. Malden, MA.

Fisher, N. (2008). 'The Bad Boyfriend, the Flatterer, and the Sykophant: Related Forms of the "*Kakos*" in Democratic Athens', in I. Sluiter and R. Rosen (eds), *KAKOS, Badness and Anti-Value in Classical Antiquity*, 185–231. Leiden.

Forsdyke, S. (2018). 'Slave Agency and Citizenship in Classical Athens', in G. Thür, U. Yiftach, and R. Zelnick-Abramovitz (eds), *Symposion 2017: Vorträge zur griechischen und hellenistischen Rechtsgeschichte*, 345–66. Vienna.

Forsdyke, S. (2021). *Slaves and Slavery in Ancient Greece*. Cambridge.

Forster, E. (1927) (ed and trans). *Isaeus*. Cambridge, MA.

Glazebrook, A. (2021). 'Female Sexual Agency and an Enslaved "Olynthian": Demosthenes 19.196-98', in D. Kamen and C. W. Marshall (eds), *Slavery and Sexuality in Classical Antiquity*, 141-58. Madison.

Gottesman, A. (2014). *Politics and the Street in Democratic Athens*. Cambridge.

Harris, E. M. (1992). Review of MacDowell (1990), *Classical Philology*, 87: 71-80.

Harris, E. M. (2013). 'The *Against Meidias* (Dem. 21)', in M. Canevaro (ed), *The Documents in the Attic Orators: Laws and Decrees in the Public Speeches of the Demosthenic Corpus*, 209-36. Oxford.

Harris, E. M. (2019). '*Hybris* nelle corti giudiziarie ateniesi: Il profilo legale dell'accusa nella *Contro Midia* di Demostene', *Rivista di diritto ellenico*, 9: 43-90.

Harrison, A. (1968). *The Law of Athens*, i. London.

Hobden, F. (2009). '*Symposion* and the Rhetorics of Commensality in Demosthenes 19, *On the False Embassy*', in C. Mann, M. Haake, and R. von den Hoff (eds), *Rollenbilder in der athenischen Demokratie*, 71-87. Wiesbaden.

Hunter, V. (2006). 'Pittalacus and Eucles: Slaves in the Public Service of Athens', *Mouseion*, 6: 1-13.

Ismard, P. (2017). *Democracy's Slaves: A Political History of Ancient Greece*, trans. J. Todd. Cambridge, MA.

Jacob, O. (1928). *Les esclaves publics à Athèns*. Liège.

Kamen, D. (2013). *Status in Classical Athens*. Princeton.

Kamen, D. (2020). *Insults in Classical Athens*. Madison.

Kapparis, K. (2018). *Prostitution in the Ancient Greek World*. Berlin.

Kapparis, K. (2019). *Athenian Law and Society*. London.

Kennedy, R. F. (2014). *Immigrant Women in Athens: Gender, Ethnicity, and Citizenship in the Classical City*. London.

Kennedy, R. F. (2015). 'Elite Citizen Women and the Origins of the *Hetaira* in Classical Athens', *Helios*, 42: 61-79.

Lanni, A. (2006). *Law and Justice in the Courts of Classical Athens*. Cambridge.

Lanni, A. (2016). *Law and Order in Ancient Athens*. Cambridge.

Lape, S. (2010). *Race and Citizen Identity in the Classical Athenian Democracy*. Cambridge.

Leão, D., and P. J. Rhodes (2015). *The Laws of Solon: A New Edition with Introduction, Translation and Commentary*. London.

Lewis, D. (2018). *Greek Slave Systems in their Eastern Mediterranean Context, c.800-146 BC*. Oxford.

MacDowell, D. (1978). *The Law in Classical Athens*. Ithaca, NY.

MacDowell, D. (1990). *Demosthenes against Meidias*. Oxford.

McHardy, F. (2008). *Revenge in Athenian Culture*. Athens.

Mactoux, M.-M. (1988). 'Lois de Solon sur les esclaves et formation d'une société esclavagiste', in T. Yuge and M. Doi (eds), *Forms of Control and Subordination in Antiquity*, 331–54. Leiden.

Meyer, E. A. (2010). *Metics and the Athenian* Phialai-*Inscriptions: A Study in Athenian Epigraphy and Law*. Stuttgart.

Murray, O. (1990). 'The Solonian Law of *Hubris*', in P. Cartledge, P. Millett, and S. Todd (eds), *Nomos: Essays in Athenian Law, Politics and Society*, 139–45. Cambridge.

Ober, J. (1989). *Mass and Elite in Democratic Athens: Rhetoric, Ideology, and the Power of the People*. Princeton.

Ober, J. (2012). 'Democracy's Dignity', *American Political Science Review*, 106: 827–46.

Omitowoju, R. (2002). *Rape and the Politics of Consent in Classical Athens*. Cambridge.

Patterson, C. (1986). '*Hai Attikai*: The Other Athenians', in M. Skinner (ed), *Rescuing Creusa: New Methodological Approaches to Women in Antiquity*. A Special Issue of *Helios*, 13: 49–67.

Patterson, C. (2000). 'The Hospitality of Athenian Justice: The Metic in Court', in V. Hunter and J. Edmondson (eds), *Law and Social Status in Classical Athens*, 93–112. Oxford.

Patteson, A. J. (1978). 'Commentary on [Demosthenes] LIX: Against Neaira'. Ph.D. dissertation. Pennsylvania.

Rhodes, P. J. (1981). *Commentary on the Aristotelian* Athenaion Politeia. Oxford.

Rhodes, P. J., and R. Osborne (2003). *Greek Historical Inscriptions 404–323 BC*. Oxford (= RO).

Rubinstein, L. (2018). 'Immigration and Refugee Crises in Fourth-Century Greece: An Athenian Perspective', *European Legacy*, 23: 5–24.

Steinhauer, J. (2014). *Religious Associations in the Post-Classical Polis*. Stuttgart.

Taylor, C. (2015). 'Social Networks and Social Mobility in Fourth-Century Athens', in Taylor and Vlassopoulos (2015: 35–53).

Taylor, C. (2017). *Poverty, Wealth, and Well-Being: Experiencing* Penia *in Democratic Athens*. Oxford.

Taylor, C., and K. Vlassopoulos (2015) (eds). *Communities and Networks in the Ancient World*. Oxford.

Todd, S. (1993). *The Shape of Athenian Law*. Oxford.

Todd, S. (2000). *Lysias*. Austin.

Trevett, J. (1992). *Apollodoros, the Son of Pasion*. Oxford.

van Wees, H. (2011). 'The "Law of *Hybris*" and Solon's Reform of Justice', in S. Lambert (ed), *Sociable Man: Essays on Ancient Greek Social Behaviour in Honour of Nick Fisher*, 117–44. Swansea.

Vlassopoulos, K. (2009). 'Slavery, Freedom and Citizenship in Classical Athens: Beyond a Legalistic Approach', *European Review of History/Revue européenne d'histoire*, 16: 347–63.

Vlassopoulos, K. (2011). 'Greek Slavery: From Domination to Property and Back Again', *Journal of Hellenic Studies*, 131: 115–30.

Vlassopoulos, K. (2021). *Historicising Ancient Slavery*. Edinburgh.

Westgate, R. (2015). 'Space and Social Complexity in Greece from the Iron Age to the Classical Period', *Hesperia*, 84: 47–95.

Whitehead, D. (1977). *The Ideology of the Athenian Metic*. Cambridge.

Wyse, W. (1904). *The Speeches of Isaeus*. Cambridge.

# 10
# Strategies of Disenfranchisement
## 'Citizen' Women, Minor Heirs, and the Precarity of Status in Attic Oratory

*Rebecca Futo Kennedy*

### Preface

Although women and children appear frequently in extant Athenian orations, we rarely know more about them than what appears in the speeches that remain. What is said about them is frequently taken at face value, as if the women were as represented: foreigners perpetrating illegal marriages, whores laying illegal claims to estates through fake marriages or illegitimate children, or nameless women and children of uncertain status. In inheritance disputes, these women and children can stand between speakers and the estates they claim; it is hardly surprising that speakers present a remarkably biased narrative about them. And yet these texts have traditionally been used to construct not only our working knowledge of laws for inheritance and heirs/heiresses, which presume women's subordination to male heirs (regardless of how distant the relation), but also the limited statuses that scholars believe women and children were able to occupy in classical Athens. In most cases, this procedure must ignore the biases of the texts and the strategies that the speakers are using to undermine the credibility and status of these women. This approach gives the speeches a level of credibility as evidence that is unwarranted, since we lack any control for their claims. Structural biases must be assessed, and these can be understood better by looking at the persistence of specific rhetorical strategies for disinheriting and, in some cases, disenfranchising women and children.

Additionally, our own biases as readers of these speeches needs to be considered. Why do we generally believe the sordid tales of these women? Part of the reason for this is the unexamined positionality of scholars. With few exceptions, the study of Athenian law and courtroom speeches has been dominated by men, and academics generally tend to be of higher socio-economic statuses. Few of us come from the working classes, even fewer are women from the working classes. As a result, there is a tendency to invest those with similar standing to the scholar with value, believing the speakers over their targets. This unexamined position of the scholar is sometimes called 'objectivity', while acknowledging one's position is considered 'political'. Claiming that the positionality of the scholar does not inform or bias our interpretations is itself a political position, which claims an unacknowledged default state of neutrality for those who identify with the status quo. My own status as a first-generation, woman scholar whose grandmother was an immigrant, single mother and worked as a barmaid has informed my approach to these texts, in part because I relate to these women and the potential harms they are being subjected to by the prejudices both of the speaker and of scholars.[1] One party in each speech is misrepresenting status, either their own or another's. Scholars have generally assumed it is the women targeted in the speeches who are lying.[2] I am assuming the opposite.

## Introduction

In 1977 *Classical Quarterly* published David Schaps's essay 'The Women Least Mentioned: Etiquette and Women's Names'. In this relatively short philological study of women named in Athenian oratory and comedy from the fifth and fourth centuries BCE, Schaps argued that women were named in public discourses like the courts and on stage only if they were dead, were non-citizens, were being presented as women of questionable sexual status (like sex workers), or if the name was essential to the argument. As a result, he concluded, if we see a living woman named in forensic oratory or comedy, with rare exceptions, we can assume the speaker viewed her not as a 'respectable' woman, but as one of 'ill-repute'. This conclusion has been highly influential, and, unfortunately, too often understood to mean that the women mentioned *were* disreputable and probably sex workers, as opposed to just being subjected to disrespectful treatment by a speaker.[3] This unfortunate interpretation of Schaps's findings stems from a fundamentally flawed assumption that forensic oratory and comic plays represent straightforwardly the reality of the people who appear in them. Searching for ways to classify the status of the women, scholars have given the weight of truth to information from women's antagonists in the courts, men whose own reputations were often either unsavoury or completely unknown, with their tendentious

---

[1] For an explanation of the interplay between my personal positionality and research on women in ancient Athens, see Kennedy (2020).

[2] There are, of course, always exceptions. They will be cited throughout this chapter.

[3] We might consider the scholarship on [Dem.] 59 *Against Neaira* generally as a primary example, but also scholarship on the Lemnian woman Theoris. See Kennedy (2014: chs 4, 5, with references). Eidinow (2015) offers a nuanced approach to some of the most well-known cases of women said in the orations to be prostitutes. Faraguna (2014: 174) on naming practices repeats Schaps's assessment that the women are being marked as 'of shady reputation' if named in the courts. And, despite the article purporting to be on 'citizens, non-citizens, or slaves', it actually provides evidence only on male citizens, providing one paragraph of discussion of slaves and metics and, other than the brief statement on women in court speeches, ignores women in epigraphic and other material entirely, where we have thousands of examples of women's identity practices.

arguments made in search of profit (or laughs). And, yet, we take their words as if they are clear evidence for the lives, behaviours, and status of the targets of their animosity and legal strategies.

We should also be suspicious of scholarship that depends on categories like 'respectable', since this is a purely subjective and historically contingent concept. What it may have been in the nineteenth century when many of our dictionaries and commentaries were written does not necessarily translate to classical Athens. Instead, we need to figure out what behaviours or situations might qualify a woman for derision in public and what such derision was intended to imply. Traditionally, on the side of 'respectability', scholars have placed the wives, mothers, daughters, and, at times, widows of the propertied classes, who were not required or expected to work outside the home and who had male representation in the courts. In most cases, these meant the wives, mothers, and daughters of citizens— though wealthy women among the metics (permanent non-citizen residents) could also acquire some trappings of 'respectability'.[4] 'Woman of ill-repute' is, of course, an old euphemism for sex worker, as if there were no spaces for women to inhabit in-between the well-to-do citizen wife and the woman who sells sex for financial support. The speakers in the Athenian courts play with this binary and construct it to their own ends, and scholars have, by and large, accepted it as reality.

There is good reason, however, to reject the simple respectability binary. Those in power frequently construct strict definitions of the 'proper' in order to silence and denigrate outsiders. An outsider can be anyone who is not a property-owning, male citizen. The silencing and denigration can be based on gender, race, ethnicity, class, or any number of other factors, alone or in combination, and we find in forensic oratory all these factors used as grounds for why a speaker should or should not be believed and supported. The speeches themselves construct the category of respectability; it is not an inherently obvious status. If we start from the common premise that speakers are giving us accurate, unbiased insight into the lives of the women, that any woman named is not a legitimate citizen but is a sex worker or scam artist (or both) whose children are illegitimate, we erase the visible traces of how law, economics, and status worked in Athens to maintain power, wealth, and property in the hands of a small group of elite citizen men. We fail to understand how speakers' strategies functioned to maintain their own status. We take their status for granted as a norm, as natural or neutral, and mistake their grasping at privilege for a justified self-defence of that norm. We reinforce their power and status by accepting their words as truth, while failing to listen to the silenced and invisible objects of their attacks, who can speak to us only between the lines.

---

[4] The notion of an easily definable idea of 'respectable' for women in our ancient Athenian sources has bedevilled scholars since the nineteenth century. It was S. Pomeroy (1975), however, who encoded the term absolutely within the framework of being a wife—daughters, mothers, and widows are all just variations of or potential wives. See Kennedy (2014) for a refutation (with bibliography) of this framework. For a more nuanced view of statuses in Athens (generally, not only of women), see Kamen (2013).

In this chapter, I examine a series of inheritance and property disputes recorded in Athenian orations from the fourth century BCE involving women and children. Each of the cases under discussion involves a male relative using the courts to gain an inheritance from a distant relation, an inheritance that originally fell to a woman or child.[5] These are not criminal cases; it is not clear that anyone in the cases has broken a law necessarily. The speakers may accuse their targets of having committed some crime along the way, but this is incidental to the cases at hand, which are disputes over inheritance. The laws of Athens surrounding inheritance and property ownership are premised on the subordinate status of women, even citizen women. In all cases, if there is a male citizen who can lay claim to the estate, this takes precedence over the needs of the woman and her children. These cases are about silencing women who resist this subordination and returning them to a more dependent state.

Central to this examination, I discuss the speakers' strategies for (or against) disenfranchisement. Even if incidental to the cases themselves, disenfranchisement could be the eventual outcome for the women and/or children involved; erasure from citizen status meant potential sale into enslavement.[6] Even though the women and children are supposedly citizens and of the propertied classes with male representation (therefore supposedly among the 'respectable'), their citizenship and position are shown in these speeches to be precarious and their claims to inheritance subordinate to those of less closely related male citizens.[7] It is necessary to remember that the speakers are not honest reporters, but deploying a strategy. They are using the language, even if slanderous, that they think will be most effective in winning their cases regardless of the truth, careless of the fact that the children and women targeted may be left bereft of resources and, in some cases, without citizenship. Athenian legal disputes rarely can be said to be aiming for a discovery of truth—they are not modern investigatory actions, but function on assumptions of plausibility that align with, reinforce, and support the status quo of elite citizen men's power and wealth, while coopting the male jurors through shared prejudices against, in these cases, a female (and supposedly non-citizen) other.

Some scholars have assumed that the citizenship law of 451 BCE increased the standing and importance of woman as citizens[8] and that, based on the arguments

---

[5] See Cudjoe (2010) for a fuller treatment of cases involving widows and orphans. His focus is on reconstructing the legal frameworks surrounding these types of inheritance cases.

[6] Proving adultery could result in a type of 'partial disenfranchisement' according to Kamen (2013: 90–1), in that the women so convicted were not protected from public abuse, a form of *atimia* (dishonour).

[7] For a brief discussion of this idea previously, see Foxhall (1996: 140). Just (1989) seems to me a bit optimistic at times in the demarcation and stability of citizen versus non-citizen statuses for women in Athens.

[8] e.g. Osborne (1997); Burton (2003); Blok (2005). Boegehold (1994) looks at the law specifically with reference to inheritance of property. Blok (2017: ch. 4) provides a fuller view of what she argues women's citizenship entailed.

made by the speaker of Dem. 43,[9] women's births and marriages would have been recorded by tribes or demes. But this seems not to have been the case at all—unlike for men, registering for women was the exception, not the rule.[10] We must be careful not to make general assumptions about all women in Athens based on speeches that are concentrated into a roughly fifty-year period in the fourth century BCE. Laws and social mores shift and change over time. Between 380 BCE and 360 BCE marriage by citizen men to metic women was banned, suggesting that mixing between citizens and non-citizens was being more heavily policed than in previous decades. This attitude is reflected in the arguments of numerous extant property disputes from the fourth century.

Further, the families involved in these cases are from a narrow subset of the Athenian population—those who have property to dispute in the courts, who could afford to pay a speech-writer like Isaeus, and who failed to come to an agreement in arbitration. How does this sample of cases reflect practices and risks among the less wealthy within Athens, especially those who did not own property? If registering women citizen births was not a common practice even among propertied families, how was women's citizenship monitored overall? Did women bear the burden of proving their citizenship at every level of society or were these battles only among the elite because the stakes were so high? The terminology of 'ill-repute' is frequently conflated with foreignness and with low economic status.[11] Thus, proving that a woman was a citizen meant proving that a woman was a daughter or wife of a citizen man, implying that propertied citizen men did not necessarily consider women among the lower classes to be fully citizens.[12] And proving status was almost exclusively done through either witnesses or appeals to character.[13] The rhetoric explored in this chapter, therefore, will be shown to deploy social and economic prejudices to undermine legal realities within the private lawsuits of the propertied, but the strategies used for trying to show how these women and children were either foreign or of the wrong class suggest that women of all socio-economic statuses in Athens were at risk of having their citizenship questioned, particularly if they worked.[14]

---

[9] Discussed below in detail.

[10] We have as evidence for female enrolment in a *phratry* only a reference in Dem. 43. We have no contemporary references to deme registration of women. It seems to be generally assumed in all other cases that this practice was either non-existent or only among certain elite families. See Patterson (1987 *passim*); Kamen (2013: 87–96).

[11] Kennedy (2014: 97–122).

[12] The debates over whether women were legally considered to be citizens has been persuasively decided in favour of citizenship with a difference (see Kamen 2013: 87–96 for summary with references; also Patterson 1987).

[13] See Humphreys (1985). Scafuro (1994) discusses a number of cases mentioned in this chapter in the light of accusations of false witnessing. Faraguna (2014) gives a brief overview of the use of patronymics, demotics, and other such markers (like phratry) in confirming identities.

[14] On prejudices against certain women's (and men) work, see Kennedy (2014: 123–161); Taylor (2017: 119–121).

Most of the cases here demonstrate that it was not just women in the working and non-citizen classes whose lives were precarious, but that even women and minors from wealthy citizen families could inhabit grey areas between citizenship and non-citizenship. For women more so than men, identity rested at an intersection of their gender, status, and perceived ethnicity, but even women at the top of the social order, who had seemingly performed the expected duties of a citizen woman by marrying and bearing citizen children, did not necessarily earn stability. They could still be subject to the whims of the citizen men in power—their uncles, distant cousins, even complete strangers. In a number of speeches, orators invoke the status of women closer to this centre of citizen power—the wives and daughters of the jurymen—arguing that their status will be preserved by convicting a foreign woman like Neaira (who was also once an enslaved sex worker) of pretending to be a citizen ([Dem.] 59).[15] But inheritance cases often attempt to assimilate women from wealthy citizen families to foreign or enslaved sex workers as a strategy for stealing their inheritances.[16] Kamen has stated that 'downward mobility was also possible, if uncommon'.[17] I suggest here that it may not be as uncommon as we would like to think. And, even if these cases are outliers owing to the wealth involved, the reasoning used in them seems to reflect prejudices that would have needed to appeal to a large citizen jury made up of all socio-economic backgrounds to work.[18]

What follows is speculative, and for a good reason: these women and children, while real people who once lived, have not left us evidence outside of the tendentious speeches of their opponents. We will never know the truth of their lives or their experiences for certain, only the plausible reality that the orators who mention them (sometimes named, sometimes not) create. We need to engage our sources with scepticism and acknowledge that 'facts' will only evade us, and so we must try to see what might be construed as the 'possible' for these women. This should be distinguished from what has been referred to as gossip—talk with 'implicit moral judgements—meant to criticize, to scandalize, or to abuse'.[19] This talk may lie behind the arguments used in court to an extent, but some of the

---

[15] After providing an extensive narrative of Neaira's supposedly lurid life, Apollodoros, especially at [Dem.] 59.110, invokes 'how-could-you-look-your-wives-and-daughters-in-the-eye' as a strategy, after also relating the history of the grant of citizenship to the Plataeans as a reason for why the jury should find her guilty of violating the citizen–metic boundary. See Kennedy (2014) for discussion and references on the policing of this boundary with respect to metic women.

[16] One case of possible interest that I will not discuss is Hyperides 1 *In Defence of Lycophron*, which presents an interesting attempt to prove adultery by a woman in the third year after her husband's death and the birth of an infant heir. The family members, after seeing that the child was unlikely simply to die of natural causes at this point, charge that the child is really the product of adultery. The text is fragmentary, so it is difficult to know the full story, but we should imagine such charges were not that unusual, even years after the fact.

[17] Kamen (2013: 93).

[18] There is debate over the composition of Athenian juries. See, e.g., Todd (1990).

[19] Hunter (1989a: 300; see also 1994: ch. 4).

material in the speeches is simply made up. Also, such talk ceases to be gossip when it is used in the lawcourts. At that point, it becomes legal (and potentially legalized) violence.

I refer to these women and children as 'real' only insofar as they really did exist in the world and lived a life of some sort, unlike imaginary women of poems, plays, philosophical treatises, and so on. But, oratory is often fictionalized, because it represents a version of people's reality, and we should not mistake the person presented to us for the reality of that person's existence. However, because there are real disputes in these texts, real outcomes and impacts, and real people involved, we can assume (in most cases) that the women and children we will discuss lived, breathed, suffered, and maybe even were involved in some of the activities the speakers say they were.

Additionally, I will be addressing only a subsection of a possible dozen cases that involve rhetoric of this type. In some cases, the texts are too fragmentary to address with any accuracy. In other cases, the status of the citizen women is so contested, as with the case of Archippe, mother of Apollodoros, that whether the inheritances do involve a citizen woman or not is hard to discern.[20] Each case here has been chosen because it clearly involves an estate that belonged to a citizen, because the women involved were citizen women, and because of the similarity of strategy involved in disputing the cases.

## The Family of Demosthenes

I begin with one of the more well-known inheritance cases from Athens, the case of Demosthenes the orator. We know the case well, because Demosthenes, as soon as he came of age, sued his guardians for mismanagement of his inheritance, leaving us several speeches, all from Demosthenes' perspective. Unusually with oratory, we know the outcome: Demosthenes won his case. Despite being delivered by a 20 year old, the scenario was plausible enough to sway the jury. Even stripping away the clear bias of a speech for the plaintiff, we can see the outline of the dangers to which mothers and their underage offspring were subject—even heirs of clearly acknowledged parentage, even when the women themselves came from elite families. The sums involved may have led, in fact, to more unscrupulous behaviour.

In *Against Aphobos I* (Dem. 27), Demosthenes explains the situation:

For my father Demosthenes, men of the jury, left behind property worth nearly fourteen talents, me aged 7, my sister aged 5, and our mother, who had brought

---

[20] Kamen (2013: 82–4, with references); Kennedy (2014: 100).

50 minae to the household. He had made plans concerning us, and when he was about to die, he placed all our affairs into the hands of Aphobos, Demophon, son of Demo (both of whom were nephews of his—one from his brother, the other from his sister) and, lastly, Therippides from Paiania, who was not related by birth, but was a friend since childhood. (Dem. 27.4)[21]

As part of the arrangement, Demosthenes' sister was to be given in marriage to Demophon along with 2 talents, possibly as the dowry, but the funds were to be given to him immediately and not upon his marriage to the then 5-year-old girl.[22] His mother, Kleoboulê, was willed 80 minae and marriage to Aphobos, who was granted the right to live in the home with Kleoboulê and the children and use of their belongings.[23] Aphobos did not marry Demosthenes' mother. Demosthenes also tells us that they administered his estates for their own profit over the years and left him with only the house, fourteen slaves, and 40 minae—a loss of nearly 92 per cent of his initial inheritance (27.8).[24]

The marriage arrangements made within the will seem not to be unusual in fourth-century Athens and were one of the primary options available for settling an estate in a will; the widow or daughter became the conduit through which the estate passed either to a close male relative or to a male child.[25] In the case of Kleoboulê, the reasoning for this type of arrangement was, according to Demosthenes, to bind his temporary guardians to them by the closer ties of family (ἡγούμενος, καὶ τούτους ἔτ' οἰκειοτέρους εἴ μοι ποιήσειεν, οὐκ ἂν χεῖρόν μ' ἐπιτροπευθῆναι ταύτης τῆς οἰκειότητος προσγενομένης; 'thinking that if he made these men still more a part of the family, they might administer my estate all the better due to the close ties of kinship' (27.5)). Events, however, did not play out the way the senior Demosthenes had planned. According to our sources (and reconstructed by both Virginia Hunter and Lin Foxhall), Aphobos moved into the house, managed to get control of Kleoboulê's dowry, but soon after moved out of the house again and lived separately and unmarried for the next decade until just before Demosthenes brought his case.[26]

Demosthenes presents the case initially as if his mother was rejected by Aphobos. Foxhall, however, suggests that widowhood was Kleoboulê's choice, that she herself rejected Aphobos—in which case, this is a strong assertion of independence by her and one that was seemingly a gamble made in the hopes of

---

[21] All translations are my own. Greek texts follow those found in the Loeb Classical Library.
[22] Δημοφῶντι δὲ τὴν ἐμὴν ἀδελφὴν καὶ δύο τάλαντ' εὐθὺς ἔδωκεν ἔχειν ('To Demophon he gave my sister and 2 talents to have immediately' (27.5)).
[23] 27.5: αὐτῷ δὲ τούτῳ τὴν μητέρα τὴν ἡμετέραν, καὶ προῖκά τ' ὀγδοήκοντα μνᾶς, καὶ τὴν οἰκίαν οἰκεῖν καὶ σκεύεσι χρῆσθαι τοῖς ἐμοῖς... 'to [Aphobos] himself, [he gave] my mother, and 80 minae, and the house to live in, and the use of our belongings'.
[24] Demosthenes goes on (27.10-11) to add up all that his father left (including in the total his mother's jewellery) to get to the total of 14 talents.
[25] Kamen (2013: 92). [26] Hunter (1989b); Foxhall (1996: 144–50).

preserving, rather than risking the loss of, both her own property and her son's estate.[27] Whatever the reason for this decision, no remarriage put her in a precarious situation regarding the protections of a *kurios* (legal guardian),[28] especially since she had no other male relatives to appeal to except her brother-in-law, her father Gylon being dead.[29] And it was the case that Kleoboulê and Demosthenes' sister were the subject of slander as a result of their unmarried and precarious legal and social position. In Dem. 21, *Against Meidias*, Demosthenes charges Meidias with abusive language against himself, his mother, and sister (21.79–81). It is likely this was not the only time he had to defend his family and their reputation, even after he had regained his squandered inheritance and become one of Athens's most important politicians. In fact, we see Kleoboulê's character questioned in political speeches against Demosthenes later in his career by Aeschines (2.78, 3.172–3) and Dinarchus (1.15), where Demosthenes is referred to as a 'son of a Scythian woman' because his mother was possibly a *metroxenê*, among other things, demonstrating how slanders and accusations in private cases could move into the rhetorical strategies of high politics.[30] Accusation of foreignness was a primary mode of attack on heiresses or claimants dependent upon descent through a woman.[31]

We will see this idea of foreign or suspicious birth leveraged by other speakers, used against women who were not the daughters of famous Athenian generals like Kleoboulê, women who were likely to be more easily targeted with such charges. Because it was uncommon even after the re-establishment of the Citizenship Law in 403 BCE to present daughters to the deme for recognition, status of citizenship for women was still based on witnesses. So, the status of the woman, any witnesses she may have, and any family she may have had were

---

[27] The only full study of widowhood in classical Athens is Cudjoe (2010). Kleoboulê's ability to maintain her own independence of action and control over her own property and her daughter's position seems to have been dependent on her maintaining a fiction of still being married to Demosthenes' father by remaining in the house and unmarried. Kamen (2013: 92) assumes that this was one of the standard options for a widow, but it seems to have come at much risk, according to Cudjoe.

[28] All citizen women in Athens were expected to fall under the legal guardianship of a male relative, who would operate for her in economic and legal matters. We do see instances of a woman being named in law 'her own *kuria*', but every instance involves a metic woman, not a citizen (Kennedy 2014: 114, 120–1, 137–8, 140). For a recent discussion of women's ability to act as *kuria* over property, see Campa (2019).

[29] Her father, Gylon, was an Athenian general accused of treason. See Davies (1971: 121–2) on Gylon's history and whether he was dead or not. Additional information about Kleoboulê, including her name, can be found in Plutarch *Mor.* 844a and *Dem.* 4.2. Technically, we should assume that Aphobos was her *kurios*, but, as Foxhall (1996: 144) points out, she seems to have acted as if it was Demochares, her sister Philia's husband.

[30] See Hunter (1989a: 305); Foxhall (1996: 140); Kennedy (2014: 107–9). Gylon supposedly married while in exile in Kepoi on the Bosporos around 408 BCE. But just because Aeschines and Deinarchus call the woman a 'Scythian' does not mean she was. As Davies (1971: 122) points out, Kepoi was a Milesian colony. Kleoboulê could have had a Greek or even Athenian mother.

[31] See Kennedy (2014) for a full discussion and evidence of how such accusations follow a gendered pattern.

savagely called into question in speeches (as we will see below).[32] The truth of the slanders to which they and the dead were subjected in these speeches was up to the jury to decide, and the slanders were typically geared towards playing on the prejudices of the juries: foreignness, sex work, and bastardy/adultery—even in cases where women were 'respectfully' not named.[33]

Further, the case demonstrates that wills could be circumvented more easily than they could be enforced. If either Kleoboulê or Aphobos was so easily permitted to disregard the will and not marry (and especially if Demosthenes' sister never married Demophon even though he took the dowry), then this shows how precarious the situation could be for a woman without a clear *kurios*.[34] If only a sense of duty or decency deterred men whose claims were superseded by the children left behind, then those children had few real protections against the seizure of their estates outside the help of their mothers and the maternal family (if there was one). Given that we have direct evidence in orations of people falsely swearing oaths (otherwise, we would not have two sides to these cases at all), it seems that fear of the gods was, at least in the lawcourts where elite estates were contested, only a minor deterrent from otherwise unsavoury behaviour. Courtroom speeches are not evidence of wrongdoing. They are evidence of a dispute. Kleoboulê may have had her brother-in-law to help her maintain her status as a widow as a form of protection against the encroachments of the uncles on her personal property,[35] but it clearly was not enough to protect Demosthenes' inheritance.

We do know, however, that Demosthenes did win his case, which resulted in belated enforcement of some of the will. Demosthenes' arguments are only minimally concerned, however, with how his guardians' behaviour impacted his mother or sister, who is barely mentioned—their suffering seems more like collateral damage while he is the true victim. In the cases that follow, the women are the central victims. We have no idea how these cases ended, making it hard to know how successful the women in them fared against legal manoeuvres designed to disinherit them.

When various slanders interact with the unenforceable nature of wills, it gives rise to what I call here 'strategies of disenfranchisement', because that is the

---

[32] On witnesses and strategies against them, see Humphreys (1985).

[33] The marriageability of Kleoboulê is another piece of evidence that the Citizenship Law of 451 BCE was rescinded during the Peloponnesian War. See Kennedy (2014: 107-9) for discussion with references. On the tensions surrounding *nothoi* (bastards) in the years before 403 BCE as unforeseen consequences of the 451 law, see Irwin (2016).

[34] Hunter (1989b: 41, n. 12) discusses the debt Gylon, Demosthenes' grandfather, still owed the state, and the possibility that the will was arranged as it was to protect the estate from being sold to pay the debt; Demosthenes suggests Gylon had accused them of this in 28.1-3.

[35] The question of her jewellery is at the centre of reasons why she and Aphobos never married. See Schaps (1981) and Hunter (1989b). Foxhall (1996: 142) does not believe there was a law banning women from owning land. See also Foxhall (1989: 26) and Eidinow (2015: 293-6).

potential result of the rhetoric employed, even if it is not explicit—to disenfranchise the women and children who originally inherited.[36] If Kleoboulê was viewed as foreign born, if Demosthenes' father was viewed as foreign born, then both her and her children's citizenship (that of Demosthenes and his sister) could have been called into question. The 'son of a Scythian woman' phrase is used later by Aeschines to impugn Demosthenes' commitment to Athens—the claim being he was infected by a foreign contaminant, he was not 'pure'[37]—but if, at his initial coming of age and trial in the courts, his circumstances had been slightly less well known (as with many of the cases discussed below), then he and his sister both stood a chance at being effectively disenfranchised. The only person standing between them and destitution was their un-*kurios*-ed mother.[38]

## Phylomachê

The case of Kleoboulê and her son Demosthenes turned out well, thanks to both the fortitude of Kleoboulê herself and the rhetorical skill of the young Demosthenes. But not everyone we see in the courts has such connections or abilities, even while they may be among the propertied elite of Athens. In these cases, where the women are of relatively unknown families (though still families with wealth enough to dispute substantial inheritances in the courts), we see attempts not just to slander the women involved and diminish their status, but to erase their status entirely. Two women who embody an extreme version of this erasure of status are found in Demosthenes 43 and Isaeus 6.

In Dem. 43, a complex case, we are introduced to two women named Phylomachê. The speaker claims the estate of Hagnias against a distant cousin, Macartatos, the son of Theopompos. This is the third lawsuit over this estate (the estate appears as a bone of contention in other speeches of Demosthenes and Isaeus).[39] In the earlier case, the younger Phylomachê gained the estate in place of the children of the elder Phylomachê's half-brothers. In the second, Theopompos

---

[36] An interesting point of comparison in this period might be Sparta and women's inheritance of property. Assumptions about the ability of women to inherit property in their own right are based on a negative assessment of the results at *Politics* 1269$^b$12–1270$^a$34, where Aristotle cites high levels of women's property ownership as a cause of Sparta's decline. The attitude expressed by Aristotle can certainly be seen within these speeches.

[37] On the notions of purity and foreign contamination in Athenian discussions of descent and citizenship, see Lape (2010) and Kennedy (2014: 38–49). On this idea within the context of archaic and classical Greek literature more broadly, see Kennedy (2016: 9–28).

[38] Hunter (1989a: 42) discusses the case of Lysias 32, which involves a widow challenging her own father's embezzling of her children's inheritance. If widows needed to guard even against their own fathers and uncles, imagine how uninterested those not related to them at all might be in maintaining their children's status and rights.

[39] See Cox (1998: 3–10) with extensive references for a discussion of the legal battles among the family for this estate.

gained the estate from Phylomachê. In that speech, Theopompos disputed Phylomachê's claim because, he argued, the elder Phylomachê (the source of the younger's claim) never existed. This accusation seems to have been successful, and the estate was thus awarded to Theopompos. And so, as part of the new lawsuit attempting to regain the property from Theopompos' son, Macartatos, the younger Phylomachê's husband, Sositheus, and son, Euboulides, must argue once again that the elder Phylomachê existed.

Theopompos was a distant relative, and his case rested solely upon convincing a jury that a woman never existed, of erasing her entirely. Here is what Sositheus tells us of the previous and current case (43.38–41):

> [38] In the previous case, Athenian jurors, when these men formed their confederacy and, being many, conspired together against this woman, we, men of the jury, neither prepared witness statements nor called upon witnesses regarding these charges, but thought ourselves secure in the matter. Our opponents, however, had contrived numerous shameful lies for the trial and concerned themselves with nothing except deceiving the jury at that moment in time. [39] These men are alleging that there was no daughter born to Polemon, father of Hagnias at all, neither of the same mother or the same father! So shameful and loathsome and misleading concerning such an important and so conspicuous matter. And they were eager to do it and made every effort in the attempt. But we are now bringing forward many witnesses to you concerning the daughter of Polemon, aunt of Hagnias. [40] Let whoever on their side bring witnesses that Polemon was not the son or Phylomachê the daughter of Hagnias son of Bouselos. Or let them testify that Polemon was not the father of Hagnias whose estate is currently under dispute [41] and Phylomachê not Polemon's sister or Hagnias's aunt. Or let them testify that Euboulides was not the son of Phylomachê, nor Philagros the cousin of Hagnias. Let them bring witnesses that the still living Phylomachê is not the daughter of Euboulides, the cousin of Hagnias, and that this child is not his son, adopted in accordance with your laws into the house of Euboulides. Or that Theopompos was not the father of Macartatos from the house of Hagnias. Let them bring witnesses to whatever they want! But I know well that no man would be so bold and desperate.

Preceding this declaration in sections 35–7 are a series of depositions from witnesses to the fact of the elder Phylomachê's existence. The paragraphs that follow are also further witnesses to it. What sort of tenuous status must a citizen woman have had that her very existence could be contested in court within only a few decades of her death? Especially given that this is the third case on the estate—the first was decided based on the fact of her existence, the second declared she did not exist, thus the need for the third. The need for depositions confirming the marriage of the elder Phylomachê to one Philagros seem minor by comparison, given that her status as wife of Philagros and mother of Euboulides is premised on the fact of her existing at all—and, in fact, the only way to prove she did exist is to prove that she was married to someone or someone's mother; she existed only as a person in relation to some man.

Compare this to the situation of Kleoboulê, who had both a famous father, Gylon, and a sister married to an Athenian citizen, whose husband would have assured the status of his own marriage and heirs by supporting Kleoboulê and Demosthenes. No one could question her existence, and no one seems to have seriously questioned her citizen status, despite the slanderous statements. But no such relatives existed for Phylomachê the elder, it seems, and, since keeping records for female children was not common, she may as well never have existed so far as their opponents were concerned. What it meant for the younger Phylomachê (and her husband and children) to have her grandmother declared by a jury as a figment of someone's imagination we can only guess, since we do not have any evidence about the final outcome. It is possible, however, that her citizenship could be declared void if someone took it upon him self to challenge it in the courts after the resolution of this case, and the verdict of the previous trial could be used to demonstrate her false claims to citizenship. Being convicted of pretending to be a citizen and marrying a citizen meant sale into slavery. We see the possibilities and fact of this in numerous speeches, including [Dem.] 59.16-17, where slavery would be the penalty Neaira would pay if she lost, and Dem. 25.55-65, where numerous women are shown to have been threatened with or in fact suffered sale into slavery for either pretending to be citizens or not registering as resident foreigners.[40] There was a lot more at stake for Phylomachê here than the speaker is telling his jury. It was not just an inheritance.

This is an extreme version of a strategy of disenfranchisement, but one that highlights the lengths that some distant relatives might go to in order to lay claim to an inheritance. Given the number of these cases, some Athenians clearly saw a female or minor heir as an opportunity, and they may have done so because the juries, to what extent we do not know, legitimized their strategy by granting such relatives victories in the courts.

## Kallippê

Isaeus 6 also shows strategies of disenfranchisement, in this case dealing with the estate of Euktemon. There are two unnamed daughters of Euktemon: the son (Chairestratos) of one of these daughters is a claimant through supposed adoption by her deceased brother to the estate of her father; the other daughter, a

---

[40] See Kennedy (2014: esp. 99-101).

widow without children, was initially sought in marriage by a cousin (Androkles) as an heiress and the next of kin. There is another woman, whose disputed identity complicates matters: she is either Kallippê, a second wife of the long-lived and virile Euktemon, or Alkê, a sex worker/companion to the clearly rambunctious nonagenarian (Euktemon died, it seems, aged 96).[41]

The speaker is a friend of the family and is defending the claim of Chairestratos.[42] He tells the jury that his opponent claims Euktemon remarried in his 70s a woman named Kallippê and fathered two sons, one of whom had been introduced to and recognized by the deme and was now around 20 and whose claim was supported by Androkles. The speaker, however, denies this: ὅτι δ' [οὐδ'] ἄλλην τινὰ ἔγημε γυναῖκα, ἐξ ἧς τινος οἶδε αὐτῷ ἐγένοντο, οὐδεὶς τὸ παράπαν οἶδεν οὐδ' ἤκουσε πώποτε ζῶντος Εὐκτήμονος ('No one is aware or ever heard a word while Euktemon was alive that he had married any other wife from whom he begat these men' (6.11)). This case is another instance of denying the existence of a woman.

Instead of simply claiming that the woman and her children never existed, however, the speaker asserts that it is a case of fraudulent identity: the mother of these children was not a citizen woman named Kallippê, he says, but a local sex worker named Alkê, who took advantage of old Euktemon. Making such a claim is not simple, because the elder of Euktemon's two male children was then in his twenties and had been recognized by the deme as a legitimate son and citizen; the speaker must try to navigate around this fact.[43] And, as Glazebrook demonstrates, the speaker goes out of his way to target only Alkê and not attack either of the sons or Androkles or to lay any blame for the situation on old Euktemon himself.[44] This is a speech designed to harm a woman (Kallippê), not the men.

The story he presents of these women is fairly complicated, so it will be helpful to include the text (6.12–15).

[12] For when the pre-trial examinations were being done in front of the archon and they had paid the court fees for their claim that these were the legitimate heirs of Euktemon, they were asked by us who their mother was and whose daughter she was. They were unable to state this information, even when we protested and the archon ordered them to answer in accordance with the law. It was rather absurd that they made a claim for legitimacy and yet were unable to

---

[41] See Glazebrook (2021: 43–62) for an in-depth analysis of the representation of sex work in the speech and for an accessible description of the complexities of the case. Glazebrook makes no claims as to whether either Kallippê or Alkê was fictional, but instead analyses the logic and the speech and the construction of the image of the sex worker.

[42] Glazebrook (2021: 44) points to *IG* II² 2825.11 as potential evidence that Chairestratos lost his claim. The inscription is for a Chairestratos, son of Phanostratos of Kephisia. Had he won the claim, he would have been listed as son of Philoktemon. The name is not so uncommon that we can assume they are the same person.

[43] Foxhall (1996: 143) accepts the accusation that the children are falsely registered into the deme and were not, in fact, the children of a citizen woman, but children of the madam Alkê.

[44] Glazebrook (2021: 52–6).

confirm who their mother was or name any relatives whatsoever. [13] But, at that time, they suggested that she was Lemnian and so procured a delay. Later on at the examination, before any question was asked, they declared that their mother was Kallippê, the daughter of Pistoxenos, as if it was enough for them merely to provide his name! So, we asked who he was and whether he was alive or not. They said he had died fighting in Sicily and had left his daughter behind with Euktemon. The children were born to him while she was under his guardianship—a shameless tale they have concocted! Entirely untrue as I will demonstrate using their own words. [14] It has been fifty-two years since the Sicilian expedition, dating from the archonship of Arimnestos. Somehow, the elder son supposedly born to Kallippê and Euktemon is 20 years old. Subtract that and you get thirty years since the expedition. Kallippê, therefore, would have been thirty years old and would not have been unmarried or without children. Long since she would have been married off properly according to law, either by her guardian or by the courts. [15] Besides that, she would have been known necessarily to the family and slaves, if she had actually been married to him and had dwelt so long in the house.

There are a number of aspects to this speech that are of interest. The speaker claims that no woman would have been unmarried and left with a guardian at thirty years of age unless that guardian were her husband (6.14). He reacts incredulously that any orphaned girl might have been improperly cared for or not appropriately married off by her guardian at a young age. And, yet, his logic is flawed. Kallippê seems to have gone under Euktemon's care fifty-two or more years earlier. The speaker deduces from the age of the elder son that she was roughly 30 when she had the first child. This assumes that the marriage and the birth of the child took place at the same time. It also assumes that this was her first marriage, but the realities of the Peloponnesian War make it highly likely that any first marriage was just as likely to have ended in widowhood as not to have happened at all. Euktemon may have married her after an earlier marriage.[45] Or, he simply may never have properly married her off to begin with, because marriages were difficult to arrange during the war, when death rates, especially among men of marriageable/military age, were high, leaving too few men for eligible women.

Further, thrown into this somewhat crazy tale of the filing of claims with the archon is a sneak attack—the speaker claims that, when asked who the father of Kallippê was, they claimed she was born of an Athenian *klerouchos* in Lemnos (6.11–13).[46] The citizenship law was reinstated in 403 BCE, so she could have

---

[45] See also Cudjoe (2010: 195).
[46] There is some debate as to whether the Lemnians could have been citizens because of Athens's imperial relationship to the island. See Ogden (1996: 71, 177–9) and Carawan (2008) for discussions.

been born of a Lemnian mother and still have been a citizen.[47] Her opponents, however, do not claim she is not a citizen at this point, avoiding the easy, expected slander. Instead, they offer a bit of a twist—Kallippê never existed. There was *a* woman, they say, who had these children and who was associated with Euktemon, but her name was not Kallippê and she was not his wife. Instead, the speaker alleges she was a local sex worker named Alkê.

Alkê is introduced as a freed woman set up by Euktemon to run a brothel he owned in Kerameikos. Euktemon, the speaker suggests, became infatuated with her (though she was old and had two children by a freed slave/metic) and he regularly dined with her. Under her influence and, the speaker suggests, under the more nefarious influences of drugs or disease (6.21), Euktemon agreed to introduce her children to the deme as his own children. The children—regardless of the strange conditions the speaker concocts—were recognized as legitimate and citizens by the deme. Euktemon then, apparently, made a will that ensured their inheritance.

Alkê—a formerly enslaved prostitute, madam, and manipulator—takes the place for the speaker of the young citizen woman whose father had died in war and who had been placed under the care and protection of a friend (or perhaps distant relative—we do not have that information). The speaker gives no evidence that Kallippê did not exist, and, in fact, we can only assume she is no longer alive to be present to dispute her non-existence. But, as the speaker points out—nearly everyone in the jury knows Alkê (ἣν καὶ ὑμῶν οἶμαι πολλοὺς εἰδέναι (6.19)). Kallippê, if we can trust the speaker's summary of the filings of the case at a basic level, was a citizen woman, probably like many young citizen women whose fathers died while she was not married or possibly widowed, who had no brothers or uncles to speak of. Who would speak for her? And, if she was 'respectable', she would have been mostly invisible already, even though the speakers suggest she would have been publicly visible as a citizen at community rituals. A citizen woman attending public rituals was probably veiled. Her presence would not mean anyone would have recognized her.

If we read against the grain of the speech and accept the reality of Kallippê (as opposed to Alkê), the scenario for Kallippê seems to have been that she became ward of a man who eventually married her and had children with her. Why would he do that? Maybe because his three grown sons had died in the various battles that marked the end of the fifth century. One would think that three sons would ensure a line of inheritance, especially with two daughters also married off. But the long years of wars probably led to many daughters, sisters, and wives ending up on their own without witnesses to their lives, and the Athenian legal system simply was not equipped to deal with large numbers of citizen women without

---

[47] See Carawan (2008) and Kennedy (2014: 12–25) with summary of previous arguments on the Peloponnesian War era abeyance of the 451 BCE law requiring two citizen parents.

legal guardians. We simply do not hear about these women in other sources (like Thucydides). Their vulnerability and the vulnerability of their children were, in fact, built into the system. In a legal structure where the births of women were not recorded and where marriages, like births, were attested only through the memories and testimony of witnesses, it seems to have been easy to attempt to erase the very existence of women. This case has all three of the strategies for erasing these women: 1. impugning any potential remaining witnesses; 2. suggesting they or an ancestor were foreign; and 3. suggesting they or their mothers were sex workers or otherwise women of questionable repute and untrustworthy to know who the father of their children were.

Given the lack of registering daughters, even with the importance of female citizenship in fourth-century Athens, we are left to wonder how many women must have been left in legal limbo at the hands of unscrupulous relatives, relatives who did not care what the law said about who was responsible for them and how they were to be maintained. In the cases of Phylomachê and Kallippê, it was their children or grandchildren who felt the impact of their erasure, but what about direct impact? This direct impact on the women themselves is the focus of the next case study, Isaeus 3.

## Philê (Kleitaretê) and her Mother

Isaeus 3 revolves around the estate of one Pyrrhos, who had died twenty years earlier. He had no son and so adopted his nephew Endios. Endios died, however, without an heir, and his own brothers are trying to claim the estate as next of kin. Pyrrhos, however, left a daughter (possibly Philê, but this is contested), whom Endios had married to a certain Xenokles with a dowry of 1,000 drachmas (against an estate of, apparently, 3 talents). After Endios' death, the daughter's husband and maternal grandfather filed a claim against the estate on her behalf and on behalf of her children. The brothers' strategy to fight the claim seems to have been to file perjury charges against the men as a way to discredit them and dispute the claims of Philê (3.3–5).

That Philê is Pyrrhos' daughter is not disputed. What is disputed is her legitimacy. According to the speaker, if she were legitimate, then the adoption of Endios would not have been permitted, as it is against the law to take an inheritance away from an heiress in such a manner. That said, both the brothers of Pyrrhos and the maternal grandfather, Nikodemos, gave depositions to the effect that Philê was the legitimate daughter of a legitimate marriage. The speaker says that these depositions should be disregarded—Nikodemos, because he was a perjurer (the actual case seems to have been a perjury case against him), and the uncles for no real reason; the speaker just thinks the uncles do not want him to have the estate (3.8–12; 30–4).

The arguments in the speech are based entirely on probability, but they play very effectively to the potential prejudices of the jury. Whether they were effective in reality, we do not know.[48] If we look at the strategies used to attack women in the speeches above, however, we see they are all again deployed here against both Philê *and* her mother in the speech.

First, we see the impugning of any potential remaining witnesses: this is a perjury case against one of the primary witnesses both to the marriage of Philê's mother to Pyrrhos and to Philê's birth. Next, the suggestion that they or an ancestor was foreign: according to our speaker, Nikodemos was charged in the past with illegally claiming citizenship. He won his case, we are told, but only by four votes (6.37). This is used to impugn him and, of course, to suggest that his daughter (the mother of Philê) was a metic, not a citizen. Also at issue is the question of legitimacy, which gets us involved in a debate over whether one must be both born of two citizens and born in a dowered marriage to count as a citizen, something scholars have not managed to resolve.[49] If the grandfather, however, is a metic in disguise, then, of course, Philê is not a citizen, and, of course, her marriage to Xenokles (if conducted after c.380 BCE[50]) is also likely not to be valid, making her children non-citizens both by ethnicity and by legitimacy (if one needs both for a legal marriage).

Finally, we see the suggestion that they or their mothers were sex workers or otherwise women of questionable repute, thus making the identity of the father of any child impossible to determine. In this case, the third strategy of erasure is taken up with gusto, and both the mother (name unknown) and Philê are raked over the coals: the mother as if she were a common whore, and Philê as illegitimate and the daughter of a sex worker. Interestingly, the text never names the mother (though this is supposedly one of the things you do to disreputable foreign prostitutes), and Philê herself is not ever directly considered responsible for the claim being filed by her husband and maternal grandfather.

The attacks go as follows. If the marriage of Pyrrhos to the mother was valid, where is the dowry contract (3.26, 28–9)? If Philê was legitimate, why would Pyrrhos have adopted Endios and why did the uncles not dispute Endios' inheritance at the time of Pyrrhos' death? Also, if she was legitimate, why would she have been married to a non-family member (Xenokles) with such a paltry dowry compared to the amount of the estate,[51] which, by rights, they say, would have been hers as an heiress (though, of course, the adoption means she was no longer an heiress)? There are perfectly legitimate (and more probable) scenarios that

---

[48] Though some scholars believe they did win the case. See Hatzilambrou (2010).
[49] Despite the valiant efforts Patterson (1990) and Ogden (1996) have made at unravelling it.
[50] See Bakewell (2009) and Kennedy (2014: 19–20) on the marriage ban between citizen men and metic women.
[51] Cudjoe (2010: 151) disputes Schaps's and others' assumptions that the size of the dowry can tell us anything about the citizen status of a woman.

would answer all of these questions, but they would expose the weakness and unenforceability of laws intended to protect women and children—to question them would be to question the laws and the will of the *demos* to follow them. But the weakness of these laws is the reality. Here are a few more likely scenarios:

First: The father had no interest in leaving his estate to a young unmarried daughter on the chance that she might have sons to inherit it; he adopted a nephew to ensure the line stayed with his name. This was technically illegal, but was likely to be practical in the eyes of many Athenians.

Second: The brothers of Pyrrhos did not dispute the adoption or the decision basically to defraud Philê of her inheritance, because they would have done the same thing in Pyrrhos' situation and because Endios was also their nephew. But neither they nor Endios were interested in marrying her—this may have cost them their own current marriage and any connections that went along with it, and the estate under debate may not have been large enough to make such a marriage worthwhile to them[52]—and, as we know from Kleoboulê, Demosthenes' mother, the person who is supposed to marry the widow or the daughter does not always do it.

Third: Endios probably agreed to marry her to someone with enough of a dowry to appease the groom if both her uncles and Nikodemos did not make a fuss— she was, after all, being taken care of; she was not getting the 3-talent estate of her father to support her, but does a woman really need that much? And do they really want to put a full talent into a dowry when they were marrying her outside the kinship circle? Her uncles, like Endios, would have had no interest in the estate potentially passing out of the family—marry her quietly to an outsider with a reasonable dowry and then move on with their lives.

If the uncles of Philê behaved badly in not dissuading Pyrrhos from adopting Endios and thus ensuring that Philê would not be heir to his estate; if Endios behaved badly by not giving her a larger dowry and, perhaps, marrying her himself; if Nikodemos behaved badly by not filing a claim and disputing the adoption himself on behalf of his sister and her child (we need to assume, however, that Philê's mother was dead already), should we be surprised? Laws protecting heiresses existed for a reason—because their families could not be trusted to protect their interests or inheritances. But the courts were made up of men who were likely to be more sympathetic to Pyrrhos adopting a male heir than to Philê.

Philê was, we can suppose, not harmed all that much so long as she went along and made no claim against Endios—she was married, had a dowry, and so on. But when she, her husband, or her maternal grandfather opted to stake their claim

[52] Taylor (2017: 132–3).

after Endios' death, the attacks by the speakers sought to delegitimize her, her mother, and her grandfather and thus also her marriage and her children's status—it is an attack root and stock with much wider possible repercussions than not getting the estate that had been owed to her. Because what happens if the jury agrees with the speaker? It means it agrees that her mother was never married to Pyrrhos, that her mother was not a citizen. Does that then mean her marriage to Xenokles is invalid? Does it also mean her children are now illegitimate? Do she and they lose their citizen status? If you are a man and declared a *nothos*, the scholarly jury is still out on whether you could exercise full citizenship.[53] But the status of the women seems unquestioned—if you are illegitimate, you get pushed out of the marriage circuit, making your citizen status worthless and putting you and your children at risk for being accused of falsely claiming it.[54]

But this is not all that the case of Philê brings up. As part of the attack on Nikodemos' credibility, the speaker questions why there was no dowry or contract that was brought up in depositions. It is assumed by all that, if there is a valid marriage—or *pallakia* (a state of domestic partnership; mentioned at 3.39)—there is some sort of contract and some sort of financial security for the woman. That Nikodemos made no claims against the estate after Pyrrhos' death for a return of a dowry is their argument against a marriage (or any sort of contracted relationship). Of course, it is quite possible that a dowry was returned—by Endios as part of his assuming the estate and dowering Philê—but Endios is dead. But the lack of a known contract and depositions to it allows the speaker to claim that Philê's mother was a *hetaira* ('girlfriend', but with implications of sexual availability[55]) and her brother Nikodemos essentially her trafficker (6.45-53).

The intent to slander and silence is clear. But perhaps more interesting is the statement that the mother had no children other than Philê (3.15). What are they insinuating? That she was potentially passing off Philê as her own child, when she was not, in fact, her child—suggesting the whole thing was a big scam to defraud them of their childless brother's estate? Of course, the more likely scenario is that Philê was her only child because she was married to Pyrrhos and had no other children and no other husbands. Why not provide depositions to contradict those who spoke against her in a previous trial? Well, apparently, the brothers of Pyrrhos did, but our speaker dismisses them, claiming they just want the estate themselves and says they claim that, if there was a child, it was named Kleitaretê, not Philê (3.34). And, in fact, the 1,000-drachma dowry and the marriage to non-kin is repeatedly used to suggest that everyone knew Philê was the child not of a marriage, but of a liaison between Pyrrhos and a *hetaira*. They seem to admit

---

[53] See, e.g., Patterson 1990; Ogden (1996, 2009).   [54] See, e.g., Dem. 57.
[55] On the meaning of this word in the fifth and fourth centuries, see Kennedy (2014: 68-74, 112-17 with references; 2016); contra Kurke (1997). The recent Ph.D. thesis by Cecilia Landau (2018) provides an extensive study of named women labelled *hetairai*, including a catalogue of references for all of these women.

repeatedly that the relationship existed but try to suggest with these slanders that it was not a real marriage.

In order to make their case (which they do not make in terms of any laws), they must get the jury to try to differentiate, as Apollodoros states explicitly in [Dem.] 59.122, between three different types of women—the type you marry (*gunê*), the type you might contract with but not marry (a *pallakê*), both of whom could legally bear legitimate children, and the type you might consider for sex, but would not have children with (a *hetaira*). Philê's mother is, they argue, the last. They can get away with this in part by undermining the credibility of Nikodemos as potentially both a foreigner and a perjurer. His citizenship, after all, exists only by virtue of four votes. If he is illegally a citizen, then Phile's mother is clearly not marriageable—she is 'common', *koinê*, and too many people to name have had 'marriages' with her (3.16).

Why not claim she was a *pallakê* instead? Because a *pallakê* had a level of legitimacy and that would mean they would have to admit to the legitimacy of the child, Philê, as well.[56] But whether the child of a *pallakê* could inherit if the mother was Athenian is not a question we can answer. We cannot even answer whether the speakers won their case or not. All we can say is that, even with male representation, Philê seems to have been unable to verify her identity with any certainty because of a lack of any record-keeping or any explicit rules on whether female infants should be presented to demes or not or whether marriages should be presented or not. The heavy reliance on witnesses means that any woman could have her identity nullified by a crooked judgement.

## Conclusions

What can we conclude? First, laws protecting women and minor heirs could, in practice, be circumvented. Second, the primary way to circumvent these laws was to call into question the validity of the line of descent through a woman. Third, undermining the validity of descent followed a well-trodden strategy: a key woman, whether dead or alive, could have her character and even her existence challenged, a practice eased by lax record-keeping even for citizen women. These rhetorical tropes go beyond gossip, because they are used in the courts in the service of stripping women and their descendants of their inheritances and possibly citizenship—an implied practical outcome if not one mentioned explicitly by the speakers. Women held an explicitly subordinate position in Athenian law and society. The practical application of laws reinforced and secured this subordinate status.

---

[56] On the meaning and status of a *pallakê* (outside the courts alternatively called a *pallakis*) in fourth-century Athens, see Kennedy (2014: 21, 113–17, 137–40); Patterson (1990); Sealey (1984); Miner (2003); Kaffarnik (2013).

This last point is worth considering further. Scholars have suggested that the citizenship law's passage in 451 BCE (and again its re-enactment in 403 BCE) increased the concern shown to citizen women. These cases, however, lead us to question whether women could have a consistent status as citizens at all. These extant orations suggest a carelessness in ensuring women's identities or in safeguarding their rights in law, both of which might have been helped by more consistent identification practices. Also, in a society that discouraged or disallowed women's landownership, women could easily be pushed out of the way by male relatives, because the laws surrounding heiresses were complicated and required the goodwill of male relatives to enforce.[57] It seems likely that some women lost their citizen status and, if very unfortunate, potentially found themselves condemned as an unregistered *metic* and sold into enslavement.[58] The more we examine the evidence, the more it seems unlikely that there were hard lines between married women, women under *pallakia*-contracts, and girlfriends.[59] Rather, any woman could be any of these at various stages of her life, or could, at the least, be represented as such during and after her own lifetime, because the boundaries were, in fact, so fuzzy; women—even elite women—were never more than a few rhetorical tropes away from precarity. Between citizen women and the metic (and sometimes the slave) there were only a blurred boundary, muddied waters, and much uncertainty. And the speakers—sometimes even their own defenders—seem to have been indifferent to the toll such precarity took.

We should also consider that precarity was part of the point of such lax record-keeping and fuzzy boundaries—it kept women in positions of vulnerability and dependence. Multiple recent studies have assessed the issue of poverty in classical Athens, focusing on both public discourses and experiences.[60] There is something in these studies that may help us understand the human toll these strategies of disenfranchisement had on the women and children involved. Cecchet distinguishes in her study between 'material poverty' and 'social poverty'. The former is poverty in terms of property ownership, income, and family support, the things these lawsuits intend to strip away from the women and children involved. We do not know that all involved would have been left materially impoverished at the outcome of these cases—the potential loss of citizenship for mothers and their

---

[57] See Campa (2019) for a more optimistic reading of women's property rights.

[58] The strange situation of the mother and sister of Aristogeiton (Dem. 25.55, 65, 78) may fall into this category. Though Aristogeiton and his brother were citizens, his mother was apparently sold as a slave for failure to register as a metic, even though she had citizen sons and a citizen husband (who died a debtor to the state), and she seems to have been prosecuted for this by Aristogeiton himself. For one theory on how this is possible, see Kennedy (2014: 99–101 with references).

[59] Just (1989: 40–75) attempted to untangle these relationships by examining the importance of marriage to the state. And, yet, it was not important enough to provide real mechanisms for protecting women's interests or identities.

[60] On public discourses, see Cecchet (2015); on experiences, see Taylor (2017). For a survey of women and poverty from Hesiod to early Christian texts, see (Kennedy 2024).

children was real, but how it would harm the male citizens who spoke for them varies. What we can discern, however, is that the impacts on the women were a feature of the system, not a bug. As I argue in a recent survey of women and poverty:

> if we think of material poverty in the same terms as modern sociologists, women are the most likely to be subject to every form of poverty simultaneously— endemic (structural), epidemic (conjunctural), and episodic—because they were frequently restricted from working, were often unable to own non-moveable assets like land or buildings, and when they did work, often did so in occupations which were unskilled (for example, in markets) or did work subject to physical capacity (for example, wet-nursing).[61]

We see these issues reflected in the speeches discussed above.

'Social poverty', on the other hand, 'the condition determined by the common imaginary and public ideology',[62] could be equally problematic for these women, as inheritance cases such as these often reflect a breakdown of the social networks for the women targeted.[63] Social poverty cuts across economic statuses and can reflect relationships to work. The women in these cases are not women who work outside the home. In fact, work is one of the ways a woman's citizen status is challenged. And, while Cecchet identifies a positive discourse of poverty in Athens ('active poverty'), women *de facto* could not participate in that discourse.[64] Rather, women seem in these speeches to fall universally into the category of 'inactive poverty', poverty that is the fault of the impoverished because of their lack of will or ability not to 'resort to the aid of others'. In most of the cases above, the women are accused of resorting to criminal behaviours to prevent their impoverishment.[65] They are viewed almost inherently as unworthy of the inheritances by virtue of being women.

That this seems to be the case is arguable based on the cases themselves. Cecchet makes the argument that many appeals to poverty in inheritance cases in the fourth century BCE were intended to invoke pathos for the person being denied the inheritance.[66] As, with the case of Demosthenes, however, these invocations of pity are almost always on behalf of the male victims. Demosthenes mentions his mother and sister only briefly in his arguments. In another example, Dem. 45, Apollodoros, the speaker, mentions that his own daughters are being

---

[61] Kennedy (2024).    [62] Cecchet (2015: 23).    [63] Kennedy (2024).
[64] Cecchet (2015: 28). In fact, Cecchet rarely discusses women in her book, even though poverty discourses almost always have a gendered component to them. See Kennedy (2024) on the intersections between poverty and gender.
[65] Though, Euxitheus in Dem. 57 defends his mother's citizen status by emphasizing the dignity of work, breaking the equation between poverty and non-civic status. See also Aristarchos in Xenophon's *Memorabilia* (2.7.1–14), who boasts about a family business in which mostly women participated.
[66] Cecchet (2015: 225–6).

impoverished by the loss of his inheritance only once. And this is not the only speech on his inheritance—they are not mentioned in the others at all. Even in Isaeus 6, the speaker does not ask anyone to pity Phylomachê for the loss of her inheritance, and she is the central figure of the speech! This suggests that a discourse of pity for the material or social loss for women was not an effective rhetorical ploy with the all-male juries.

The lack of a discourse of pity surrounding these women in the ancient texts, however, does not authorize us as scholars to ignore the possible human impacts and experiences of these cases on those involved. These lawsuits represent crises that can precipitate not only cycles of temporary poverty but multigenerational poverty as well. For these reasons, it is important that we see these women, or, at least, try to see them, not as their enemies or courtroom adversaries presented them, but as they might have been outside of the tropes and outside of the ideological constraints these tropes placed upon them. Ideologies and practical realities rarely match up. Taylor argues that women could 'use their social networks to resist the discourse that valued their labour'.[67] The women in the cases discussed here did not labour outside the home (if we believe their side of the story and not their accusers), but we can see in their attempts to contest the strategies a resistance to the social realities that allow their disenfranchisement and disinheritance in the first place.

## Works Cited

Bakewell, G. (2009). 'Forbidding Marriage: *Neaira* 16 and Metic Spouses at Athens', *Classical Journal*, 104: 97–109.

Blok, J. (2005). 'Becoming Citizens: Some Notes on the Semantics of "Citizen" in Archaic Greece and Classical Athens', *Klio*, 87: 7–40.

Blok, J. (2017). *Citizenship in Classical Athens*. Cambridge, UK.

Boegehold, A. (1994). 'Perikles' Citizenship Law of 451/0 BC', in Boegehold and Scafuro (1994: 57–66).

Boegehold, A., and A. Scafuro (1994) (eds). *Athenian Identity and Civic Ideology*. Baltimore.

Burton, D. (2003). 'Public Memorials, Private Virtues: Women on Classical Athenian Grave Monuments', *Mortality*, 8: 20–35.

Campa, N. (2019). '*Kurios, Kuria* and the Status of Athenian Women', *Classical Journal*, 114: 257–79.

Carawan, E. (2008). 'Pericles the Younger and the Citizenship Law', *Classical Journal*, 103: 383–406.

---

[67] Taylor (2017: 115 ff.).

Cecchet, L. (2015). *Poverty in Athenian Public Discourse*. Stuttgart.

Cox, C. A. (1998). *Household Interests: Property, Marriage Strategies, and Family Dynamics in Ancient Athens*. Princeton.

Cudjoe, R. (2010). *The Social and Legal Positions of Widows and Orphans in Classical Athens*. Athens.

Davies, J. K. (1971). *Athenian Propertied Families, 600–300 BC*. Oxford.

Eidinow, E. (2015). *Envy, Poison, and Death: Women on Trial in Classical Athens*. Oxford.

Faraguna, M. (2014). 'Citizens, Non-Citizens, and Slaves: Identification Methods in Classical Greece', in M. Depaux and S. Coussement (eds), *Identifiers and Identification Methods in the Ancient World*, 165–84. Leuven.

Foxhall, L. (1989). 'Household, gender and property in classical Athens', *The Classical Quarterly*, 39: 22–44.

Foxhall, L. (1996). 'The Law and the Lady: Women and Legal Proceedings in Classical Athens', in L. Foxhall and A. Lewis (eds), *Greek Law in its Political Setting: Justifications not Justice*, 133–52. Oxford.

Glazebrook, A. (2021). *Sexual Labor in the Athenian Courts*. Austin.

Hatzilambrou, R. (2010). 'Isaeus' Art of Persuasion: The Case of his Third Speech', *Wiener Studien*, 123: 19–35.

Humphreys, S. C. (1985). 'Social Relations on Stage: Witnesses in Classical Athens', *History and Anthropology*, 1: 313–69.

Hunter, V. (1989a). 'Gossip and the Politics of Reputation in Classical Athens', *Phoenix*, 44: 299–325.

Hunter, V. (1989b). 'Women's Authority in Classical Athens: The Example of Kleoboule and her Son (Dem. 27–29)', *Échos du monde Classique*, 33: 39–48.

Hunter, V. (1994). *Policing Athens: Social Control in the Attic Lawsuits, 420–320 BC*. Princeton.

Irwin, E. (2016). 'The *Nothoi* Come of Age? Illegitimate Sons and Political Unrest in Late-Fifth-Century Athens', in P. Sänger (ed), *Minderheiten und Migration in der griechisch-römischen Welt: Politische, rechtliche, religiöse und kulturelle Aspekte*, 75–121. Paderborn.

Just, R. (1989). *Women in Athenian Law and Life*. London.

Kaffarnik, J. (2013). 'Pallake', in R. Bagnall et al. (eds), *The Encyclopedia of Ancient History*, 5009–10. Malden, MA. doi: 10.1002/9781444338386.wbeah22216

Kamen, D. (2013). *Status in Classical Athens*. Princeton.

Kennedy, R. F. (2014). *Immigrant Women in Athens: Gender, Ethnicity, and Citizenship in the Classical City*. New York.

Kennedy, R. F. (2016). 'Airs, Waters, Metals, Earth: People and Environment in Archaic and Classical Greek Thought', in R. F. Kennedy and M. Jones-Lewis (eds), *Routledge Handbook of Identity and the Environment in the Classical and Medieval Worlds*, 9–28. Routledge.

Kennedy, R. F. (2020). 'The Epilogue I Never Wrote: On Finally Coming to a Conclusion', *Classics at the Intersections*, https://rfkclassics.blogspot.com/2020/08/the-epilogue-i-never-wrote-in-finally.html (accessed 9 February 2023).

Kennedy, R. F. (2024). 'Women and Poverty', in C. Taylor (ed), *The Cultural History of Poverty*, i. *Antiquity*. London and New York.

Kurke, L. (1997). 'Inventing the "Hetaira": Sex, Politics, and Discursive Conflict in Archaic Greece', *Classical Antiquity*, 16: 106–50.

Landau, C. (2018). 'Les Courtisanes dans la Grèce Classique: Entre réalité et representation: Approche prosopographique, philologique et rhétorique'. 2 vols. Ph.D. dissertation. Strasbourg.

Lape, S. (2010). *Race and Citizen Identity in Classical Athenian Democracy*. Cambridge.

Miner, J. (2003). 'Courtesan, Concubine, Whore: Apollodorus' Deliberate Use of Terms for Prostitutes', *American Journal of Philology*, 124: 19–37.

Ogden, D. (1996). *Greek Bastardy in the Classical and Hellenistic Periods*. Oxford.

Ogden, D. (2009). 'Bastardy and Fatherlessness in Ancient Greece', in S. Hübner and D. Ratzan (eds), *Growing up Fatherless in Antiquity*, 105–19. Cambridge.

Osborne, R. (1997). 'Law, the Democratic Citizen and the Representation of Women in Classical Athens', *Past and Present*, 155: 3–33.

Patterson, C. (1990). 'Those Athenian Bastards', *Classical Antiquity*, 9: 40–73.

Patterson, C. (1987). '*Hai Attikai*: The Other Athenians', *Helios*, 13: 49–67.

Pomeroy, S. (1975). *Goddesses, Whores, Wives, and Slaves: Women in Classical Antiquity*. New York.

Scafuro, A. (1994). 'Witnessing and False Witnessing: Proving Citizenship and Kin Identity in Fourth-Century Athens', in Boegehold and Scafuro (1994: 156–98).

Schaps, D. (1981). *Economic Rights of Women in Ancient Greece*. Edinburgh.

Schaps, D. (1977). 'The Woman Least Mentioned: Etiquette and Women's Names', *Classical Quarterly*, 27: 323–30.

Sealey, R. (1984). 'On Lawful Concubinage in Athens', *Classical Antiquity*, 3: 111–33.

Taylor, C. (ed.) (2017). *Poverty, Wealth, and Well-Being: Experiencing* Penia *in Democratic Athens*. Oxford.

Todd, S. (1990). 'Lady Chatterley's Lover and the Attic Orators: The Social Composition of the Athenian Jury', *Journal of Hellenic Studies*, 110: 146–73.

Rebecca Futo Kennedy, *Strategies of Disenfranchisement: 'Citizen' Women, Minor Heirs, and the Precarity of Status in Attic Oratory* In: *Voiceless, Invisible, and Countless in Ancient Greece: The Experience of Subordinates, 700–300 BCE*. Edited by: Samuel D. Gartland and David W. Tandy, Oxford University Press. © Rebecca Futo Kennedy 2024. DOI: 10.1093/9780191995514.003.0011

# Index

Because the index has been created to work across multiple formats, indexed terms for which a page range is given (e.g., 52–53, 66–70, etc.) may occasionally appear only on some, but not all, of the pages within the range.

Aegina 9–10, 76 n.32, 164–6
Aeschines 196, 245, 251–3, 256, 272–5
agriculture/husbandry 2–3, 23–5, 37, 42–3, 48–9, 90–1, 101, 103–4, 107–8, 131–3, 139, 143–6, 149, 168, 172
Apollodoros 156, 253–6, 270–1, 285, 287–8
aristocracy/ies 11, 13–30, 32, 37–40, 42–5, 52–60, 68–74, 89–93, 99–100, 104, 110–11, 118, 120, 127–8, 135–6, 139, 141–8, 164–6, 170–2, 174–5, 189–90, 211, 221–2, 230–2, 234, 249, 267–9, 271, 274–5, 286
Aristophanes (comic playwright) 23 n.29, 81 n.60, 111–12, 120, 166 n.43, 175 n.90, 196, 199, 201–2
Aristophanes (of Byzantium) 138 n.54, 159–62
Aristotle 28–31, 45, 84 n.63, 101–8, 118, 130–1, 145, 156, 161–3, 166, 169–70, 172, 243–4
Askra 4, 6–8, 11, 169–70
assembly 100–2, 104, 119–20, 130 n.16, 147–8, 254–5, 258–9
*Athenaion politeia* 101, 105, 108, 130–1, 139–43
Athens/Athenians passim
  agora 25, 75–80, 90–1, 103–4, 117–19, 165–6, 209–10, 211 n.17, 247 n.29
  Acropolis 74 n.24, 77, 105–7, 113 n.59, 115–16, 196 n.38
  Kerameikos 77, 79 n.47, 90–1, 218–21, 225, 280
Attica 7, 30, 42–3, 75 n.27, 79 n.47, 90–1, 103, 108, 110–11, 115–16, 128, 130–1, 135–6, 139, 142–4, 156–7, 165–6, 172 n.77, 194, 208, 209 n.6, 210–11, 216–21, 225–6, 233–4, 254–5

Bacchios the potter 84–5, 114–15, 118–20
*banausos* 67–98 *passim*, 104–5, 119–20
Boiotia/Boiotians 1–16 *passim*, 167–8, 218–19, 227–8, 234–5

child/children 79–80, 115–16, 118, 137–40, 142, 212, 217, 224–6, 230–1, 236–7, 248, 255–6, 265–90 *passim*

citizens/citizenship 11–14, 27, 29–31, 40–7, 55–6, 59, 70–1, 73–4, 86–7, 99–112, 127, 133–7, 144–50, 167, 169–71, 174–5, 187 n.11, 197, 203, 207–10, 217–18, 224–7, 232–5, 238, 243, 245–9, 252–3, 255–60, 266–71, 273–87
class 17–18, 40 n.6, 47–9, 52 n.38, 57–8, 60–2, 67, 69–70, 73–4, 99–126 *passim*, 127–54 *passim*, 155, 166, 172–5, 209 n.4, 269
community 2–13, 21–2, 25, 27, 29–31, 39–40, 43–4, 47, 51, 72–4, 79, 91, 93, 101–2, 114–15, 127, 130–1, 174–5, 201–2, 207–10, 212–14, 218–19, 225–6, 234, 238, 280
Corcyra/Corcyraeans 145–6, 173 n.82, 194
Corinth/Corinthians 28–9, 81–3, 85, 89, 164–6
Crete 155, 157–9, 162–4, 170, 173 n.82
  *see also* Gortyn

debt/debt slavery 6, 21–2, 24, 30, 37, 41–2, 103, 133, 139–44, 190 n.18, 274 n.34
Delphi 10, 86–7, 164, 169–71, 217–18
*demos* 22–6, 37–66 *passim*, 102–6, 172, 208–9, 216
Demosthenes 106–7, 117–18, 148, 165
Diogenes, Laertius 142
Dodona 167–8

Eleusis 9–10, 139, 146–8, 251, 254–5
Elis 28–9
elites, *see* aristocracy/ies
Ephesos 175 n.90, 197
Epidauros 79–80, 167–8
Epirus 90–1, 217–19
Epizephyrian Lokroi 28–9, 167–70
Erechtheion 70 n.8, 106–7, 110–11, 146, 148 n.92, 190, 244 n.4, 248–9, 251–2, 256–9, 271–7, 283–5, 287–8
ethnicity 86–7, 99, 115–18, 162, 165–6, 171–2, 174–5, 194, 208–11, 214–15, 218–19, 233–5, 238, 267, 270, 282
Euripides 100, 104–5
exiles, *see also* refugees 7–10, 29, 41, 138, 142, 246–7

Finley, M. 3 n.5, 160, 163–4, 169–71, 173–4, 176–7, 210
free(dom), *see also* manumission 2–5, 23, 41–2, 58–9, 160–2, 167 n.48, 191–202, 208–11, 228–30, 232–3, 246 n.20, 251–6, 280

gender 20–1, 68, 93, 176, 213, 226, 259–60, 267, 270
Gortyn
  law code 201–2
  slavery 163–4

*hektemoroi* 25 n.32, 28–9, 139–44
Helots/helotage 8, 28–30, 42–3, 143 n.74, 155, 157–65, 167–8, 173, 196, 198
Herakleia Pontike 171–5, 219–22, 224
Herodotus 73, 89, 103–4, 198
Hesiod 2–7, 17–22, 24–8, 30–2, 72–3, 133 n.30, 137–8, 145–6, 165, 168–70
Homer 2–3, 5, 25, 30–1, 43 n.15, 59, 72, 137–9, 141, 164–5, 170
hubris, law of 197, 243–64 *passim*

inheritance 4–5, 20–1, 29, 61, 107, 111–12, 118–19, 129–30, 131 n.22, 132 n.26, 245–6, 255–8, 265–90 *passim*
Isaeus 269, 275–8, 281, 288
Isocrates 104–5, 141
Isthmia 86–9

Khios 146 n.82, 155–6, 158–9, 162–4, 173–5, 194, 236–7

labour 2–6, 30, 37–8, 40–5, 47, 58–9, 70–3, 90–3, 99–100, 102–6, 112, 116–18, 120, 127–54 *passim*, 156–7, 170, 174–6, 288
Laconia, *see also* Helots 196, 198
Lemnos 131 n.21, 232 n.85, 266–7, 278–80
Lesbos 170
Leucas 28–9
liturgies 114, 128, 131, 134, 148–9
Lokris/Lokrians 83, 90 n.91, 158–9, 164, 167–71, 220–1
Lysias 118–19, 136 n.46, 194–5, 208–9, 226–7, 234–5, 238, 257–9, 275 n.38

Macedon 10, 170, 228–30, 251–2
Manes the woodcutter 116, 118
manumission, *see also* free(dom) 41, 103–4, 167 n.48, 171, 176, 187 n.11, 198–9, 215, 230, 252–3
Mariandynoi 171–3
Megara/Megarians 22–5, 28, 30–1
Menander 146, 196 n.36

Messene/Messenians 8, 42–3, 155, 157–8, 190 n.18, 218–21
metics 78, 146, 207–42 *passim*, 245–8, 253–6
Mikion 75–7

Neaira 11, 253–4, 266 n.3, 270, 277
neighbours 2–4, 8, 21–2, 22 n.26, 24–5, 25 n.37, 43–4, 48 n.31, 49, 77–8, 133, 143, 146 n.83, 170, 201, 221–2
Nemea 76 n.32, 86–7
Nikarete 117–19

Old Oligarch 100
Olympia 75–6, 81–3, 86–9, 170
Olynthos 228, 251–3
ownership
  land 17–18, 46–7, 108, 111 n.44, 117–18, 127 n.1, 129, 133, 138–41, 207–8, 234, 268, 286–7
  means of production 2–6
  ship 3–4
  slaves 5, 21–2, 118–19, 155–6, 158–9, 163–4, 166, 185–9, 191–2, 198–9, 202–3, 245–6, 248–50, 252–3
  workshop/tavern/brothel 79–80, 104–5, 118–19

Peasant/peasantry 2–4, 17–19, 21–4, 26, 28, 30–1, 70, 103, 127, 155
Peisistratos 22, 55 n.45, 144, 161 n.24
Peloponnesian War 7–8, 101, 106–7, 117–18, 170–1, 194, 237, 279
Penestai 29–30, 42–3, 162–7
Phoenicia/Phoenicians 171, 216, 218–19, 235–6
Phokis/Phokians 167–71, 226
Phrygia 116, 164, 171, 174–5, 237
Phryne (Mnesarete) 9–11, 13
Piraeus 119, 218–19, 222–4, 247 n.29
Plataia/Plataians 7–9, 12–13, 227–8, 230–1, 234–5, 256–7
Plato 23, 84 n.63, 100, 103–4, 118–20, 138, 161–3, 171–3, 188–92, 203
Plutarch 8, 10, 23, 24 n.31, 37–9, 42–3, 45, 52–3, 72–3, 77, 79–80, 103, 130–1, 139–40, 142, 143 n.73, 176–7
polis 1–16 *passim*, 2–13, 37, 39 n.4, 50, 52, 54–5, 111–12, 114 n.60, 114–15, 117–18, 148–9, 156–7, 162–3, 173–4, 175 n.92, 197–8, 203, 207–8, 210, 213–14, 226–7, 232–5, 237–8, 248–9, 252–3, 259–60
Pollux 107–8, 130–1, 140, 157–64, 190–1
Polybios 169–70
poverty and the poor 17–18, 22–6, 30–1, 40–4, 52, 60–2, 93, 99–101, 103–5, 108–12, 118–20, 127 n.1, 131 n.22, 133, 137–9, 141–6, 216, 247–8, 255–6, 286–8

rape 186–7, 256–7
refugees, *see also* exiles 7, 9, 195–8, 200–1, 234–5, 252
Rhodes/Rhodians 86–7, 170, 172 n.77, 173 n.82, 232 n.83
rich(es), *see* wealth(y)

Samos 197–8, 217–18, 221 n.54
sanctuaries 10, 72–3, 75, 86–9, 91, 146, 195–203, 216, 234
sex
  sexual abuse 10, 193, 257 n.71
  sex workers/sex work 9–10, 266–7, 270, 273–4, 277–82, 284
slavery/enslaved persons 2–3, 5–8, 12, 21–2, 29–30, 37, 40–5, 48–9, 51, 55–6, 58–9, 73, 101–11, 117–18, 139–41, 146, 148, 155–83 *passim*, 184–206 *passim*, 209–10, 215, 224–32, 245–6, 248–59, 268, 277, 286
Solon 7–8, 29–30, 37–66 *passim*, 72–3, 99–126 *passim*, 127–54 *passim*, 189
Sparta/Spartans 6–8, 10, 28–30, 157–8, 161–7, 170–1, 173–5, 184 n.1, 190–1, 194–6, 198, 203, 234–5, 275 n.36
subaltern/subalternity 1, 18, 69–72, 75, 184, 188

Thebes/Thebans 2, 6–10, 28–9, 218–19, 228–30, 234–7

Theopompos of Khios 155–83 *passim*
Thespiai/Thespians 2–3, 5–11, 254–5
Thessaly/Thessalians 42–3, 155, 157–9, 161–4, 167–8, 172, 174–5, 227
thetes 2–4, 40 n.6, 48 n.31, 74 n.24, 99–126 *passim*, 127–54 *passim*, 164–8, 172, 174–5, 209 n.4, 227
Thompson, E. P. 18–19, 26–7, 30–2
Thucydides 100, 105–7, 119–20, 134–5, 162–3, 168, 173–96, 280–1
trade 61, 108, 165–6, 171–3, 200–1, 228 n.74
Tyrants, tyranny, *see also* Peisistratos 22, 28–9, 44–5, 52–9, 195–6
Tyrtaeus 46

wages 2–3, 6, 70, 102–5, 127–9, 133–50, 247–8
wealth(y), rich(es) 9–10, 23–5, 39–40, 49–53, 58–62, 73, 84–5, 92–3, 103, 105–11, 119–20, 127–30, 134, 136, 139, 142–3, 164–6, 170–1, 218, 220–2, 224–5, 238, 247–8, 252, 259–60, 267–70, 275
  wealth and poverty in opposition 18, 22–4, 26–7, 40, 52, 54 n.42, 60–2, 93, 100, 109–12, 143, 247–8, 255–6

Xenophon 28, 100, 108–10, 116–20, 134, 138, 145, 148, 185 n.6, 190–1